SILK
PAINTING
Techniques and Ideas

SILK PAINTING

Techniques and Ideas

Jill Kennedy

Jane Varrall

B.T. Batsford, London

First published 1991 by
B.T. Batsford Ltd
583 Fulham Road
London SW6 5BY

Published in paperback 1997

A catalogue record for this book is available from the British Library.

0 7134 6482 8

Typeset by Keyspools Ltd., Golborne, Lancs
Printed in Hong Kong

Acknowledgements
We would like to thank our husbands and our families for their continued support and encouragement. We would also like to thank Catherine for typing, Sarah and Jean-Pierre.

Photographs
J. P. Van Den Wayenberg
Fotostudio Jean-Pierre
Mechelsesteenweg 232
1960 Sterrebeek
Belgium

CONTENTS

INTRODUCTION

If you, like many others, have recently become interested in the art of painting on silk, you may have asked yourself this question: having produced a beautiful design on a beautiful material, what are you going to do with it? This book will help by giving practical advice on how to make the most of the opportunities silk painting offers to create your own clothes, accessories, furnishings and decorations.

The first section is a brief but comprehensive description of the equipment and techniques used in silk painting. The main body of the book, however, comprises the 'projects' and has been organized into three sections: fashions, home furnishings and accessories. (We are using this last term as a 'catch-all' to cover everything from jewellery to Christmas decorations, and we hope you will find a few novel ideas here!)

You should be able to achieve professional-looking results by following the detailed instructions and diagrams on planning, sewing or finishing any of the projects. We have used as many pictures as possible to help you envisage the finished articles, and to illustrate some of the methods. Scale drawings are included for the reader who lacks the confidence to 'design', but we hope that the original work we have shown will stimulate your imagination and creativity.

PART ONE

TOOLS and MATERIALS

EQUIPMENT

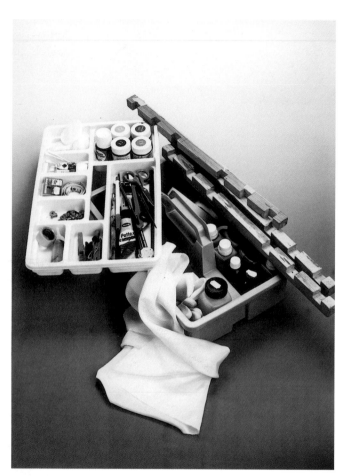

Silk painting equipment

To begin painting on silk, you will need the following:

- Silk
- Frames, pins
- Brushes and applicators
- Gutta
- Wax
- Salt, sugar, alcohol
- Dyes and thinning agents
- Scissors, pencil, masking tape, cotton wool, tracing, graph and drawing paper, hair dryer

Silk

Silk is a superb fabric to work with and can be used for all the projects shown in this book. It can be woven in various ways to produce fabric of different types and textures. The following types can all be used for the projects described in this book:

pongée no. 5–10 (habutai or jap silk)

twill

wild (raw or tussah, soie sauvage)

crêpe de Chine

brocade

chiffon

satin

shantung

organza

taffeta

Pongée no. 9

Pongée or habutai, a lightweight lining material, is most commonly used for silk painting and can usually be found in your local department store or fabric shop. This lightweight silk is ideal for the beginner as the dyes flow easily and gutta penetrates the fibres creating a fast barrier. Smooth and shiny, it is an ideal fabric; it is sold in a variety of thicknesses from nos 5 to 10: the higher the number, the thicker the silk. It also has the advantage of being the cheapest silk available. Choose white silk initially as the dyes will show up in their true colours. If you choose cream, beige or any other colours you must test your dyes on a sample to check the end results. Pongée no. 5 is very good for experimental techniques such as salt, alcohol and watercolour, mainly because it is less expensive, but also because the dyes react well on the fine fabric. No. 9 we find is the most useful as it works well for scarves, lampshades and pictures; no. 10 can be used for cushions, ties, blouses and fashion projects.

Wild or raw silk is much thicker and more textured and is ideal for ties, jackets, blouses and cushion covers.

Crêpe de Chine drapes and hangs beautifully and makes wonderful clothes and exclusive scarves. **Brocade** and **satin** are also favourites for lingerie and clothes.

Caring for your silk

It is advisable to clean the silk before painting, to remove any dressing; some silks may have had an application of size to increase their weight. Before painting, wash the silk thoroughly in warm soapy water, rinse in warm water and roll in a tea towel to remove excess moisture. Iron with a steam iron while still damp. The dyes will then penetrate the fibres evenly and thoroughly. Also use this method when washing a finished article; do not use a harsh detergent, as it may cause the colours to fade.

Frames

A wooden frame is an essential piece of equipment when painting on silk. The fabric must be raised above the work surface, so it is necessary for it to be stretched taut over a rigid frame. There are several types of frame available: fixed, sliding and adjustable. The fixed wooden frame is easy to make: just cut four lengths of

Fixed, adjustable slot and sliding frames

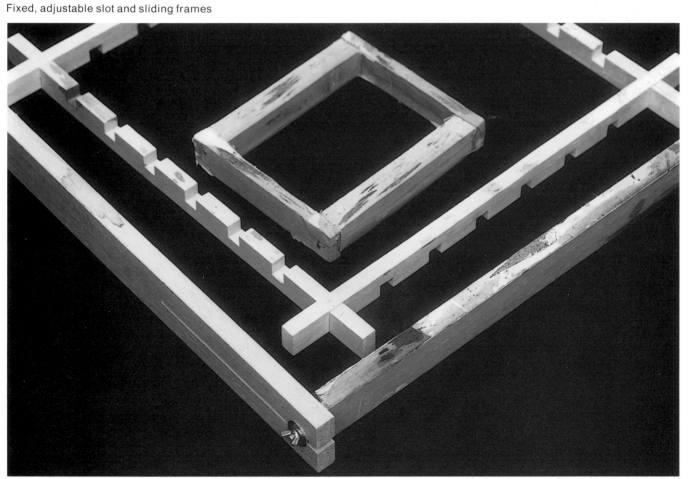

soft wood to the required size and fix together with butt or mitred joints. An old picture frame could be used. The adjustable wooden slot frame or sliding frames are very useful as they can be used for various sizes of fabric. We have found that the soft wood adjustable frame which accommodates a 90 cm × 90 cm (36 in × 36 in) fabric is the most useful; many projects of different sizes can be painted using this frame.

When working with a large piece of silk which needs to be painted in one piece, for example a kimono or sarong, it is a good idea to improvise a frame by securing two planks of soft wood between two wooden trestles, or to join two adjustable wooden slot frames end to end. If, however, you intend to paint a lot of large scarves or sarongs of the same size, it may be worth your while to buy a large sliding frame; or make a frame 150 cm × 90 cm (60 in × 36 in), or the size you will need for your chosen project.

Pins

To stretch the silk you need special fine pointed pins which will not tear the silk when it is secured to the frame. Architect's pins are ideal, as they have three small points which hold the silk firmly on the frame. They can be removed easily by using a small lever. If you cannot find these, look for push pins or drawing pins with long fine points.

Stretching silk on a frame

Before stretching the silk on the frame it is a good idea to protect the frame by covering the top surface with masking tape. This tape may become dye stained but can easily be removed and renewed before each project. Place the silk design side uppermost and begin pinning along one side, following the grain of the fabric. Some people prefer to place pins in all four corners or start in the middle of each side. Whichever method you choose, be sure to stretch the silk tightly using the grain of the fabric as a guide. When you have finished pinning, the silk should be as tight and firm as a drum.

Masking the frame with tape

Silk being stretched on the frame

Firmly stretched silk

Brushes

A selection of silk painting brushes, wax brushes and applicators

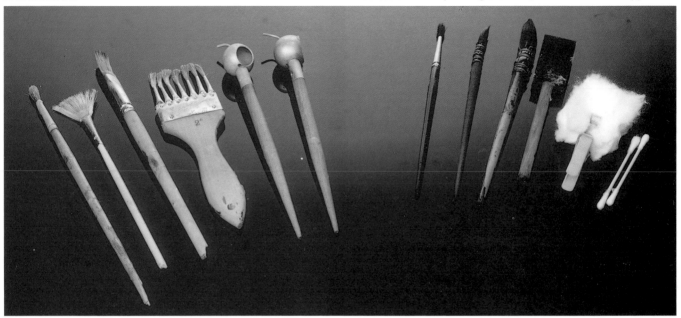

There are many types of brush available, but you can manage with just three brushes of different sizes. Wash brushes and specialized silk painting brushes are ideal. Depending on their size, they are able to hold enough dye to cover large areas. Cottonwool can be used as an alternative, and foam pads are handy when covering large areas. Brushes are expensive, so take great care of them. Never leave them soaking for long periods in water and store them with their tips uppermost.

Gutta

Gutta or resist is the liquid you use to transfer the outline of the design to the silk. There are two types of gutta: rubber based, which can be diluted by a solvent, and water-soluble. When the gutta penetrates fibres of the silk it creates a barrier which is waterproof and therefore dyeproof. After the gutta line has been applied to the silk it remains soft and pliable, even when it has dried. The colour of the silk will show through the gutta lines, unless of course you are using a metallic or coloured gutta.

Coloured gutta is usually sold in smaller containers and is more expensive. It is possible to make your own coloured gutta by adding stained glass colour or typographic ink to the colourless variety. To prepare this, mix a small amount of colour with the solvent and then add to the colourless gutta. Coloured and metallic guttas should not be dry cleaned, as this dissolves the colour.

Preparation of gutta

The consistency of the gutta is very important: if it is too thick or too thin it will not create a fast barrier and the dye will flow over or under the gutta line. It is possible to thin down the gutta, if it has become thick and sticky, by using one of several thinning agents, depending on the type of gutta you are using. The gutta must be diluted using the solvent the manufacturer suggests on the bottle, lighter fuel or white spirit. If you add too much solvent by mistake, leave the bottle open for a while and some of the solvent will evaporate. Always do a small sample to check the gutta and dyes.

Pipettes, gutta and nibs

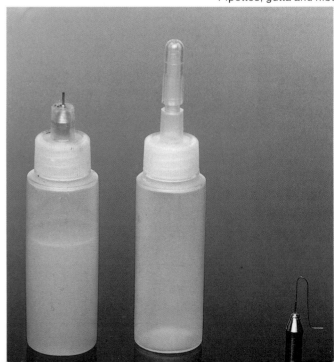

Containers for the application of gutta

To draw the gutta line a pipette or cone is needed (see opposite, below). It is much easier to use a pipette, which is a small plastic bottle with a long spout. To fill the pipette, remove the screw top and spout and slowly pour the gutta into the bottle. The plastic spout can be pierced with a fine needle, but the best way is to affix a nomographic nib (metal-tipped spout) which produces a perfect, even line. These nibs are available in sizes from nos 4 to 10 (the lower the number, the finer the hole). We suggest a no. 5 or no. 6 unless a very thick line is required, when a no. 9 or no. 10 should be used. The nib can be secured to the plastic spout with tape or placed inside the screw-on top after cutting off the plastic spout. To keep nibs clean they should be placed in an airtight container of thinning fluid after use. Gutta will start to harden if left out overnight, so drain any remaining solution back into the original bottle.

Wax

Hot wax can be used in the same way as gutta (see pages 24 and 25). When applied to the silk it creates a barrier to any dye by penetrating the fibres. This process of applying molten wax and dyes is traditionally known as batik. We will explain a method called false batik which will enable you to create exciting and original results. The wax used is a mixture of paraffin wax and beeswax. These can be obtained from hardware stores, craft shops or candlemakers' suppliers.

Heating wax

The wax must be heated slowly. This can be done by one of the following methods: a thermostatically controlled wax pot, an electric ring or a gas burner with a double boiler, saucepan or aluminium tin.

When melted, the wax is applied to the silk. If it is the correct temperature, it will leave a transparent line. If the wax sits on the surface of the silk and looks white, it has not penetrated and the dyes will flow under it. If the wax is too hot, it will spread too far and the brushes will burn.

Equipment for the application of wax

Brushes of any size and shape can be used to apply wax. The brushes can be cleaned in white spirit, but it is best to reserve a few brushes for wax use only. Tjantings can also be used. A tjanting is a small copper bowl attached to a wooden handle with one or more spouts. It is dipped into the hot wax to fill the copper bowl and then the molten wax is applied to the fabric through the spout.

Wax pot, wax and candles

Salt, sugar and alcohol

Salt, sugar and alcohol can be used to create different and exciting textures when used in conjunction with silk painting dyes (see pages 26 and 27). Medicinal alcohol, methylated spirits and surgical spirit can all be used and are available from chemists or hardware shops. Salt is available in several qualities: fine table salt, sea salt, dishwater salt and rock salt. These all produce different unusual textures. Sugar can also be used, either white granulated or icing sugar.

Table salt and sea salt

Dyes

There are many silk-painting dyes now on the market. We have placed them into three categories, depending on their method of fixing. Check the manufactuer's instructions. These should be clearly marked on whichever brand of dye you buy.

Dyes, palette and markers

Steam-fixed dyes

These are transparent and penetrate the material thoroughly. It is fun to experiment superimposing one colour over another while the first colour is still wet. The brightness and permanence of colour is excellent, and once fixed by steam the silk is washable and dry cleanable. These dyes are non-toxic and odourless. They are available at art and craft shops under a variety of brand names. Pastel-type silk painting crayons can be used to sketch and draw on the silk. These also need to be fixed by steam.

Heat-fixed dyes

These are thicker and less transparent than the steam-fixed dyes. They do not penetrate the fibres of the silk completely unless watered right down and therefore the reverse of the design may not be as clear and bright as the front. The great advantage of these dyes is their easy fixing method using a hot iron. There are many types, available under a variety of brand names. Once fixed, these dyes are washable and dry cleanable.

Special dye-filled pens with felt tips are also available to draw on silk, and these are great for children.

Liquid-fixed dyes

These dyes are water-based and are fixed using a liquid fixer. They are non-toxic and after fixing are washable and dry cleanable.

Mixing the dyes

All of the dyes are available in a wide range of vibrant colours. For all the projects in this book we have used either the steam-fixed or the iron-fixed varieties. The dyes can be mixed with each other and diluted with water and alcohol, or with a special commercially available diluent. Do not mix dyes from different manufacturers. Try to stay with one brand throughout your project.

When mixing dyes, use white palettes and pots. If you are mixing small amounts, do not pour from the jars: use a dropper instead. When paler shades are required, it is necessary to dilute the dyes using water, alcohol or diluent. You may need to use distilled water rather than tap water, since in some areas tap water contains chemicals and minerals which may affect the colours. When diluting the dye it is best to use a 50% water/50% alcohol mix.

Be sure to check the instructions from the manufacturer on the dye bottle. We recommend that at least 10% of this 50/50 mix is added to the dye, even when a vibrant colour is required. Diluting the dye by this ratio will not change the shade, but will save money and avoid the over-saturation of silk with dye. (Over-saturation can cause problems on washing later on: 'bleeding' sometimes occurs, especially with reds and black, if too much colour has been used; excess dye is rejected on to the fixing paper or runs in the wash.) Obviously paler shades require more of the mixture. Water alone can be used, but we find that the diluent helps smoother applications, especially on large areas.

Iron-fixed dyes differ from the steam-fixed ones in that

Test colour chart for dyes

there is a white dye available which can be mixed with coloured dyes to create pastel shades. When you have decided on and mixed your colours, we suggest that you draw a test grid with gutta and make a test chart like the one above. You will notice that once the dye has dried out the colour becomes lighter; after fixing it also becomes much more vivid.

When not in use, all dyes should be stored in airtight containers in a cool place. Save diluted and mixed colours in sealed glass or polythene containers for further use.

Fixing

The dye needs to be fixed permanently into the silk to allow it to be washed and to prevent fading. Depending on the dyes used, there are three ways of doing this: steaming, ironing and liquid fixing.

Steam fixing

You can steam your own work at home using a pressure cooker (see picture overleaf). Few people have access to professional steamers, which are expensive and only viable if you are producing a lot of work. It is, however, worth asking at your silk painting suppliers if they run a steaming service or enquiring at your local dry cleaners, as they usually have a steam box.

The pressure cooker is ideal for smaller amounts of work. Each piece of painted silk must be placed flat on top of several layers of lining paper, craft paper or newsprint without type. Roll the silk and paper together and flatten and seal the ends using strong tape. Tuck the ends towards the centre, then roll and flatten again to form a firm package. The package should be small enough to not touch the sides of the pressure cooker. Fill the bottom of the pressure cooker with about 2 cm (1 in) of water. Place the package in a basket so that the condensation runs down into the water. Seal the lid and cook under pressure for 45 minutes. Turn the heat off, carefully open the lid and remove the package.

After steaming, the colours are more vibrant, and texture of the silk is softer and has a lustrous sheen. If the silk has had inadequate protection in the steamer, water marks or rings may appear on it. Once water marks have been made little can be done to remove them.

Fixing equipment and steamer

Fixing equipment and pressure cooker

Heat fixing

Iron-fixed dyes are fixed by pressing thoroughly with a hot dry iron on the reverse side of the fabric. Set the temperature of the iron as recommended by the dye manufacturer. After heat fixing the silk can be washed and dry cleaned.

Take care when ironing, as coloured and metallic guttas may print on your ironing board; protect with a layer of newsprint without type, or an old pressing cloth.

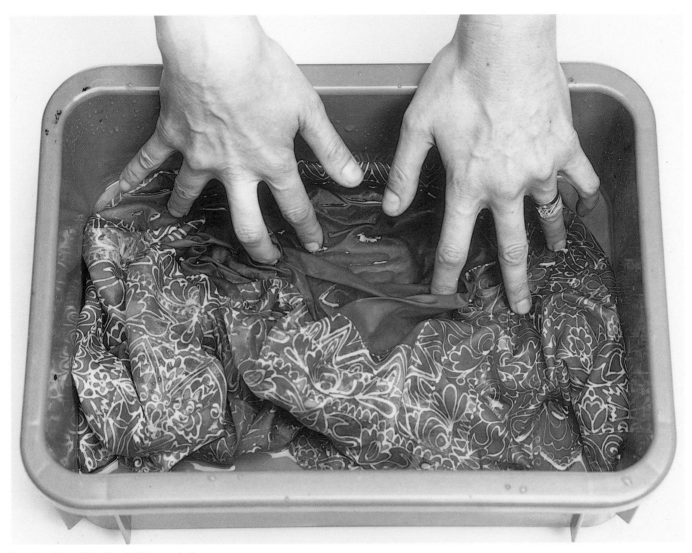

Soaking the silk in liquid fixing solution

Liquid fixing

Liquid-fixed dyes are used in conjunction with silk paint liquid fixer to make them light fast, washable and dry cleanable. Make sure that the silk is dry and then coat on or soak in (depending on the brand) the liquid fixer for approximately one hour. Again, the manufacturer's instructions must be followed, as some fixers need different methods and longer fixing times than others. The silk is then rinsed in cool water to remove excess dye and fixer.

Washing instructions after fixing

After fixing rinse the silk thoroughly in warm water. If water-soluble gutta has been used this will be removed at this stage, leaving a sharp, clear outline. To remove gutta that is not water-soluble, the silk can be dry cleaned or soaked in white spirit. Finally, wash the silk in warm soapy water, rinse and lay on a clean tea towel, roll up and pat to remove the excess moisture. The silk can be ironed while still damp as creases are then easily removed; a fine sheen will appear on the surface of the fabric. If you have used coloured gutta or metallic gutta, do not dry clean the fabric and iron on the reverse side only.

If you have used wax on your silk it will be necessary to wash in white spirit first to remove the last traces. Then wash and iron as normal.

PART TWO

DESIGN and
TECHNIQUES

DESIGN and TECHNIQUES

The designs

Any design can be used when silk painting, but you will soon find that certain designs lend themselves to particular painting techniques. You do not have to be a great artist to try your hand at this craft. Certain techniques, for example the salt technique, require no drawing whatsoever. When using gutta, simple, bold designs work very well. Seascapes and snow scenes are very effective when wax is used, and landscapes lend themselves to the watercolour technique.

Photographs and sketches can be enlarged or reduced in the following way.

Enlarging your design

In this book some of the projects are accompanied by drawings and grids. Enlarge each square to the size indicated and transfer the design to the larger grid. Where drawings are not supplied sketch a design, using our ideas as inspiration or your own. Draw a grid of approximately 2.5 cm (1 in) squares on your original sketch. Decide on the size of your finished work and draw another, larger, grid. This grid must have exactly the same number of squares as are on the original sketch. Working square by square, reproduce the sketch on the larger grid. The same process can be used to reduce the size of a design.

Another way to enlarge or reduce a design is to use a pantograph. These are available at most art and craft shops.

Transferring your design to the silk

Your design must now be transferred to the silk. It is a good idea to make the outline bolder on the paper, using a permanent ink pen, so that the design shows clearly through the silk. Trace the design onto the silk using a soft pencil or a fade-away fabric marking pen (see opposite). The ink disappears after 72 hours – sometimes sooner! – so remember to finish the gutta outline before it vanishes.

To help when tracing, it is best to tape the design and silk to a flat surface to prevent it from moving. The silk is now ready to be stretched on to the frame.

Sometimes clear, simple designs can be seen through a fine silk and it is not necessary to trace the outline. The design can be placed under the frame, close enough to be seen without touching the silk.

Gutta technique

This technique is also known as serti or resist. It involves drawing fine lines of gutta on the silk to outline the design. These lines stop the dyes from spreading into each other. The liquid dyes are then painted directly onto the silk and fixed into the fabric.

Enlarging a design

Faults that may occur when applying gutta

1. The gutta line may appear thick and uneven and start and finish with a big blob. This is because your nib is too large. Replace it with a smaller one.

2. The silk may become smudged or marked with gutta. This may have been caused by a badly-stretched frame, meaning that the silk has touched the work table, or you may have smudged the gutta with your arm or cuff. To prevent these smudges stretch the silk taut; start at the top and work down, or make sure cuffs and loose-fitting clothes do not get in the way.

   To remove unwanted gutta marks, place a folded tissue under the area and rub gently using a cotton bud dipped in the appropriate solvent. This process can be repeated several times to dry and remove the smudge, but sometimes the only way is to cover it and camouflage the mistake by enlarging the design.

3. The gutta may not work properly, causing the dyes to flow over or under the line. The reason for this is that the gutta may have been too thick or too thin. To achieve the correct consistency, see page 12. If the gutta is of a poor quality, there is really no remedy other than to buy another brand. The gutta needs to be more fluid when working on thicker, heavier fabrics.

4. The gutta does not form a continuous line. This may be because of carelessness in the application, meaning that tiny gaps have been left in the gutta line. Check that the line is continuous and go over any opening again before you paint. Be careful not to press too hard or go too fast, as this may cause gaps in the line. Thicker fabrics may need a second application of gutta on the back of the silk.

Tracing the design on to silk

Application of gutta

After deciding on the colour of gutta to be used and the nib size, check the consistency of the gutta. Assemble the pipette, nib and gutta. Holding the pipette like a pen and at an angle of 45 degrees, squeeze steadily and gently so that the gutta flows forming a continuous line (see page 22). Try to pull the pipette towards you, otherwise the top of the pen may catch in the silk. To check that the gutta has penetrated the silk, turn the frame over: you should be able to see a transparent line. It is useful to keep a tissue in your hand as excess gutta sometimes collects around the nib.

Application of dyes

When the gutta is dry you may start painting your design with the dyes (see page 22). For preparing and mixing the dyes see page 14. Paler colours should be applied first, and you will be able to see if you have any 'leaks' of dye seeping over or under your gutta line. Never overload your brush as a little dye goes a long way. The dyes must be worked into the fibres of the silk using the tip of the brush, otherwise uneven colouring may occur. When shading, paint the lighter colours first; then introduce the darker tones while the light ones are still wet. Blend together with the tip of the brush.

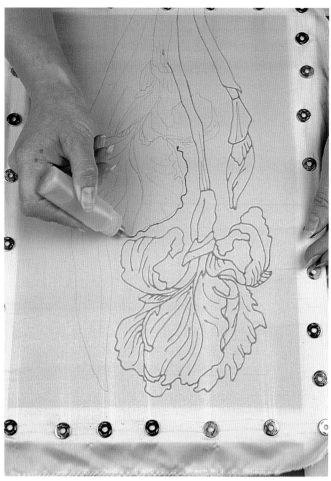

Application of gutta

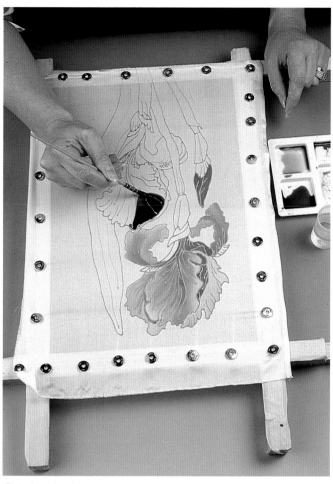

Painting the design

When painting large areas and backgrounds, speed is essential, otherwise water lines or rings will appear on the silk. Large foam brushes or cottonwool can be used. Never re-touch areas that have already dried or paint next to dry paint unless there is a gutta line between the two areas, otherwise a dark line, which is almost impossible to remove, will appear. When you have finished painting and your work is dry, it is ready to be fixed.

Faults that may occur when applying dyes

1. Spots of dye may spill accidentally on either white or an already painted area. Try to remove spots of unwanted dye using cotton buds, tissues and alcohol. Be careful not to use too much alcohol, or the stain will spread. Sometimes this proves unsuccessful. If so, use some creative flair and change your design to incorporate the mistake as a part of the new design. If the cleaning did not work, and on repainting the silk still looks patchy, wet the whole area and sprinkle with salt.

2. The dye may bleed through the gutta line where it is not wanted. This is because of the way the gutta has been

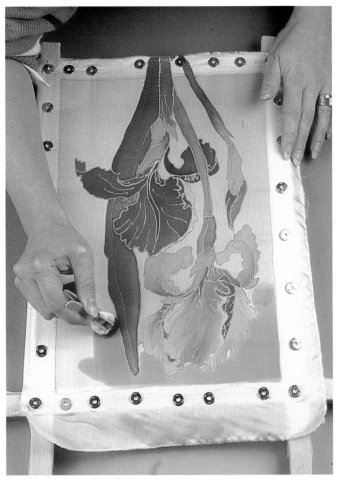

Painting the background

Completed design

applied, although sometimes the dye flows over the lines because the brush is overloaded with dye or through sheer clumsiness. If bleeding occurs quick action is needed. Seal the hole where the dye is escaping with gutta, or sometimes hot air from a hair dryer will stop the flow. Try to remove the dye as in point 1, or improvise.

3. Uneven painting of large areas can result in water-marks. This occurs when the proportions of dye, water and alcohol are incorrect or the dye has been re-applied to areas that have already dried. If the uneven area is a pale colour, it can be repainted using a darker, stronger dye. If this does not work the only solution is to repaint and add texture using salt or alcohol (see pages 26 and 27).

4. Streaks or changes of colour may appear on the silk. This is because the brush or applicator has not been cleaned properly.

5. Marks may be caused by the silk touching the work surface. When painting large pieces of work the wet silk sometimes stretches. To prevent this, keep adjusting the pins to keep the silk taut on the frame.

Wax technique

There is an easy way to get a batik effect without the inconvenience of repeated dipping of the silk in dyebaths as used in the traditional method. This easier method is known as fake or false batik. As with the gutta technique the silk must be stretched taut on a frame. Using molten wax as a resist, apply it to the silk using a brush or a tjanting. Then using a large brush or foam pad, paint the entire surface of the silk. Different colours can be applied to different areas if desired. When the paint is dry, apply more wax to cover the areas you want to remain the first colour and paint again. Keep repeating this process. It is not necessary to remove the fabric from the frame, unless you want a crackled effect, in which case remove the fabric from the frame before applying the final dye colour and crinkle the fabric. Re-pin the fabric and coat with the final dye colour, which will penetrate the cracks to give you the distinctive crackle effect of traditional batik.

Daisies showing the use of wax and cracking

Faults that may occur when applying wax

1.   The dye may penetrate the silk under the wax. This is because the wax is not hot enough. Re-wax the reverse side if necessary.

2.   The wax may spread too far over the surface of the silk where it is not wanted. This is because the wax is too hot and it has become too fluid. To prevent this, use a test sample to try out the flow of the wax. The only way to remove wax is to soak the silk in white spirit or dry clean, which means that the whole project would need to be re-waxed.

3.   Discoloration of the wax may occur if it has not been allowed to harden and cool before the application of the dye. Make sure the wax is cool and hard before applying the dye or unwanted staining may occur.

4.   Drips or blobs of wax may have fallen in the wrong place. This often happens, especially when using a tjanting. It is difficult to remove these drips, so keep a tissue underneath to catch them. If mistakes do occur, try to modify the design to include the blobs. Wax must always be ironed off before fixing. Place the silk between clean sheets of brown or absorbent paper and iron until most of the wax has disappeared. A double layer of fixing paper is necessary.

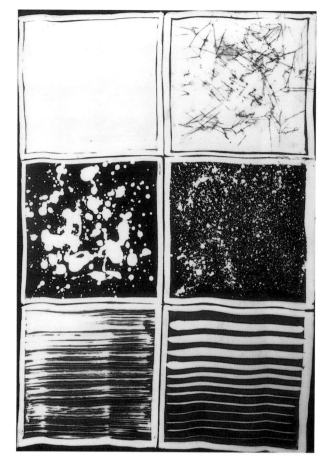

Wax textures, including cracking, dripping, spattering using a brush and tjanting

Using a tjanting

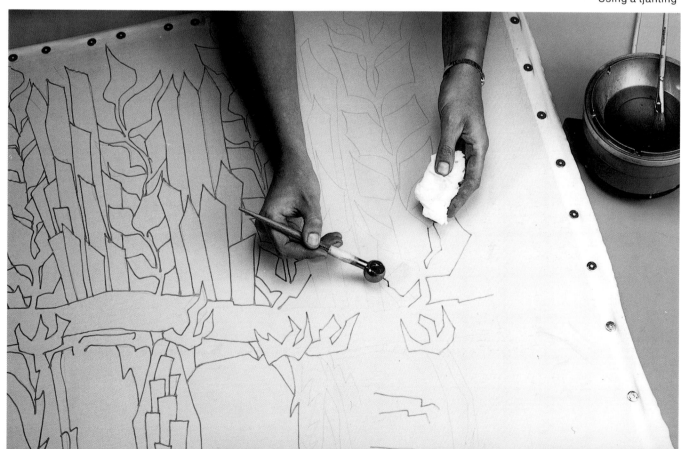

Salt, sugar and alcohol techniques

The effect of salt crystals on dye

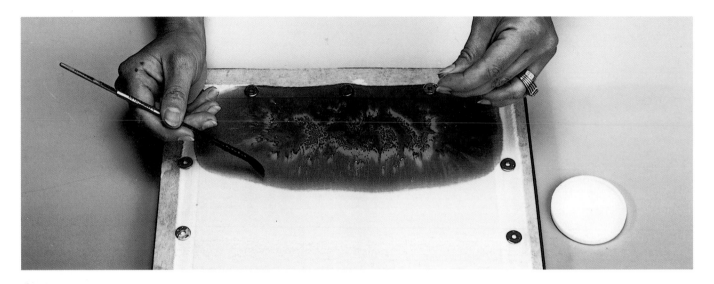

Salt

Place salt on the wet or damp painted colours and allow them to dry. You can see the colours flow as the salt crystals soak up the dye and leave the colour pigments as dark-tones and spots. The salt technique requires the use of water rather than alcohol, which evaporates too quickly and so dries the silk. The end result is always different, depending on the following: the colour and the strength of the dye, the weight and type of silk, the dampness of the fabric and the type of salt used. Even the humidity and room temperature can affect the results. It is difficult to control what happens, but be sure not to use too much salt or to have the silk too wet or the effect will be lost. The salt technique works best with strong, darker dyes or mixed colours. Some colours give far more exciting results than others. It is wise to test them beforehand if the results are vital to a project. Scattering salt at random is effective, especially if several colours are used, as this will produce a mottled effect. You can try to control the results by positioning the salt to produce a specific pattern, for example circles, flowers or bands. The silk should be entirely free from salt before fixing. Once the dyes are dry, brush the salt off.

Silk can be painted with a salt solution to create further effects. Use 250 g (9 oz) salt to one litre (1¾ pints) of warm water. Dissolve the salt for one hour and then strain the solution through a filter paper. Paint this solution on stretched silk using a Large brush. Leave the silk to dry naturally so the salt texture can form.

Stripes of colour moved using rock salt

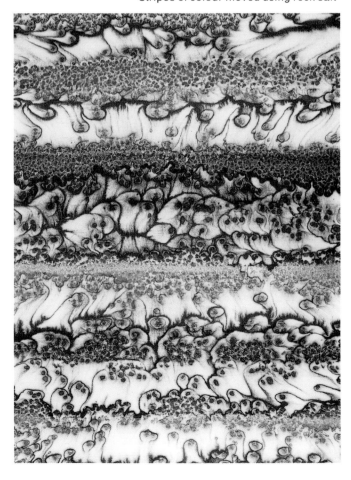

Sugar

This is not quite as exciting as salt, although the sugar crystals do have an effect on the dye if sprinkled on the surface, creating an interesting texture.

The sugar syrup technique can give unusual flowing forms, but be prepared: the drying time of the silk projects can be several days. The sugar solution is made from equal quantities of icing sugar and water. Boil the mixture without stirring until it is reduced by half. The liquid can be used hot or cold. It can be stored in an airtight jar for some time. Re-heat if it goes solid. Drop the thick syrup from a brush or pipette on to the silk. The frame can be horizontal or even upright so that the sugar trickles downwards. Immediately apply the dyes in the gaps beside the syrup. Place the frame flat and leave it to dry. Make sure when fixing that a double piece of paper is used on the silk; this should prevent the concentrated dye from printing through the fixing paper onto the silk during the fixing process.

Effect of sugar syrup on dye

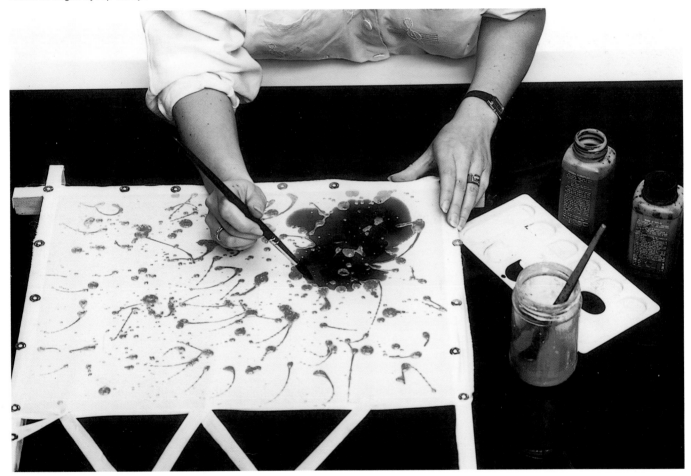

Alcohol

You will find that the stronger the alcohol and dyes, the more effective the results. The textured effect created by the use of alcohol is opposite to the salt technique, as the alcohol disperses the pigment, whereas the salt attracts it (see overleaf). When alcohol is applied to a painted shape or line, the centre becomes paler and the pigment layers itself to the edges. If the process is repeated several times the centre becomes paler and the outside more defined.

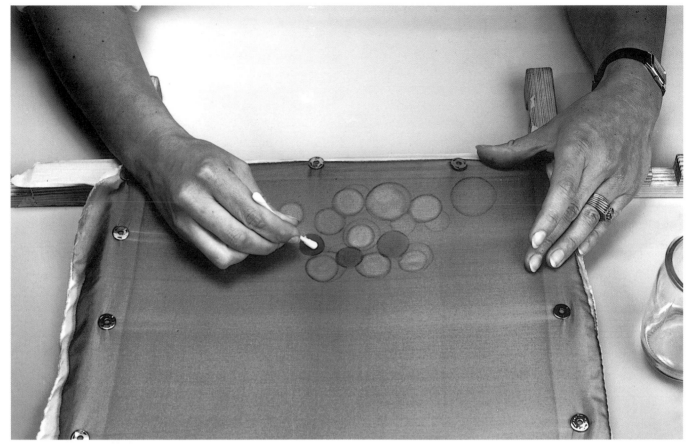

Effect of alcohol on dye

Watercolour technique

The dyes are unrestrained by the barriers of gutta or wax when using the watercolour technique. First paint the surface of the silk with clear or tinted water, with a diluent, or with a 50/50 alcohol/water solution. Remove excess water with a paper towel. Paint your design while the background is still wet; you will find that the colours move less on a wet background than on a dry one. When two colours are placed close to one another on the fabric, see how they run and blend into each other. The wetter the fabric, the more the colours will run. If you do not want the colours to blend, let the first colour dry before applying the second. A larger line will then form. Try painting with one colour on a wet background, then dipping a second or third colour onto it when wet. The variations to this technique are endless and it is great fun to experiment. Try painting the dyes on dry silk. The dye spreads quickly across the fabric, and by working at speed you can produce some very original work.

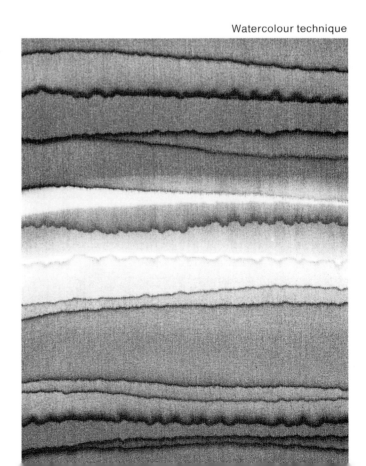

Watercolour technique

28

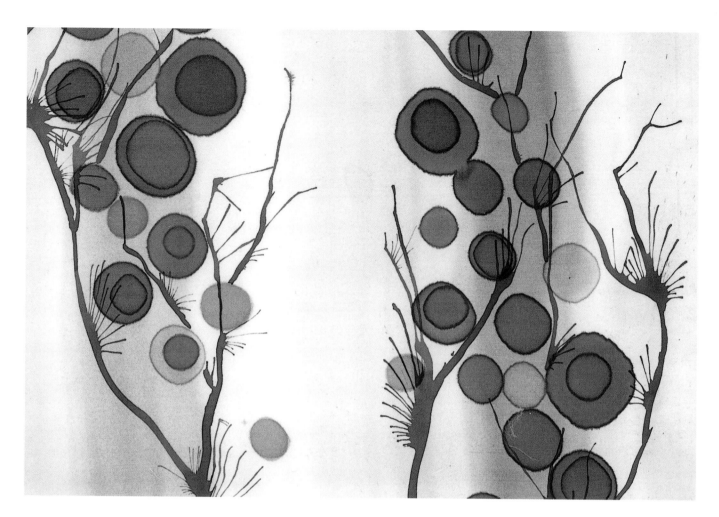

Dye on the surface of the silk after antifusant

Antifusant or anti-spread

Antifusant is also known as stop flow or anti-spread. It is a starch-like fluid used to prevent dyes from penetrating or spreading through the fabric. This allows you to paint directly on to the silk without the dyes spreading. This product is available ready prepared, but it is possible to make your own by mixing solvent and gutta together (we suggest one part of gutta to six parts solvent). The higher the proportion of gutta, the more resistant the silk becomes to the dye.

Coat the silk with anti-spread and allow to dry. Use a cottonwool pad for this; if a brush is used it then has to be cleaned with solvent to remove the gutta. When the anti-spread is dry you can paint directly on to your silk.

Fantastic results can be gained from using this technique with overlaying dyes and combining it with watercolour and salt.

Epaississant or dye thickener

Epaississant, also known as dye thickener, is a colourless glue-like substance. When mixed with the dye this thickener makes it possible to paint directly on the silk without spreading. This is useful when painting fine, detailed work, but its glue-like quality makes it hard to use on large areas when a smooth effect is needed. Alternatively, there is an iron-fix dye on the market which has proved very useful for finer details as it has so thick a consistency. Some of the colours have a slight metallic sheen which is quite attractive.

Stencilling

This technique has always been difficult with steam-fixed dyes, but the new, thicker iron-fix dyes have improved the results tremendously. Some have a metallic sheen which adds to the interest of the colours and enables a greater degree of shading. When the stencil has been prepared on oiled card or acetate, the silk can be stretched out firmly underneath and taped flat to the work surface. Using a flat stencil brush, firmly dab a small amount of dye through the holes. A professional finish can be achieved if more than one colour can be shaded on the same motif. These new dyes do not require the first colour to dry out before others can be added. An interesting combination of techniques is a watercolour or salted background with stencilling on the top.

Christmas design stencil using iron-on dyes

Thick iron-on dyes used for stencilling

Spraying

A spray gun is necessary to achieve even results with this technique, although very interesting textures can be created with a mouth diffuser. Instead of painting a wash background, sprayed colours can give a muted richness to a large area. Quite strong colours can be used, as they lose their strength when sprayed.

Spraying dye through flower stencil

A soft effect is achieved by using a spray design on this wisteria

PART THREE

PROJECTS and

IDEAS

FASHION

SCARVES and SARONGS

Coral reef, hydrangea head and sweet peas. These scarves illustrate sugar syrup, wax and gutta techniques and the projects can be found in this section

Never out of fashion, a scarf is an important accessory. Painting on silk is a splendid way to make your own fashion statements. Rolled and twisted at a whim, the scarf is worn more as a fashionable decoration than as a cover-up.

Pure silk, with its infinitely varied weights and textures, can be painted to suit every occasion. Some of the world's most famous artists have been attracted to the magic of a moving canvas. In the 1940's the Hungarian textile designer Zika Asher commissioned work from Henri Matisse, Jean Cocteau and Henry Moore, and the scarves they designed were later displayed in picture frames. You may wish to frame your own scarves, but in this section we hope to inspire you to create wearable art.

The techniques are varied, as are the types of silk used and the sizes of the scarves. The patterns form a guide, but can of course be modified and interchanged to make your own individual creations. Do not be afraid to sign your work: every time a scarf is painted it is an original, because the colours and techniques can never be repeated. The Paris fashion houses of Coco Chanel and Hermes sign their printed scarves, so why not you? Create your own 'Designer' label!

Types of silk

There are many silks that can be used for scarves. The weight and quality must be considered carefully at the beginning of a project, taking into account the finished effect you wish to achieve.

The most effective silk we have found for scarves is pongée no. 9; it is firm but still drapes beautifully without being too expensive.

If luxury is what you are aiming for, then crêpe de Chine is a perfect choice. It is heavier than the pongées and falls into deeper folds. The dyes are enhanced by the twisted yarns which increase the surface texture. Some people find shading more difficult initially with crêpe de Chine, because the dyes need to be worked well into the fabric.

Brocades, too, are luxurious but rather expensive. Often the self-coloured woven pattern can detract from a complicated silk painting on top. Keep the colours and the design simple so that the fabric itself can impress. Scarves needing a lighter, more 'floaty' effect should be made in something like no. 5 or no. 7, or even lovely crêpe georgette or chiffon. These are much more transparent and are ideal for evening stoles or fine summer scarves.

A more traditional look can be gained by using a pongée no. 10, or a twill. The diagonal grain of the twill can be seen on the most exclusive scarves in the shops.

Organza and taffeta are rather stiff silks, but look quite effective as neat neckline scarves or collars, perhaps even edged in fine lace, or beaded.

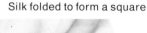

Silk folded to form a square

Scarf sizes

The size of your scarf depends very much on the finished effect required. The silk is usually cut along the straight grain line which runs parallel to the selvedges. It is easy to make a snip at the selvedge and then the silk can simply be torn across. The tear will be along the grain line.

The normal width of pure silk is 90 cm (36 in). A true square will be the width of the silk. To cut an exact square, fold the corner over to the opposite corner, to form a diagonal. Clip at the point where it touches the selvedge (see picture on page 35).

Here is a list of suggested scarf sizes (in metric):

Large	90 cm × 90 cm
Medium	75 cm × 75 cm
	70 cm × 70 cm
Small	60 cm × 60 cm
Long	45 cm × 150 cm wide
	30 cm × 150 cm narrow (3 per scarf width)

Shawl	120 cm × 150 cm
	90 cm × 90 cm
	120 cm × 120 cm – triangle from 120 cm square
	115 cm × 110 cm – cut on the cross
	115 cm × 150 cm – cut in half lengthways and joined – long
Sarong	90 cm × 150 cm
	120 cm × 150 cm – wide
	120 cm × 200 cm – long and wide

Methods of finishing scarves

Once your silk has been painted and fixed by one of the methods described in Part One, it is ready to be made up into a scarf.

If the gutta is to be removed, the silk should be cleaned at this stage. All scarves should then be washed and ironed (see page 17). Painted pin marks and unwanted edges should be cut away from the silk prior to hemming. Place the silk flat on the work surface. Using a pencil or a fade-away marker pen, rule a line along the

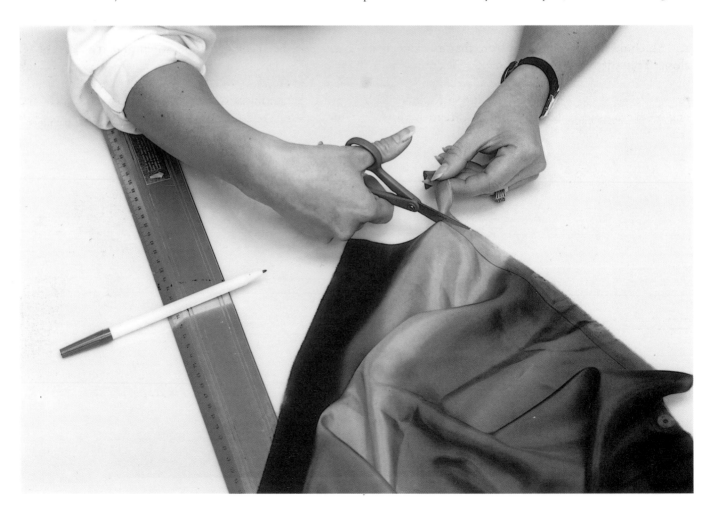

edge of the silk, following the straight grain of the fabric. Remember that at least 1 cm ($\frac{3}{8}$ in) will be taken into the hem if it is hand rolled or machine stitched.

Once it is tidied up, the silk is ready to be hemmed using a fine matching thread. Usually a slightly darker shade of pure silk is recommended, but an ordinary cotton thread could be used instead. Synthetic thread tangles when used for hand sewing and therefore makes the rolling process more difficult.

Silks and sheers require the couture touch of hand-rolled hems. The first thing to catch your eye on any exclusive item is the finish; it takes very little extra effort to impart this same touch and fine workmanship to your own scarves.

Hand-rolled narrow hems

Use this hem to finish your scarves. There are two popular methods, both rather time-consuming and needing practice, but well worth the effort. Never tack this hem or press it heavily afterwards; it should remain fine, soft and rounded.

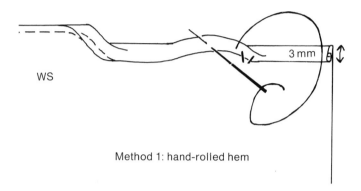

Method 1: hand-rolled hem

1. Machine stitch 6 mm ($\frac{1}{4}$ in) from the raw edge; trim close to the stitching. Roll approximately 3 mm ($\frac{1}{8}$ in) of the edge between the thumb and forefinger, concealing the stitching. Stabilize the roll with the third and fourth finger and slipstitch, taking a single thread with each stitch.

2. For the second method stitch and trim as above. Turn the edge about 3 mm ($\frac{1}{8}$ in) and crease sharply. Pick up a thread alongside the raw edge. Work in a zigzag pattern, making stitches 6 mm ($\frac{1}{4}$ in) apart. Repeat the process for about 25 m (1 in), then pull up the thread to tighten the stitches and create a roll.

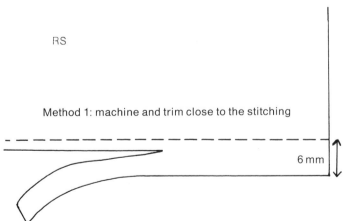

Method 1: machine and trim close to the stitching

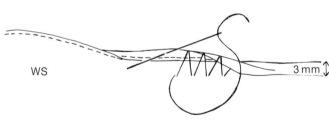

Method 2: zigzag hand-rolled hem

For those who cannot face rolling a hem, some, pre-rolled Chinese silk scarves are available.

◄ Cutting off excess silk

Bright yachts sarong

This sarong measures 90 cm × 150 cm (36 cm × 60 in). The surf is painted first of all, using wax, then the yachts are outlined with opaque gutta. A cloudy look is created in the sky by using diluent with pale grey, blue and a touch of pink. The sand is painted using yellow and brown, then salt is sprinkled on to create texture. Finally, the yachts, sea and landscape are painted in.

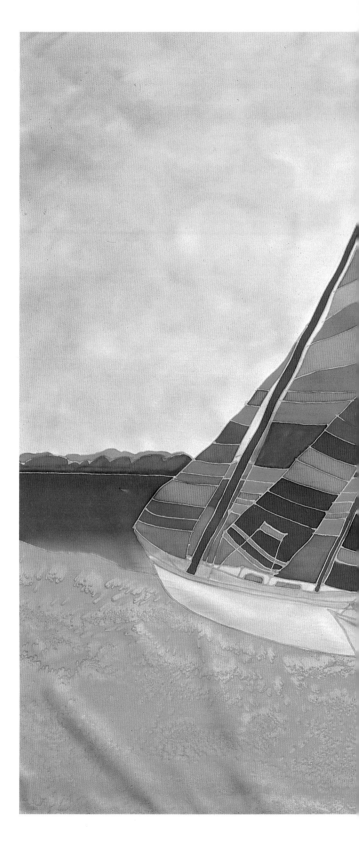

Machine hemming

For those who feel they are unable to hand roll, there are several neat machine methods of rolling a hem.

1. **Narrow straight machine stitched hem.** Turn under 6 mm ($\frac{1}{4}$ in) on raw edge and stitch with a small stitch length close to the fold. Cut away the fabric close to the stitching. Turn under again, encasing the raw edge. Machine stitch the hem in place.

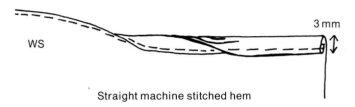

Straight machine stitched hem

2. **Narrow zigzag machine stitched hem.** Alternatively, a narrow zigzag machine stitch can give you a fine, quick hem. Turn under on the raw edge 1 cm ($\frac{3}{8}$ in). Press with an iron. Using a fine, close zigzag setting, machine on the edge of the fold line. Trim off the excess to the edge of the zigzag with sharp pointed scissors.

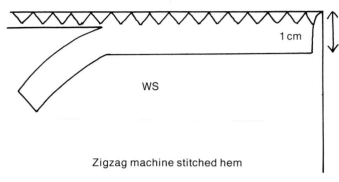

Zigzag machine stitched hem

3. **A narrow hemming machine attachment** could be used on the sewing machine to turn a fine straight hem. The foot double folds and machines at the same time. (See the manufacturer's instructions provided with the attachment.) On the fine silk fabric great care must be taken that the corners do not disappear down the throat plate.

Other finishes

Fraying edges. The two vertical sides of a long scarf could be hand rolled leaving the bottom edge to be frayed out for a natural look.

Take a sharp needle or pin and carefully tease out the fibres of silk, leaving the warp threads behind (see picture opposite). It may be difficult to get started, but once the threads are evenly removed there should be no further problems. The fraying could be from 3 cm ($1\frac{1}{2}$ in) or even longer depending on your patience and the desired finished effect.

Double-sided scarves

This is an interesting idea for a long or a square scarf: it could be lined with a co-ordinating or contrasting colour. You might even have a plain side and a patterned side; the scope is endless. Bear in mind that the scarf may not drape so well, as it is thicker, but against that, it will certainly be warmer.

Method

Place the two scarves right sides together.
Tack 1 cm ($\frac{3}{8}$ in) from the edge on all sides.
Machine on this line leaving a 10 cm (4 in) opening in the middle of one side (preferably not a short side on a long scarf).
Remove the tackings and trim off the corners diagonally.
Turn to the right side and slipstitch the opening together invisibly.
Press flat, rolling the seam line right to the edge.

Designing your scarf

This is very personal and depends on many factors, including the purpose for which the scarf is intended, the skill of the painter and also the technique to be used.

Most designs for scarves benefit by having a border. It seems to bring the whole idea together. Sometimes the design can break into a border to cut across the solid line. A much lighter effect is gained when background colour

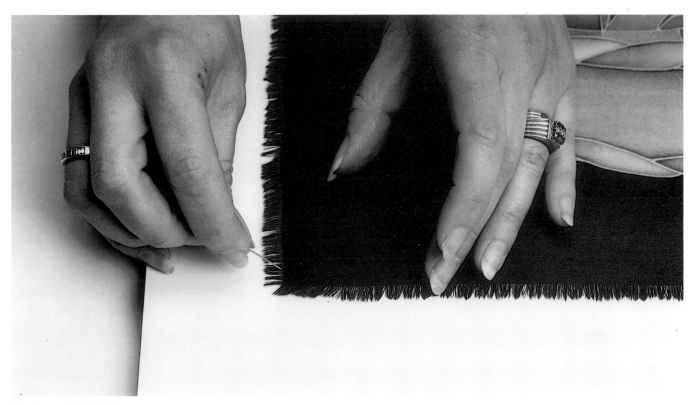

Fraying out silk fabric

goes to the edges; it seems less formal.

Many times a complicated design is lost because the main design or pattern is placed in the middle of the scarf. Bear in mind that the scarf is usually folded into a triangle so that it is from the centre of the bottom corner. Try drawing your design on tissue paper exactly the same size as your scarf. You can then fold and drape it to see what the effect will be like.

PROJECTS

The following scarf projects are accompanied by brief descriptions of their design and method of painting.

As many of the ideas use the same techniques, we have simply shown photographs in some cases.

Gutta technique	Autumn leaves and fruit
	American patchwork sampler
	Tropical bird
	Sweet peas
	Hot air balloons over
	Connecticut–sarong
Gutta/watercolour	Boatmen's sunset
Gutta/spray	Cellular forms
Wax	Hydrangea heads
	Red poppy
	Lightning
	Ripples
	On the beach
Pastel crayons	Squares and squiggles
Sugar syrup	Coral reef
	Blue lagoon

41

AUTUMN LEAVES and FRUIT

Material used: Pongée no. 9
Dimensions: 90 cm × 90 cm (36 in × 36 in)
Technique: Gutta (gold), no. 5 nib

Colours: Bright red, orange, warm brown, dark brown, olive, ivy green

Method

Apply the gutta design (see chart overleaf). Paint one group of leaves at a time and shade using two or three tones of green. Change the shades for another set of colours on contrasting leaf shapes. Do not overload your brush with dye or there will be no opportunity for shading.

The fruit should stand out clearly from the leaves but should also be delicately shaded. Place a deeper tone consistently to one side to round off the shapes.

Remember that the colours of autumn can be quite vivid and varied. The background is painted last in a deep chocolate brown using a large brush or pad of cottonwool.

AMERICAN PATCHWORK SAMPLER

Material used: Pongée no. 9
Dimensions: 90 cm × 90 cm (36 in × 36 in)
Technique: Gutta (gold), no. 5 nib
Colours: Burnt orange, light tan, airforce blue

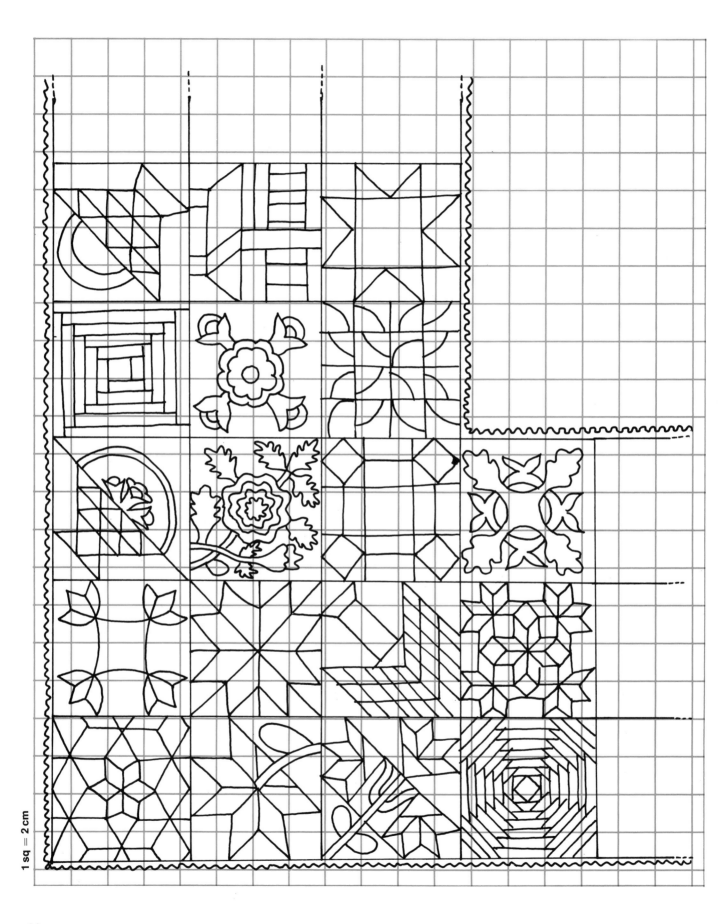

1 sq = 2 cm

Method

The patchwork design is very complicated as a whole: we have drawn out a combination of squares for you to use (opposite). These can be used systematically or can be drawn on to your silk at random.

The depth of the patchwork design is three full squares with a border of 6 cm (2½ in) at the edges. The thicker gold gutta lines in the centre and on the outside of the design are simply broader scalloped bands of the gold gutta.

The three colours are a combination of burnt orange, light tan and a deep airforce blue. Again, the choice is yours. Alternate the three to make different interesting effects. Here the centre of the design is painted in burnt orange and the outside border in airforce blue.

TROPICAL BIRD

Material used: Crêpe de Chine
Dimensions: 70 cm × 70 cm
Technique: Gutta (gold flower and foliage, navy bird), no. 5 nib; alcohol texture
Colours: Yellow, pale cream, peach, orange warm brown, pale turquoise, leaf green jade, burgundy and navy

1 sq = 3 cm

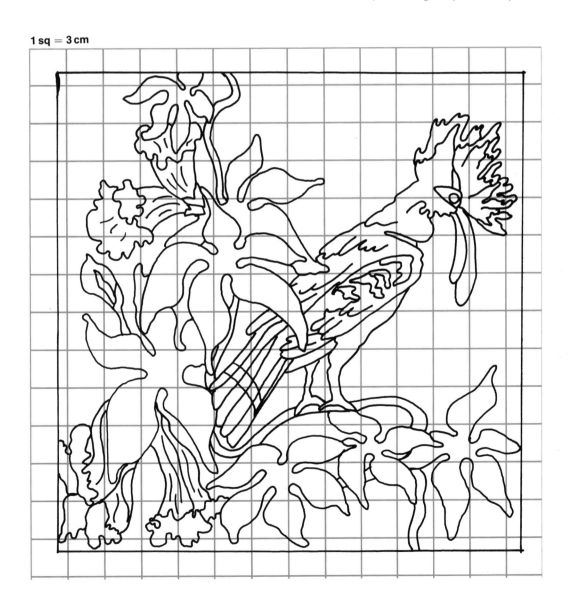

Method

Using the gold gutta first, outline the flowers and foliage. When dry, outline the bird in navy.

Paint the bird in the paler colours first (the yellow and the turquoise/green). Add to it the warmer peach brown tones with a touch of burgundy to enrich the colour. Finally, fill in the dark navy on the wings, tail and head.

The flowers are shades of cream, peach and orange. Do not overload your brush with dye or shading will be difficult; the light edges of the flower tips should be wetted with a little alcohol or water first to stop the dyes from creeping up to the outline.

Use the leaf green with a little yellow for shading on the uppermost leaves. Change to the jade green and add a little navy for the shading on the stems and background leaves.

The centre is a warm peach/brown tone. Dry thoroughly. Then, using the tip of a brush or a cotton bud, dot the surface at the corners with alcohol to create a light texture.

The border is two colours merging, with the navy nearest to the leaves and the burgundy on the outside.

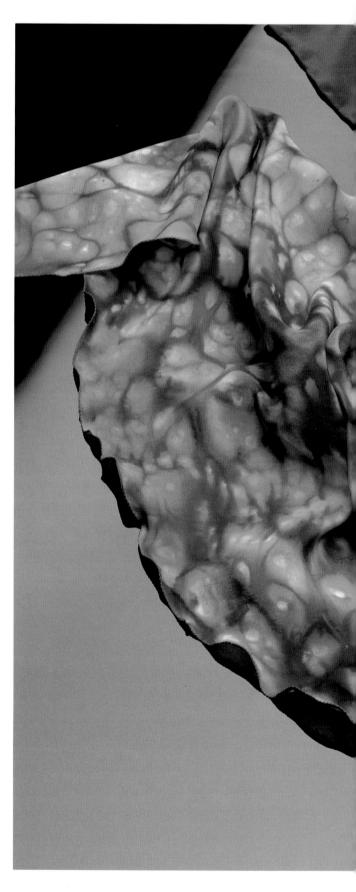

Tropical bird and blue lagoon scarves (see page 63)

SWEET PEAS

See finished design on page 34

Material used: Pongée no. 9
Dimensions: 30 cm × 150 cm (12 in × 60 in)
Technique: Gutta (green on stems, red on flowers, grey on trellis), no. 5 nib
Colours: Pale and deep purple, pale and bright pink, pale and bright red

1 sq = 2 cm

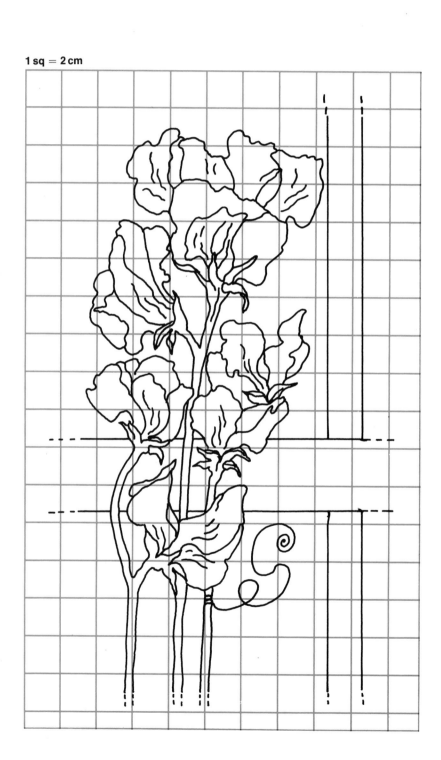

Method

Using the green gutta, outline the stems and sepals. Follow by changing to the red gutta for all the flower heads. The trellis border is in dark grey gutta.

Continue, when dry, to paint the sweet pea flowers. They will need to be painted using a fine brush to achieve the subtle shading. Start with the red on the inner flower, then change to shades of pink, and finally use the purple and minute touches of pink on the outer heads. To help retain some white silk, place dots of either diluent or water on the edges of the individual petals. This painting cannot be hurried if you want to achieve fine, detailed shading.

Paint in the cross stripes in bright pink and deep purple. Tone down these colours with diluent and paint in the background colours pale pink and pale purple.

HOT AIR BALLOONS SARONG

See finished design on pages 50 and 51
Material used: Pongée no. 9
Dimensions: 90 cm × 150 cm (36 in × 60 in)
Technique: Gutta (clear), no. 5 nib
Colours: Pale blue, yellow, red, green, pink, purple, turquoise, light and dark.

Method

Apply gutta as shown below. Dry thoroughly. Paint the sky first using a pale blue dye mixed with diluent. Try to give the idea of distance by lightening the colour near to the skyline. Paint straight over the balloons (the stronger colours will cover these tones).

Using the entire range of bright colours, paint in the balloons as you wish. The people and the baskets are painted in grey and brown. Finally, paint in the hills, again using lighter shades of green in the distance and bottle green in the foreground.

1 sq = 5 cm

Hot air balloons over Connecticut sarong

GUTTA WATERCOLOUR

BOATMEN'S SUNSET

See finished design on page 54
Material used: Crêpe de Chine
Dimensions: 70 cm × 70 cm (28 in × 28 in)
Technique: Watercolour, gutta (black) no. 5 nib;
sea salt
Colours: Pale yellow, blue, pale grey, pale
orange, blue, burnt orange, dark
brown

Method

Using the black gutta, draw over the design and the
border lines. Dry thoroughly.

Wet the entire piece of silk with diluent so that the
dyes used for the watercolour effect will go on smoothly.
Mix the pastel shades of the blue, grey, yellow and
orange tones and apply smoothly with a large brush over
the background. Keep the sky in predominantly orange
and yellow tones to represent the sunset, moving down
into the blues and reflected orange by the boats.

You can paint on top of the boats, as these will later be
painted over in a darker colour. Never let the background dry as you are working it, as lines will form.

When the watercolour is complete, dry using a hair
dryer, then paint in the boats using deeper tones of
brown. The sails are stronger tones of burnt orange and
brown.

Finally, paint the narrower border burnt orange and
the outer border in dark brown. Whilst the dark brown
border is damp, sprinkle it with crystals of salt. Wait for
these to draw up the dye (usually this process continues
until the silk is dry).

1 sq = 4 cm

GUTTA SPRAY

CELLULAR FORMS

See finished design on page 55
Material used: Crêpe de Chine
Dimensions: 90 cm × 90 cm (36 in × 36 in)
Technique: Spray and gutta (colourless), no. 5 nib
Colours: Lemon yellow, pale grey, grey, pale purple, deep purple

Method

Cut out the square of silk and pin loosely into folds on an upright frame. Prepare three shades of dye (lemon yellow, pale grey and pale purple) ready for spraying the background. A spray can was used for this, but an airbrush or even a mouth diffuser would create the same effect. Holding the can at least 25 cm (10 in) away from the silk, start to spray. Try to follow the folds to re-create them with colour. Do not overspray so that the silk becomes wet; several light layers are better than one heavy one. Change your dye to the second colour and try to spray from the underside of the fold this time, rather than on top of the first colour. Unpin the silk and recreate folds and drapes from another side. This will add an extra dimension to your work. Spray with the third colour on these new folds and on the plainer areas.

Carefully remove the folded silk from the frame and stretch it on your frame as normal. Make sure that the silk is dry. Gutta abstract cellular forms on the less interesting areas of the scarf. Using a broad ruler, draw in the border about 6 cm (2¼ in) from the edge. Gutta the border and dry thoroughly.

Paint in the cellular forms using pale and deep purple. Shades of grey can be added to give definition. The border is painted last in a dark grey.

1 sq = 5 cm

Boatmen's sunset scarf

Cellular forms scarf

HYDRANGEA HEADS

See finished design on page 34
Material used: Pongée no. 9
Dimensions: 30 cm × 150 cm (12 in × 60 in)
Technique: Watercolour, wax, sea salt
Colours: Pink, pale and deep purple, navy

Method

Position groups of flower heads and leaves randomly on the length of the scarf. Make sure that the leaves and flowers vary in direction. Draw on the silk lightly in pencil. Mix up two shades of pink, a lilac and a pale blue for the wash background colours. Using a large brush, cover the background with random stripes of these colours across the width of the scarf. Heat the wax and paint over half the flower head design, sealing in the first layer of colour. Paint over this with a second wash of stronger pink and blue tones. Dry carefully using a hair dryer, being careful not to melt the wax. Add the final petals to the full hydrangea heads in wax. Also place on the leaves in wax.

Mix up the final purple colour and, using a large brush, cover the entire scarf in an even wash. As the scarf is painted, sprinkle on sea salt crystals. When the silk dries, these will create a random texture. Leave the scarf to dry naturally. When dry, remove the salt and iron off the wax between sheets of absorbent paper. The scarf is now ready for fixing.

1 sq = 2 cm

Lightning and ripples scarves

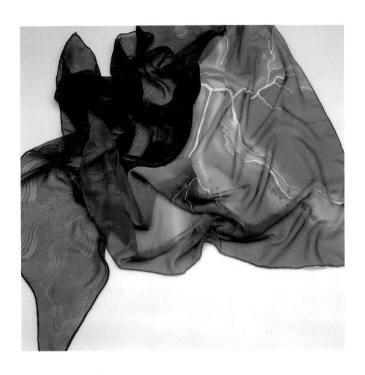

On the beach sarong

RIPPLES

See finished design on page 59
Material used: Crêpe georgette
Dimensions: Triangle cut from 120 cm × 120 cm
                 square (48 in × 48 in)
Technique: Wax
Colours: Tan brown, pale blue/grey, navy blue
              with a hint of purple

Method

Paint the whole scarf with a wash of two colours (the grey blue and the tan brown). They can be applied in rough, rounded shapes of colour. Take care not to leave any white areas unpainted. Dry with a hair dryer.

Using a fan-shaped wax brush, wiggle light lines of wax over the whole area of the scarf. Some can cross over at right angles. With a large brush or cotton wool pad, cover the entire scarf with navy blue. Leave to dry naturally. Remove the wax. The scarf is now ready for fixing.

ON THE BEACH – SARONG

See finished design on page 59
Material used: Pongée no. 9
Dimensions: 90 cm × 150 cm (36 in × 60 in)
Technique: Watercolour, wax, sea salt
Colours: Turquoise, navy, royal blue, jade,
              yellow, light tan, brown

Method

Wax in the white parts of the sunshades and the deck chairs using a medium-sized wax brush. At this stage you also need to wax in the waves at the shoreline. They need to form a continuous barrier for the blue dye, but should not look too solid; try flicking the brush tip with your fingertip to spray the wax upwards on to the sea area.

Mix a pale turquoise blue shade with diluent and paint across the top of the silk to a depth of about 20 cm (8 in); try to vary the tone to indicate clouds. Dry carefully with a hair dryer. Do not melt the wax.

Apply a broad band of wax across the skyline on top of but at the base of the sky colour. Then paint the darker blues of the sea below this line, up to the waves. (**Note**: There should be no white line between these two sections.)

Paint in the jade, blue and turquoise of the sunshades. Wipe off any colour which falls on the white wax.

Finally, paint in the sand using the bright yellow and light tan. Vary the shading over the beach; sprinkle salt on while wet for extra texture. Iron off the wax and fix between two sheets of paper.

PASTEL CRAYONS

SQUARES and SQUIGGLES

See opposite and finished design on page 62
Material used: Crêpe de Chine
Dimensions: 90 cm × 90 cm (36 in × 36 in)
Technique: Dye pastel crayons, steam fix, dyes
Colours: Crayons: beige, turquoise, purple,
              mauve, black
              Dyes: tan, pink, purple, olive, navy
              blue

Method

Stretch the silk out on a frame. Using a dye pastel crayon, firmly draw the framework of the design using the chart opposite. Change colours frequently and add the shapes and symbols within the squares. The crayons must be applied strongly, or they will not form a resist for the dyes. Melt the lines with a hair dryer. Paint in your dye colours randomly. Try to space them out evenly. Do not paint the dyes on too heavily, or they will creep under the barrier created by the crayons. Also, for the same reason, try to paint beside a squiggle or motif rather than over it. Remove the silk when dry. Remember when fixing to add extra paper to absorb the wax.

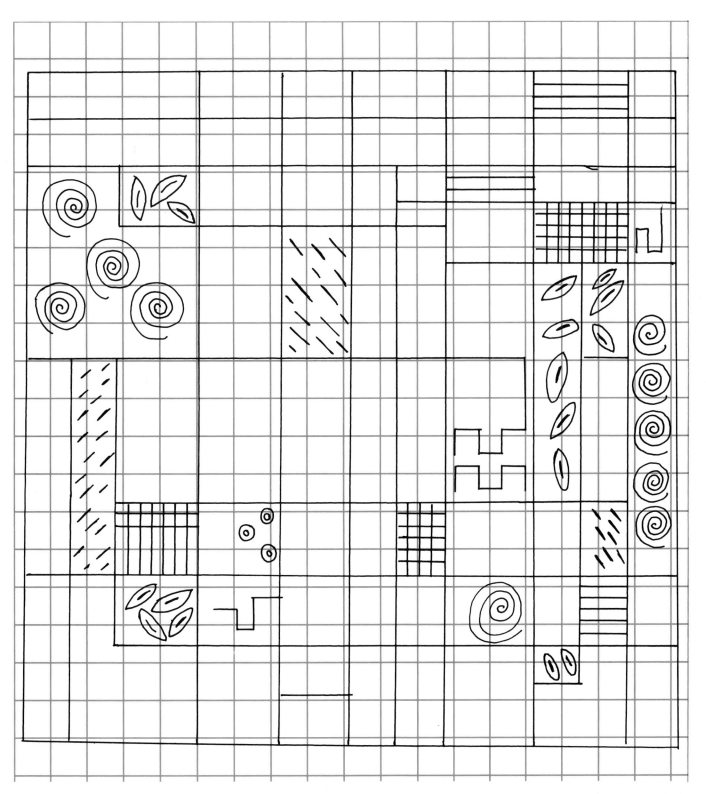

Squares and squiggles

1 sq = 5 cm

Squares and squiggles scarf

$\mathcal{S}$UGAR $\mathcal{S}$YRUP

CORAL REEF

See finished design on page 34
Material used: Crêpe de Chine
Dimensions: 2 pieces 30 cm × 150 cm (12 in × 60 in)
Technique: Sugar, syrup, watercolour
Colours: Tan brown, red, pink/burgandy, grey

Method

Warm up the sugar syrup (use the recipe on page 27). Stretch the two pieces of silk 60 × 150 cm (24 in × 60 in) as a whole on the frame. Draw a pencil line down the centre for the back and front. Stand the frame upright on the floor resting against a wall. Using a large brush, not necessarily an expensive silk painting brush, drip the sugar syrup down one half of the silk. Make sure you have placed newspaper underneath the frame as this technique is rather messy! The idea is to create long streaks at random and of varying lengths and thicknesses.

Pour your colours into jam jars and then drip these down the silk on top and beside the sugar streaks. Make the silk quite wet with the dyes so as to create a reaction with the sugar. Leave the frame upright for several hours. Keep the colours used on the front half of the scarf; they can be used for the second half which will be shaded using the watercolour technique.

Lay the frame back on a table and, using a large brush, paint soft stripes of all the colours along the length of the second side. Try to blend the colours smoothly where they join. Pale colours should always be mixed with diluent for smooth shading. (See information on water-colour techniques on page 28.)

Allow the sugar syrup to dry; this may take up to three days. The silk can then be fixed, using a double piece of paper, separately from the other work.

BLUE LAGOON

See detail below and finished design on page 47
Material used: Crêpe de Chine
Dimensions: 115 cm × 90 cm (46 in × 36 in)
Technique: Sugar syrup
Colours: Emerald, turquoise, ivy green, purple/blue, navy blue

Method

Warm up the sugar syrup (use the recipe on page 27). Stretch the silk on a frame. Keep the frame flat on the table. Drip the sugar syrup on the silk, using an old brush; put plenty on in blobs of different sizes. Paint around the sugar with all the colours. Make the silk quite wet with the dyes, so that the whole piece is painted.

Continue to drip more sugar syrup on top of the wet dyes; they will continue to react for some time. Leave for two or three days until the syrup has dried. Fix separately from other work. Use at least double thickness of paper.

Blue lagoon scarf – detail

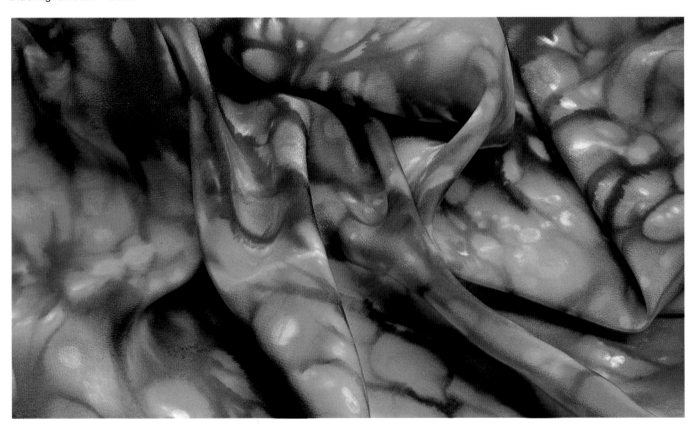

CAMISOLE and TOPS

Silk fabric feels wonderful next to the skin and is ideal for special tops, either for day wear or for the evening. We have chosen some very simple styles which can be sewn easily by the average dressmaker.

Patterns

The pattern layouts are intended as a guide for your silk painting rather than as an accurate cutting layout. They will help you decide on placing of colours, textures and motifs on the fabric. Remember that all the painting is done on square or rectangular pieces of silk with the pattern shapes drawn on. These are then cut out accurately to size after the fabric has been fixed.

Try to choose a very basic pattern for your first attempts. Avoid darts, pleats and tucks. Often, the simpler the pattern, the more effective your silk painting will be. Silk drapes so well and has such a natural sheen that it will not be necessary to incorporate elaborate sewing techniques.

Commercial patterns are available in styles similar to those we describe here. Simply cut out the pattern shapes and lay them on your silk fabric as shown on the commercial pattern layout. Draw on your pencil and gutta outline at least 2 cm ($\frac{3}{4}$ in) larger than your pattern so that the seam allowances will be painted in coloured dye. Nothing looks worse than white background creeping into your garment or pin marks from the silk painting.

Design

Keep your designs simple. Colours can be vibrant for stunning impact – see the camisole top and bag on page 66 – or subtle for tasteful classical styles, as shown in the jackets. The designs can be minimal, to show one or two painting techniques to great effect: gutta, watercolour, salt, antifusant and wax have all been used in this section. The placing of a motif is important: make sure it is not too low on a blouse so that most of it is tucked away into skirts or trousers. On a top, remember that the seam allowances encroach into a neckline shaping, so do not place a motif too near an edge. The eye can also be drawn away from areas which you may not want to accentuate – for example, place a bird or flower motif on the shoulder and neckline rather than on the bustline if you have a heavy bosom. Remember the back of your garment. The design could continue over the shoulder on to the back, or a small part of the larger front design could be placed on the back for eye-catching detail.

Draw the design on to the actual pattern piece to ensure the correct positioning; the proportion of the design is important.

Type of silk

We have used crêpe de Chine as the main fabric in most of these examples, as it is slightly thicker than the pongée and therefore not so 'see through' when painted in pale shades. It also hangs and drapes beautifully because of its extra weight.

Pongée no. 9 was used for several of the simpler tops and also for the lining of the jackets. A heavier pongée could also be used for any of the tops. Other silk types could include satin brocade, twill and soie sauvage. The latter does not drape softly, but is ideal for jackets and skirts.

Any materials that you use with the silk should be dry cleanable or washable. Pre-shrink cottons if they are to be used as lining fabrics.

Sewing silk on the machine

Many people are afraid to use a fine fabric such as silk, claiming that it is too difficult to sew. This is not the case if a few points are considered beforehand.

- Always cut out the fabric using very sharp scissors to avoid snags.

- Carefully pin and tack the seams so that they do not move under the presser foot.

- Choose a suitable seam for the garment. Flat seams with small zigzag finish or french seams are recommended. We prefer to see the neat finish of a french seam on tops which are unlined (see diagrams opposite).

- Make sure that your needle is fine and has a sharp point. Renew regularly if snags occur.

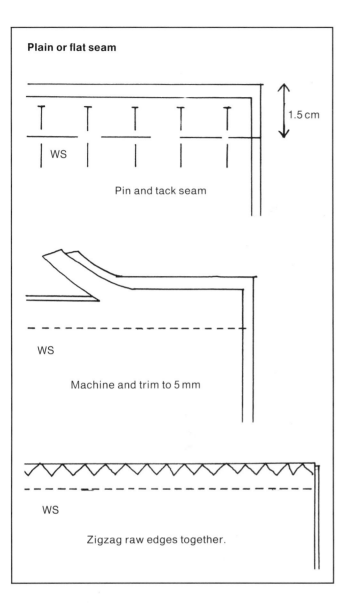

Plain or flat seam

1.5 cm

WS

Pin and tack seam

WS

Machine and trim to 5 mm

WS

Zigzag raw edges together.

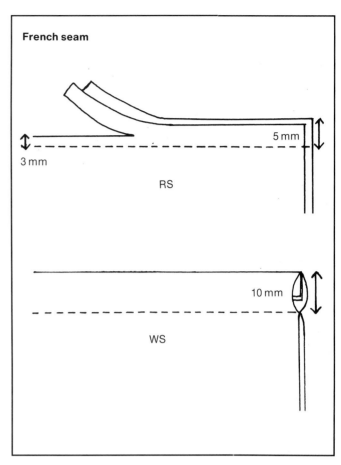

French seam

3 mm

5 mm

RS

10 mm

WS

- Use a small stitch length and stretch the silk slightly as you feed it under the presser foot. This will allow a little extra 'give' so that the seam line does not look too tight.

- Sewing thread should preferably be of pure silk although, if this is not available, a good quality cotton and synthetic mixture could be used instead.

- Always use a steam iron and press regularly throughout the construction of the garment.

- Hems and necklines on blouses can be machined using a narrow, fine straight stitch edge or by hand rolling the edge (see page 37). Those of you with machines which have the facility of special embroidery patterns could simply sew a decorative finish on the neckline or hems for a pretty and unusual edging.

PROJECTS

BUTTERFLY CAMISOLE

See finished design on page 66
Finished size: Dress size 10–12 (38–40)
Material used: Crêpe de Chine
Fabric requirement: 45 cm × 92 cm (18 in × 37 in) – bodice
15 cm × 92 cm (6 in × 37 in) – straps straps and butterfly
30 cm × 90 cm (12 in × 37 in) – wadding
70 cm × 92 cm (28 in × 36 in) – bag
Technique: Salt – bodice, straps and bag
Antifusant – butterflies
Appliqué – butterflies
Colours: Fuchsia, pink, bright purple

Method

Paint the whole piece of bodice silk, strap and bag in shades of purple and fuchsia pink. Salt the wet surface to create textures. Allow to dry. Coat a small square of silk, 10 cm × 10 cm (4 in × 4 in) with antifusant and delicately paint on butterfly shapes. Paint three or four so that the better two can be chosen. Fix as normal. For methods of appliqué, see opposite.

Sewing up the garment

1. Cut out the bodice and strap pieces.

2. Machine along foldline as shown in diagram.

3. Press to form a fold.

4. Tack centre back seam. Adjust the size at this stage.

5. Machine back seam (see diagram on french seam, page 65)

6. Machine length of the straps, wrong side facing. Turn to right side. Tuck under ends. Hem. Adjust to fit.

7. Sew on to bodice at front and back. Machine under fold line. Hand sew invisibly at the top edge.

8. Machine narrow hem on bottom edge of camisole.

9. Sew on detached appliqué butterflies.

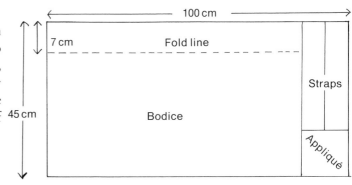

Pattern layout of camisole top

Camisole top and matching piped clutch bag. Separate painted butterflies are applied to the shoulder

Appliqué

This is a separate piece of fabric which is sewn to a larger piece of fabric as an extra decorative motif. There are two ways in which you could make your appliqué and apply it to the background fabric:

Detached appliqué

1. Paint the silk motif, fix, wash and iron flat.

2. Sandwich three layers of material together – the painted top piece, the wadding in the centre and the silk or backing fabric underneath. Using a pointed needle and working from the middle, baste (large tacking) the layers together. Keep all the layers smooth. This stage of preparation is very important to the final finish of the piece.

Preparing and sewing butterflies for appliqué

Effective gutta graffiti in gold and black enhances these three tops (see Method on page 70)

3. Using the zigzag setting, machine a satin stitch around the motif. The stitch length is nearly o and the stitch width approximately 2 mm ($\frac{1}{16}$ in).

4. Clip off the ends of the machining and trim excess silk very close to the machine stitches, using small sharp pointed scissors.

5. Small pieces of appliqué finished in this way will tend to 'curl'; either lightly steam flat or leave to give a three-dimensional effect, as with the butterfly.

6. Sew by hand on to the garment. Appliqué could be easily removed if sewn to garments which cannot be washed. The silk is washable.

Appliqué trapunto

1. Roughly cut out your shapes to be appliquéd.

2. Tack to the background fabric in final position.

3. Using small satin stitch, zigzag around the motif. Trim to stitches using sharp, pointed scissors.

4. Turn to the inside of the garment and make a small slit in the centre of the shape following the grain. Gently push in padding from behind with a knitting needle. Fill until the surface is sufficiently raised.

5. Close the slit by oversewing the edges neatly together.

6. The shell design below was then quilted along the centres in running stitch to create extra texture.

GREEN and BLUE STRIPED TOP

Finished size:　Dress size 10–12 (38–40)
Material used:　Crêpe de Chine
Technique:　Watercolour
Colours:　Jade green, dark blue

Method

Paint the whole silk green. When dry, apply one layer of pale blue stripes down the length of the silk. Dry with a hair dryer. Using slightly stronger blue dye, paint on some more stripes to create fluted edges. Dry with a hair dryer. Fix as normal.

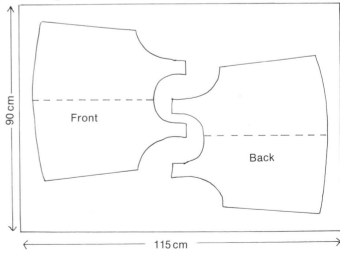

Pattern layout for green and blue top

Sewing up the garment

1. Cut out as in the diagram.

2. Machine shoulder and side seams using french seam (see page 65).

3. Roll neck and armhole edges. Roll up the hem (see page 40).

4. Press lightly.

'LADY'S LACE' TOP

Finished size: Dress size 12–16 (40–42)
Material used: Crêpe de Chine
Technique: Gutta (clear), watercolour
Colours: Pale yellow, peach, green

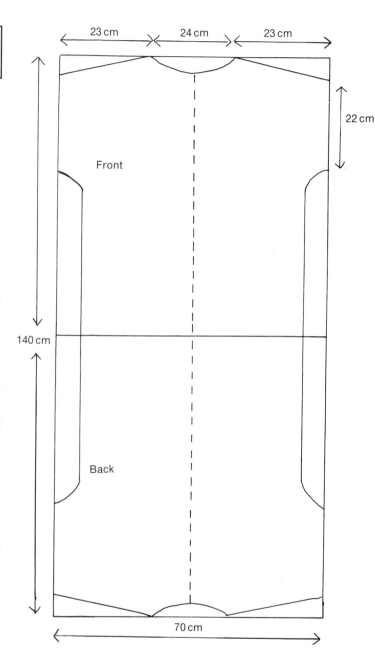

Pattern layout for 'lady's lace' top

Method

Using a wide nib, no. 7, draw on the 'lace' effect for the front design in clear gutta. Allow to dry. Paint the three colours in broad bands across the silk, allowing the dyes to dry between the application of each colour so that some interesting edges are created. Fix as normal.

Sewing up the garment

Follow the instructions given for the striped top opposite.

RED WHITE and BLACK GRAFFITI TOPS

See finished designs on page 67
These three tops are included to show the effect of simple gutta designs on silk. The silks themselves were not hand painted, but bought and used in their original colours.

Very dramatic designs can be created using gutta:

1. The red top has a black gutta 'squiggle' repeated all over the surface both front and back.

2. The white top uses black and gold gutta alternately, forming a triangular design both back and front.

3. The black silk top looks exceptionally good with a large gold gutta design repeated all over the front and back of the silk. Great care should be taken when ironing – always use a steam iron on the wrong side of the fabric. Do not dry clean gold or coloured gutta, as the particles will be removed.

Sewing up the garments

Follow the cutting layout for 'lady's lace' top on page 69 and sewing instructions for the top on page 68.

Quilted daffodil top

QUILTED DAFFODIL TOP

Finished size: Dress size 10–12 (38–40)
Fabric requirement: 90 cm × 90 cm (36 in × 36 in) crêpe and pongée
Material used: Crêpe de Chine (outside), pongée no. 9 (lining)
Domette for quilting
Technique: Wax, quilting
Colours: Cream, yellow, green, purple, navy

Method

Using a few daffodils as inspiration, roughly draw their shapes on the front square of crêpe de Chine. Paint in pale cream and purples for the outer petals. Dry, then wax over the cream in petal forms. Add dye in bright yellow to the centres of the flower trumpets. Paint some purple and green in the very middle. Allow dyes to merge and flute out at the edges. Paint leaves in cream and green. Dry, then cover all areas to be kept in wax. Paint over the background in dark navy with flashes of green and purple. Paint the back of the top in navy, green and purple as for the front. Paint lining for the top in navy.

Sewing up the garment

1. Follow the cutting layout for 'lady's lace' top on page 69. Baste together the front and back sections in their three layers: the painted silk on top, the domette wadding, and the pongée lining as the backing. Do not cut out the pattern pieces at this stage as the quilting will shrink the fabric.

2. Lightly quilt the front of the top on the flower petals and in some of the centres using a running stitch.

Method of quilting

There are several stitches which can be used for quilting:
    straight machine stitch
    machine zigzag stitch
    hand back stitch
    running stitch
    reverse chain stitch

The choice of stitch depends on the finished effect required. In many cases the simple running stitch is the most useful, as it is quick and easy to sew. It also makes a less definite outline which does not detract from the silk painting but just adds to the decorative texture.

The type of wadding used depends again on the final effect required. Usually the garment needs to remain soft and supple, so a domette would be preferable. Terylene wadding can also be used, although it is much thicker.

3. Cut out the back and front. Machine together across the shoulders and down the sides.

4. Neaten inside seams by making a flat fell seam.

5. Turn under the hem, armholes and neckline and sew neatly to the lining.

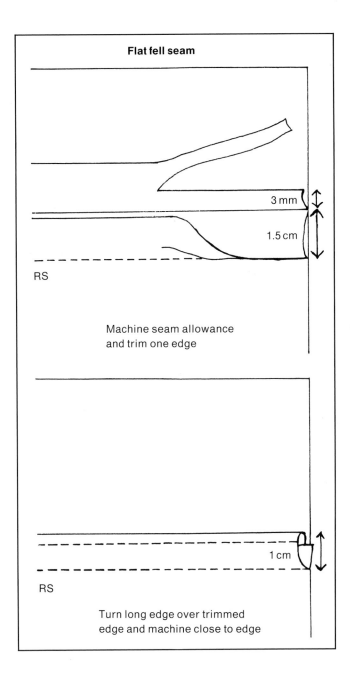

Flat fell seam

3 mm

1.5 cm

RS

Machine seam allowance and trim one edge

RS

1 cm

Turn long edge over trimmed edge and machine close to edge

KIMONO and JACKETS

These three stunning garments show the full potential of silk painting and using the fabric to make original pieces of work. We recommend that you buy commercial patterns of similar designs to create these unique garments accurately, although we do give approximate fabric requirements in all three projects. Draw your designs in the pattern pieces and trace them in the correct position on your silk.

WATER LILY KIMONO

See finished design on page 74

Material used:	Crêpe de Chine, pongée no. 9 lining
Fabric requirement:	Approximately 4 m × 90 cm (4½ yd × 36 in) each
Technique:	Gutta (gold), no. 6 nib
Colours:	Vivid greens, cream and yellow. Navy background

SHORT ART NOUVEAU JACKET

Method

Draw the waterlily design on the back and two fronts of the kimono. You will need a 1.5 m (1¾ yd) length frame to do this. Gutta the outline in gold and paint in the subtle shades of the cream and yellow waterlilies. Paint in the bright apple green and emerald of the waterlily pads; shade to create interest. Paint the whole of the background navy. Paint a piece of silk bright green to edge the arms and bind the neckline. The waist ties could be in either green or navy.

Material used:	Crêpe de Chine, pongée no. 9 lining
Fabric requirement:	Approximately 2.5 m (3 yds) each
Technique:	Gutta (black), watercolour
Colours:	Pinks, red, grey blue

Method

Paint as for jacket opposite, but when the background is dry lightly paint some abstract lines in blue.

THREE-QUARTER LENGTH ART NOUVEAU JACKET

See finished design on page 75

Material used:	Crêpe de Chine (jacket), pongée no. 9 (lining)
Fabric requirement:	Approximately 3 m (3½ yd) each
Technique:	Gutta (black)
Colours:	Avocado green, pinks, lilacs and navy blue
Diagram:	Design taken from an original Brussels fresco

Method

Draw the stylized lady in her flowing gown on the left front of your pattern. The flowers were placed at random on the sleeves, front and back of the garment. The lady was painted in subtle shades of pinks and lilacs with the deeper pinks on the formal roses. The base and leaves are in navy and green. The background was painted using a pale avocado green. The contrasting lining is pink with a hint of grey.

1 sq = 4 cm

A bold waterlily design is applied in gold gutta onto this full-length kimono

Art Nouveau three-quarter length jacket in Crêpe de Chine, lined with contrasting pink pongée

Waistcoats have seen a fashion revival over the past few years. The three models here are each in a different style using a variety of silk painting techniques.

Your waistcoat will certainly be an original and can be specially made to link with other items in your wardrobe to create a co-ordinated designer touch. It can be worn either in the daytime or for a special evening occasion.

It is not necessary to paint the whole waistcoat yourself. Maybe you could paint the front and buy a matching or contrasting lining for the back and inside. We have painted the whole garment to make it that little bit special.

You may want to buy a commercial pattern to make up your waistcoat, as they vary in cut from season to season. Try to find a pattern that does not break into the front pieces with darts or bust shaping, as this may spoil your design when it is sewn up. If it is not possible to do this, try to take into account where the darts will come and calculate the design around it, or paint an all over pattern that will not show up the shaping so much.

A simple motif carefully placed on a front can look interesting. Complicated designs are often just not necessary.

QUILTED GRAPES WAISTCOAT

See finished design on page 78

Finished size: To fit size 10–12 (38–40) approximately

Material used: 90 cm × 80 cm (36 in × 32 in) soie sauvage, back and front
90 cm × 80 cm (36 in × 32 in) crêpe de Chine, back and front lining
50 cm (20 in) wadding for quilted areas
Matching thread
Synthetic lining behind quilting

Technique: Gutta (black), salt

Colours: Deep purple, pale greens and pinks, amber

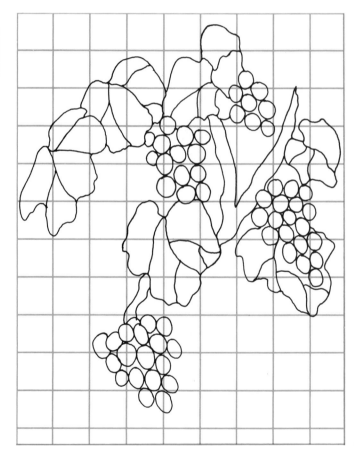

1 sq = 2 cm

76

Method

1.   Mark out the pattern pieces with a good margin for seam allowances and allowing extra for shrinkage with the quilting. Draw the design on to the soie sauvage.

2.   Stretch the silk, and gutta the leaves and grape design. Use a large nib (no. 7 or no. 8) so that the gutta will penetrate through the thick silk. Check the back and re-gutta if necessary.

3.   Paint in the leaves and branch in greens and pink tones and shade the grapes carefully in pinks and purples. Dry thoroughly.

4.   Mix up a large quantity of pink and amber dyes. Using a large brush, paint evenly across the background, starting with the pink and gradually changing to the amber for the main body of the waistcoat. A touch of purple may be added at the points. Sprinkle sea salt lightly on the waistcoat, from the middle to the base, to add texture and a rich colour variation. Leave to dry. Paint the crêpe de Chine lining a plain deep purple.

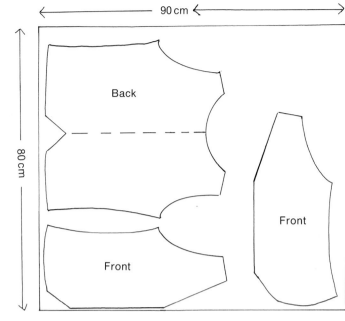

Quilted waistcoat pattern

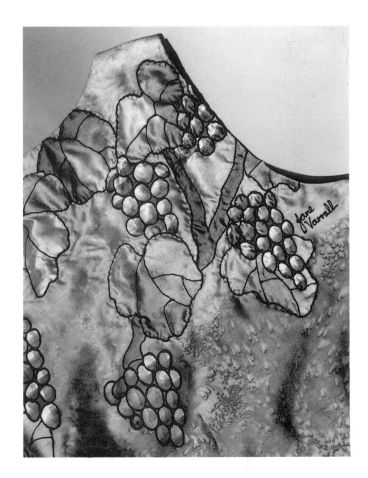

Close-up of waistcoat back

Sewing up the garment

1.   Cut out the soie sauvage allowing 2 cm ($\frac{3}{4}$ in) extra for quilting. Cut out the lining according to the pattern to make it slightly smaller.

2.   Quilt some of the leaves and grapes to give an extra dimension to your work (see quilting on page 71).

3.   Adjust the front and back size of the waistcoat after quilting. Pin, tack and stitch the fronts to the back at shoulder seams. Do the same to the lining.

4.   Matching shoulder seams, right sides together, pin, tack and stitch the lining to the waistcoat at the armhole, neck, front and lower edges. Clip the seams well at the curves.

5.   Turn the waistcoat to the right side, pulling the garment through the shoulder and out through the side seam.

6.   Press. Pin, tack and stitch the front and back of the waistcoat together at the side seams.

7.   Press under seam allowances on the lining and neatly oversew together to finish off the seams.

8.   Give a final press to the waistcoat.

Different styles of waistcoat using wax and gutta techniques: quilted grapes waistcoat, waistcoat A (left), waistcoat B (right)

WAXED WAISTCOATS A and B

The two waistcoats, right and left, have different patterns, but use the same wax techique.

Finished size: To fit size 10–12 (38–40)
Material used: 65 cm × 90 cm (26 in × 36 in) soie
               sauvage, fronts and belt
               150 cm × 90 cm (60 in × 36 in) pongée
               no. 9, back and lining
Extras: 4 buttons
Technique: Wax
Colours: A: purple, bright pink, bright blue, olive
               B: cream, pale pink, bright pink, grey

Method

1.   Mark out front pattern pieces on soie sauvage.

A: paint all over – areas of bright blue and pink using a cotton wool pad or a large brush. Dry thoroughly. Heat the wax and using a fan-shaped wax brush whisk over the surface at random, forming half-moon shapes. Mix up a large amount of olive green as this will be your lining colour too. Paint over waxed silk with the olive dye. Leave to dry with dots of dye remaining on the surface of the wax. Iron off wax. Fix as normal.

B: paint pale cream and pinks all over the background using a cotton wool pad or a large brush. Dry thoroughly. Heat the wax and use a fan-shaped wax brush to make circles all over the silk. Do this lightly. Mix up pale grey dye and paint over the wax. Dry carefully with a hair dryer.

Heat up the wax again. Re-apply circles all over the silk in the spaces and overlapping some of the original ones. Mix up a large amount of strong grey dye (this will also be your lining colour). Paint over the waxed silk with the grey dye and wipe off some of the excess dots of dye with cotton wool. Remove wax and fix as normal.

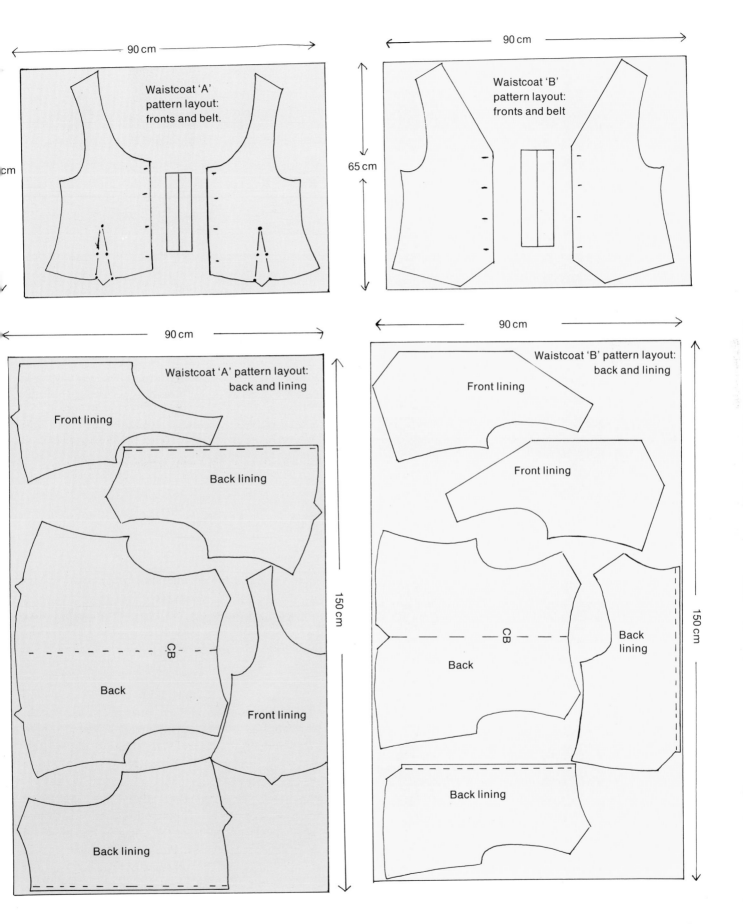

90 cm

Waistcoat 'A'
pattern layout:
fronts and belt.

90 cm

Waistcoat 'B'
pattern layout:
fronts and belt

65 cm

90 cm

Waistcoat 'A' pattern layout:
back and lining

Front lining

Back lining

150 cm

Back

CB

Front lining

Back lining

90 cm

Waistcoat 'B' pattern layout:
back and lining

Front lining

Front lining

150 cm

Back

CB

Back
lining

Back lining

Finished back of waistcoat

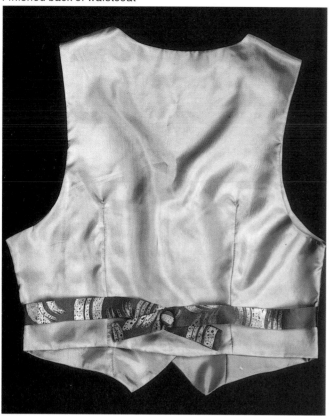

2. Paint the back and lining of waistcoats. Ours are plain, but they can be shaded or salted for extra interest. Fix as normal.

Sewing up the garments 'A' and 'B'

1. Cut out the front pieces and two belt pieces in soie sauvage. Cut out the backs and lining pieces from the pongée.

2. Waistcoat 'A'. Sew darts in fronts and lining fronts.

3. Waistcoats 'A' and 'B'. Place interfacing on wrong side of waistcoat fronts.

4. Sew two belt strips right sides together and across one end. Turn through and press. Tack to the outside seams of waistcoat front.

5. Continue following the 'grapes waistcoat' method nos. 3–6 on page 77.

6. Cover buttons to match in the leftover pieces of soie sauvage. There should also be enough for brooches and earrings; maybe even a hair bow. Work four buttonholes on the right fronts. Sew buttons on the left fronts. Sew a button on the overlapping back belt pieces.

7. Press the garment.

ᛏIES and ᛒOW TIES

A man's appearance can be made more individual by a silk-painted tie. It is often easier to co-ordinate with his existing wardrobe because you may choose your own colour combinations.

We have some samples here painted on soie sauvage (wild silk) which show you a wide variety of techniques and colour combinations. We recommend that you choose a strong, firm silk such as soie sauvage or a good heavy quality of crêpe de Chine. Bear in mind that the creases formed by the knot could spoil a tie made of a lighter weight of silk. We also suggest that the tie is dry cleaned so as not to reduce the 'body' of the fabric.

Designing your tie

Any pattern can be painted on a tie: stripes, dots, dashes, abstract designs. The main point to remember is that the

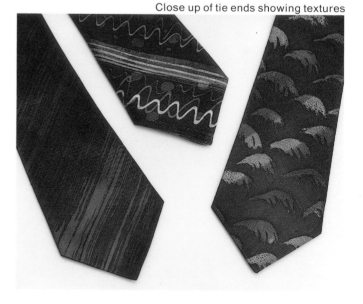

Close up of tie ends showing textures

tie must be cut out on the cross so that it will fold and hang properly. When planning the design, take this into consideration. On our pattern layout we show the centre front position of the tie so that you can even work out where an individual motif or signature would need to go.

Another point to consider is that one tie will be cut out from the bottom left-hand corner of silk, but the other tie will be cut from the top right-hand corner. If you are painting one motif regularly over the whole silk, then the right-hand tie might end up with a motif upside down. Try to create a motif that has no top or bottom; or one that can be painted in both directions. Stripes are ideal as they can be painted along the horizontal so when cut out they form the diagonal stripe down the tie. You can draw a gutta line down the diagonal of the silk and paint two different ties, one on each side.

Painting your tie

As you can see from the variety of effects we have created, ties can look very individual. The techniques used here are:

watercolour
wax
salt

You could also use gutta in combination with the above methods, although you must take care with a thick fabric like soie sauvage that the gutta penetrates the whole way through. You may need to gutta on the back of the silk, as well.

PROJECTS

1. **Watercolour stripe** *(see page 82)* Stretch up your silk. Choose two colours; here we have selected a bright red and grey, but any combinations can be used. Taking a narrow and a wide brush, paint evenly across the horizontal width of the silk, starting from the top. Try to blend the edge of the next colour into the one above. Work smoothly and quickly so that each band does not have time to dry out. Alternate the widths of the stripes to add interest when the tie is cut out.

2. **Salted stripe** *(see page 82)* Four colours were chosen – pale and dark grey, burgundy red and navy blue. This time the tie was painted in two stages. The pale grey, dark grey and burgundy were painted in stripes as above. As they were painted, sea salt was sprinkled randomly on the silk to create a texture when it dried. To create more interest, the fourth colour, navy, was very lightly painted over the top of the original stripes with a fine brush when the first layer was dry.

3. **Peacock feathers** *(see page 82)* The techniques used here are wax and watercolour. Two shades of jade green and emerald green were painted on the whole background area of the silk, using a large brush. The colours were painted at random but blended in where they joined. The background was then dried thoroughly and the wax heated. The heads of the feathers and spines were painted on using a fine wax brush. Make sure that your design has the heads of the feathers quite close together and in different positions so that when the tie is made up they can be seen.

The wax will have retained all of the background colour. Now simply paint over the whole piece of silk with a dark colour (we have used black). If you want a crisp, clear effect, wipe off any surplus dots of dye which may be resting on the wax with cotton wool. Sometimes it is nice to leave these on as they create extra texture: the choice is yours. When the painting is dry, iron off the wax and steam fix as instructed.

Bow ties showing wax and watercolour textures ▶

Ties showing different techniques: grey (salted), peacock (waxed) and striped (watercolour)

Making up a tie

Material used: Painted silk
Interlining for the centre of the tie
Matching lining for the end sections

Extra materials: Matching thread

Method

1.   Place the pattern pieces for one tie on the silk. It is sometimes easier to draw the layout on using a ruler and marker pen. The tie is made up of three sections cut on the bias (see Figure c).

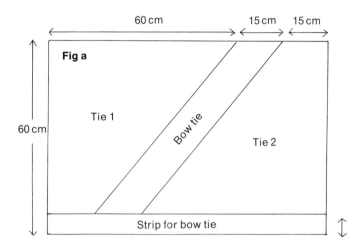

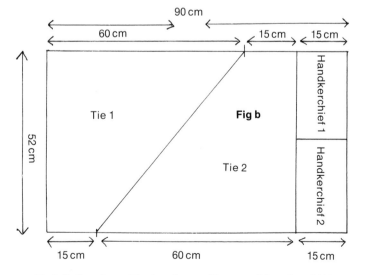

Fig a Pattern layout for two ties and one bow tie

Fig b Pattern layout for two ties and two small handkerchiefs

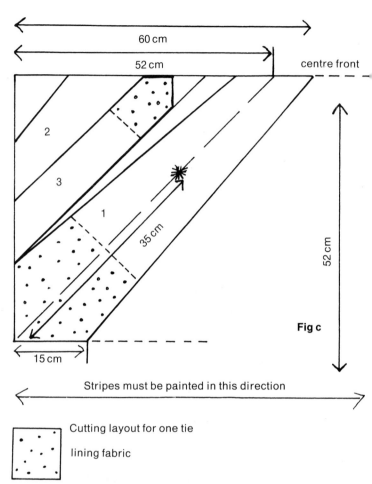

Fig c

Stripes must be painted in this direction

Cutting layout for one tie

lining fabric

* Top of motif 35 cm from point.

2.   Pin the sections together numbers 1, 2 and 3 using a 1 cm ($\frac{3}{4}$ in) seam allowance. Machine and press the joins open.

3. Cut out the centre interlining piece (see below). This can be made of any pre-shrunk woven fabric of a firm body. Tack into position down the centre of the tie.

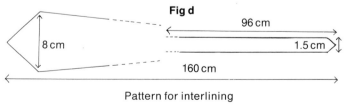

Fig d

Pattern for interlining

4.   Cut out, in the lining fabric, the two lining end sections (see the spotted shading on Figure c). Tack on to the tie ends right sides together and machine carefully around the points. Trim across the points and turn through to the right side. Press the points carefully.

5. Press under 1 cm ($\frac{3}{8}$ in) down the length of one side of the tie.

6. Fold over the top of the other side and loosely slip-stitch the edges together. Take care that these stitches do not penetrate through to the front.

7. Lightly press with this seam down the centre back of the tie.

Fig e

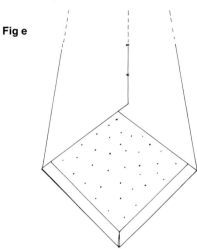

Back of tie showing lining

Making up a bow tie

Bow ties are very fashionable at the moment, both for evening and for day wear. They tend to vary in size as fashion dictates.

The instructions given below and overleaf are for two small evening bow ties. You could allow extra material for making up a bow tie while making ordinary ties (see Figure a).

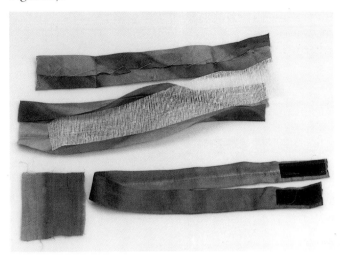

Pieces required for making the blunt-ended bow tie

BLUNT-ENDED BOW TIE

Final size: 30 cm × 30 cm (12 in × 12 in)
Material used: Painted silk cut in the following measurements:
        Bow – 2 pieces 10 cm × 23 cm (4 in × 9$\frac{1}{4}$ in) cut on the bias
        Knot – 1 piece 6 cm × 7 cm (2$\frac{1}{2}$ in × 2$\frac{3}{4}$ in) cut on the straight
        Neckband – 1 piece 45 cm × 5 cm (18 in × 2 in) cut on the straight
        Interfacing (if using soft silk) 2 pieces 4 cm × 23 cm (1$\frac{1}{2}$ in × 9$\frac{1}{4}$ in)
Extra materials: Matching thread
        Velcro fastening – 4 cm (1$\frac{1}{2}$ in)

Method

1. Place interfacing down the centre of the two bow sections. Press the edges of the silk over the interfacing. Oversew the join lightly using large stitches.

2. Fold bow pieces into three, making the upper bow very slightly smaller than the lower one.

3. Machine the long neckband right sides together 1 cm ($\frac{3}{8}$ in) from the edge. Turn through to the right side. Press with the seam down the middle. Tuck under the ends and slipstitch.

4. Attach a small strip of Velcro fastening to the wrong side at one end and the right side at the other end.

5. Take the knot piece and press under 1 cm ($\frac{3}{8}$ in) on both of the long sides. Fold almost in half, enclosing the raw edges, and press again. It will be quite effective if when sewn together, the knot shows two little edges on the right side.

6. Pinch the bow sections together in the middle and hand sew securely.

7. Place the neckband behind the bows and fold the knot piece over these. Try to hold the centre tight while you overlap the back of the knot. Hand stitch neatly.

POINTED BOW TIE

Final size: 40 cm × 30 cm (16 in × 12 in)

Material used: Painted silk cut in the following measurements:

Bow – 2 pieces 6 cm × 40 cm (2½ in × 16 in) – cut on the bias, pointed at both ends

Knot – 1 piece 6 cm × 7 cm (2½ in × 2¾ in) – cut on the straight

Neckband – 1 piece 5 cm × 55 cm (2 in × 22 in) – cut on the straight

Extra materials: Matching thread

Velcro fastening – narrow stip 15 cm (6 in) narrow strip

Metal hook and ring for fastening

Method

1. Place the two pointed sections right sides together. Machine 1 cm (⅜ in) from the edge. Leave a small gap for turning in the centre of one side. Trim at the points.

2. Turn through to the right side. Press carefully.

3. Machine a narrow strip of hook Velcro 5 cm (2 in) long to the neckband silk approximately 2 cm (¾ in) in from the long edge (see below). Machine the narrow fluffy strip of Velcro on to the silk at least 10 cm (4 in) away from the first strip and approximately 10 cm (4 in) long.

4. Machine the long neckband right sides together 1 cm (⅜ in) from the edge. Turn through. Press with the seam on the edge.

5. Tuck under one end and slipstitch in place. On the other end insert the metal hook facing uppermost.

6. Slide the metal hook into position between the two Velcro sections. The neckband is now complete.

7. Take the knot piece and press under 1 cm (⅜ in) on both the long sides. Fold almost in half, enclosing the raw edges. Press again.

8. Concertina fold the bow so that one point sits from right and the back point is back left.

9. Complete as from stage 6 on page 85.

Pieces required for making the pointed bow tie

CRAVATS and HANDKERCHIEFS

These can be painted on a softer fabric: a crêpe de Chine or twill would be suitable. The cravat below can be cut out on the straight grain if fabric is short, but hangs better if cut on the bias.

Material used: Painted silk for the front and back, *or* silk front and lining back
40 cm × 90 cm (18 in × 36 in) – if cut on the straight grain.

Cravat pattern layout

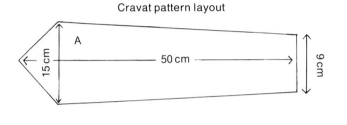

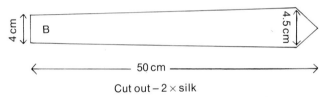

Cut out – 2 × silk

Add 1.5 cm seam allowance.

Cravats with top pocket handkerchiefs

Method

1. Cut out two 'A' pieces and two 'B' pieces. (One set will be the lining.)

2. Place right sides together on both sections and machine 1 cm ($\frac{3}{8}$ in) from the edge around the point, leaving the straight narrow end open. Turn through to the right side and press.

3. Tuck under 1 cm ($\frac{3}{8}$ in) on the narrow edge of piece 'B'. Press.

4. Gather up the wide straight end of piece 'A' and push into the end of piece 'B'. Arrange the gathers neatly.

5. Either machine across this join to secure, or hand sew invisibly.

Top pocket handkerchiefs

These are a bit of fun to link up the tie with a suit. Using the leftover end sections of silk, cut out a rectangle and neaten the raw edges with either a straight stitch or a small zigzag stitch (see Figure b on page 84).

Ladies' handkerchiefs

Painted on a fine pongée no. 7 or no. 9, handkerchiefs could make pretty, personal gifts. They are squares of silk 45 cm × 45 cm (18 in × 18 in) which when hemmed form a square of 40 cm × 40 cm (16 in × 16 in). Four handkerchiefs could be painted at one time on a 90 cm × 90 cm (36 in × 36 in) square of silk.

The handkerchiefs could include a person's name or be painted to match a special outfit and worn in a jacket pocket. Even children could paint a special one for a granny or aunt.

Ladies' floppy bows

Brighten up the neckline or collar of a plain blouse with a bow tie. Floppy bows are best made in crêpe de Chine, but other soft silk fabric could be used. We paint several at one time. The length needs to be 1.5 cm ($\frac{3}{4}$ in) and the width of each strip 20 cm (8 in). When machining up you can either form a point at the ends or sew straight across.

HOME FURNISHINGS

PICTURES

Any one of the techniques for painting on silk can be used to create an original picture for your walls. If you combine a few of the techniques, you will find you have created something truly personal and unique. Even a beginner can produce work to be proud of, from miniatures to large abstract paintings which will look wonderful on your walls.

Always sign your work; this can be done in gutta or wax, or alternatively a gold or silver permanent marker can be used.

Once you have completed your silk painting and decided you would like to display it on a wall, you must decide how to present it. There are several methods of displaying your silk paintings:

- Traditional wood and metal frames
- Flat glass or perspex box frames
- Silk stapled over a wooden frame
- Wall hangings

Backing

Before mounting and framing your painting, it needs to be placed on a backing. We find a piece of cardboard or mount board ideal for this. Choose white board, as brown or grey will dull the colours on the silk. Another piece of card or hardboard can be used as a final backing sheet when placing the picture in the frame. For larger paintings, hardboard must be used to keep the picture rigid. The silk can be attached to the backing sheet by various methods:

1. The silk can be attached to the backing sheet using a spray adhesive. Great care must be used when doing this; if too much adhesive is applied it will soak through the silk. Hold the spray can 15–20 cm (3–4 in) away from the surface of the silk and coat with a fine spray. Place the silk gently into position on the backing sheet.

2. The silk can be stretched and taped to the backing board using masking tape or double-sided sticky tape. Again, this is easier with a smaller piece of silk; large pieces sometimes crease or wrinkle.

3. We find this method the best as it always eliminates any wrinkles, bubbles or creases that may occur. A sticky backing paper made for lampshade-making is used. The best method of sticking the silk to the sticky backing is to stretch it on a frame or a flat wooden board. Make sure it is right side down and that no wrinkles or bubbles are present. Then peel the covering off the backing and roll the paper on to the silk, sticky side down, rubbing with your hands as you go. Unpin the silk, turn over and make sure there are no bubbles on the right side.

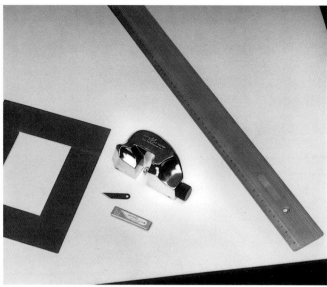

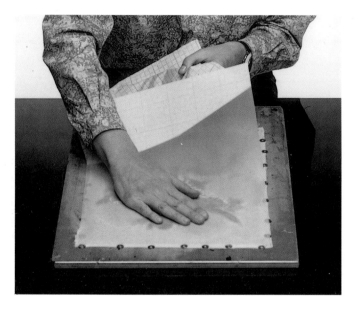

centre, which will give a similarly attractive edge.

As a general rule, good proportions when cutting mounts are 6 cm (2½ in) at the top and sides and a little more at the bottom. Obviously larger pictures can tolerate a wider mount. The mount can now be placed over the silk painting on the backing, and the picture is ready for framing.

Mounting

There are hundreds of colours to choose from when selecting your mount. Some subjects can be improved by the use of a coloured mount, but be careful and try to select a colour which will enhance your painting (see the baby picture on page 91). The purpose of a mount is to separate the painting and the glass, and to cover the edges of the silk where it has been pinned to the frame for painting.

Cut your mount board to the size of your frame. The centre piece of the mount board is then cut out, forming a window for viewing your silk. Be sure to measure and mark the rectangle on the mount board before cutting so that just the right amount of picture is showing.

A steel ruler and craft knife or an angled cutting blade are needed to cut the mount. The cutting blade is ideal for this, as a perfect 45° angle cut is obtained. However it is possible to hold your knife at an angle away from the

Framing

Traditional picture frames

Picture frames have two purposes: to protect the silk from dust and stains and to enhance the picture. The correct frame is important and can make or ruin a picture. To choose the frame for your painting, it is best to take it with you to the frame shop and try various styles. A frame that is too narrow may spoil the picture, while a frame that is too large will smother the painting. Today there is a wide choice of frames available. You can buy ready-made frames, or pre-cut self-assembly frames, or even build your own.

Ready-made frames

Ready-made frames are available in a wide choice of styles and many different sizes. It is worth checking on these before you mount your painting; if you have a difficult size you will have to build your own frame or take your picture to a professional frame-maker.

A traditionally mounted baby birthday picture (see page 96)

Pre-cut self-assembly frames

Pre-cut frames which you can easily assemble yourself are available in most art and craft shops and hardware stores. They clip or screw together at the corners. We find this method very economical if you have a few paintings to frame, are hesistant about building your own and don't want to spend a lot of money at a specialized shop. These pre-cut frames are available in wood, metal and plastic, and come in a wide variety of colours and finishes.

Two sets of lengths are required in the sizes appropriate for your painting. You will also need a piece of backing board and glass.

Building your own frame

One advantage of building your own frame is that you can decide on the exact measurements you need for your painting. If you decide to do this, it is worth investing in a mitre box so that you make accurate 45° corner cuts. A

Miniature pictures showing different techniques

set of four clamps is also a good idea, as it allows you to glue up all the frame at once.

There are hundreds of different mouldings to choose from but try to select one which will complement your painting. First saw off the end of your moulding at a 45° angle, then carefully measure the longest side of the mounted picture and add 0.25 cm ($\frac{1}{8}$ in) to this measurement to allow the silk painting to fit into the frame easily.

Measure the moulding and starting from the edge of the mitre cut at a point where the picture inserts into the frame. Mark and cut a 45° mitre at the other end of the piece you have just cut. Repeat this process, as you will need a piece exactly the same for the opposite side. Next measure the short sides of the picture and cut two pieces of moulding this length, not forgetting to add the extra 0.25 cm ($\frac{1}{8}$ in) to allow your painting to fit the frame. Now the parts are all ready to assemble.

Take one side piece and the bottom piece and coat with glue the ends which are to be joined. Place carefully in the clamps and tighten while you nail the corners together. Check that the pictures will fit the frame. Repeat this process in the other three corners and allow the glue to dry thoroughly.

Glass

When buying the glass for your frames, you will find there are two kinds: single-strength picture glass, and non-reflecting (sometimes called non-glare) glass. Perspex can also be used: it has the advantage of being much lighter in weight than glass, which can be useful in a very large painting; however, it does tend to scratch easily.

Primulas in a flat glass frame (see page 96)

To assemble the picture

Check that you have everything in the right order and the right way up, and that the glass is clean. You should have: frame, glass, picture, mount, whiteboard, hardboard.

Place everything into the frame and use brads or glass points to hold the backing in place. Insert these all around at 10 cm (4 in) intervals. The back of the frame can be sealed using brown paper. This can be taped to the frame using gummed paper or masking tape, or you can wet the brown paper before applying. As it dries it will shrink to a tight finish.

Fix some screw eyes to each side and fasten wire or heavy cord across. Your silk painting is now ready to hang and enjoy.

Flat glass or perspex box frames

These are very easy to use. Perspex box frames can look particularly effective with a silk painting inside, as you can see through the sides and do not need a mount. Flat glass frames, sometimes called poster frames, can be used with a mount or you can display your silk painting using spray adhesive and the frayed edge look (see p. 40).

Staple the silk over a wooden frame

This is an inexpensive method for framing your silk. The silk is stapled around a wooden frame and backed with a cotton lining to strengthen it. This has the same appearance as the perspex box in that you can see the sides of the painting, but has the disadvantage of giving no protection from glass or perspex so that in time your painting will get dusty and may stain and fade in the sun. If you have padded, quilted and beaded your silk picture, this is an ideal way to display it as the effect you have created may be lost if you put it behind glass.

Wall hangings

Wall hangings can be supported by a pole which runs through a casing. This is formed by sewing approximately 3 cm ($1\frac{1}{4}$ in) away from the top edge of the

Materials required to assemble and hang your picture

Domes in a perspex box, 40 × 60 cm (16 in × 24 in)

hanging. Sew the layers of fabric together with small running stitches. Turn under the fabric ends and sew by hand to finish off. Then simply slide the pole through the opening formed. Attach the pole to the wall with hooks.

The base of the wall hanging can be held together by two wooden battens. These are glued together using a rubber-based glue with the layers of fabric sandwiched in between. The battens need clamping firmly until the glue dries. An alternative method is to simply turn under the lower edges and sew together neatly by hand. Weights can be inserted before sewing to make your work hang evenly.

Stapling silk and lining around a wooden frame

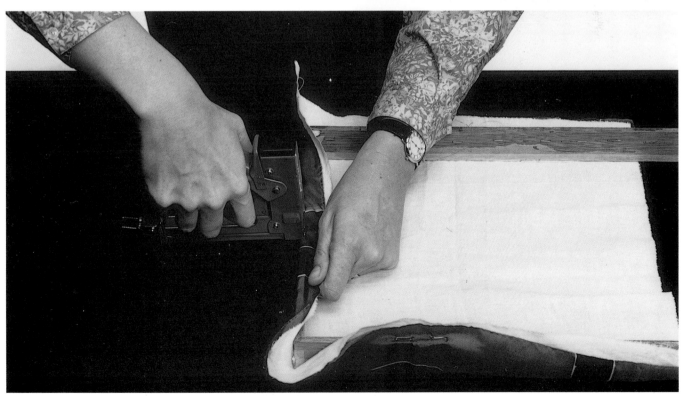

painted using brown dye diluted to a pale beige with diluent. Paint the leaves and flowers using a variety of reds and greens to create interesting shading effects. After fixing, remove the wax by ironing (remember not to dry clean the silk as this will remove the gold gutta). This picture has a backing layer of white cotton and has been stapled over a wooden frame.

Quilted flower wall hanging (see page 96)

CHRISTMAS WREATH

Material used: Silk pongée no. 9
Dimensions: Cut your silk 75 cm × 90 cm (30 in × 36 in)
Finished picture 60 cm × 75 cm (24 in × 30 in)
Technique: Wax and gutta (gold), no. 5 nib
Colours: Brown, red and green

Method
After drawing the wreath on the silk, the delicate white flowers are painted using molten wax and a thin brush. Gold gutta is then used to outline all the flowers, berries, leaves, etc. When the gutta is dry, the background can be

EDELWEISS FLOWER SHOP

Material used: Silk pongée no. 9
Dimensions: 90 cm × 60 cm (36 in × 30 in)
Technique: Wax, antifusant
Colours: Red, green, yellow, blue, purple, orange

Method

This painting uses a combination of wax and antifusant techniques. When painting either traditional or false batik it is very difficult to obtain reds and greens on the same painting without a long process whereby the picture must be dry cleaned and re-waxed halfway through the work. Here, by covering the silk with a solution of antifusant, many coloured flowers can be painted directly on to the silk. Wax any flowers, pots, lables, etc. which are to remain white, and then wax over all the coloured flower heads you have painted. The work then continues as a false batik, waxing and drying as many times as you wish. Finally, remove the wax by ironing and dry cleaning or by soaking in white spirit. Wash and iron the silk; cut a mount and frame using one of the methods shown earlier. We chose to use a sticky backing on this picture (see page 89).

QUILTED FLOWER WALL HANGING

See finished design on page 94

Material used:	3 m (3¼ yds) crêpe de Chine
	1.5 m (1¾ yd) lining
	1.5 m (1¾ yd) wadding
Dimensions:	85 cm × 140 cm (34 in × 56 in)
	Cut silk 90 cm × 150 cm (36 in × 60 in)
Technique:	Gutta (black), watercolour, salt, alcohol, antifusant
Colours:	Beige, purple, orange, red, brown, grey

Method

The design for the wall hanging is loosely based on a flower. Half of the silk area will form the front of the wall hanging, hay will form the back. The design was sketched lightly on to the front of the wall hanging and grew as the paint was applied.

The gutta lines in black were drawn as an indication of the design, but were not intended to inhibit the progression of the painting.

The background is painted first. In order to get an even wash, paint the silk in diluent. Using very muted tones of beige, orange, grey and brown cover the whole background area. Sprinkle a little sea salt in selected areas to create a texture. Dry.

Strong tones for the leaves, stems and hillsides can now be painted in using grey, brown, tan and cinnamon colours. Allow the dyes to creep over the silk to create interesting shapes. Halt the movement by drying them quickly with a hair dryer.

Continue to fill in the trumpet-shaped flower heads using purple and many tones of red. Dry and repaint to create decorative outlines. When the basic shape has been painted, dry thoroughly. Coat the flower area and its surround with antifusant (see page 29). Now you can paint further delicate colours on top of the initial ones to create more depth in your work. These will show up much stronger when the silk is fixed.

Paint the back of the hanging in pale cream, tan and grey tones to link up with the front. Quilt selected areas (see page 71) and complete the hanging as on pages 92 and 93.

BABY'S BIRTHDAY PICTURE

See finished design on page 91

Material used:	Silk pongée no. 9
Dimensions:	80 cm × 65 cm (32 in × 26 in)
Technique:	Gutta (gold), no. 6 nib
Colours:	Iron-on dyes: white, red, yellow, blue, green, purple

Method

Draw the design on to the silk and outline using gold gutta and a no. 6 nib. When the gutta is dry, paint using iron-on dyes. A white dye is available which can be mixed with other colours to obtain lovely pastel shades. When fixed, the picture can be stuck on a sticky backing (see page 89), mounted using blue mount board, and framed in a traditional wooden frame.

PRIMULAS IN A BASKET

See finished design on page 91

Material used:	Silk pongée no. 9
Dimensions:	60 cm × 50 cm (24 in × 24 in)
Technique:	Gutta (gold), no. 5 nib
Colours:	Brown, orange, red, green, yellow

Method

This is a straightforward gutta painting. Try to create shading on the basket and leaves. When painting the flowers, add a second colour while the first is still wet to obtain the distinctive primula look.

When the painting has been fixed, carefully tear down each side and then fray the edges. Spray the back with adhesive and stick on the mount board before framing in a flat glass frame.

LUPINS IN A VASE and FIELD OF SUNFLOWERS

See finished designs on page 98
Material used: Silk pongée no. 9
Dimensions: Lupins in a vase – 70 cm × 90 cm
(28 in × 36 in)
Colours: Pink, red, maroon, brown, olive green, black
Field of sunflowers – 85 cm × 70 cm
(34 in × 28 in)
Colours: Yellow, olive, salad green, brown, black
Technique: False batik

Method
These two pictures have both been painted using the false batik method described on page 24.

NEW YORK SKYLINE

See finished design on page 99
Material used: Silk pongée no. 9
Dimensions: Cut your silk 90 cm × 45 cm
(36 in × 18 in)
Finished picture 85 cm × 40 cm
(34 in × 16 in)
Technique: Gutta (clear), no. 5 nib
Colours: Blue, grey and pink

Method
Draw your design on the silk, and use a no. 5 nib and clear gutta to outline all the buildings. When the gutta is dry, paint the sky in any combinations of colours you like – sunsets, stormy clouds and night skies can all be attempted as backgrounds. Proceed by painting all the buildings and the river in tones of grey and blue. After fixing the silk is washed, ironed and mounted on a sticky backing (see page 89) before framing.

ABSTRACT

See finished design on page 99
Material used: 90 cm × 90 cm (36 in × 36 in) Crêpe de Chine
Dimensions: 80 cm × 80 cm (32 in × 32 in)
Technique: Salt, spray, antifusant
Colours: Turquoise, green, blue, purple, red

Method
Drawing shapes on the silk is not necessary, but you must have a firm idea of the picture design before starting to paint.

The background is first sprayed in pale jade and green. The silk is then coated with antifusant – this may need a second coat when used on crêpe de Chine. The stronger colours are then painted on the silk and salt applied sparingly to create texture on the left-hand side.

When dry, some areas are overpainted to create further dimensions.

Lupins in a vase

Field of sunflowers

Abstract

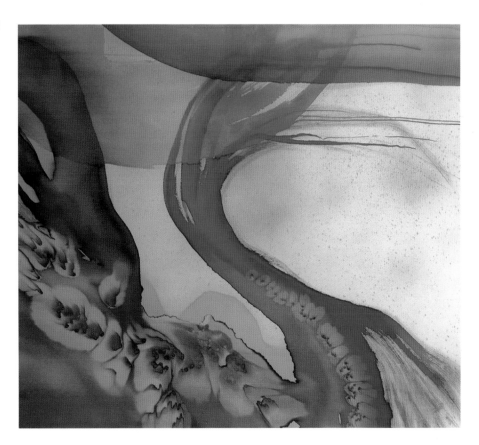

New York skyline

$\mathcal{C}$OT $\mathcal{Q}$UILT

A rocking horse design and delicate pastel shades are used on this pretty cot quilt. The finished design can be seen on page 102.

Material used: Silk pongée no. 9 145 cm × 190 cm (56½ in × 75 in)
Wadding 110 cm × 140 cm (44 in × 56 in)
Backing material

Technique: The rocking horse squares were all painted separately; however, time can be saved by painting four at once on a frame. The dyes on the rocking horse quilt are the iron-on variety, in which a white is available, making lovely pastel shades possible. A long frame is needed to paint the border pieces. Again these can all be painted on one frame.

Colours: Pastel blue, pink, yellow, green

Method

Cut 12 single squares 35 cm × 35 cm (14 in × 14 in) allowing for hems, or three 70 cm × 70 cm (28 in × 28 in) allowing for squares to be painted at once. Paint your design in a 30 cm × 30 cm (12 in × 12 in) box in the middle of the squares. Paint the border strips; you will need 6 lengths as shown in the diagram below.

When all the silk has been painted and fixed, the squares need to be sewn together, taking care to match the edges and corners. Sew the three outer borders around the squares. Add the wadding and backing material and quilt (see page 71).

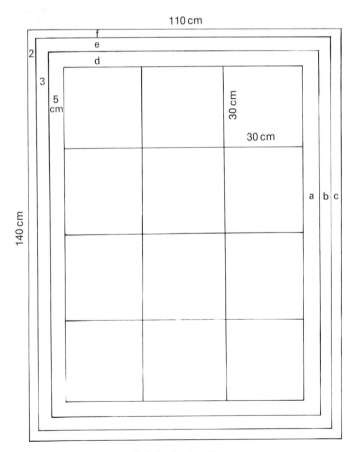

Finished cot quilt size

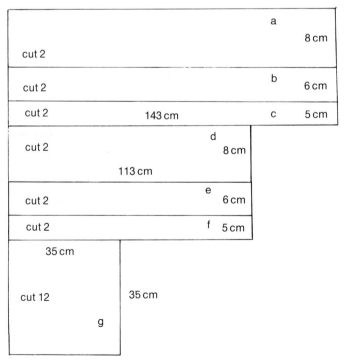

Pattern pieces for cot quilt

Silk cushions give the impression of something rather fragile and delicate, but are in fact surprisingly strong and versatile, depending upon the weight of silk used and their position within a room scheme. As floor cushions with regular use, they certainly would not last very long, but on sofas, window recesses, or piled in masses on beds or chairs, they can create wonderful effects. Try to place informal shapes and sizes together, maybe linked by a similar motif or toning colour (see the picture of the boudoir cushions, on page 103.)

This section shows a large variety of silk painting techniques combined with many ways of constructing and completing the cushions. Once again we hope that these will give you the opportunity to put your ideas into practice.

Cushion pads

The easiest way to decide on cushion sizes is to paint your silk according to the size of the cushion pad. These are now available in many different sizes and with a variety of fillings. Failing this, you can use one of a number of loose fillings which can be put into a similar-sized casing. Old feather cushions can be recycled; try damping the old cushion with water and then putting it into the tumble dryer until the feathers are dry and fluffy. When putting feathers into a new casing keep the doors and windows closed if indoors, alternatively on a calm day, do it outside.

Suggested pad sizes:

30 cm × 30 cm (12 in × 12 in)	very small square
35 cm × 35 cm (14 in × 14 in)	medium square
40 cm × 40 cm (16 in × 16 in)	standard cushion size
45 cm × 45 cm (18 in × 18 in)	old English square size
90 cm × 90 cm (36 in × 36 in)	floor cushion
40 cm (16 in) across	heart
appropriate size	bolster

The pads are available in feather and down, and synthetic fibres. Feather pads are best for silk cushions, as they seem to give weight and elegance; they also 'plump up' well.

Stuffings are also available in a variety of forms, although the cheaper foam chips really do not look as nice. Try to obtain a good quality acrylic or polyester wadding for a smooth filling. A normal 40 cm × 40 cm (16 in × 16 in) cushion should take approximately 600 g (21 oz) of fibre filling.

Rose cushion with lace insert

Fabrics

Most of our samples here use pongée no. 10, which we find is strong and withstands a fair amount of wear. We have also used pongée no. 9 and crêpe de Chine. Wild silk is also ideal for painted tones and colours, although it is rather stiff for frills.

The cushions are all lined to give extra strength. In the case of the paler cushions, a white lining underneath the silk shows off their subtle colours to a greater advantage. We use nylon lining as it will not shrink and is strong. Fine cotton can also be used, but must be pre-shrunk before being made up into cushions. The linings are mounted on the silk and the results are used as one fabric rather than inserted separately.

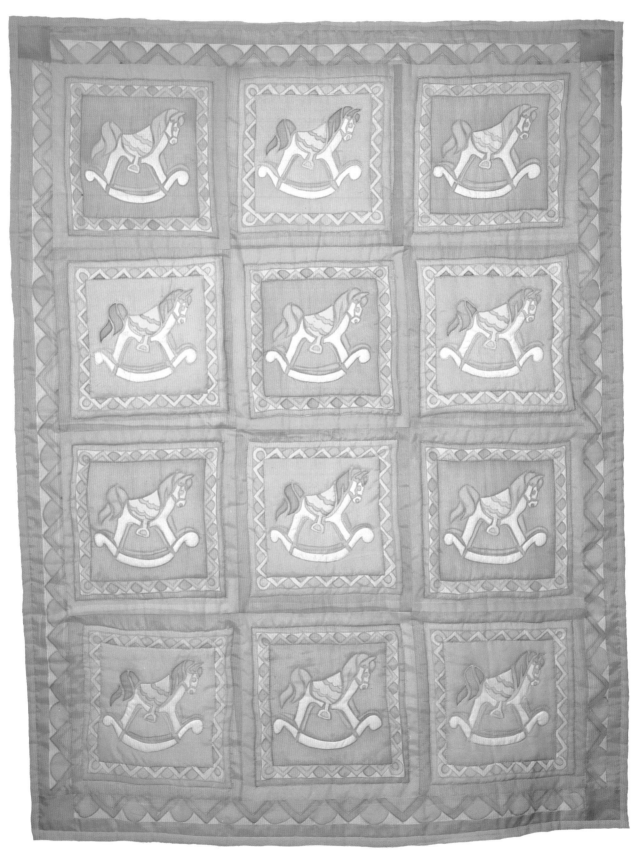

Cot quilt painted in squares then assembled

Boudoir cushions using various silk painting techniques and with a variety of edge finishes

Estimating fabric

Once the cushion pad has been chosen or the final size decided upon, use a tape measure to calculate the size of the cushion cover, which should be the same size as the cushion plus the turnings, which need to be 5 cm (2 in) extra. This will give each seam 2.5 cm (1 in) extra. This will enable you to paint your silk comfortably and in the construction you will be able to cut away any unwanted pin marks or painting problems. If you are painting more than one cushion with a similar design, it is sensible to paint at least two at a time so that the colours will match. From a 90 cm × 90 cm (36 in × 36 in) square you can paint two 40 cm × 40 cm (16 in × 16 in) square cushions (see diagram).

Here are approximate suggestions of fabric sizes for individual cushions. There are many commercial patterns available these days with interesting cushion features, which are highly recommended.

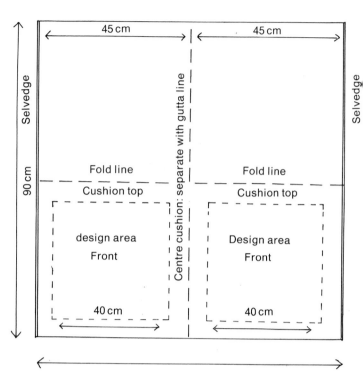

	Final size	Fabric
Square	30 cm × 30 cm (12 in × 12 in)	35 cm × 70 cm (14 in × 28 in)
	35 cm × 35 cm (14 in × 14 in)	40 cm × 80 cm (16 in × 32 in)
	40 cm × 40 cm (16 in × 16 in)	45 cm × 90 cm (18 in × 36 in)
	90 cm × 90 cm (36 in × 36 in)	95 cm × 190 cm (38 in × 76 in)
Round	35 cm (14 in) diameter	40 cm × 80 cm (16 in × 32 in)
	40 cm (16 in) diameter	45 cm × 90 cm (18 in × 36 in)

Heart	See diagram below	
	40 cm × 50 cm (16 in × 20 in)	60 cm × 90 cm (24 in × 37 in)
Bolster	See diagram below	
	100 cm × 35 cm diameter (40 in × 14 in)	

All extras such as frills and contrasting pipings should be calculated separately. These will be discussed in detail on pages 108 and 109.

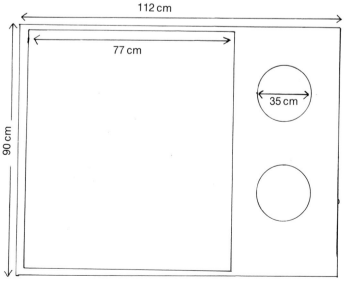

Layout for round bolster – contrast pleated frill needed

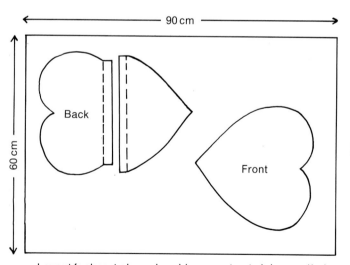

Layout for heart-shaped cushion – contrast piping needed.

Fastenings

The method of finishing off a cushion needs to be considered before it is painted. The following need no further addition of fabric; slipstitch finish, side seam zip insertion, side seam Velcro insertion, press-stud tape. **Note:** when a closure is required in the centre back of a cushion rather than at the edge, *an extra 5–6 cm (2–2½ in) of fabric is needed* on the back piece for the turnings (see heart-shape diagram opposite, below).

Methods of fastening

• *Slipstitch*

Allow an opening no less than 10 cm (4 in) shorter than one side of the cushion. Insert the pad and, using a matching thread, slipstitch the edges invisibly together closing the hole. The disadvantage of this method is that the cover will need to be unpicked and re-sewn every time the cushion is washed.

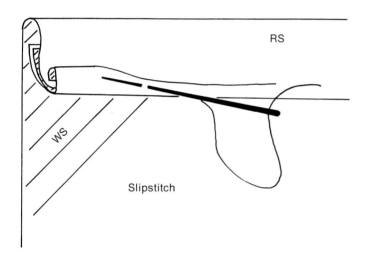

• *Zip fastening*

This method is neat and ideal for silk cushions. Place right sides of fabric together. Tack along the seam line and press open. Place the zip face down on the tacked seam line. Machine down the centre of the tape, and to the ends of the cushion. Neaten inside the seam allowance. Oversew neatly from the end of the zip tape to the cushion edge to join up the seam.

Inserting zip: edge to edge method

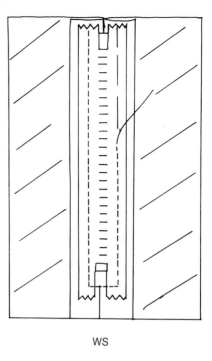

WS

Place zip right side down on opening then tack and machine in place

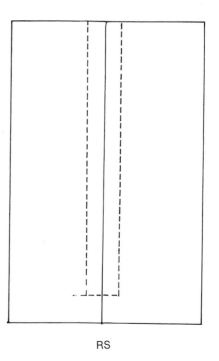

RS

Zip in position

● *Ties*

For this technique, extra matching or contrasting fabric will need to be painted. Cut out at least 4 ties for a 40 cm × 40 cm (16 in × 16 in) cushion (less for a smaller one). The width of the ties can vary according to taste: a final size of 2 cm ($\frac{3}{4}$ in) would require a strip of 10 cm (4 in). The length can also vary, but a minimum length of 25 cm (10 in) for each side is necessary. Therefore 100 cm ($39\frac{1}{2}$ in) of fabric would be needed for your ties. Press under 1 cm ($\frac{3}{8}$ in) towards the centre on both edges of the tie strips. Fold in half and machine along the edge turning under the ends neatly. Position on cushion on both side edges of the opening. Machine neatly in place along the length of the seam.

● *Strip/press-stud fastening*

These methods can be attached by hand and are very strong; however, they are rather bulky for silk cushions. Turn under the seam allowances. Tack each Velcro strip or fastening to the opposite edges of the cushion opening as shown below. Make sure that the overlap will face the back of the cushion so that the opening does not show. Machine stitch neatly in place. Construct cushion.

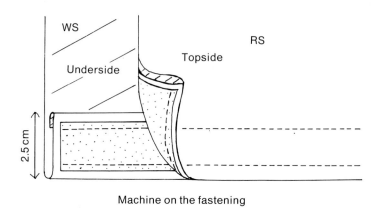

Machine on the fastening

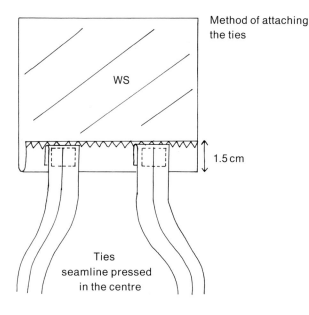

Method of attaching the ties

Ties seamline pressed in the centre

1.5 cm

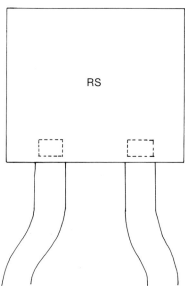

Completing cushions

Square cushion

1. Iron the silk fabric flat. Lay it on an even surface. Using a fade-away marker pen draw the cutting lines (cushion size + seam allowances). Carefully cut out the pieces in silk. Cut the lining pieces to exactly the same size.

2. Tack lining and the silk together – use together as one fabric.

3. Insert fastening at this stage.

4. Place front and back pieces right sides together. Pin and tack around the remaining three sides on seam allowance: 1.5 cm ($\frac{5}{8}$ in).

5. Machine stitch. Trim seam allowances and clip the corners diagonally.

6. Zigzag raw edges to neaten.

7. Turn to right side and roll seam line to edge. Press carefully.

8. Insert cushion pad. Fill the corners and 'plump up'.

Round cushion

This can be constructed in the same way as the square cushion although a fastening should be inserted across the centre of the cushion, rather than at the curved seam edge. Always clip the seam allowance well so that a round shape is formed. See measurements on page 104.

Bolster

Two circles of silk and lining are cut out (see diagram on page 104). The central panel is a rectangle. Insert the zip down the length of the rectangle. Attach pleated frill to sew on the end circles (see page 109). Machine, clip and finish off the edges.

Fancy edgings

Silk cushions can be given many interesting edge decorations. These can be made from commercially-produced haberdashery such as lace, cords and braids, but it can make a cushion much more attractive if you add a silk painted edging. We have shown several different treatments in this chapter.

Fancy cushion edgings: piping, frilled, ruched and tied with raised pintucks

Bias binding

The fabric is cut on the bias to give flexibility when bent around a corner, as with the piping used on cushions.

Cutting and making the strips

1. Fold the raw edge which is cut across the grain parallel to the selvedge. Cut strips of material of the required width following the lines shown in the diagram below. Narrow strips for piping are usually the finished width of the cord × 4 (approximately 3 cm, $1\frac{3}{16}$ in).

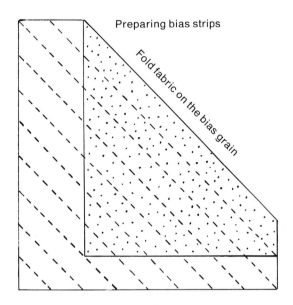

Cut strips along parallel lines

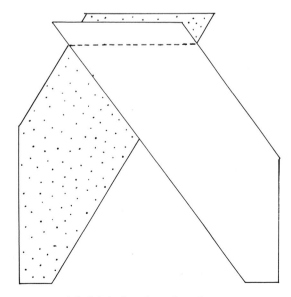

Join fabric 1 cm from the edges

2. Join the seams to make a continuous strip. A flat seam of 1 cm ($\frac{3}{8}$ in) is usual along the straight grain (see diagram below, left). Press seams open and clip off corners.

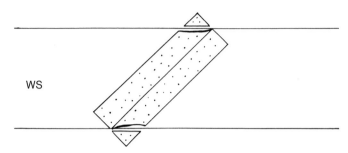

Press seam open and clip off corners

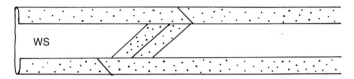

Bias strips showing turnings

Piping

This decorative edge is often used in soft furnishing to add a contrast and professional look to a cushion or quilt.

The fabric strip is cut on the bias and moulded around a cord. The cord is usually of white cotton synthetic fibre. Always boil cotton cord to shrink it before use, otherwise you could end up with puckered cushions.

Making the piping

1. Cut and prepare the bias strip. Do not press the turnings under.

2. Lay the cord down the centre of the wrong side of the bias strip and fold in half.

3. Tack the two sides of the fabric together close to the cord.

4. Machine the fabric using a zip foot so that the cord is tightly trapped inside the fabric.

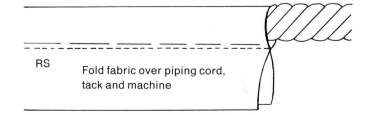

Fold fabric over piping cord, tack and machine

Using the piping

The piping is sewn into the seamline.

1. Sandwich the piping in between the right sides of the outer fabric.

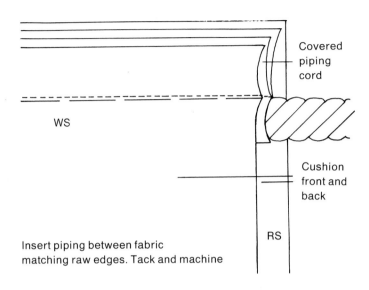

WS

Covered piping cord

Cushion front and back

RS

Insert piping between fabric matching raw edges. Tack and machine

2. Tack close to piping and machine. Try to round the corners of a cushion slightly so that the piping forms an even curve. It may be easier to tack the piping in place on one right side of a cushion first, then tack the second on top.

3. Trim seam allowances to reduce the bulk.

4. Turn and press.

Ruched piping

This is a fancy decorative edging for cushions.

1. Cut and make a bias strip double the width of the cord to be covered and two and a half times the length needed.

2. Lay the piping cord in the centre of the wrong side of the fabric. Tack 1 cm ($\frac{3}{8}$ in) away from the cord so that it is loose inside.

3. Gather the bias strip evenly as you tack so that the cord is covered by ruched fabric.

4. Insert as usual.

Frills

These can be any width, but as silk is so fine it is better to make them double the fabric width plus the seam allowances.

The silk can be evenly gathered or pleated (see diagram below).

Cut the fabric on the straight grain for gathered frills. If enough fabric is available, cut the strips on the bias for pleated frills, which gives a better effect.

Decorative finishes on the surface of cushions

Use your silk painting as a basis for various decorative treatments to the surface of your cushions. The examples shown in this section include a wide variety of techniques, some more complicated than others, but all giving interesting effects: lace insertions, pin tucking on the diagonal, machine Italian quilting, machine embroidery.

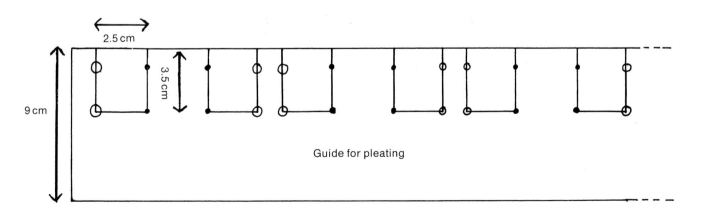

2.5 cm

3.5 cm

9 cm

Guide for pleating

PROJECTS

KNOT CUSHIONS

Finished size: 40 cm × 40 cm (16 in × 16 in)
Material used: Pongée no. 9
Dimensions: 2 pieces 90 cm × 90 cm (36 in × 36 in)
Technique: Gutta
Colours: Red, blue, yellow, green

Method

The effect of these four cushions is created by the juxtaposition of the colours within the set. Each has a different background colour and the knot is filled in using the remaining colours. The design can be repeated on the back of the cushion, or the same background colour can be used over the whole area.

1 sq = 5 cm

ZOO ANIMAL CUSHIONS

Finished size: 40 cm × 40 cm (16 in × 16 in)
Material used: Pongée no. 10
Dimensions: 2 pieces 90 cm × 90 cm (36 in × 36 in)
Technique: Wax
Colours: Black

Method

Draw the animal motifs carefully on each cushion front. Heat the wax. Using a fine brush, cover over all the areas which are to remain white. A smooth wax outline is necessary to give a sharp contrast of colour. When it has hardened, paint over the wax with black dye. It may be necessary to put on a second coat to ensure a deep, strong colour. Dry thoroughly and iron off the wax between paper. Fix using a double layer of paper for protection.

1 sq = 5 cm

TULIP STENCIL CUSHIONS

Finished size: 40 cm × 40 cm (16 in × 16 in)
Material used: Pongée no. 10
Dimensions: 1 piece 90 cm × 45 cm (36 in × 18 in)
Technique: Spray and stencil (iron fix dyes)
Colours: Pale cream, peach, pink, turquoise, green

Method

Stretch out the plain silk on a frame. Stand the frame upright and, using a mouth diffuser or spray, lightly colour the background with cream and peach dye. Do not go too close to the silk or the dyes will merge. Allow it to dry completely. Prepare the tulip stencil; using the thicker, iron-fix dyes, stipple the petals and leaves delicately with shades of peach/pink and green/turquoise. Dry thoroughly and iron on the wrong side. Steam fix the silk as normal.

1 sq = 8 cm

BLUE LACE CUSHION

Finished size: 40 cm × 40 cm (16 in × 16 in)
Material used: Pongée no. 10
Dimensions: 1 piece 90 cm × 45 cm (36 in × 18 in)
Technique: Spray
Colours: Pale blue

Method

This effect is created by stretching the plain white silk on a frame. A piece of lace curtaining is pinned over the top of the silk. Pale blue dye is then sprayed on the silk through the holes in the lace. The piece of lace is lifted away from the silk, taking care not to smudge the dyes. Once dried, the lace can be used for successive sprayings.

The blue frill is painted on a separate piece of silk but the same colour dye used.

Blue lace cushion (left) and pastel rose bolster (back). Watercolour technique is used on the heart cushion and on the lilac cushion which has a salt impregnated background

PASTEL ROSE BOLSTER

Material used: Pongée no. 10
Dimensions: 112 cm × 90 cm (44 in × 36 in)
 90 cm × 90 cm (36 in × 36 in) – frill
Technique: Sugar
Colours: Pale/deep pink, pale/deep yellow, pale/mid blue

Method

See the diagram on page 104 for cutting instructions. First paint the frill, using subtle tones of pink all over the silk. Stretch the piece of silk for the sugar technique separately (see method of making syrup, on page 27). Heat the liquid. Paint bold strokes of syrup in large rose-like shapes all over the silk. Liberally paint on the three pale dye colours, keeping each colour within a rose motif. Add the stronger colours to the centres. Join all the unpainted areas with very watery colours. Do not be afraid to splash it on, but avoid painting over the syrup itself, only up to it. Add more strokes of syrup to the centres and drop it on bare patches. Leave flat to dry for one or two days. Steam sugar pieces separately from other work. Wash thoroughly to remove the sugar.

Painted silk can look wonderful as handsome lampshades. Different atmospheres can be created by choosing from a range of painting methods and by varying the colours.

Your lampshades can create charm by both day and night, reflecting the character of your room. It can also be extremely useful in linking separate colours within a room. How often have you wished that you could find a subtle and unusual lampshade in the shops? Now you can paint your own extremely personal and effective room accessories. Link the colours of the cushions and table covers with those of the lampshades and create a harmony within your room.

Types of lampshades

You must decide which shape of lampshade would suit your room, taking several conditions into account:

● The position in which it is to be situated; is it to be high up or low down?

● Is the lampshade to hang from the ceiling, or have you a specific shaped base to utilize?

● The base of the lamp will often suggest the form and the dimensions of the shade.

● Will the lampshade be mainly an effective decoration, or is it a necessary light source?

● Which shape will suit the style of your furniture?

Straight-sided drum shades suit most situations; the conical 'Chinese hat' shape often suits a 1930s style and a square or rectangular shape blends well with modern, more geometric lines.

The trend at the moment is for oval or tapered conical shades, with a smaller ring at the top. Such shades are ideal for tables, as the light bulb is not so visible from above and the design shows more effectively.

It is quite easy to renovate an existing lampshade. Simply remove the old backing from the two rings. Try not to cut into this too much, as it is the template for your new backing and shade. Clean the two rings using a little sandpaper, and you are ready to start.

Colour and design

Once the position and shape of your lampshade is decided, then the importance of the design and final effect need to be considered. Any light bulb behind the shade will allow some light through, whatever the colour, even if it is only from the top or bottom.

In most rooms the colours are extremely important, whether they are used to link or contrast with the existing ones. If the effect is to add warmth to a room, any yellows, oranges, reds, pinks, creams and light browns will add a glow. The cooler tones are citrus yellow, greens, blues, purples, greys and black. Vibrant effects can be gained by adding a touch of contrasting colour.

Your design can be simply bands of colour in stripes or gutta lines, or flowers and birds. Salt and wax effects can be striking. The pattern can be placed all over the shade or just in the centre. Our ideas in this chapter are merely suggestions of different styles that can be created to suit a variety of situations.

Try to link the design up at the back of your shade. This is not easy, as even a minor adjustment to the position of the silk on the backing can affect the final join. It is probably simpler not to have any motif or definite line by the actual join; certainly a half tree or bird would look very odd. Think carefully about the edges at this stage. The darkest and strongest colour is usually used at the base of the shade to give the final result stability; this naturally happens with landscapes. A motif in the foreground will also give the same effect.

Plan the design position carefully before drawing on the silk so that the chosen image actually shows where it is wanted. This is especially important with squares and ovals. Do not overwork your design. Once the finished shade is constructed, even simple colours and washes become incredibly effective.

Calculation

There are many shapes of lampshades available in good craft shops or furnishing stores. Sometimes it is possible to have specific sizes made up for you. If you are not sure about proportions, look at ready-made shades and take their dimensions – while no one is looking!

We prefer not to use strutted frames, as the effect of the silk in conjunction with pastel colours is often marred by the strong vertical lines which show through when the lampshade is lit. Top and bottom rings can be used with the stiff, clear, sticky parchment which is available for mounting the fabric on. This easily supports the rim and frames, and is used on all of the following lampshades: squares, oval, drum, conical, tapered conical ('Chinese hat'), and wall.

Assortment of frames for lampshades: square, oval, drum, conical and wall

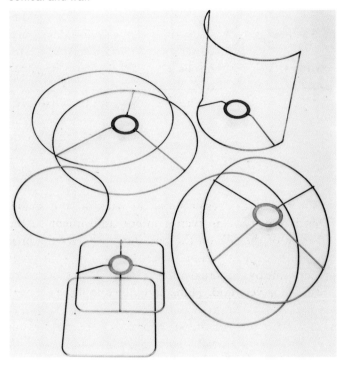

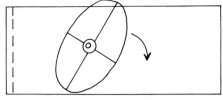

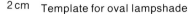

2 cm   Template for oval lampshade

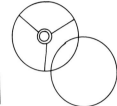

1 cm   Template for drum lampshade

The backing will be an exact measurement of the perimeter of the frame or ring, plus 1–2 cm ($\frac{3}{8}$–$\frac{3}{4}$ in) for the overlap join, multiplied by the height required. This is important, as if the backing is cut too short the shade will be ruined. It is sometimes possible to trim off excess on the underside of the join if the overlap is too great, unless you are trying to get the perfect match of a design.

With the square and wall frames, remember that a little length is always lost when turning a corner; the backing does not always attach so tightly, so allow 1 cm ($\frac{3}{8}$ in) extra in length.

Conical shade. This tapered shade has a smaller ring at one end and a wider ring at the other. The different diameters of these rings vary the slope of the sides. This creates problems, which can be overcome if the construction is tackled stage by stage. The silk and backing will not be straight but will form a curve. Draw the shape using the following method:

1.   Following the diagram below, measure the diameter of top ring AB, and the bottom ring CD.

Calculating the backing
It is essential to make a template first. The following shapes are straight-sided, and therefore easier to construct.

Square, oval, drum and wall. Two frames of exactly the same diameter are needed, one of which will support the light fitting. Equipment required: ruler, paper, tape measure, pencil and card.

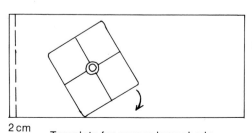

2 cm

Template for square lampshade

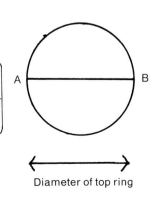

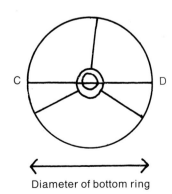

A ——————— B   C ——————— D

Diameter of top ring   Diameter of bottom ring

2. Decide on the distance between the upper and lower rings and measure this vertical height, EF.

3. Take a large sheet of paper, preferably plain but newspaper will do, and make a drawing of the dimensions measured, as shown in fig. 1 below. Extend AC and BD until they intersect at point G.

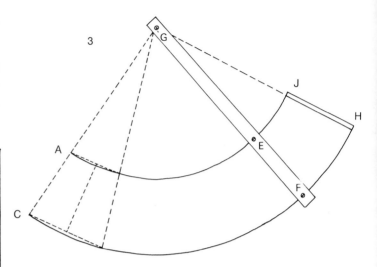

Making template for conical lampshade

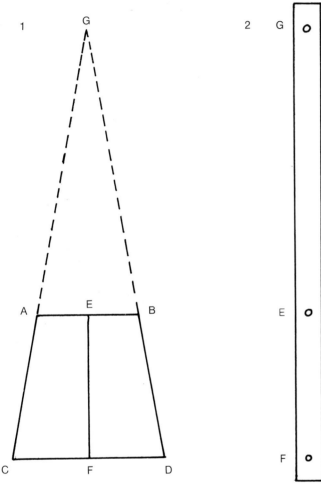

Measurement diagram and 'compass'

4. Make a large 'compass' whose length is at least equal to the distance FG. This can be made from a strip of stiff card with two holes in it through which a pencil can be passed. The holes are placed corresponding to distances E and F, from G as shown in fig. 2 above. (An alternative is simply to use a piece of string with a pencil tied at one end.)

5. Fix one end of the 'compass' at G using a pin. Ensuring that the pivot at point G does not move, trace two arcs corresponding to the top and bottom of the lampshade (see fig. 3).

6. Measure the circumference of the bottom ring (it is possible to calculate this dimension by multiplying the diameter by $\frac{22}{7}$ or 3.14).

7. Take a piece of string and measure a length equal to this circumference.

8. Fix one end at C; lay the string around the bottom arc and mark off the correct length CH.

9. Repeat steps 6, 7 and 8 for the upper rim.

10. Add an extra 15 mm ($\frac{1}{2}$ in) to upper and lower arcs, AJ and CH, to provide the necessary overlap at the join.

11. Cut out the correct shape for the lampshade template.

Calculating the size of the silk and applying the design

Once the template has been made, the silk can be cut and the design drawn larger in pencil on the template. It is a good idea to draw an outline larger than the final lampshade on your silk, 2 cm–3 cm ($\frac{3}{4}$ in–$1\frac{1}{2}$ in). You will paint up to this line so that, should the backing move on application, the colour of the silk will be continuous.

Do not cut out the shaped silk pieces, but pin up and paint as a rectangle. The silk will be trimmed to size later.

Tape the silk carefully into position over your design, (see page 120). Paint as needed, dry and fix. Remove gutta at this stage if necessary. Wash and iron.

Salt and wax textured square lamps with matching cushions ▶

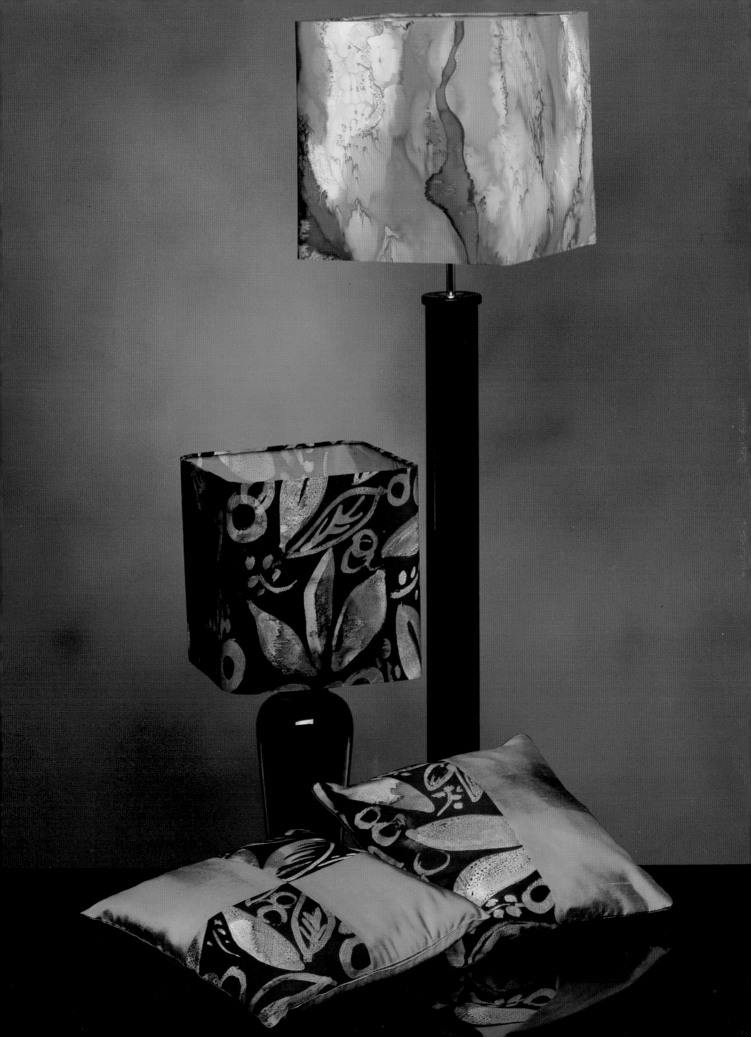

Constructing the lampshade

Equipment: Painted silk
           Sticky paper backing
           Two rings for top and base
           Ruler, tape measure
           Pegs
           Scissors
           Glue or double-sided sellotape
           Board

1. Cut out the sticky backing accurately. Try to make the edges even and smooth.

2. On a clean, firm surface such as chipboard, stretch out your painted silk. Make sure your work is right side down, i.e. you are looking at the wrong side. You can tape this on the surface or stretch it out using three-pronged pins. (This second method ensures that the silk is perfectly straight and taut.)

Stretching the silk over the design

3. Roll back 5 cm (2 in) of the protective sheet from the backing and position it on the silk. Using smooth, even movements, with your free hand press the backing on to the silk a little at a time. Unroll the backing paper until it is securely attached. There should be no air bubbles if this process is done carefully. Be warned, the backing cannot be removed once it is in position.

4. Unpin the silk and turn to the right side. Check that all the edges are secured by pressing down with your hands.

5. Decide which of the two side edges is to be the overlapping one. Using sharp scissors, trim off the surplus silk from this side to 0.5 cm ($\frac{3}{16}$ in) from the edge.

Stretched silk pinned upside down; with the backing cut to size for attaching

Lightly glue this edge over to prevent fraying, using a strong rubber-based glue (see below). Trim the other side edge exactly to the backing.

Edges trimmed and glue being applied to top and bottom

6. Trim the upper and lower longer sides to 1.5–2 cm ($\frac{5}{8}$ in–$\frac{3}{4}$ in). Lightly glue the outside edges of the top and bottom rings. Place to one side. Lightly glue the top and bottom edges only of the lampshade backing. The glue must not touch the silk, but must be clos to the edge. Do not rush; the glue can harden slighty before bonding the rings to the backing.

7. Starting with the lower ring, roll it carefully along the bottom of the glued backing. Press it against the table as you roll to get a good bonding. Pegs can be placed at intervals to keep it in place. When attaching the square and oval shapes make sure that the centre of your design will be correctly positioned on the ring when assembled. Attach the top ring the same way.

    The conical frame is tricky at this stage, as one ring is much smaller than the other. You may need to peel back the lower ring a little to insert the upper one. Have patience: it will work in the end! Re-glue sections if necessary.

Make sure that the top and bottom edges are aligned before the glue sets, otherwise the back join will look messy.

Rolling the frame on to the sticky backing

8. Lightly glue the back edges together with the folded-over side uppermost. Press the glue until set.

9. Using a blunt screwdriver or fingernail, tuck all the excess silk up under the rim of the ring. Try to do this as neatly and smoothly as possible, as the finish affects the look of your lampshade.

Tucking under the silk to make a neat edge

10. Assemble your shade with the base or light fitting, and there you are – perfect.

Completed landscape design lampshade and matching cushion

It is possible, instead of using glue, to attach the silk with double-sided tape. This means you replace the glue with tape at each stage. We worry that in the long term the tape will wear and lose its sticking power. The choice, however, is yours; this method is certainly less messy.

PROJECTS

ROSE LAMPSHADE

Material used: 32 cm × 100 cm (13 in × 40 in) crêpe de Chine
28 cm × 94 cm (11¼ in × 38 in) sticky backing
94 cm (37½ in) circumference oval rings, 1 top, 1 base
Rubber-based glue

Dimensions: Finished height 28 cm × 94 cm (11¼ in × 37½ in) length

Technique: Gutta (gold)

Colours: Pink, pale blue, yellow, pale green

1 sq = 1.5 cm

Method

Carefully draw the design on the crêpe de Chine. It is important that the silk is stretched taut and evenly so that when it is mounted the lines in the design remain straight. Position the three roses, one in the centre and two at the sides. Gutta the outlines. When these are dry, paint in the colours. Try to keep them pale but also introduce some careful shading. The roses in particular need this, otherwise they can look rather flat. Fix the silk and complete the lampshade as on pages 120–121.

TULIP LAMPSHADE

Materials: 170 cm × 90 cm (67 in × 36 in) pongée no. 9
160 cm × 90 cm (63 in × 36 in) sticky backing
1 × 25 cm ($9\frac{3}{4}$ in) diameter top ring and bulb support
1 × 50 cm ($19\frac{3}{4}$ in) diameter base ring
rubber glue

Dimensions: Finished height 29 cm ($11\frac{1}{2}$ in)
Circumference 160 cm (63 in)

Technique: Gutta, black

Colours: Peach and shades of pale green

1 sq = 1.5 cm

Method

Use the tulip motif at random to create an overall design on the lampshade shape. Gutta the outlines using a large nib so that the black shows up as a clear feature of the design. When dry, paint in the colours. Shading is not necessary but several leaf colours could be used to make the effect more interesting. Fix the silk and complete the lampshade as on pages 120 and 121.

A tulip conical lampshade and matching cushion using black gutta and a stencil tulip cushion

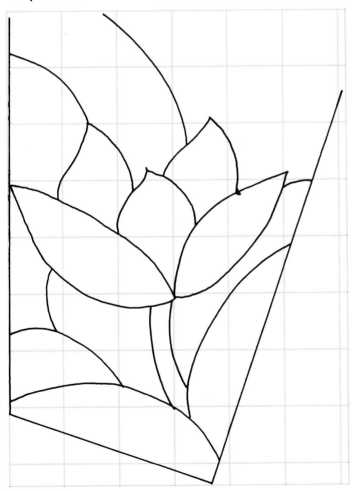

LANDSCAPE LAMPSHADE

See finished design on page 121

Material used: Pongée no. 9 50 cm × 90 cm
(20 in × 36 in)
Rings: top 15 cm (6 in) diameter; base
18 cm (7¼ in) diameter
Sticky backing
Rubber-based glue

Dimensions: Top diameter 18 cm (7 in), base 30 cm
(11¾ in), Height 21 cm (8¼ in)

Colours: Peach, green, cream, grey, navy

Method

The effect of this landscape is achieved by subtle application of dye in the initial stages. Very lightly sketch in hills and sun. Wet the stretched silk with diluent first.

Using cream and palest grey, paint the sky in an arc of these colours. While this is still wet, roll a pale peach colour on a fine brush over the surface. Try to build up cloud forms. Add slightly stronger peach and grey to the base of the clouds. Dry thoroughly.

Paint the hill forms upwards from the base in pale green. Allow the dyes to creep up. Dry quickly once the crinkled effect has been achieved. Paint up from the base again on top of the green using the stronger peach tone; this will now turn more of a brown tone. Dry again when the dye approaches the green. Finally, paint in navy from the base as the last deep colour. Dry thoroughly. Using a cotton bud, dot the surface of the navy dye with alcohol to create an interesting texture. The sun is formed by using alcohol and a cotton bud. Lightly dip the cotton bud into alcohol and a minute amount of navy dye and apply to the silk. Rub carefully from the centre of the sun until a halo of dye is formed on the outside of the circle. Dry quickly once the correct size is achieved.

Complete as described on pages 120 and 121.

ACCESSORIES

GREETINGS CARDS

A hand-painted greetings card is an ideal first project if you are a beginner and reluctant to embark upon something larger. You can try your hand at any one of the silk painting techniques to make your own original card which can be mounted and framed. Bookmarks, postcards, gift tags and notelets can also be made.

A large section of ready-cut mounts and blanks are available with matching envelopes, and it is worth investing in a selection of these for professional looking results. It is quite a simple process to cut your own mounts, however; all you need is the card, a craft knife and a steel ruler.

A selection of pre-cut mounts

Cutting your own mounts

To make your own mount you must choose the paper or card very carefully. If the paper is too thin it will curl and your card will fall down. Card comes in many qualities and textures. Cloud effect, metallic, parchment style, marbled and glossy are all available, so choose one that will complement your silk painting.

Before you decide on the size of your card and cut the paper, make sure you can find an envelope of the appropriate size. Of course, you could make your own envelopes too!

One-fold card

The easiest type to make is from a rectangular piece of card simply folded in half. The silk can be stuck to the front using spray adhesive or bonding web.

A more professional method is to cut a window opening in the front of the card. Different shapes can be cut: squares, rectangles, hearts, or even real window shapes.

One-fold card with window

To work out the size for a one-fold card, measure the size of the silk painting plus a margin of approximately 2 cm ($\frac{3}{4}$ in) all the way around, and then multiply the width by two. Fold the card in half by scoring it lightly on the right side with a craft knife or compass point. You will then obtain a neat, straight fold. On the left-hand side, cut out a window about 1 cm ($\frac{3}{8}$ in) smaller than the silk painting. Cut another piece of card to cover the back.

Two-fold card with window

The card can also be folded into three. This way, the back of the silk can be neatly covered. Decide on the size of your card: it should be the size of the silk painting plus a margin of at least 2 cm ($\frac{3}{4}$ in) all the way around, multiplied by three. The height remains constant. Measuring carefully, divide the card into three. Score the two fold lines on the right side using a craft knife, taking care not to score too hard or you will cut right through the card. In the middle section, cut out the window large enough to display your silk painting, leaving about 1 cm ($\frac{3}{8}$ in) of silk to allow for gluing. Finally, cut a thin strip off from the left side of the card so it will close easily when folded.

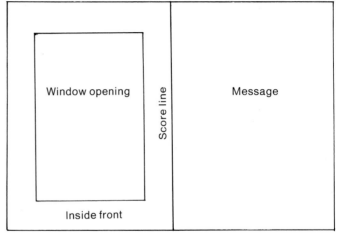

One-fold card

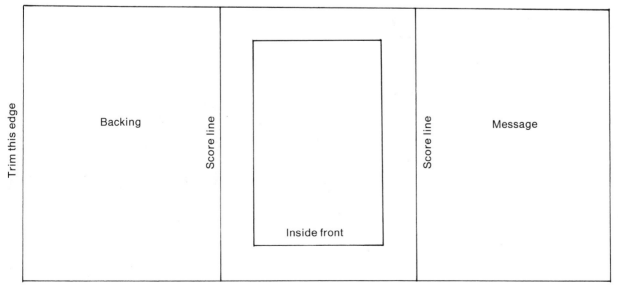

Two-fold card

Mounting your card

There are three different ways of gluing the silk painting into the card: rubber-based glue, spray glue, or bonding web.

Rubber-based glue

A rubber-based glue is the best to use, as any excess can be rubbed off the card when it has dried. With the right side of the silk facing uppermost, glue lightly around the edges of the silk painting. Place the silk face down on the back of the window opening you have cut. Make sure it is in the correct position as it is difficult to re-position it, and take care not to get glue on the front of your card. Wait until the glue is dry before folding the card along the lines you have scored. Sometimes with this method the glue puckers the silk and so if you are using a one-fold window card it is advisable to use another piece of card to cover the back and prevent puckers and bubbles. If you are using a two-fold window card, glue the backing segment (the left-hand side) around the edges and fold over immediately.

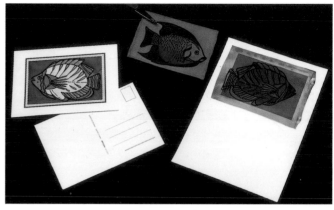

Adhesive-backed postcards

Spray glue

Spray glue is ideal for mounting your cards. Spray the silk and carefully place the painting in the correct position. If you have positioned the silk incorrectly, it can be easily lifted and re-positioned using this adhesive.

If you are using a folded piece of card with no window, you can tear the silk and fray the edges. Lightly spray the card with adhesive and gently place the silk in position.

Glueing silk into a one-fold card

Tearing, fraying and spraying the silk

Flower cards using the salt technique

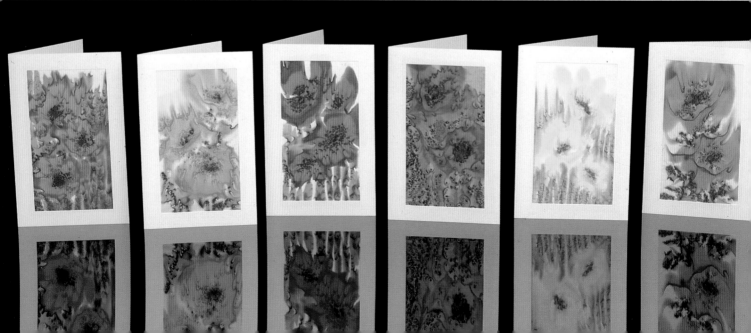

Bonding web

The silk can also be fixed to the card with bonding web. This is a fine mesh of glue with paper stuck to it. The paper is peeled off the glue and it can then be ironed on to your card using a warm dry iron. This is a good way to glue the silk if you do not want a frayed look, as the glue web binds the edges and even enables shapes to be cut.

Fish postcards using the gutta technique

A selection of birthday cards, notelets, tags and bookmarks

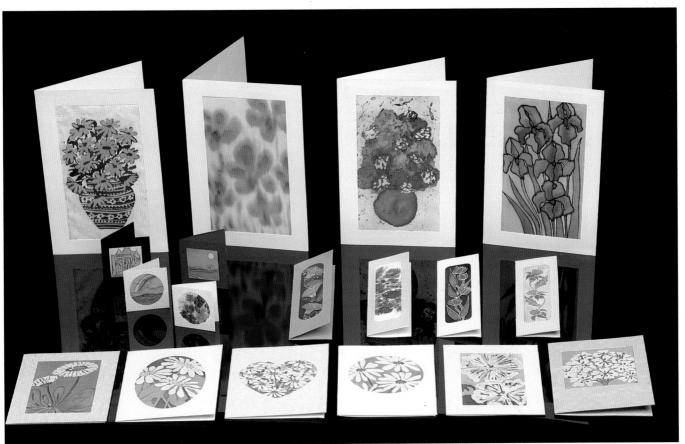

PROJECTS

surface, as the silk should be entirely free from salt before it is fixed. After fixing, cut each painting along the gutta line. Cut mounts and make the cards as shown on page 125.

SALT FLOWER CARDS

See finished designs on page 126

Material used: Silk pongée no. 9
Cards and matching envelopes

Dimensions: Each painting is 10 cm × 18 cm
(4 in × 7¼ in), but it is a good idea to use a larger frame and divide the silk into squares using a gutta line to paint several cards at one time.

Technique: Rock salt

Method

Salt flowers are easy to paint and the results are always different. Individual circles or flowers can be produced by painting the background with water or one colour. Then place a circle of salt crystals on this background and add a few drops of dye to the middle. If you paint the flowers too close together, they will run into each other. You can add a further colour to the centre if desired, and then add stems and leaves. Leave the work in position until it is completely dry, as any movement will spoil the pattern. When it is dry, brush the rock salt from the

WAX DAISY NOTELETS

See finished design on page 127

Material used: Silk pongée no. 9
Notelets and matching envelopes

Dimensions: Each card is 10 cm × 12 cm (4 in × 4¾ in). As you are making a set of 6 notelets, use a large frame and divide the silk into 6 using a wax line.

Technique: False batik

Method

The daisies are painted on the silk using melted wax. Dye is then applied using a large brush. After the silk is dry, repeat the process of waxing and dyeing with each of the colours. When the final colour has dried, remove the wax by ironing the silk between sheets of newsprint with a hot dry iron. Steam or heat fix, depending on the dyes you have used. (See page 24 for more detailed information on false batik.)

After fixing and cleaning, cut the silk into rectangles and mount into the notelets. These can be put into a box and make a wonderful gift.

Painting several greetings cards on one piece of silk

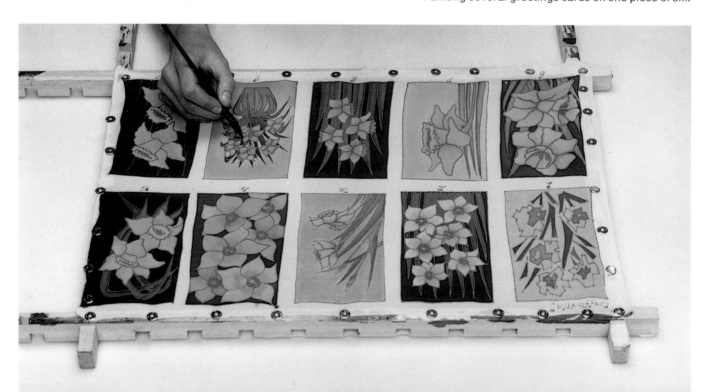

1 sq = 1 cm

Use these designs to create your own cards

GUTTA FISH POSTCARDS

See finished designs on page 127

Material used: Silk pongée no. 9
                          Postcards

Dimensions: Each postcard is 8 cm × 14 cm ($3\frac{1}{4} × 5\frac{1}{2}$ in). You can paint several cards on one frame by dividing the silk into rectangles with gutta

Technique: Gutta (black)

Method

See page 20 for the gutta technique. Use the brightest dyes you have for these gaily coloured tropical fish. Cut mounts and make cards as shown on page 125.

BIRTHDAY CARDS

See finished designs on page 127

The stencilling, gutta and wax techniques (see Part Two of this book) have been used to create these original cards which your friends will love to receive. Some diagrams for you to copy are illustrated on page 129. Just enlarge them to the size you require by using the method described on page 20.

A display of brooches, earrings and a pendant
The techniques used include salt, salt impregnated background, wax and antifusant

BROOCHES, PENDANTS, EARRINGS and SCARF CLIPS

The charming pieces of jewellery seen opposite can easily be made to co-ordinate with your outfits. They require such small pieces of silk that any leftover scraps can be used. Why not make earrings to match a silk-painted top or link a scarf clip with a hand-painted silk scarf? A lovely gift idea is a matching card and brooch, ideal for a small birthday present.

A kit for making brooches and the other items is available in some good art and craft shops. It generally consists of a metal front or 'window' with two or three flanges on the side, a convex centre piece of metal over which the silk is stretched and a metal back piece with a fastening for the brooch.

The following description refers to the assembly of a brooch, but also applies to the other items.

When choosing a section of silk to 'frame' in your brooch, look for some interesting effect: maybe a change of colour or a contrast of textures created by wax or antifusant. Place the shape over your silk so that you can see what the finished effect will be through the 'window'.

Equipment for making brooches

A colourful collection of hair accessories. Many silk painting techniques and types of silk are used (see overleaf)

Materials: Small pieces of pongée, crêpe de Chine, soie
sauvage, twill, etc.
Rubber-based glue
Wadding

Method

1.   Choose an interesting piece of your silk. Place the 'window' shape over the area you wish to mount and draw lightly 1 cm ($\frac{3}{8}$ in) away from the shape.

2.   Cut out your silk.

3.   Using a rubber-based glue, lightly coat the surface of the inner rounded metal mount.

4.   Turn the mount upside down and place it on a piece of wadding. Trim around the wadding exactly to the edge of this mount. Leave to dry.

5.   Glue all around the edge of the underside of the mount. Leave for one minute so that the glue will go 'tacky'. Then place the silk on top of the wadding and pull evenly over to the underside of the mount. This should stick into place neatly. Do not pull the silk over too tightly, as it is nice to leave the top side of the brooch slightly rounded.

6.   Place the 'window' over the top of the silk-covered mount and the back fastening section behind. Using a small hammer, tap the small metal fastening keys to hold the brooch together.

The same method of assembling the jewellery applies to the earrings, pendant and scarf clip. If you wish the silk to be flat in your mount, omit the wadding. We have also seen these assembled using double-sided sticky tape on the front and back of the mount as an alternative to glue.

$\mathcal{H}$AIR BANDS, $\mathcal{S}$CRUNCHIES, $\mathcal{B}$OWS and $\mathcal{S}$LIDES

Hair ornaments are an important fashion accessory these days, and can often be rather expensive to buy. If you make your own luxury items, not only will you be wearing an original bow or slide but they will cost very little. All techniques for painting on silk can be used, creating a variety of effects for both day and evening wear.

HAIR BANDS

See finished designs opposite and on page 131
Material used: Soft silk, such as crêpe de Chine or
pongée – cut a strip double the length of
the hair band and the width plus 3 cm
($1\frac{1}{4}$ in)
Hair band

Method

1.   Paint, fix and cut out the strip of silk.

2.   Fold, right sides together, and sew across one end and up one side. Round off the end so that the tip of the hair band will fit in snugly.

3.   Turn through to right side. Feed on to the hair band. Flatten silk for 5 cm (2 in) at the ends, then sew to secure a flat area.

4.   Allow the silk to ruffle and gather across the centre, then flatten at the other end.

5.   Sew up the open end close to the tip. Secure flat area.

SCRUNCHIES

See finished designs below and on page 131
These can be of varying widths and lengths, depending on the effect required when worn. The following instructions are just one suggestion.

Material used: Soft silk, such as crêpe de Chine or pongée. Cut a strip 1.50 m × 25 cm (60 in × 10 in)
Narrow elastic 10–15 cm (4–6 in)

Method

1. Paint, fix and cut out the strip of silk.

2. Fold the silk lengthwise, right sides together, machine the length of strip. Turn through to the right side.

3. Lightly press the seam, but do not flatten the folded edge.

4. Turn in the raw edges 1 cm ($\frac{3}{8}$ in) on one end. Feed the elastic inside the tube and sew very securely across the end.

5. Pull the silk through the tube, gathering up the silk as you pull.

6. Pin this loose elastic to the other end of the scrunchy. Turn under the raw edges and push inside the other, already sewn, end.

7. Trap both ends and elastic with a secure line of machine stitching.

BOWS

Fashion often dictates the size of bows in the hair. Ours are fastened to metallic clips which have two holes at the ends. These enable you to sew the clips securely onto the underside of the bow.

The bows can be made up in many ways. Look at the section on bow ties and see the construction there for the blunt ended method (see page 85). The method is the same, but the measurements were enlarged to suit your finished bow size. The result is rather like the grey and pink bow illustrated on page 131, rather a formal shape.

For the larger bow with pointed ends, simply enlarge the underside and cut diagonal points at the ends. Sew together as for bow tie, omitting, of course, the neck-band section.

A pongée silk will probably need stiffening if you are making a large bow. Either an iron-on vilene or cotton would be suitable. If using soie sauvage, there is no need for stiffening.

SLIDES

We were lucky enough to find slide kits in our local craft shop. They are similar to the brooch kits in that they consist of a metal plate, over which the silk is stretched, and a back section which has the metal clip attached.

The method for making up these slides is the same as for the brooches (see opposite). Alternatively, if you can obtain just the metal clips, why not make a long tube of silk and sew it in loops along the length? We show this example in the colour picture on page 131 painted bright turquoise and pink.

A variety of hair accessories using silk painting techniques

Hat Boxes

Material used: (for large oval box)
Cardboard or pre-cut cardboard kit
Bonding web or glue gun and glue
Scissors, pencil, steel ruler and craft knife
Bonding web 2.50 m (100 in)
Wadding 30 cm × 40 cm (12 in × 16 in)
Painted crêpe de Chine 70 cm (28 in) for outside
80 cm (32 in) pongée no. 9 for lining

Technique

Any of the silk painting techniques can be used to paint the silk used to cover the hat boxes. Opaque gutta on crêpe de Chine and watercolour on wild silk have been used in the picture. Covering the hat boxes inside and outside takes a great deal of painted silk – you may like to use your painted silk on the outside only, and line the box with another material. For best results, we recommend that you use bonding web or a hot glue gun when covering the boxes; however, it is possible to use just fabric glue.

Choose a thicker silk to cover your box, as the thin pongées are too difficult to work with. When you have painted your silk, remember to fix it before covering your hat box.

Method

Hat box kits containing pre-cut cardboard pieces in round, oval and heart shapes are available, but you can cut your own using cardboard, craft knife, scissors and a steel ruler.

1.   You will need to cut your card pieces for each hat box: a base, a lid slightly larger than the base, a wide base side and a narrow lid side.

2.   If you want to pad the top of your hat box, cut a piece of wadding slightly smaller than the lid.

3.   When covering all the pieces of card with your painted silk, the easiest method is to use the iron-on bonding web. A glue gun is also ideal for this. Cover all the pieces of card, clipping the edges of the silk on the round oval or heart-shaped pieces as shown on the photograph frame (see page 136). Glue down carefully. When they are all dry, the lining can be fused in place.

Oval and heart shaped boxes covered in soie sauvage and crêpe de Chine

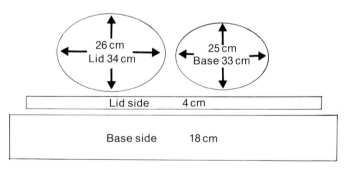

4.   Next, working on a flat surface, form the wide base side around the base and mark the overlap with pins or draw a faint pencil line at the top, middle and bottom. Remove the base side and check that the overlap is even all the way down; if it is not, a misshapen box will result.

Equipment needed for covering a hat box

5. Apply glue to the overlap and hold together until dry. Glue the base into the bottom of the shaped base side. Continue by repeating the same process with the lid and lid side. Make sure that the overlap line matches the overlap line on the base.

6. Piping, cording, ribbons, tassels, etc. can be used to finish off your hat box.

PHOTO FRAMES

Material used: Mount board or old used photograph
frame
Wadding
Glue
Painted silk
Scissors, pencil, steel ruler, craft knife

Technique

Any of the silk painting techniques can be used to paint the silk needed to cover the photograph frame. Gold gutta, salt, watercolour and wax techniques have all been used in the photograh shown on below.

A selection of silk covered photograph frames using salt, gutta and wax techniques

Method

It may be possible to buy pre-cut mount board photograph frame kits at your craft shop. If not you can easily cut your own from mount board using a craft knife and a steel ruler, or find an old cardboard photograph frame which you can cover.

1. First of all you must work out how much silk you will need to paint. This will depend, of course, on the size of photograph frame you wish to cover. If you intend to cover both sides of the back board and make a stand, you will need approximately four times the size of the back board plus 5 cm (2 in) all around. However, twice the size of the mount plus 5 cm (2 in) all around is enough for a frame with no stand. Remember to fix the silk before starting to cover the frame.

2. Before cutting and gluing the silk, measure and cut the wadding. Cut the wadding 0.25 cm ($\frac{1}{8}$ in) smaller than the outside measurement of the frame. Trace the opening shape on the wadding and cut it out.

3. To cover the front board of the frame, cut the silk 5 cm (2 in) larger on all sides of the board. Place the board in the middle on the wrong side of the silk. Trace around the oval, round or rectangular opening. Draw another line 2 cm ($\frac{3}{4}$ in) inside the first line. Cut out the shape on the second line.

4. Place the cardboard mount on top of the silk using the traced line as a guide. Clip the curves as shown in the diagram, fold them over and glue. Continue around the opening until all the edges are glued.

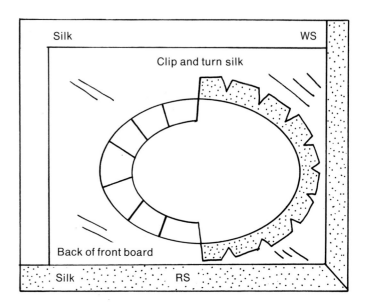

5. If you have decided to pad your photograph frame, now is the time to add the wadding. When the glue is dry, turn over the board, lift up the silk and put the wadding down on the board. Lay the silk evenly over the wadding and turn the board over. Spread glue along the edges of the back of the card and fold the silk around it, making sure that the corners are finished with a neat tuck. If you have an oval or round frame, clip the edge of the silk as you did for the window opening.

6. The back board can now be covered in the same way as the outer edge of the front board. Both sides of the back board can be covered if you wish.

A stand can be covered with silk and glued on to the back of the frame if you plan for the photograph to stand on a table. The back and front boards are now ready to be glued together, leaving enough space to slip your photograph into the frame.

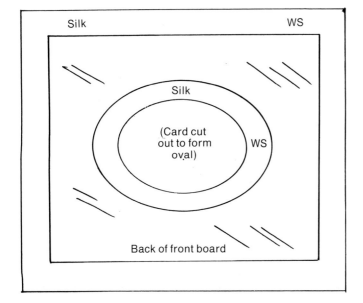

COATHANGERS, POMANDERS, LAVENDER BAGS and TISSUE HOLDERS

These small items will take almost no time to make up and require very little silk. They look so attractive, you will not only want to give them as gifts but also to use them to ornament your own bathroom and dressing room. Your finest evening wear can be hung on matching padded coathangers and the pot pourri in the pomanders will freshen up a toilet or stuffy wardrobe. Lavender sachets in drawers will keep your clothes fresh.

Once you start, you will find it difficult not to continue producing small decorative items from leftover scraps of silk. Some can be made without a sewing machine.

Any silk painting technique can be used to colour your silk. Often the colours themselves are very pretty, so a lot of time spent on detailed work is not necessary. Salt impregnated background flowers, sea salt on toning colours, or background colour washes with dots of colour on the top could all make interesting textures.

COATHANGER

See finished designs on page 138
Material used: A good quality wooden coathanger
Wadding
Painted crêpe de Chine 15 cm (6 in) wide × 3 cm (1$\frac{3}{16}$ in) longer than hanger
Matching narrow ribbon
Fake silk flower
Rubber-based glue

Method

1. Wind the wadding evenly around the coathanger until it is 15 cm (6 in) in circumference. Make sure that the ends are covered well.

2. Using ribbon, cover the coathanger hook. A dot of glue will hold the ribbon to the end while you wind downwards. Towards the base, tuck in a pretty silk flower and secure by winding further over it to the base of the wire. Glue carefully and securely.

3. Cut out the rectangle of silk 15 cm (6 in) wide and 3 cm (1$\frac{3}{16}$ in) longer than the wooden hanger. Iron inwards turnings of 1 cm ($\frac{3}{8}$ in) on all four sides.

4. Pin the folded edges together over the top of the squashy wadding. Tack carefully, making sure that the ends are nicely rounded.

5. Using a matching thread, neatly oversew the length of the seam. An alternative is to use little running stitches, although oversewing is neater.

POMANDER

See finished design on page 138
Material used: Painted silk, pongée or crêpe de Chine 24 cm (9$\frac{1}{2}$ in) diameter
Circle of wadding 18 cm (7$\frac{1}{4}$ in) diameter
Handful of pot pourri
1.5 m (60 in) narrow satin ribbon
1 m (40 in) decorative lace
Pretty silk flower

Method

1. Draw a large circle, 24 cm (9$\frac{1}{2}$ in) diameter or large dinner plate size, on the silk.

2. Zigzag the lace to the outside edge of the silk circle. (This stage could be hand sewn).

3. Cut out a smaller circle of wadding and place in the centre of the circle. Place a handful of pot pourri on top.

4. Gather up the circle of silk and tie the ribbon firmly round to form a ball shape. The pomander will need a hanging loop and a bow.

5. Before tightening the ribbon, slip a flower into the middle of the pomander. Trim the ribbon ends diagonally.

LAVENDER BAGS

Lavender can be put into any shaped sachet of silk and tied with pretty satin ribbon. This design looks attractive using salted silk and a pretty edging of automatic machine embroidery pattern.

Material used: Pongée or crêpe de Chine 26 cm × 13 cm ($10\frac{1}{2}$ in × $5\frac{1}{4}$ in)
Matching thread
Satin ribbon for bow
Dried lavender

Method

1.   Cut out two circles of silk approximately 12–13 cm (5–$5\frac{1}{4}$ in) across. Draw on a centre circle of 8 cm ($3\frac{1}{4}$ in) across using a fade-away marker pen.

2.   Pin the two pieces together. Set the machine stitch to satin stitch zigzag. Join the two pieces together on the centre circle line, leaving a small gap.

3.   Firmly stuff the centre with lavender, then zigzag over the opening to seal the lavender in.

4.   Set the machine stitch to automatic scallop design. Zigzag over the outside circle line in the scallop pattern. Using sharp, pointed scissors cut round the edge close to the scallop to show a pretty edge.

5.   Sew a satin ribbon in the centre bow to decorate.

TISSUE HOLDER

Material used: Rectangular piece of painted silk
Plain white silk for the lining
Wadding
Lace for the edging

Method

1.   Cut out one rectangle each of painted silk, plain silk and wadding. These should all be the same size. The rectangle needs to be the length of the bought tissue packet plus 3 cm ($1\frac{3}{16}$ in). The width of the rectangle is double the width of the packet plus 3 cm ($1\frac{1}{16}$ in).

2.   The finished design has two bands of lace on the inside edge. Cut two pieces of lace the same length as the tissue packet, plus 3 cm ($1\frac{1}{4}$ in). Place the layers on the table: wadding, painted silk, lace (frilled edges towards the centre) and plain silk on the top.

3.   Machine down the two shorter sides, catching the lace in the middle. Turn through to the right side.

4.   Place on the table with the lace and painted silk uppermost. Fold the two lace edges to meet in the centre. Machine and neaten across the ends.

Pretty covered coathangers, pomanders, lavender bags and a tissue holder

CHRISTMAS STOCKINGS, TREE DECORATIONS and CARDS

CHRISTMAS STOCKINGS

Finished size: 25 cm × 40 cm (10 in × 16 in)
Material used: Two pieces painted pongée no. 9
30 cm × 45 cm (12 in × 18 in)
Two pieces cotton or silk lining
30 cm × 45 cm (12 in × 18 in)
2 pieces wadding 30 cm × 45 cm
(12 in × 18 in)
Red loop for hanging
Technique: Gutta (gold)
Colours: Red, green

Method

1. Gutta the motifs across the silk, putting the name at the top and continuing downwards in bands of varying widths.

2. Paint alternate rows in reds and greens.

3. Fix as normal.

Sewing up

1. Make a cardboard template of the stocking shape plus 1.5 cm ($\frac{5}{8}$ in) turnings.

2. Draw round the template on the painted silk and cotton lining. Cut out a pair of each. Cut out one pair in wadding without the seam allowance.

3. Pin, right sides together, the top of the stocking front and back to their cotton linings. Tack, machine and turn over so that the right sides are uppermost.

4. Place the wadding between the stocking front and back sections.

5. Pin and tack the front stocking to the back stocking section, right sides together. Machine around the leg and toe. Zigzag the edge to neaten. Clip at the corners.

6. Turn through to the right side and press.

7. Sew on hanging loop in top right-hand corner.

Bright cards, tags and Christmas stockings

Unusual tree decorations, baubles and angels

CHRISTMAS CARDS and GIFT TAGS

See finished designs on page 139
See details on how to make cards on page 125. Look at old cards for design ideas – Christmas trees, angels, doves, baubles, presents, robins, snow scenes, poinsettias, bells; all could be utilized for your personal cards.

Any of the silk painting techniques could be used: gutta, watercolour, stencilling, spraying, wax and salt.

TREE BAUBLES

See finished designs on page 139
These perspex tree decorations are great fun to make. They depend on the availability of the round and heart-shaped decorations in your craft shops. It is easiest to paint a few at a time on one square of silk. Each bauble only needs a circle approximately 10 cm (4 in) of silk.

Material used:	Perspex shapes – ball or heart
Dimensions:	Small square of silk 45 cm × 45 cm (18 in × 18 in) (8 balls)
	Transparent glue
	Gold or coloured braid
	Cord for hanging
Technique:	Gutta (gold or black)

Method
Draw around the half globe or heart to obtain the correct size. Your design must fit neatly into this shape. Gutta and paint the designs. Try to use concentrated dye, so that the colours are strong and bright when fixed.

Assembling your shape

1.   Using sharp pointed scissors, cut neatly around the shape allowing 0.5 cm ($\frac{3}{16}$ in) extra for joining.

2.   Glue the rim of one half of the shape using a transparent glue. Place the trimmed silk on top and allow to dry. Press lightly with your hand to make sure it is in contact with the edge.

3.   Push the other half of the shape over the first to seal together. Carefully match up the hole at the top.

4.   Glue lightly around this join and disguise it using a narrow gold or coloured braid.

5.   Attach a loop through the top and your decoration is ready for display.

PADDED GOLD ANGELS

See finished designs on page 139
These three-dimensional silk angels are effective as a group display. Design them so that each one is in a different position. They need to be sewn and padded, so their outline must be easy to machine around.

Material used:	For eight angels you will need approximately 90 cm × 40 cm (36 in × 16 in) pongée no. 9
	Cotton lining fabric of a similar size
	Wadding
	Gold card for hanging
Technique:	Gutta (gold)

Method
Draw out matching back and front designs on the silk using the designs opposite. Our angels are about 10–12 cm (4–5 in) finished height. Use gold gutta for the outlines and paint in the angels using shades of yellow and brown dye. The shading is very important on these pieces to add visual interest.

Assembly

1.   Cut out round your angel shape leaving a 1 cm ($\frac{3}{8}$ in) seam allowance. Cut out a matching lining for both the front and back in cotton.

2.   Tack the front and back to their lining pieces.

3.   Pin right sides together; machine around the angel shape. Leave a gap on straight section for turning.

4.   Clip and trim carefully and turn through to the right side. Press.

5.   Pad the angel using a small amount of wadding at a time and push into place using a knitting needle. Oversew the opening neatly together.

6.   Attach a small gold loop of card to the top of each angel ready for hanging.

PERFORMER NON GRATA

Brian Alessandro is savagely calm, fiercely erudite, and fully determined to show us everything – everything – he sees. —**Kathe Koja**, Bram Stoker Award-winning author of *Under the Poppy, Dark Facotry* and *The Cipher*

A madhouse novel, both scathing and unforgettably tender, in which the real and the absurd are one…Alessandro is a virtuoso.
—**Junot Díaz**, Pulitzer Prize-winning author of *The Brief, Wondrous Life of Oscar Wao, Drown,* & *This Is How You Lose Her*

Brian Alessandro's *Performer Non Grata* is a face-meltingly perverse satire-cum-farce, a sort of contemporary love child of Wilde and Burroughs, streaming with blood, splooge, booze, snot, bitcoin, litcoin—and prancing with turgidity. Theater as novel, and vice versa, with no guide for determining the gaslight from the candelabra, the performance from the performance-within-the-performance, colonized from colonizer, faux-minist from feminist, ancient myth from YouTube voyeurism, victim from perp. Who, or what, is there to root for beneath the effluvial wreckage? In a novel whose allegory is the bullfight, I ended up cheering for the bull!
—**Diane Seuss**, Pulitzer Prize winning author of *frank: sonnets*

By turns biting and grotesque, audacious and cruel, *Performer Non Grata* pierces through the absurdity of how and why we keep deifying masculinity.
—**Manuel Munoz**, three-time O Henry Award winner and author of *What You See in The Dark*

In sharp, nuanced prose, Brian Alessandro cuts to the core of the human psyche. Strident and imaginative all at once, this novel is a welcome throwback to the kind of unchained fiction that makes so many readers want to write in the first place. As such, Performer Non Grata offers itself up as a vivid, necessary montage of desire, narcissism, and toxic masculinity.

—**Chris Campanioni**, editor-in-chief of PANK
& author of *The Internet is For Real*

Hold on tight. Brian Alessandro's *Performer Non Grata* is a bucking bull ride of a novel. Placing an American family in the milieu of the Spanish toreadors, Alessandro deftly makes a scathing commentary on the most toxic manifestations of traditional masculinity, homophobia, and society's obsession with spectacle. Like Genet's *Querelle of Brest*, *Performer Non Grata* takes Oscar Wilde's famous quote, "each man kills the thing he loves," and runs with it, pushing the dynamics of sexual relationships to the very limits of morality. One can place Alessandro's work among the most irreverent satires of Roth, Albee, and White. And even though the trajectory of Alessandro's lovers' entanglements is a proverbial train wreck, Alessandro skillfully and compassionately imbues his characters with an uncommon humanity. As the novel centers on the world of Spanish bullfighting, with taut, muscular prose, one cannot help but recall Hemingway—only Alessandro turns Hemingway's antiquated machismo on its head and kicks it directly in its manhood. *Performer Non Grata* is a tour de force of satire for our times.

—**David Santos Donaldson**, playwright & author of the Carnegie Medal
for Excellence shortlisted novel, *Greenland*.

Alessandro has written a psychoanalytic farce on our strange political moment, using the Bonaventura family as a decoder. I laughed and groaned my way through this family's mishaps. Alessandro is working in an endangered queer genre; it's rare to find such Sadean wickedness and wit in a contemporary novel. —**Garrard Conley**, author of *Boy Erased*

A wild sex-soaked ride! —**Iris Smyles**, author of *Droll Tales*
& *Iris Has Free Time*

PERFORMER NON GRATA

A NOVEL

BRIAN ALESSANDRO

REBEL SATORI PRESS

New Orleans

Published in the United States of America by
Rebel Satori Press
www.rebelsatoripress.com

Cover by Igor Karash © 2023

Library of Congress Cataloging-in-Publication Data

Names: Alessandro, Brian, 1977- author.
Title: Performer non grata : a novel / Brian Alessandro.
Description: New Orleans : Rebel Satori Press, [2023]
Identifiers: LCCN 2023000017 (print) | LCCN 2023000018 (ebook) | ISBN
   9781608642465 (paperback) | ISBN 9781608642472 (ebook)
Subjects: LCGFT: Satirical literature. | Novels.
Classification: LCC PS3601.L35359 P47 2023 (print) | LCC PS3601.L35359
   (ebook) | DDC 813/.6--dc23/eng/20230103
LC record available at https://lccn.loc.gov/2023000017
LC ebook record available at https://lccn.loc.gov/2023000018

"Faber est suae quisque fortunae"
(Every man is the architect of his own fortune).
Sallust, *Speech to Caesar on the State*

PART I
THE MINOR
ADDITIONS

I

Theodore Bonaventura's parents weren't bad people. Misunderstood, maybe. Self-involved, possibly. Vain, at the very least. Morally complex, only when he was feeling charitable. When dealt with on an individual basis, they could be downright pleasant, even enjoyable. It was when they were together that they formed a chimeric beast, an unstoppable monster on parity with creatures of Greek myth.

The sixteen-year-old had hoped that the unauthorized "documentary" he'd been shooting about them, intending to capture their marriage in all its heightened melodrama, would go some way in mitigating his contempt. He was wrong. The behavior of Risk Bonaventura and Lorna Hall-Bonaventura was anything but predictable.

Early on, Theo learned that diversion was an effective self-preserving exercise. In addition to the movie about his parents, he also designed and constructed costumes for his drag queen friend (his *straight* drag queen friend), Charlie. Intermittently, he edited a video series of clumsy strangers taking public spills down flights of stairs or into park ponds or off benches and uploaded them onto his YouTube channel, which had become increasingly popular. Less often, he drew perverted cartoon characters (Bugs Bunny and Daffy Duck did the most heinous things to each other in his warped universe) to work through rare creative blocks. And when he wasn't engaged in any of those activities, Theo fussed with his fabricated online persona.

That evening, Theo had been on project number five: editing the profile of "Tristan Goodman" on Instagram. At first blush, the photo of the man looked enough like Theo, though with more enviable, testosterone-laden features: a strong jawline, a cleft chin, a prominent brow, a Romanesque nose, thicker hair, and a more developed body. Tristan's skin tone was tawny, whereas Theo's was ashen. Tristan looked to be in his late thirties with a thick, hormonal five o'clock shadow; Theo was still only sixteen with a porcelain complexion. The silhouette Tristan cut was brawny with long, fibrous sinew, showy vascularity worthy of a *GQ* or *Men's Health* cover. Because Theo was a wonder with retouching, augmenting, and reshaping images in Photoshop, and possessed the impetus to envision himself as something greater, he executed startling transformations. At least, in cyberspace.

The pseudo-profile had been created two years ago, and its inventor was currently adding biographical detail in the form of current events. Theo posted on the social media app a photo of his latest drawing, a gangbang with supple *Whos*—in the Seussical sense—quartering a naked Grinch, with disarming sex appeal, as they took turns burrowing into his Whoville. Theo conceptualized the piece as a *Gulliver's Travels*-type scenario, in which the Lilliputians bound and tormented—and in this case, penetrated—their invasive giant.

In the text section, Theo wrote: "Just won first-place prize in the Northeastern Erotic Satire contest." Of course, this was a made-up award in a phony competition, but whoever even bothered to fact-check anymore. In addition to Instagram, Theo also posted the drawing and text on Facebook, Twitter, Tumblr, Tik Tok, and Vine, though he anticipated that they'd be flagged and taken down at some point, once one narc or another reported the "lewd" art. It was a routine to which he'd become accustomed.

Being a member of Generation Z, even less impressed with everything than their forebears, Millennials and Generation X, and in search of perpetual entertainment, or at least distraction, Theo switched gears once again and returned to the documentary about his parents. He had been covertly recording them on his iPhone for several weeks and had dumped over ten hours of uncut footage onto an external terabyte drive. Theo reviewed the last "scene" he had surreptitiously shot, replaying the short clip three times. This magnum opus would be presented as "A Film by Theo Bonaventura."

The Tristan Goodman alter ego could be compartmentalized, after all.

"That's mother, *Doctor* Lorna Hall-Bonaventura, editing her book about rape and how important tough guys are in modern society and crap," Theo had whispered into the camera as he framed his parents at the dinner table, lazily reviewing work documents, and drinking wine. "Everyone's been giving her shit about it, but I think she gets off on the attention, honestly. And then, dear ole dad, Risk Bonaventura—my grandparents actually, really named him *Risk* because, supposedly, his father, my grandad, always saw risk-taking as the greatest, noblest virtue of a man, a quintessentially American character trait to an Italian immigrant—who must *always wear the pants*, though mother wears them a lot better. He's the rich one. An investment banker who *just had to* open a network of charter schools! And even, get this—hire himself as a history teacher! Trying to live out some white savior fantasy or something lame! Like teaching poor kids in the ghetto is going to make him like himself. Or impress anyone. He doesn't even like poor people! I guess it looks like he's grading papers now or whatever."

Risk was speaking to Lorna about Spain. Though they were down the hall in Risk's den, Theo could hear them. His father's conversations, over the phone with business associates or in-person with mother, were audible when Theo wasn't listening to music or watching TV, and they always sounded like a put on. The acoustics in the old apartment were sharp and voices carried. Theo paused his movie and moved to the door, opened it, and crept down the hall with his camera-phone ready. He was an expert eavesdropper.

"Madrid? Really?" said Lorna, loitering in the threshold of her husband's home office. "And I'm just supposed to do what? Drop *my* career?"

"I'm not saying I want to go anytime soon, *dear*, but eventually, I thought it might be a nice place to spend some time, you know, once Theo is out of high school, and in college."

"Yeah, and that's now fewer than two years away, Risk."

"Well, maybe not *right after*..."

"Maybe not at all." Even with her back turned toward him, Theo could tell that his mother was making *that face*. A cross between a smirk and a scowl, an expression that she reserved for moments where she hoped to both humiliate and intimidate. It was a face she reserved mainly for Risk, and on occasion, a student or colleague.

Theo must have made a noise—maybe his foot brushing against the door frame or his shallow, out-of-shape breathing as he attempted to creep closer—because Lorna stepped out of the office and turned to him, expecting him to be there. She was not bothered by his snooping—she'd gotten used to it at this point—and waved him over. She'd require an audience for her sermon, anyway.

"Theo, come here, would you, and listen to this."

Theo shuffled into the office with his chin tucked into his chest and his iPhone still recording. He'd kept the camera's lens trained on his parents, poised from the hip.

"Your father wants to move to Spain! Of all places! What do you think of that? What do you guys say now? How 'rando'!"

Theo turned to his father. "Alone?"

"No, silly." Lorna's impatience covered the room. "With us."

"But not now." Risk did a hurried half stand, awkward crouch, leaning forward on his desk. "Or even anytime soon, son."

Theo pursed his lips and nodded. He hadn't cared all that much about when or where they'd be going.

"Hey," said Risk, mussing his son's hair, an unfamiliar, studied gesture that made Theo cringe. "Remember when we went to Spain? Remember Pamplona?"

Theo nodded. He had been thirteen the first and only other time he'd been to the country with his parents. They'd spent a week driving from city to city. He and Risk had been impressed—disgusted and intrigued—by the gore left behind in Pamplona. Shopkeepers hosing off their storefronts hours after the annual Running of the Bulls. Blood had stained the mortar between the cobblestones.

"And how about La Tomatina in Valencia? All those people hurling tomatoes at each other. So much fun!"

Lorna remembered the festival in Bunol, the mess and the stink and the roaches and rats it invited. She moved closer to her husband, which sent him back to his seat, safely behind the mahogany desk. "And who is this man you keep talking about?"

"His name is Javier Forza, he's a pretty famous matador. Lives in Madrid. A kind of favorite son. He's like what Derek Jeter was to New York before he retired. Or Carmello Anthony, before Kristaps Porzingis came into the picture."

"Right, of course." Lorna sighed, dismissing the esoterica espoused by her husband. "*Them.*"

Theo turned to her. "You don't get those references, Mom."

Risk waved his Mont Blanc. "It's not important! Suffice to say, this guy is like a really big deal. And I've been following his matches online. And I think it's something I'd like to maybe pursue in the next couple years."

"Don't these guys start out when they're still boys?" Lorna shifted her weight, put a hand to her hip. "This Javier person was probably just a kid when he began training."

"Yeah, and?"

That face, again. "You're old, honey," said Lorna. "*Too old* for something this hairbrained."

Risk shook his head and returned to checking his stock margins and financial news on his laptop. Theo had already turned away and was heading toward the door. He couldn't see the silent surrender, but the clacking of keys on his father's keyboard signaled a retreat. The conversation was over, and mom had emerged victorious, if only for the moment.

"Don't forget our appointment with Worthingham tomorrow night," said Lorna to Risk as she continued to loiter in the threshold, allowing Theo to brush past her. "And we should discuss this with her."

Before Lorna could make Theo any more complicit in her frustrating discussion with her quixotic husband, he was back in his bedroom and already at his computer, typing "Javier Forza" into Google. Within seconds, pages of links to articles and photos of the athlete in tantalizing poses, drenched in brine and blood, showcasing an ample cod section, appeared. Theo quickly found his social media profile, began following him on Instagram, and posted a flurry of comments (as Tristan Goodman) beneath a series of photos.

A studio lit photo of Javier posing in boxer briefs while wrapping his arms around a pair of bull horns coming at him from behind, an ad for underwear in some European fashion magazine. The image had "398,000 likes" and "32,000 comments." The things that had revolted Theo when he was a child would stir him as a teenager.

Theo-as-Tristan: You're a true specimen!

An intentionally distressed photo of Javier snapping a red cloak past a charging bull, a lovingly photographed action shot that could have been published in *LIFE* and won a major prize for viscerally, corporeally capturing adroit and life-threatening sportsmanship. The image fetched "409,000 likes" and "47,000 comments."

Theo-as-Tristan: Brutal and balletic!

A paparazzi photo of Javier leaving a club in Barcelona, playing the fool with a powdered face, rouged cheeks, red lips, black eyeliner, donning a white silk scarf, a pair of under-sized dark glasses, a black bowler cap, a maroon blazer with no shirt underneath, too-tight gray jeans, and ruby Oxfords. On one arm was a bald black woman who was definitely a couture model in a slinky orange and brown dress and on the other a Herculean Filipino man who was dressed in a skin-tight mustard suit that accented his bodybuilder frame. The shot boasted "820,000 likes" and "187,000 comments."

Theo-as-Tristan: #Lifegoals!

Theo then found Javier's Facebook page and wrote him a message as, once again, Tristan Goodman, a fellow aesthete, athlete, and bon vivant.

> Javier, I'm NOT gay and I'm NOT hitting on you. You are awesome, though, and I just wanted you to know. I'm sure you must get thousands of emails a day!!! I don't expect to hear back from you anytime soon. Or even ever!!! But I just wanted you to know that someone in New York City (I'm sure a lot of *someones* in NYC, lolz) thinks you're pretty fucking special!!! And I can tell there is more to you than meets the eye. You're a lot smarter and deeper than your public image makes you seem. Keep slayin' 'em—the girls, the guys, AND THE BULLS!
>
> From Tristan Goodman

Theo hit "send" and took a breath. He finished dinner (Lorna, abiding by traditional gender norms as a sacred rite, had made a meat and chickpea stew, Cocido Madrileno, that she'd found a recipe for online, which made Theo and Risk wonder if she'd been seriously contemplating Spain as it was a popular Madrid dish), masturbated to wrestling videos from the early-1990s on YouTube (he was most fond of the young Sting tussling with a young Ric Flair), showered (he also washed and conditioned his hair), and finished his latest doodle (the Hulk with a python-like erection devouring a petite, fetching Thor), and considered his motives. The boy was old enough to have self-awareness; after all, his mother had stressed the virtue of "knowing thyself" since before she started homeschooling him freshman year. His intentions were not only to one-up his father—claiming victory by making first contact with the international athlete he'd admired—but also to bridge a sentimental gulf that had widened between himself and Dad during the past few years. Though the sport was ghoulish and had become politically unpopular, he and Risk shared a memory of its culture, something that soldered them. It wasn't nothing.

Theo reconciled his actions and then checked his Facebook account. Though it had been only three hours since he had sent the message and it was, by his calculations, the middle of the night in Spain, Javier had responded in endearingly broken English.

Tristan, Great profiles, man! You drawings is fucking sick! Thanks
for the love! Later,
Javier

Blood rushed to Theo's head, and he thought he might have to masturbate again before bed.

I I

Whenever it occurred to Risk Bonaventura to inventory his innumerable failures, he always began with the ones most people would discount as insignificant. Too miniscule to matter. Too trivial to mention. But matter, they did. Mention them, he invariably would, if only to himself. Of course, if anyone else ever confronted him with his failings, he'd deny them, attribute them to some other poor sap, or lash out in animalistic fashion at the unfortunate accuser.

That time he chickened out three quarters up the mountain in Zion National Park just before he would have reached the summit of Angel's Landing, some 1,488 sheer feet above Utah's red craggy earth. His friend, fellow-trekker, and coworker, Darnell, naturally, was able to complete the hike and reap the glory of having made it to the terrifying peak, something he'd remind Risk of nine years later. And then there were all those tiny instances of disproved manhood in which he was incapable of boring a screw through a plank of softwood, inelegantly and chaotically shuffled a deck of cards, botched the casting of a fishing line, misused a handsaw to the point of nearly severing a finger. And in almost every case some man or another— a cousin, a friend, a colleague—was there to witness the error, the incompetence, the clumsiness. And the shame would take hold. Followed swiftly by a rage-rich trigger.

Risk considered his routine catastrophes most fervidly, and somewhat ritualistically, during his weekly professional development sessions at Perseverance High, the South Bronx charter school where he taught History, both World and American. The tone of the meetings evoked the subjects of futility and inadequacy. His assistant principal, Reginald Finn, principal, Velma

Sanchez, executive director, Howard James, and occasionally even colleagues ran the "PD workshops" as though they were addressing recalcitrant scholars.

The worst of them was Dominick Truman, a charismatic biology teacher originally from Arizona who at thirty-six was twelve years Risk's junior (though Dominick could pass for even younger than his reported age mainly due to his athleticism, beauty, vigor, and spirit) and who was one of the insufferable people who excelled effortlessly at everything. He was the school's star and he reveled in the adoration. Risk romanticized his many attributes as often as he imagined ways of defeating him.

The discussion that afternoon centered on assessment and school culture. Mr. Bonaventura had inherited the school's toughest "cohort" in its short history (that is, since its inception only a few years back), and even though he had developed a class conduct and culture rubric to get them in line with the threat of impacted grade point averages, they still resisted becoming model pupils. The teens, all Hispanic and black from the surrounding neighborhoods, persisted in covertly texting during lectures, submitting to hushed side conversations during "Socratic seminars," sneaking snacks during group work, and even dozing when gifted a study hall.

The big not-so-well-kept secret was that Risk had founded the network. The schools were his. He gave himself the teaching job on day one and insisted upon the students never knowing. His colleagues and "superiors" performed well as per his orders and treated him as just another teacher. The obnoxious faux-beat poet café snaps had been his brainchild, too.

"Some of us here are young, only a few years older than our seniors, and are maybe seeking to revisit our glory days, that is, relive high school vicariously through them," said Mr. James, robust, bald, black, with a gray beard, but a child's face, even at fifty-seven. He paced back and forth before his staff with gargantuan hands clasped behind a hulking back and quick eyes that threatened to pop out of his shiny skull as they darted from one obedient educator to another. "Mr. Truman said it best during last week's PD: We need to act like the role models our scholars expect us to be."

All twenty-two faculty members and administrators snapped in unison as though they were a world-weary audience in an East Village café coolly applauding a beat poet slamming his iambs.

As for scholar evaluations, Risk was often penalized for not offering more rigorous feedback on essays. He merely cursorily scanned each assignment and gave it a number grade. In his defense, the network—a governing body assembled early on by him, a meddling board of directors—did pressure their teachers to enter some five scores a week into its electronic grade keeper. When accounting for eighty-five students, that demand averaged out to 425 assessments per week. Who had the time or energy to gallantly face such numbers and deadlines? Yes, the board was technically under his control, but like the standardized exam prep he routinely oversaw, Risk sought "actual conditions" for his "profession".

Naturally, Dominick excelled here, too. And he was teaching his fellow educators how.

"Just to echo what Mr. Truman said a few moments ago," began Ms. Sanchez, wide-faced with light skin and a bullish frame. Her red and blue, polka dot dress made her look more like a PTA mom in the Midwest than the principal of a top-performing New York City charter. She stood firm, arms nearly akimbo and her strong, square chin turned upward in a patronizing sneer. "Your facial expressions, tone of voice, and body language speak loudest, and effectuate more attention than words ever can. Be aware of your performance. Your space. Your own self."

More snaps. The fingers were animated and adoring.

Risk dismissed his wife's rare efforts to make him realize that his missteps were normal. That everyone, even towering intellectuals like himself, goofed at the tedium of everyday life. And that no one was keeping score. She didn't understand, he'd balk. There *were* scorekeepers. Lorna was wrong. Risk was not the only one keeping stock. The world's many managers lurked in shadows and hovered overhead, they whispered in dark corners and logged their observations. He'd be confronted by his failures, repeatedly. Anyway, whenever they fought, which was with increased frequency, she'd toss all the consolations out the window and dig right in like the rest of them.

Really, Risk only relished the trappings of being a teacher. He hated to admit it, but he would have much rather spent his time doing almost anything else than reading and grading the poorly written research essays by his students. A waste of his time.

"Mr. Truman focused on this during his graduate studies," began Mr. Finn, caramel skinned and densely packed with uneven musculature like a boxer's. His dark, ready eyes and hunched shoulders matched his scowl and gait. He bobbed and parried nervously as he stood up and strolled the aisles, his bulbous gut leading the slow rampage, his stealth and speed belying his fifty-two years. "The science shows that if we repeat the same question multiple times, differentiating the phrasing throughout, and the longer we wait, the closer the attention to the lesson the children will pay, and the more arms will go up to volunteer an answer. It's scientifically valid, people."

More snaps. The fingers were galvanized and furious.

Risk had achievements, sure. Wrestling trophies from middle school and high school filled two shelves in his den. A bachelor's degree in history from Penn State and an MBA from NYU's Stern Business School hung behind his desk. A beautiful wife who was also famous because she was smart if not always compassionate. A creative and clever son who didn't always loathe him and who was maintaining a solid B average during his sophomore year, even if he was being homeschooled. A body and a face that at forty-eight-years old still felt vital and not unattractive. Sure, his wrists and ankles were too boney, his salt-and-pepper hair was thinning, his four-pack had become obscured by a layer of hard fat, and his crow's feet had deepened, but his arms, legs, back, and chest were still rich with muscle, and his skin still held tight and even glowed when he got adequate sleep and maybe a little sun.

"And as for the grading procedures you proposed earlier this afternoon, Mr. Truman," began Ms. Priscilla Jourdain, the thirty-one-year-old Spanish teacher with purple hair, Betty Page eyelashes, Disney-character-tattoo sleeves, and pear-shaped silhouette. "It really promises the most pragmatic solution to the workload. Using Turn-It-In and No Red Ink to scan for plagiarism and grammatical errors would cut my time reading and researching in half. I mean, if you can manage to grade as many research papers on cancer and HIV in so short a time with such diligence and depth, then I can surely handle the demands of my classes."

More snaps. The fingers were enthusiastic and warm.

It was a hell of a thing to lose skills, talents, looks, and knowledge. Risk had read about how it was to be expected, the loss of such things once one reached a certain age. The forties were supposed to be the decade where mastery of details and accumulated abilities were supplanted by a quiet and satisfied wisdom, a mature insouciance. And yet, on the verge of leaving the decade and hitting 50 like a brick wall, all Risk could feel was despair and panic. The construction of character took a lifetime and now in a mere few years it was all being dismantled.

"Just to return to your work with conduct and classroom culture, Mr. Truman," said Mr. Warren Desmond, black, sixty-two, tall and thin, and always in a designer suit. He'd been the dean of students from the very beginning. "You've really done most of my job for me. You're an example of how to manage and lead. I'd say a natural leader. Other teachers should take a note from your book and study your method. What you do in your classroom is special and is leaving an indelible mark on our scholars."

More snaps. The fingers were sharp and aggressive.

Risk also wouldn't allow himself to forget—mainly because he maintained an extensive list—the many instances where he misspoke or forgot a fact or made a grammatical error in a piece of administrative writing, a memo or email or some such irrelevant thing, or in casual conversation. Writing "on attendance," instead of "in attendance," forgetting in front of his class of juniors what the 15th amendment did during a seminar on *Huck Finn*, conflating "disparate" with "dispirit" in one of his very infrequent essay critiques, saying "orchard" when he meant "orchid" during a game of *Clue*, mistaking Shelley Winters for Rosemary Clooney during a screening of *Lolita* with Lorna and her snarky colleagues from Merriweather.

Lorna accused him of being egotistical about such gaffes: "Only a narcissist who believed himself above error and strove for perfection would care so much about laughably unimportant mistakes!"

It was unnatural how attractive Mr. Truman was, thought Risk. His forearms bulged like Popeye's. His legs seemed intent on bursting from their form-fitting burgundy khakis. His movements were fluid and athletic, and he exuded an easy rhythm even when only gesturing at the projection on the Smart Board behind him. The bulk in his arms and shoulders twitched and pulsated with every gesticulation and pose. He was a model and a cult leader, and his colleagues and superiors duly fawned and worshiped. Risk imagined that based on Dominick's considerable bulge, his genitalia was likely outsized, too. Of course. An impeccable specimen extant for the witnessing by the inferiors. And Risk was the prime inferior. The chief mediocrity. Someone villainous sent into the shadows by the brightness of someone heroic. Contrast was cruel.

"We love our children, right," said Dominick, with a self-satisfaction that bordered on autofellatio. "But we must remind them that we are *not* their friends, even if we are friendly. I mean, we mustn't lose sight of the Broken Windows Theory on which our charter was founded, to nip in the bud minor infractions before they become unmanageable felonies."

The snaps were now in a rage. The devotion to the speaker was that of a fanbase for an icon. And he hadn't even yet mentioned how he guided his twin twenty-two-year-old world wrestling champion brothers from troubled gang-affiliated roughs into scholar-athletes "through sheer will and grit and fortitude".

The complex fascinated and unnerved Risk. For every idealization of Dominick that he would make there would be found, or forced, a related devaluation of himself. The science teacher was vampiric. The energy he pulled from the room in the form of applause, laughter, enthusiastic nods, vigorous back pats, chants, and handshakes sucked from Risk, who could only marvel at the champion crack jokes, imitate administrators, master impressions, break into a tap dance, and even sing with a surprising vibrato. Dominick was a hungry performer, and every room was a stage, every person a prospective spectator. He compelled. He commanded. His audience was always captive. And the history teacher felt a chill in the shade he cast.

The ones who didn't proffer their adulation verbally at least nodded with a fiery focus and snapped with the most verve.

English teacher, Mr. Roy Schwartz, was bald and white, forty-five and mildly overweight, bespectacled and fond of vests. Chemistry and Physics teacher, Ms. Susan Kim was fifty-five and Korean with a heavy accent and a black bob. Math teacher, Ms. Marielle Granite was a WASP and from Florida with rosy cheeks, frizzy red hair, and ditzy good humor.

Risk, the odd man out in this family dynamic, feigned well enough minimal respect and attention, even if his thoughts were elsewhere. Like what impact his insecurities and self-loathing might be having on Theo. His son had only recently turned sixteen and was nothing if not impressionable. His new obsession with recording strangers in compromising situations and uploading them on social media was disconcerting. It was a quiet aggression that creeped out Lorna, though unapologetically fascinated Risk. His boy's obscene drawings and eventual graffiti were other matters, entirely.

When Dominick concluded his presentation the woots and snaps that followed culminated in an explosion of actual applause. It was then that the lower-intestinal pang Risk always anticipated when in Truman's presence struck. His testicles tightened and rose into his pelvis. An emasculation so consistent and unfailing that when Risk didn't feel it, he searched in a reserved panic, knowing it imminent.

"What'd you think of the presentation, Risk?" asked bloodthirsty Dominick, fangs deep in neck.

"It was, the usual, you know, Dominick." Risk had been in mid-rise from his desk when the vampiric golden boy approached him, catching him off-guard, and the stammer was more obvious than usual. "You're good at this sort of thing."

"Yeah, well, you know what passion does, right? Gotta push the rigor!"

Risk smiled goofily and feigned as well as he could that kind of glad-handed, fraternal approval that people like Dominick Truman demanded from all who were graced with their attention.

"I've done something horrible," Risk, in a rude fugue state, mumbled unintelligibly to Dominick.

"Huh?"

Risk put himself back in order. "Right, I've done something *comparable*."

"I'm sure! You should try one, sometime. Give it a crack! It's a lot of work to prep, but man, does it feel good to develop people. To serve as a leader. But you sort of know that already, right, boss? To bring an organization from good to great, right, captain? Have I ever told you about how I mentored my twin twenty-two-year-old brothers, world college wrestling champions—"

"Yeah, sure! We'll see. Someday!" Risk thought he would vomit but managed to beat back the tuna sandwich he'd just wolfed down at the corner bodega an hour before PD. "Overloaded with lesson planning and grading, and so, you know …"

"You can always make time for what's important, no? *This* is, right?" Dominick smiled so wide that the pinks of his gums and the whites of his teeth seemed to jockey for the spotlight.

Risk nodded furiously now and pushed away from the desk, straightening himself out, and pretending well that he truly did have an urgent matter to which to attend. "I really do have to run, Dominick. Good work, again. As usual, you know."

Dominick's radiant smile relaxed into a mere smirk, however still wide and ebullient. It toed the line between sinister snark and earnest endearment. "Never too late to have an impact. Effectuate change. Kick mediocrity in the nuts."

Was the little fucker teasing him? Throwing his own mottoes in his face? Could he have been earnest?

Other teachers and administrators swooned around them, buzzing like gadflies in need of plant exudates. Dominick would feed them. Risk wanted to know all his secrets. Like what he did to earn his enchantment, his favor with fate, his bargain with the universe. Why should he, Risk, be the damned one, the cursed one? Or maybe he was just a buffoon who acted absurdly, carelessly, with a foolhardy conceit. And downfall would always be the likely, deserved outcome.

Dominick seemed to possess an implicit understanding of astral planes, the unseen magical realms. He alone was granted access to these spaces that no one else could see let alone know. And it touched him, lifted him. Cast a light on him. Gave him voice. Made him Salient. Ensured his Presence. Risk would remain mute and invisible and absent. Never mind his ingenious business dealings and subsequent discreet wealth.

Never mind that the whole fucking endeavor— the goddamned school itself—was his!

Risk turned away from his too-galvanized colleague as if it were a grave emergency, as though he were dodging some dire menace, in a fit of panic, and moved to the classroom's threshold with one mission in mind: escape the toxic condescension before some murderous rage took hold and drove him to an action from which there would be no return.

And faintly from the hall, he could hear Dominick still talking to his coterie, his band of admirers, gifting them with banal revelations.

"Don't you just have the need to be better today than you were yesterday?"

III

Class was still twenty minutes out and Lorna was reluctant to grade papers. She instead read an article in the online edition of the *Washington Post* about an NYU professor—a clinical psychologist put on the map by her empathy analysis of "good Germans" who passively witnessed the holocaust. The professor's office had been vandalized with anti-Semitic insults, including the words "YID" and "KIKE." And no fewer than six swastikas. Dr. Leah Rabinowitz disclosed that this had been the second such defacement in under ten years.

Lorna looked around her own office and imagined a similar cultural travesty befalling her solace space.

"There's going to be some trouble." She whispered the words without thinking about them, a mindless ramble. She would not think about them again until she arrived in Europe not too long after.

And then she checked her email. One suspicious note commanded all her attention now. As a rule, Lorna deleted emails from unknown senders, though few ever made it past her spam filter. She felt safe opening this one. The subject line read:

Dr. Hall-Bonaventura, I am NOT a Robot! Please read me! EOM.

Lorna clicked the embedded URL, a YouTube destination, and watched herself give a lecture from two days ago. She recalled that it was the day she'd slipped up and gone on a rant in her *Gendering Culture* class about how rape is evolutionary, how it could be avoided by exercising common sense, and how many women—and men—possessed an unconscious desire for it. She'd also gone after the gays and feminine men too.

"I mean, who doesn't like a show of strength?" Her blank-faced pupils were too appalled to react with any animation. "I'm not saying the act is a downright myth, but come on now, there are parts of the violation that could be construed as desirable."

"Without ascribing blame, we should, at least, consider the complicity of females in their own degradation." Her young audience squirmed. "Rape is really an issue of common sense and magical thinking. And by that, I mean you can't change human behavior by lecturing it about political correctness!"

"As I see it, the 'problem' with, not necessarily gay, but certainly effeminate men is that ..." A wall of agape mouths and bugged eyes stared back at her. "... they're much too soft to go into combat and fight for anything other than the perfect outfit or fabulous living room or sex, and I have gay friends and they'd agree!"

"There is something inherently sovereign about heterosexual masculinity." The audible gasps and moans prompted her to raise her voice. "So-called *toxic masculinity* is what keeps us safe and the world spinning forward!"

She had held these views for years and written about them in numerous articles and books, but pushback had historically been confined to civil discourse between academics, lively and respectful debates in university auditoriums. Her new book, *The Wanton Feminine*, forthcoming in a few months from Dowling House, her most high-profile publisher, would set the record straight.

The clip had only been posted a day ago, but already yielded four hundred and twenty thousand views and eighty-seven thousand comments, almost all of which excoriated Lorna. Some even demanded a livestreamed suicide.

"Though I consider myself a progressive, my gripe with the left is that they *absent* things like common sense, basic biology, and ancient history."

Lorna watched herself address the students in the remainder of the five-minute clip.

[19]

"Girls need to smarten up and start acknowledging human nature—and especially *male* nature—as something concrete, *not* theoretical or elastic. *Not* something that will bend to the whims of political correctness. The brain tends to mistake pursuit for desire, but that's not entirely what I'm talking about here. I *do* believe that we're built this way on an evolutionary level to perpetuate the species, though. It follows that those alpha men who effectuate change and keep the world spinning forward are also inclined to conquer sexually. *Without* beta permission, *without* omega timidity. They are biologically pushed to spread their seed. To propagate. Shaming those men into believing that there's something wrong with that impulse will surely extinguish their flames. The constructive fires that build cities and cure diseases and produce great art. Women are neurologically wired to accept the conquest because they know on some unconscious level that they're welcoming in an alpha seed and thereby helping civilization advance. And for the last time, please stop writing about the fluidity of gender in your papers. Gender is *not* fluid. It's as fixed as metastatic brain cancer."

Lorna looked around her austere office and wondered if she'd been playing the clip too loud, worrying that someone in the hall might have heard it. She lowered the volume and put on closed captioning for the duration of the video as she searched her memory for which student might have had his or her phone out during class. As there were over eighty students in attendance, the clandestine recorder was as much a mystery as the anonymous sender of the email.

Lorna weathered the stares and sneers with admirable indifference as she walked across the Morningside Heights campus. The muffled comments and audible hisses were more *impactful*—how she loathed this neologism or more precisely the back formation of the word into an adjective— blows to withstand. CUNY Merriweather's faculty and students were nothing if not up on their viral video sensations. And all the chatter that would follow. Multiple Twitter storms and Facebook fusillades erupted. She had happened upon them after closing the YouTube video and researching the national witch hunt playing out online. It all left her dazzled. She almost chimed in but decided she'd better not.

Even the barista at her favorite café across the street was awkward when handing her the receipt. She'd been an affable young woman, a graduate student who was fond of Lorna's work and conversation, if not tips. Her name tag read "Sam," but Lorna always thought she looked more like a Sue. The young woman flashed a half-smile and busily moved on to the next customer waiting in line, eyeballing Lorna with unease, if not impoliteness. Were so many people really that plugged into YouTube? Did such media trend so swiftly? It's not as if the clip had been broadcast on any of the major networks or 24-hour news channels. Not yet, anyway.

A group of protestors, politically active doctoral candidates that Lorna had recognized from past colloquia, had gathered at Merriweather's main entrance, and held placards that read "No Room for Hate Speech!" and "Beware Traitors Infiltrating from Within!" and "Stop the Sexists!" and "#MeToo is NOT a Passing Fad!" and "Toxic Masculinity is a Cloak That Even Women Can Don!" They shouted their slogans with theatrical brio.

Lorna sipped her hot black coffee, not realizing that the demonstrations had been organized in her honor, even though they'd coopted one of her phrases—donning the masculine cloak. It became clear that she was the butt of the joke—that's what this whole farce was, after all, a *joke*— when one of the protestors saw her and began hissing. The others followed suit. Lorna turned away, red face and wide-eyed, took the long trek around the building to the side entrance, passing a dumpster, and ran into a smaller faction of demonstrators anticipating her attempted escape. She grimaced hard and brushed past them, spilling some of her coffee on her pants and scuffing the side of her shoe on the base of a nearby concrete planter.

◆ ◆ ◆

Lorna's eighty-four pupils listened with a rapt attentiveness. Their tacit enthusiasm would electrify Merriweather's largest lecture hall. Or so she had relished believing. She got off on the energy that her seminars had elicited in undergraduates, apparently. Prided herself on telling the kind of truth missing from contemporary academia: that of the ugly, offensive variety. She owned her ugliness. Cuddled her offensiveness. Cultural studies as a subject was still relatively new, and students were eager to learn as much critical theory as possible, if for no other reason than to show off their creative connections between disciplines and earth-shattering insights at cocktail parties.

She should have tried to move on and away from the YouTube clip, but the cold war brewing between her pupils, ghoulishly bathed in the blue-white glow of laptop screens, and herself was a battle from which she'd not shrink. Though the circumstances couldn't be more awkward, Lorna would make the video the centerpiece of today's *Gendering Culture* class. And it being a lecture, there'd be fewer opportunities for talkback or scrutiny.

"Good afternoon. You have by now all seen this YouTube clip of my lecture last week, which has been circulating on social media, I'm sure? You were all at that session." Lorna paused with a delightful smile and jubilant eyes. "And one of you even recorded it."

Some students shifted in their seats, others leered, ready for an apology or a confession or a gloriously well executed excuse.

"What I said wasn't new. I've been writing about it for the past twenty years. You've all had time to read my book, *The Civilized Masculine: Unnecessary Crisis in The Age of Traumatized Selfhood* and should know my positions by now. None of this was done for shock value. Or to hurt anyone."

A male student, black, preppy, bespectacled, and likely a senior based on his age, raised his hand but began speaking before Lorna had a chance to call on him. "You really think that women ask for rape? Are you for real with that garbage?"

Lorna sighed and hunched a bit, approximating well the mien of an embattled woman. "I see my comments were taken out of context. Tragically, you all couldn't detect the nuance and subtext of my delivery. If only you had been keeping up with the reading, you'd have been able to better understand what I meant."

Lorna caught them, the faces, the expressions made by newly educated kids who liked to prove street credibility by schooling others, usually older and in modes of power, like parents or employers or teachers. They rolled eyes and shrugged shoulders and curled lips into mocking smirks. Many hurled expletives loud enough for Lorna to hear.

She could never be sure if their sneers were for her or her intended targets.

"So, then, a summary." Lorna reviewed her book, thumbed through the dog-eared pages, then put it down. "Listen, I'm less interested in dwelling on the role of women in all of this. The so-called victims or 'receptacles.' They'll get their hearing in my new book, *The Wanton Feminine*, coming in a few months. No, no. We'd be better served understanding the so-called perpetrators, the 'violators.' Men. When scrutinizing the behavior patterns and reactions exhibited by males today one is wise to consider the archetypal roots found in male icons of centuries and millennia past. Ramses II. Alexander the Great. Caesar Augustus. Henry VIII. Napoleon. King Herod. King Solomon. Hitler. Though their pride ultimately led them to ruin, it also fueled a quest for greatness, and here we are after all this time still discussing their indubitable glories. Consider Nietzsche and his 'master morality,' in which the master transcends the mediocrity of the common person, right?"

Some of the students, those who weren't busy muttering foul sentiments under their breath, jotted notes or punched keys. They annotated copies of her article. They wrote immediate responses, rebuttals. They logged their triggers.

"Envy between even heterosexual, masculine males spawns a strange desire. The second-fiddle beta or lowest-rung omega endeavor *not to* just steal the alpha's place, but to supplant the alpha himself! To *be* him. Or defeat him. This odd craving generates a disruption in the beta's or omega's ego. The disrupted ego occasions bizarre role plays, toxic theater, and dangerous charades. These role plays, theater, and charades foster varying humiliations. Their humiliations cause carnage. The tools of their combat and disaster are now voyeuristic, judgmental bystanders, ever-recording cell phone cameras, and an omniscient internet. Before, it was a coliseum. The envy cuts deep. A need to assert and prove oneself arises. Women, caught in between, become collateral damage. Remarkable this masculine toxicity."

Some of the young students sniggered but admitted uneasy truths, anyway, Lorna thought. Others shifted again with a detectable agitation. The notetaking and keyboard clacking persisted. Lorna paused for a dramatic beat, seductively, sweetly eyeballing the front row, all of whom looked up at her with a dense air of uneasiness. She diffused with a gentle disposition. Maternal, soothing.

"What the hell?!" A student, female, blonde, and petite, spoke up. "This is sick and offensive! And triggering!"

Lorna continued without a reaction, without even looking at the young girl who stomped loudly out of the lecture hall. "Men, not broadly mankind, but *masculine* men specifically, are prone to self-immolation. They are ruled by the command to conquer and create. When they find themselves unable to do either they choose destruction and death over surrender and submission. And there always remains one obstacle too insurmountable to fathom for the great heroes of history, be it India for the Macedonian emperor or Waterloo for the French emporer. All supreme men are hungry dogs seeking domination. And, yes, I realize that Alexander was bi, but this not about sexuality, as I will continue to reiterate."

Lorna felt the ions shift in the lecture hall, the eagerness to share thoughts and push back against theories that didn't sit well was in the dense, uneasy air. And yet she could make the suspense linger, even after considering that some of her students might be sexual assault survivors. She would push the lesson and her students' nerves further. The tension was necessary for facilitating concentration and remembrance. She was a professor who demanded absolute concentration and complete remembrance, if not fondness.

These lectures were her art, and she would somehow reclaim that goddamn, motherfucking YouTube video.

"It takes literal balls to build a culture. Sorry to *gender* the assertion! The bold push from the testes produces civilization and advancement. My blend of feminism permits worship of men who have made the world their own and those few women who have ... *donned the masculine cloak* ... and done so for themselves: Cleopatra, Elizabeth I and even her ruthless half-sister Mary, Victoria, Thatcher, Clinton. I mean, consider the great renaissance woman painter, Artemisia Gentileschi, and all that she endured, the victimhood, but how she owned it, and turned it into art on a parity with Caravaggio's best. Essentialism has its limits as a philosophy. As a science it is an experiment intended for ceaseless empirical research."

Whereas it had been the more delicate men who were most vocal in their braying at her pronouncements up until this point, the women in the room had now suddenly found themselves jeering their teacher's pseudo-defense. Lorna enjoyed this the most. To trouble young girls, to upend their new, ill-informed feminism, to chip away at the patina of their self-congratulatory activism and performative outrage. But still, she worked toward disarming with a loving glow.

Several female students were now shaking their heads and had crossed their arms, silently and in solidarity refusing to take notes, protesting anymore propaganda from this *self-loathing woman*. Lorna's calculations were not off; by her estimates two thirds of the whole class will have joined them by the time her session was up.

"Several volumes of this epic could be filled with the data amassed on the transformations undergone by the alpha and his beta. And their omega. Their change is seemingly ineluctable. It must be a demoralizing revelation indeed when these men find out that they are unable to control their own personalities, and that they had seized control of them like angry poltergeists, intent on either breaking them or recreating them."

Lorna could tell at this point that several of her scrawnier, meek pupils were searching the auditorium for the jocks, the models, the physically superior specimens. The inadequacies screamed. The jocks, the models themselves basked in the silent adulation. Lorna imagined that the bitter atoms between the alphas and betas and omegas caused the female students to tingle in all the appropriate places. In her perverse fantasy, Lorna tingled, too.

"Finding comparisons between the 'tournaments' held by the competing men and idolatry and the ancient gods requires no leap of faith. Even as the beta and omega succumb wholeheartedly to nihilism and even anarchy in their self-loathing-fueled destruction. He who shirked the dictates of logic and abided by the commands of delusion. Fastidiously, and with fetishistic relish, the beta and the omega work toward the solution to his problem: debilitating self-doubt in the shadow of their alpha."

The small, quiet, bookish boys—the first to have been audible in their disagreement— had begun to rock back and forth in their seats, their knuckles white, their cheeks flush. Lorna imagined that the jocks, the models were by now fluffing their feathers, their tumescence likely apparent had she looked closer. She couldn't be sure who'd recorded her, but she could manage the temperature in the room. And when tactical, quiet them with congeniality.

"The lazy analysis suggests that men are inherently sadistic and women masochistic. This is one of life's great fallacies. Men, not women, are the true masochists as their failure is inevitable and the suffering their conceit is destined to afford them will reveal itself as the humiliation for which they implicitly thirst. For more on this see my previous examination of self-importance, *Theater of Violent Happiness* published in 2010 by Lakehouse Ltd."

Rumor among the Merriweather faculty had it that Lakehouse Ltd. was a vanity press.

The females in the classroom scribbled with personal grudges. Lorna wondered what criticisms they were inventorying, what caricatures of her they were drawing, what phallic symbols they were sketching. She made eye contact with one student, an East Asian girl whose expression ambiguously bordered on scorn, or maybe *rapt attentiveness*. Lorna averted her eyes, set them on her notes.

"Please understand this. The beta and the omega do *not* pine for success or power in the conventional Western sense. He seeks no fame or grandeur for its own sake. Rather, he is after a deeper-dwelling fish. He plumbs depths, leagues-beneath the surface. He fights murderously for self-acceptance. His introspection is so focused and pointed that one would feel a sense of shame when in proximity, first for themselves for not digging as ardently, and then for him, for the beta and the omega, for doing so. A man—"

"Yeah, but recent evidence suggests that the concepts of the alpha, beta, and the omega are arbitrary," said the East Asian student. Lorna swung around with curled lips. It was fine that the girl had spoken up, but downright rude that she'd interrupted her sermon. "I mean, I'm sorry to cut you off, but these things you're saying are wrong, like, false dichotomies or something."

Lorna chuckled that this was the offense that prompted her students to speak up, not any of the earlier explosive assertions, and continued. "A man of his time and at a certain age ought to turn his attention to others, elsewhere, outward. He should come to the cold realization that he and his contentment or sense of achievement or worth no longer matter. The alpha is so satisfied with who he has manifested into that self-reflection is to him a vain, pointless exercise."

Lorna thought about Risk and Theo, and their designations. How would she rank them? Among the alphas? Certainly not, though Risk would like to think of himself as worthy of the station. He was no omega. Beta, then. And what about Theo? Her son was firmly planted amid the omegas. The lowest. She'd someday write about how her theories had originated as a response to her marriage and were developed as a reaction to her son. Risk engendered an intolerance with faux, forced manliness, while Theo implanted an impatience with a complete disavowal of natural states. The subtext had always been there, if not spelled out.

A young female student—Hispanic, short, overweight, and mod stylish in pink and black plaid—raised her hand with a fiery ardor, waving a paperback novel in the air; she sighed irritably. "Oh, so, like we're reading this in our *Against Cultural Cybernetics* class!"

So, it's a pissing contest you're after, then? On instinct, Lorna scowled and then caught herself. She softened as her eyes rounded. She paused, clasped her hands, and stood with a cocked head and warm smile like an unthreatening grandma. "Yes, my dear?"

"Herman Hesse's *Narcissus and Goldmund?*" said the girl, thumbing through the book to a dog-eared page. "Here. 'We are sun and moon, dear friend; we are sea and land. It is not our purpose to become each other; it is to recognize each other, to learn to see the other and honor him for what he is: each the other's opposite and complement.' Why does there have to always be such a contest?"

Lorna swallowed hard the irony, made a funny face in so doing. "Well, Hesse meant well as a permissive fiction writer, but that's really all his work is. Fiction. Also, his blend of pseudo-spirituality is to blame for this awful wave of nonsensical New Age pop psychology. He was a fraud and a weakling, I'm afraid. A narcissistic coward."

The ardent student looked down and closed her copy of Hesse's novel. This business of analyzing student psychology in the moment of intellectual delivery was a tricky affair. It had never thrown Lorna before, but these days, what with the video burning down her reputation, the steel had run from her nerves, and she was becoming distracted and driven off course. She redirected her gaze once again and fixed it on a crack in the wall, found comfort in its inevitability.

Lesser critical theorists—*typical* critical theorists like Judith Butler or Michel Foucault—relied solely on the narrow and limited tradition of the cultural Marxists. It's all magical thinking, not honest, comprehensive life. Lorna couldn't stomach the hypocrisy.

A thin-boned boy swaddled in oversized sweaters and pants, clashing patterns, and uncombed hair, twitchy and bothered, raised his hand, and began to sweat. Lorna nodded in his direction.

When the thin boy spoke, it was with shallow breaths. "But, like Elaine just said ..." He pointed a nervous finger at the East Asian girl two rows down and across the aisle. "... I think these are false equivalencies. Effeminate men, beta and omega. Masculine men, alpha. Feminine behavior, beta and omega. Masculinity, alpha. I just ... I think they're ... *false!*"

Lorna landed her grandmotherly posturing with a kindly smile that soon gave way to breathlessness and a rosy blush.

"What's your name, dear?" The lecture hall was large, and she hadn't memorized all of her students' names, yet.

"Jordan," the boy replied, lacking steel, warily holding up his iPhone, the screen of which displayed a *Business Insider* article with the headline, "There's No Such Thing as An Alpha Male." "And this is what I mean, this *Business Insider* article suggests that there's no such thing as an alpha male, and they studied—"

"*Jordan*. I don't think so, Jordan. That article is specious, at best. They looked at wolves in the study, *not* humans. And I just believe that effeminate men ought to resign themselves to their beta and omega statuses. They have their place in the culture, but it's just not behind the wheel of the big ship, is all. And masculine men must embrace and even protect their masculinity, because it is the primary engine that drives civilization. It's nothing to feel ashamed about and it's not about sexuality, rather manner. Don't buy into this ridiculous new narrative that they're selling you! Look, the Left produces victimhood, plain and simple! They require an oppressor and an oppressed for their *industry* to thrive. You, my sweet child, are *not* a victim."

Even though she had wanted to have sex with him (she wanted to have sex with all her young male pupils, especially the scrawnier ones like Jordan),

[29]

the boy had reminded Lorna of her son. It's why she wasn't moved by his trembles, pouting, and deep breathing.

Risk had been his most self-absorbed. Most childish in his pursuits. Playing at boyhood aspirations. And Theo was getting smaller by the day, shrinking into himself, into a cowed and embarrassing boy. They had failed her. She had failed them. Everyone had broken contract.

"Family is a sort of business, a corporation, in which matters of facilities and operations must be attended to. It is a concept that a leader must internalize to keep the institution running through supervision and execution of daily functions, accountability, and principles of growth and improvement. If the omega or beta is the manager of his company, the head of his household, he is remiss in his responsibilities and derelict of duty. And the employees, that is, the wife and child, duly suffer. A culture of criminal neglect and routine embarrassment is one that will not persist."

Students grumbled to one another, the hall reverberating impatient hisses, as the session was almost over, and lunch was to be had. Lorna needed a strong finisher. She always ended her classes with a punch, something for the kiddies to mull over until the next session. Three hands were raised. She ignored them. Two students had already left early, probably to use the bathroom or smoke a cigarette. No matter, she had plenty of others to populate her captive audience.

"What grief—the episodes unfurled by the child, the child of the beta or omega, his own depraved public outreach, echoing that of his father—the inherited tendencies toward exhibitionism and self-defeat rear ugly heads. On parity with the tragic Greeks or saddest Shakespeare. And the wife—her own petty, spiteful journey away from kin and into sin. Astonishing, truly, how the dissolution of a perfectly normal and well-adjusted family is begotten by such infinitesimal insults and small, needy flashes of unwise pride."

Lorna closed the book—*her* book—and turned away from her students. It had been a long, pregnant pause, awkward and tense. She'd secured tenure off the steam of earlier books published by a university press, but her views

[30]

and writings had become unorthodox and university support had wavered. And despite her tenure, she remembered that her contract had been rife with clauses about indecency and professional misconduct. These loopholes haunted. They precipitated the anger and defensiveness; Lorna had deserved the third degree from her students. She'd done them wrong. Put out into the world hateful, hurtful words. But she wouldn't be able to take any of it back now.

Lorna turned back to her students but looked at an ink stain on the floor before her. "Consider Emerson and Thoreau." Lorna got a kick out of eschewing the obvious references to Nietzsche or Hobbes or other Determinists, except on rare occasions, and instead reclaiming and subverting the transcendentalists to prove her harsh, inconvenient truths about nature. The transcendentalists, though bowing to nature, were also egalitarians, peacemakers, vegetarians, and social justice warriors, so to make them her own and use their wisdom to justify her cynical philosophy was a thrill that bordered on the ecstatic.

She continued, "The transcendental way. Consider their grave admonishments. Not to stray too far from nature, God, the humble soul. Modest needs. They warned of disingenuousness, of flinging yourself too far from earth. The disconnected face unhappy ends. They fail at grace. Nature scolds them for their hubris. It's a note worth taking."

The students at this point had become lost in the maze Dr. Hall-Bonaventura had built around them. Finding themselves in the middle of the labyrinth, the students turned and stared blankly at one another, waiting for a roadmap out, but Lorna had already packed up for the day. The lecture had ended, and she would leave no compass.

I V

Though they were good friends and Theo usually welcomed unexpected drop-ins by him, Charlie Lee was not welcomed. In fact, Theo had hoped that he would soon leave. Theo had received an email from Javier and desperately wanted to read it, but there was Charlie, at the buzzer in the lobby, demanding a warm greeting. Theo would have to delay his gratification until after Charlie left. Before Javier, Charlie had been Theo's fascination. Chinese and Irish with a swimmer's build but an awkward gait and a stoner's mien, the childhood chum captured Theo's imagination. And there he sat across from him, strong legs spread wide, looking at his sketches. But Javier's email awaited, as did what would be his first "spank session" for the day.

Theo's drawings were concept sketches for a drag contest inspired by marine life. Charlie contemplated a joke about keeping the look *fishy* but was too mesmerized by the art to properly formulate the setup. Koi. Mandarin Gobi. Anemone, even. Charlie's eyes widened at his friend's efforts. A tangerine and white pant suit with scales and giant fisheyes for nipple buttons and a ribbed neck shaped like a mouth. A plum and coral sequin gown with cerulean polka dots along the arms, shoulders, and back, finished with a turquoise turtleneck. A scarlet club kid-worthy cocktail dress with intermittently flaccid and erect appendages.

"These are really wild, man," said Charlie, again thumbing through the stack of colored pencil renditions. "Are you sure you don't mind? It looks like a lot of work"

Theo slid off his bed and tinkered with a box of colored pencils on his desk. "No way. I love doing stuff like this. When's the competition?"

Charlie reclined on Theo's bed and crossed his legs at the knee. "Two weeks from Saturday. The Stonewall Inn. It's, like, this historical gay bar in the Village."

Theo looked back at Charlie and nodded. "I know about it. I saw this documentary about the drag queen, or transwoman, or whatever, who started the riots there for gay rights."

"I have to lie about my age."

Theo stared at Charlie's legs, supple and long. Wonderfully full calf muscles. The perfect amount of hair. "Well, it *is* a bar."

"Yeah, yeah." Charlie sat up suddenly, and Theo looked away. The promise of his friend's lingering scent and Javier's email were too much of a pair. He was winded.

The tension was weird, and the weirdness was palpable. Charlie studied his friend with a coy smirk. Theo had behaved with too much urgency. There had been too much to look forward to, too much jerk off material. A therapist had once told Theo that he was a habitual masturbator who denied himself real porn—finding substitutions in wrestling and superheroes—because he was afraid of genitals. The therapist, a soft-spoken middle-aged man with a paunch and pink cheeks and receding hairline, had claimed that perhaps he'd been denying his homosexuality, suppressing his desire to be with a flesh-and-blood man. Theo shot back. He was merely a horny teenager! He also reminded the therapist of doctor-patient confidentiality. His parents would never know.

"I'd better go. Have a shit ton of homework to finish for tomorrow. You're lucky you get to be homeschooled. I'd give anything to stay up late and sleep in and not have to deal with assholes all day."

"It has its upside," said Theo, fist bumping Charlie, nervous that he might catch a glance of his stiffness.

He didn't. "Later, man."

Charlie left, and Theo breathlessly checked Javier's email. The rough grammar made him even more manly.

Tristan!!!! What up, ACEEEE? You pecs look killers!
You must nail all ladies! -J.

Theo had read it three times, memorized it, recited it as he collapsed into his bed, sticking his nose into Charlie's impression, the comforter still warm and smacking of his cheap cologne and sweat, and jerked off. Javier's words. Charlie's odor. The combination made him quake. New textures of Charlie's scent presented themselves: clean laundry and "fresh breeze" deodorant. Theo remained atop his bed for a moment, sinking into his comforter, only to inhale the molecules left behind by his friend. To take in some part of him, however infinitesimal. Charlie topped Javier, wrangled him like a bull. Theo thought his head would explode.

After a brief nap and lunch, Theo scanned his drawings onto his computer, uploaded them, and posted them to all his—that is Tristan Goodman's—social media profiles. He racked up the "likes" quickly. Javier had friended him and begun following him after their first PM exchange and "loved" the work on both Facebook and Instagram.

These are pretty amaze, Tristan. Have you ever consider doing
costumes that are culture specific? Like, maybe, Spanish type drag?
I don't mean matador and flamenco, but maybe also wardrobe
inspire by paella or bulls? BTW, how do you afford your staff?

Just some thought, ACE!

Best,
Javier

His grammar was quickly improving. And Theo smiled at *ACE*.

Theo went to work. He sketched a new collection of drag for Charlie, three outfits based on Spanish culture. Doing this would certainly curry

Javier's favor. It would cement their friendship and then Theo would have something to impress his father with. More than that, he would have something to lord over his father. He had made contact and connected deeply with the athlete his father envied and desired to be. The relationship with Javier left Theo ambivalent. He still respected his father, even if he wanted to defeat him.

The first outfit was a bronze, brown, and black ball gown in the silhouette of a bull, the horns swept around the neck like a collar that plunged into a revealing neckline, showcasing hoisted breasts, or in Charlie's case, a breastplate. The second was an evening dress patterned after the shapes and colors of paella—crescent and coiled, shrimp-like, draped beading, rice-influenced, and black shell-coated breasts with shells—calculated bursts of yellow, orange, red, green, and black. The third was a blouse and skirt based on both matadors and flamencos, a gender-fucking mix of ornate gold dripping from outsized shoulder pads, a black cap, fanned wide on the sides, a red cape, but the skirt plumed at the knee instead of at the ankle, and featured black and red floral prints. The upper half was all male, but the lower was unapologetically vixen. He barely cared what Charlie would think but hoped for Javier's approval.

At the end of the message in which he enclosed the images, Theo wrote:

BTW, even though I could afford a full staff, I do all the work on my own. Pride!

"Reyes!" wrote Javier after Theo sent him his scans of the Spanish drag that next morning; Theo had worked through the night on the designs. "That mean, royal! These is killer! And you work so fast, man! You should be professional artist, Tristan!

Much love!

J.

[35]

It was all happening so fast. It felt cinematic. Theo, as he jumped up and down on his bed giggling maniacally, never knew things like this to happen in real life, but only in the movies. He immediately took photos of the work and texted them to Charlie, who said he was impressed, and why wouldn't he be, but insisted upon Theo creating the aquatic motif, anyway.

Theo texted back: Dude, don't be so rigid. I think these are, like, deeper. More mature.

Charlie: I don't care about being "mature"! I want the fish outfits. They're more creative! Way cooler!

Theo paced his room and began to stress-sweat. It stank immediately. He texted with breathtaking speed and accuracy. "I'm the one who came up with all of this and I'm the one who will have to sew all this shit by myself!"

Charlie made typos when angry texting: Fine. Do what you want. But it's my half-naked ass on the line. My repiutation!

So did Theo: Whatq reputation? This is yor first drasg show and your only sixteen!

Charlie responded: Fuck off!

Ungrateful shithead! Couldn't he see how unreasonable he was being? How basic? Theo tossed his phone onto his bed and watched porn to calm down. It didn't work.

Lorna knocked but pushed the door open before Theo could answer anyway. Two things hit her at once: The virtual landscape he had playing on his wall of computer screens, including wrestling matches on YouTube, emails, social media feeds, and scans of drag costumes. The other was the

[36]

smell. The rank odor of boyhood. She'd avoided his bedroom as often as she could and Risk never seemed to mind the stench, or if he did, he pretended not to just to aggravate her.

Theo scrambled, fumbled with buttons, slamming shut laptops, turning off screens. It was all a secret, whatever he'd been exploring on the Internet.

"Do you ever fucking knock?"

Lorna looked away with a graceless smile. "I think I just did."

"But I didn't answer."

Lorna rolled her eyes and turned away. "Dinner is almost ready."

Theo pushed the door closed behind her and locked it.

As Lorna made her way down the long hallway back to the dining room, she knew she'd somehow failed as a parent, too. Hadn't provided Theo the proper tools to navigate this confusing new world of inauthentic exhibitionism and desperate voyeurism. She and Risk hadn't been prepared themselves for the digital age. Her son was no different from her students. He'd misunderstood her as much as they had. In all their eyes she was tone deaf, out of touch, and maybe even a bad person. There was little room for moderate titles, these days. The only labels left were saint and sinner. But she couldn't let go of the old orientations. The mind-body gap only widened due to her increased, instead of diminished, expectations.

Mom. Charlie. Conspirators in the ruination of his perfect afternoon. Theo switched to YouTube and found old wrestling videos of WWF superstars Kerry Von Erich and Ravishing Rick Rude pounding it out and flexing under a glistening gossamer of sweat. In adulthood, a therapist would tell Theo that he had become a "digital junkie" in his adolescence and that he'd constructed such an elaborate life online because he was afraid of real people and real interactions. Theo would be a man of thirty before realizing that had he understood these defenses at an age any younger, he probably would have hated himself. He would be grateful for having been a stupid kid. Never understanding until he was old enough to get it. Too helpless to have gotten it any earlier, despite all his introspection. Too caught up in the grid of image enticements and unrealistic expectations.

After orgasming, Theo surrendered to sleep. The dream was grand. Theo had become Tristan and he pounded it out with Javier under a glistening gossamer of sweat.

V

The workweek moved at a snail's pace and teemed with encounters that varied from frustrating to humiliating to downright compromising. Short of publicly shaming Risk, Dominick challenged, questioned, and discreetly reprimanded his "slightly" older, readily perturbed colleague throughout the day during virtually every interaction in the hallway, during assembly or grade team meetings or in the staff lounge for coffee breaks. Beyond his usual wisecracking, two-stepping, song-singing, satiric imitating, fact-dropping, enthusiasm-flaunting cabaret show that was his general joie de vivre, Dominick was also quick with a correction or enhancement of anything Risk would utter in passing. It had reached a fever pitch when Risk suddenly realized that he would rehearse things to say in Dominick's presence to impress him or at least redeem himself—proof of competency. The self-consciousness tripped up his script.

Risk was troubled by the level of scrutiny he afforded Dominick. It was surely an obsession at this point. His life was now being lived in comparison to another person. Holistically. On every level. Dominick had become to Risk the true measure of a man. Darnell, the school's college counselor who boasted the distinction of being Risk's longest-term friend and whose job was secured by Risk when he applied all those years ago, had become increasingly alarmed by the attention his good friend, *best* friend, had paid to the hotshot science teacher. It was unhealthy and beneath him. He should be focused on his own career, his own family, his own virtues. And besides, he was too old for this chickenshit nonsense!

A sample of the exchanges between Risk and Dominick went down in transcription like a variety hour comedy show wherein the host shepherded the guest through a labyrinth of awkward gags and nerve-wracking shocks. The topics ranged in scope and flavor. Seemingly an epic series of non sequiturs, the discussions included American royalty, calorie burn, sex reassignment surgery, the nature of evolution (in comparison to transition or change), petroleum extinction, psychoanalytic lingo, camel types, differences between verandas, gazebos, porticos, and vestibules, and countless other details that Risk generally hadn't considered important and so whose accuracy was decidedly off. Dominick, a stickler for data who fixated on precision and was fetishistic about fact, was always quick with the pronouncement of a misnomer.

"Jeez, Risk! Everyone forgets about Joe Kennedy, the oldest son, the first to die on a secret mission during World War II," said Dominick in the cafeteria during lunch duty after Risk innocently mumbled something about how tragic it was for the Kennedy patriarch to watch his *two* sons—Jack and Bobby—die.

"No, no, Risk, women burn between 1,800 to 2,200 calories daily, passively, depending on how much they move around through the course of a day, their routines and such, and men burn between 2,800 and 3,000 a day, again this is contingent upon how active they are," said Dominick after Risk presented incorrect figures during a casual stroll down the hallway on the journey back to their neighboring classrooms.

"You see, Risk, I know these things because I'm a master science teacher, right? Phalloplasty involves delivery of hormones to the labia to help it grow into a penis, non-functional, of course, and merely for decorative, or aesthetic, purposes, and the labia into testicles, again, just for appearance-sake," said Dominick, correcting Risk's scientific inquiries while visiting Mr. Bonaventura in his classroom during their prep. Dominick knew about these things, as he informed Risk he'd just watched a special on transgenderism on *The New York Times* website. "They also augment with flesh from the thighs."

Risk had all to do to maintain his bearings throughout the day, let alone field intellectual small talk. For Dominick, the banter was fraternal, fun, healthy. And considering Risk's insecurities, the conversations had a new, sharper point.

"I thought you were good at dissecting films," said Dominick after Risk brought up *Grey Gardens* and a recent speech about the state of movies delivered by the filmmaker David Cronenberg as Risk made coffee for himself just outside the principal's office. Dominick had been exiting a meeting with Velma Sanchez and the network's director of operations, and had, of course, left them in stitches; his humor was always appreciated by the schools' otherwise stern bigwigs. "I wouldn't say that the Maysles Brothers captured a 'transition' because that's too weak a word for what went down. Big Edie and Little Edie didn't just change, they evolved. I'd say it was an *evolution*, out of squalor and hoarding. Now, to connect it to the speech Cronenberg made about the new cinema, he did use the words 'change' and 'evolve,' but I wouldn't agree with you and call it an 'evolution,' exactly, because that's a value judgment, and I don't think it's evolving, or getting better, it's just changing from the theatrical experience to the at-home streaming experience. Not better, not an evolution. Just different. Only a change. Right? See? Do you get it?"

Risk nodded, smiled, gripping his black coffee. He was much too rankled to fumble through the undersized bin beside the pod-insertable instant coffeemaker for creamer and required immediate escape from the pedantic blowhard blowing hard beside him. Maybe he would toss the scalding hot beverage in the blowhard's pretty, blowing face.

"Crude oil, fossil fuel, dead stuff," said Dominick. "It's all carbon. I subscribe to the belief in 'peak oil.' We're currently at the fifty percent mark. We're running out. Scarcity of resources. Carbon emissions. Not a pretty future. You should know these things, Risk."

The last diatribe was elicited by a CNN 10 segment on petroleum that Dominick had streamed for his morning advisory. Risk was co-advisor and so was treated to a daily dose of Mr. Truman's know-it-all-athon! The pupils feigned interest well enough. It was a game, proving to their teacher that they were engaged, and Risk, especially *not* a pupil in his associate's classroom, played poorly.

Darnell nodded with a peaked left eyebrow, his lips pursed, and his body inert in a reclined serpentine pose. He was masculine though every now and then permitted his feminine tyrant free rein. With a Jamaican father and a German Irish mother, Darnell looked decidedly Latino on some days and Polynesian on others. His close-cropped hair, nearly a buzzcut, accented his cheekbones that were themselves complemented by almond doe eyes with long, thick lashes.

"And then he felt the need to explain the differences between transference and countertransference and dromedary and Bactrian camels and that's not all, he also went in on the differences between vestibules and porticos and verandas and gazebos. He's so damn insufferable! And everyone loves him, of course! Mr. Personality! You were lucky to have been absent during that last PD, Darnell! The way he was sounding off about class culture and assessments! Boy, was he in rare form! Or should I say *common* form!"

Darnell sighed and rubbed his eyes. Risk watched and waited. "What?"

"Risk, I've been your friend for longer than I can remember, and I'm still grateful to you for recommending me—ahem, *hiring* me—for this job, but you realize that all you talk about is Dominick Truman, right?"

Risk's frown was enriched by his droll tone. "That's an exaggeration."

"I don't think it is. He's an asshole. We both know it. Who cares? Let him live his asshole life. You live yours. Or, failing that, fire him! You keep forgetting you own all this shit. There's no honor in suffering for nothing!"

"It's just that ..." Risk's tension caused new wrinkles to form around his eyes and mouth. He looked down and balled his fists, kneading them against his thighs. "He's so ... I don't know. I just don't know."

Darnell detected a new urgency in his friend's demeanor, a signifier of crisis. Risk had always been a little bit tragic about himself and his life, but the vagaries that pushed and pulled him, the capricious sea that was his mental unwellness, threatened with a renewed determination to drown not just the captain but also his passengers. The friendship endured because Darnell was a sturdy sailor always ready with a life preserver.

"I've been thinking about doing something," said Risk, his eyes on the array of college flags lining Darnell's classroom, arranged as a border. Yale. Merriweather. Harvard. Dartmouth. Brown. Stanford. And Risk's self doubt surfaced as he considered his talents minor, his intellect limited, his successes barely worth touting. "Just something to ... I don't know."

Darnell put a large, hot hand on Risk's knee and stared him in the eye with a seriousness that caused Risk to snap out of his fog. "You're in a worrisome funk, dude."

Risk sighed hard and winced. "I'm sorry. I hate to bother you with this."

"Don't say 'sorry.'"

Risk nodded and patted Darnell's hand, still fixed on his knee. Darnell saw it all, and plainly. His friend had been slipping through the cracks of a dark room and back into a brightly lit meadow. Risk could feel himself stumbling into a subdued hysteria in which he would be made an outsider, paranoid and fussy, accusatorial, and protective. Risk's words were as glorious and right as they were inflamed and distressing.

"We're the same person. Dominick and I are the same. This isn't imagination. There is a man who is me and who is celebrating his better version. This man is Dominick Truman."

Darnell's panic was quiet as he was a street-smart obfuscator of truth. "Okay, Risk. Could you maybe elaborate, please?"

How to articulate to his dear, unsettled friend that the man down the hall was his shadow, his clearer, improved iteration, the revision. It was as though the core of Risk's insecurities, all his misfires and disasters, his inadequacies and neuroses were assayed and then corrected in the lovely, impossibly perfect science teacher. Risk's punishment would carry on as he was forced to carry on, by facing everyday all day the reflection of who he might have been had he the aptitude to get out of his own way. He would exhaust the obsession. Or at least snuff himself out in trying.

"I can defeat him," said Risk, rising, drifting away from Darnell, whose tepid worry gave way to impatient resistance. "I can restore myself by defeating him. If I can't become him, I can destroy him. I can find a way."

The butterflies in Darnell's gut were on a mad tear. They always fluttered haphazardly in times of siege. "Risk, you're sounding like a damned madman. What are you talking about?"

Something in Darnell's tone and body language succeeded in cowing Risk into sanity. Or at least some semblance of it. He stammered and shook the cobwebs free. Scoffed at Darnell, but really at his own daft proclamations, laughing them off, the whole ordeal a folly.

"I just need to sleep. I haven't been sleeping very well lately, and uhm, I'm just tired. Forget everything I said. I don't know what's come over me. Extraordinary. Really. This exhaustion."

Before Darnell could push the issue any further the bell had rung, and students were already pouring into Risk's classroom, taking to their seats, flipping open textbooks and notebooks or laptops, and jotting down the aim for the day— "Scholars Will Be Able to Determine and Critique the Qualities of an Effective Leader." Risk was in the front of his classroom before his Smart Board, onto which projected the lesson for the day.

Darnell began to exit but something compelled him to loiter in the back of the room for a moment and observe his friend and colleague's lesson, something teachers and administrators would do daily at Perseverance Charter High School, as improved performance was only possible when the threat of public—and documented—embarrassment loomed large.

Risk spoke in a listless, monotone pitch about John F Kennedy, Richard Nixon, George Washington, Abraham Lincoln, and Bill Clinton. A measurement with multiple categories was now on the Smart Board, a rubric of sorts, the criteria of which determined what made a "true man" and an "effective leader." The classifications included organization and management, role model worthiness, intellectual rigor, common sense/ practical intelligence, handiness/ craftiness, creativity, strength, appearance and style, eloquence, and athletic ability.

The eighteen scholars that sat between Risk and Darnell were all either West African or Dominican. They wore uniforms, gray and blue, and frequently broke into hushed side chatter, note writing, and Internet-surfing via covertly placed cell phones. Darnell knew that Risk's inattention to these small infractions would earn him a negative evaluation, and so he floated around the classroom touching the elbows or shoulders of violating teenagers, prompting them to roll their eyes but correct their behavior. Risk noticed, and it engendered a shame that he could not hide. His eyes saddened, and a lump formed in his throat. He could not control his own pupils. The humiliation was sharp.

Darnell, knowing the grief, looked away and retreated once more to the back of the classroom, all the while racking his brain trying to figure out why his rich friend/ secret leader of the whole fucking network subjected himself to this level of entirely unnecessary stress and embarrassment. He lingered at the threshold, promising a much-delayed exit.

"And so, what makes a man great, then? What makes a leader effective?"

"Why's it got to be a man?" asked one female student, beautiful with caramel skin, huge kohl eyes, lips like a bruised apricot, and sleek ebony hair. Her makeup was perhaps too heavily administered, but it did little to obscure her natural effervescence. "Why can't it be a woman?"

"It *can* be a woman, yes, of course, Ana, sure, but for now we're focusing on the forebears of the United States, all of whom were men, right?

"All dead *white* dudes, right, I got it." And her dismissive hair toss and finger fanning elicited a wave of chortles which moved Risk to redden and clench his jaw. "The crackers who stole this country from the Indians. Where's Obama on that list?"

"Uh, Ana!" snapped Darnell, unable to help himself. Risk continued to stare at the chart on the board and resisted turning to his students who were now studying the tension between Darnell and the recalcitrant schoolgirl, who straightened out at the weighty pronouncement of her name by the teacher who was cool but no-nonsense.

"So, look at these categories and consider what we've learned about these presidents and carefully fill out the worksheets I gave you yesterday. Who measures up? Who's a true man and has proven himself an effective leader?"

By the time Risk glanced back at the threshold Darnell had already left.

VI

They had been seeing Dr. Patricia Worthingham for eight months, on a weekly basis, and for fifty minutes at a time, and neither of them had regarded their commitment to her psychotherapy sessions at all effective. This would be their last session before finally heading to Madrid.

Risk shifted on the sofa, further away from Lorna, whose mouth had been wound small and tight. She tried not to make her eyeroll obvious, but failed, as both Risk and Worthingham had seen it. Their therapist, ensconced in silk tangerine, billowy faux fur, and oversized buttons, folded her hands over her knees, and smirked widely. Her chunky cheeks had been bunched and her beady black eyes penetrated. Risk was always critical of her appearance.

"Last time, you said you'd like to give the primal scream another shot," began the rotund, blushing doctor, her mellifluous English accent dancing through the room. "Maybe we can—"

"He wants to move us to Spain to pay his way into bullfighting," said Lorna, urgently but with a managerial tranquility.

"Risk, this is a departure from your current lifestyle." Dr. Worthingham gripped her notebook and leaned forward. "What prompted that?"

Lorna shrugged and made another dismissive face as if to suggest that Dr. Worthingham had not asked the right question. "It's certainly not sensible."

"Speaking of bulls!" Risk cracked, his lip twitching, his eyes glassy. "She keeps throwing that goddamn myth in my face!"

"*The Bull of Heaven*," said Lorna, corrective.

"It's so fucking berating!"

"Lorna," said Dr. Worthingham. "We spoke about this."

Lorna nodded and began: "It's a Sumerian fabled figure, Taurus in the Zodiac. He was sent by the gods to take vengeance upon Gilgamesh for rejecting Inanna, who was a goddess whose sexual advances had repelled him. Gugalanna, the bull, had feet that could shake the earth. But he was slain and dismembered by Gilgamesh, anyway."

Risk turned to Dr. Worthingham and threw his hands in the air with a goofy expression. He knew that his face had probably looked worn with fatigue but also of exasperation, as though he'd been repeatedly gut-kicked but had become accustomed to the battery.

Dr. Worthingham sighed and nodded. Instantly sympathetic to the husband, no doubt. Abused, and with his toxicity being used against him, imprisoning him, binding his hands in this unclean fight. "So, then, Lorna, who is Risk in the fable? Gilgamesh or Gugalanna?"

"I don't mean to be cruel. Risk ... he tries so hard at everything ... but he's always leading us, me and Theo, around ... to satisfy his needs and fantasies ... We're expected to just drop everything and accommodate him ... It's not fair ..."

Risk was instantly, eerily steady and spoke with a flippant matter-of-factness. "She can't fucking help herself. She must say this once a day."

"You see, my husband has this habit of celebrating himself without merit. He's his own biggest fan and I find it off-putting. And he's still going carelessly after things. He's not a coward, my husband. That's not what I'm saying. He clearly pursues what he wants. But so clumsily. Without adequate preparation. Gugalanna made his clumsy attempts, too, but also failed."

Dr. Worthingham removed her glasses and tapped them against her knee. She'd been big on therapeutic affectations. "You know, Lorna, historically you have criticized Risk for being *too* self-critical, and *not* having enough bravado. Perhaps this is his way of working through insecurities or responding to your criticisms."

To this possibility, Risk frowned. The notion had been absurd.

Instant revolt. Lorna cringed. "A midlife crisis, you mean. I thought those didn't exist."

"They're uncommon, maybe only ten percent of the population suffers from them, but *they do* exist. And he's of age. Actually, maybe what Risk is experiencing is the much more likely midlife *ennui*."

Risk glared at the two women. "Uh, I'm in the room."

"I know, dear," said Lorna. "I know."

Dr. Worthingham wore her glasses, again. "Maybe we should try the primal scream approach as you—"

"You see, doctor, my wife has built her career and reputation on extolling the virtues of machismo and aggression, all but worshipping at the altar of big cocks and rape!"

"I understand your anger, Mr. Bonaventura, but maybe curb your—"

"Big cocks and rape! Big cocks and rape! Big cocks and rape!"

Lorna touched her forehead and looked to the floor.

Dr. Worthingham leaned forward and smiled. It was as though she thought he'd maybe required this dramatic regression, this "cleansing performance," and she'd been a grand pretender in this theater of empathy.

"He's an infant," said Lorna, cool and reclined, her legs crossed. "I married an infant. I mean, he started out as a full-grown man, but grew into an infant. *Shrank* into an infant, actually."

"If anything on me shrinks, it's because of you."

Dr. Worthingham fumbled with her notepad but regained it before it could fall off her lap. "We haven't actually discussed your sex life today. Maybe we should pivot there?"

Lorna sighed. "We don't have one."

Risk stood up and began pacing. Dr. Worthingham nervously readjusted her glasses once again.

"Mr. Bonaventura, please be calm and take a seat. Mr. Bonaventura, I will not continue until you—"

"Fine!" Risk squatted on the floor. "I'll fucking sit!"

"Let's try an exercise!" exclaimed Dr. Worthingham, channeling her neuroticism into a proactive cognitive behavioral assignment. "Lorna, I'd like for you to share a core belief that you regard as a non-negotiable and then I'd like to challenge you to explain why you're unwilling to change it.

Risk, I'd like for you to do the same thing once she's done. But *actively* listen to each other in the process, okay?"

Lorna stared at Dr. Worthingham as if she were simple. Risk scoffed but then studied his wife to see if she'd take the bait. Dr. Worthingham faked a weak smile, her eyes never in agreement with her mouth.

Lorna went full-on professor: "I believe that men in our culture, especially straight, masculine men, are caught in the nexus of the new wave of feminism that demands they apologize all the time to everyone for everything and that every facet of their being is somehow toxic and corrupt and dangerous, and while the conventional world still maintains men should 'go make a killing' and 'toughen up' and 'be a man'. They can't win even though they're pressured to keep only winning! Poor, poor Risk. He means well and has the loftiest of ambitions, like this bullfighting business, but he's just … ineffectual. And this is not a belief that I feel requires challenging. It's a stark reality, Worthingham."

Risk was again on his feet and again he paced. "Ineffectual? Are you fucking kidding me? I made a fortune for our family! All of our money is *my* money, babe!"

Lorna looked at Dr. Worthingham. Her hands upturned. "Why should I challenge my beliefs about this kind of behavior?"

Dismissing Risk's eruption, Dr. Worthingham carried on, answering Lorna's maybe rhetorical question. "Well, because you're an intellectual, right? And aren't intellectuals supposed to challenge their own assumptions? Also, because I've asked you to on behalf of this exercise, Lorna."

Lorna exuded authentic reticence. "I have nothing. I'm sorry."

Risk sat back down on the sofa and twitched with anticipation. "Well, I can go!"

Dr. Worthingham nodded at Risk but caught Lorna sneering. Risk was sure the doctor was glad she had never married. She'd likely been doing this long enough to know that there could never be a clear winner.

Risk began on an emboldened note with brio. "Your body, Lorna, is—"

"Is *what*, dear?" For the first time Lorna's tone, demeanor, and language had all aligned.

Risk's own tone had sunk, softened, and surrendered, though the words still cut. "Your body ... well, it doesn't do it for me anymore. That's why I have such trouble getting aroused by you. And being a *true man* for you."

Lorna seemed unfazed by her husband's aspersions, and she'd even managed to smile at them, though the menace in her eyes had suggested a swift and merciless retaliation. "Is that the excuse you're currently using, or have you always had an aversion to my body? Or do you think you might be gay? Could maybe that be the truth? Is it just that my body is *lacking* something? I mean you go on about this Javier Forza character like he's some sort of god, so, I don't know maybe ..."

Dr. Worthingham sat upright and again fumbled with her glasses, which were again off her face.

"Let's just be careful about making judgements here, Lorna. And who is Javier Forza—"

Risk derived a secret kick out of his therapist chastising Lorna, but giving him a free pass for blaming his impotence on Lorna's body.

"I'm not making judgements. I'm asking questions. Seeking solutions. And I hate being mean like this! This is *not* me! I am not a mean person! And you, Dr. Worthingham! You let him get away with telling me that I am the reason for his erectile dysfunction, but I can't question his sexuality? I don't see how that's fair."

Had Dr. Worthingham not been so flustered she would have allowed Lorna to go on uninterrupted, as Lorna had been uncovering a reality about Risk.

"Your belly has gone flabby, and your thighs are heavier, and your arms are not as toned, and I hate the way you never trim your pubic hair anymore and allow these little tufts of armpit hair to grow and are too lazy to wax your mustache, and, and, and your breasts, well, they have always just been too small for me."

It looked as though Dr. Worthingham suddenly became self-conscious of her own body and psychically inspected every imperfect nook and cranny. "Well, that's quite a specific inventory, Mr. Bonaventura."

Risk calmed down and literally stuck his nose up at his wife, approximating the superior miens he'd observed among her retinue at Merriweather. "Well, I've had a lot of time to think about it."

Lorna laughed, likely relishing her own meanness. "He's really a clown, isn't he? Talking to me about bodies. *Middle aged* bodies!"

Risk beat his right breast and patted his flat stomach and flexed his left bicep. "I'm at the gym four days a week lifting heavy weights and sprinting and on occasion doing yoga or pilates. My physique is still good. People still comment on it. I put in the work. Strong enough to fight bulls!"

Looking back, Risk would find the self-congratulatory outburst embarrassing. And in that moment, Lorna had never been more embarrassed for her husband or for herself.

"Not strong enough to stabilize our lives, though."

"We've been through this! And stop digging into me!"

"I'm not digging into anything, dear. And that's another thing, Dr. Worthingham, why don't we discuss Risk 's unreasonable sensitivity anymore? It's only getting worse! Just the other day he accused our cleaning lady of making fun of his skinny fingers. She had only made a comment in passing about how elegant his hands were, good for playing piano. And he snapped at her, challenged her husband and son and all her male cousins and uncles from Guatemala to an arm-wrestling competition! I don't know, you're the professional here, but I think it's either paranoia or maybe a giant ego, right? To think that everyone is always having a go at you. Hey, babe! No one cares enough to disrespect you!"

"I don't believe in disrespect," Risk snapped. "Disrespect is a matter of perception. It's subjective."

After the session, Lorna had been sure to tell Risk that he'd elongated his jaw and bobbed his head in a sassy sway when he'd said that; it was something she'd added he did whenever he'd made pronouncements about human behavior, as if he thought he might have had an advantage over common people who didn't watch any number of the popular streaming procedurals about micro-expressions and forensic profiling. Her criticisms were specific and long winded.

"Good lord. He reads this self-help crap and actually believes it. The garbage they sell you in middle management or in retail. 'Disrespect is subjective.' "Intention doesn't matter, only action.' What do you people call it? *Gaslighting?*"

Dr. Worthingham's glasses were back on her face, firm against the bridge of her long, sharp nose, and now she started in on the fringed hem of her arabesque shawl. "Oh, well, I don't really—"

"You even agreed with me last week. You said it was something we should have been working on from the beginning, but you took too long to identify it. That Risk needs to always be either the victim or the hero and he's never wrong. Always makes everyone else the bad guy. I blame his abusive father. And so comical what he's doing in that charter school. Performing for what? For whom? Why don't you ever press him on those choices?"

Risk said nothing, but turned to Lorna in such a way, with such a look, that Dr. Worthingham began to perspire.

"How does it make you feel to say these things about your husband, Lorna?"

To Risk it looked genuinely like Lorna had pondered the question, and then after a long, pregnant pause, she'd sighed, shook her head, as if she were at the mercy of a truth that didn't sit well, but there it was, undeniable, nonetheless.

"It makes me feel … *right*, doctor. To see through his manipulative bullshit. To be smart enough, at least, to see *that*."

Dr. Worthingham wrinkled her mouth. "Then, I must ask, why did you marry him, Lorna?

Lorna's answer to this ostensibly more complex question had come faster. She hadn't required a pause to reveal the reason for this one. "I suppose to punish myself. I guess I also suffer from self-loathing."

"Rotten," Risk mumbled. "So rotten. Such a rotten fucking person."

Lorna turned to Risk, grabbed his big, clammy hands. She looked at him with a kind of pity that could be read as pitilessness. "No one is thinking less of you, darling. And your complex is really becoming a problem. I think it's pathological. Am I right, doctor? Egotistical, even. Your chronic misperceptions engender nothing but unhappiness for you and for me! Back me up here, Worthingham. All the inadequacies of your sexual and athletic and mechanical performances. The very unreliability of your performances! God! We haven't even begun to talk about boredom and disappointment."

Unbearable were Lorna's accusations and Risk could no longer contain himself. He grabbed Lorna's soft, delicate hands and before he knew what he was doing, his mouth had been wide open and running a mile a minute.

"I know! I know! I know!" He gasped.

Lorna recoiled, but she'd been caught. "Risk, you're hurting me!"

Nevertheless, Risk continued: "I can't do anything! You're so fucking right!

He could tell that Dr. Worthingham hadn't been able to decide what to do—hit the panic button for the local police precinct probably located under her desk or reach for the pepper spray probably in her top desk drawer. Instead, she froze and watched.

But then she forced the words out: "Risk, I will be forced to discontinue the session if you don't unhand her!"

Risk had been in Lorna's face now and spat when he spoke in staccato starts and fits, stabbing at her with words.

"Catch a fly! Assemble a bench! Dance at parties! Shoot a basketball into a hoop! Carry a stack of heavy wood planks! Fish successfully! Catch the big fish! Care! Be attentive! Do the family thing! Lead business with measurable results! What else, Lorna? What else?! Remind me of all my fuck ups and short comings! Wretched bitch!"

When Risk released her, Lorna gasped and crawled back to the other side of the sofa. She composed herself rather quickly and looked at Dr. Worthingham who'd been herself in the throes of a little panic attack.

Lorna gathered herself, shrugged, said the first thing to come to mind, likely: "The whole notion of alpha males is completely fallacious, anyway. They just disproved it in this empirical wolf study."

"I think we should try that primal therapy business you were talking about earlier, Dr. Worthingham," said Lorna, plainly.

Risk caught his breath. Dr. Worthingham had stared at him as if he were a rabid dog that just attacked a child. "Mr. Bonaventura?"

Risk spoke with a deflated, exhausted sigh, his hands tucked between his legs, covering delicate and fragile things, and hung his head, a whipped schoolboy. "Whatever my wife wants, doctor."

"Okay, then, on three," said Dr. Worthingham, slowly, hesitantly, eyeballing them, the saddest couple. "One, two … three."

And on "three" Lorna and Risk had drawn deep breaths and screamed. They screamed long and loud and hard and messily with spit and snot and big, throbbing neck veins and red, raw throats and sanguine cheeks and bugged eyeballs and trembles and wet fists and twitching shoulders and beads of sweat and with the only temporary expulsion of all the accumulated demons of resentment and blame and secret hatred and hoped-for failure and petty grievances and planned-on spite work and even death.

It exhausted them and they'd grabbed each other's hands as they caught their breaths and Risk cried and Lorna held him and cradled him and shushed him sweetly like a mother would a toddler after a fall and a scraped knee and kissed his forehead and whispered nice things in his ear and assured him that they would keep going.

VII

Tristan! Your whole collection just blow me away, man! I
speechless!!! I mean, you drawings are brilliant, but these videos
of imbeciles take humiliating falls is best, ACEEEE! Maybe I can
send you some footage of matadors getting fucked up and you
can add these to you play list?

Well done, amigo!
Talk later, J.

Theo had sent Javier the link to his *Future of the Species* You Tube video
collection a night earlier in hopes that the gifted bullfighter would be as enamored of his video artistry as he was of his drawings, and as it turned out,
he was. And Theo was giddy.

Theo looked over the six costume concepts he'd sketched out for Charlie and felt bad that he would not be actualizing them for his friend. It was
cool that he wanted to do drag but unacceptable that he wouldn't allow the
designer, Theo, in all his visionary competencies, to select which "clothing"
he ought to wear. Javier was right, the Spanish outfits were more couture,
sophisticated in their refinement, and less gimmicky. Theo's laptop dinged
and he checked his private messages. Javier had already written him back.

Tristan! I just had wild brainstorm! Have you ever considered
staging some accidents yourself? Like, set people up and shoot
them get fucked up? That would be even better because it would
be, like, you vision alone. You be, like, the director of your own

world, ACE.

Just an idea!
Bye, J.

And what an idea! Theo—"ACE"—forgot about Charlie and the costume controversy and set off for Fort Tryon Park with his iPhone and a bag of accoutrements, including olive oil, screws and nails, a paintball gun, and bundle of balloons from his birthday party earlier in the year.

Over the course of that afternoon, when he should have been finishing homework that his mother had assigned him, Theo hid behind a thicket and recorded various passersby, plotting his first sequence of shenanigans. The inaugural unsuspecting stars of his new series of films would be the two men bicycling together along the winding, downward sloping path that ran from the Cloisters deeper into the woods-like park. Theo had doused the pavement with his mother's olive oil, creating a slick trap. Seconds later, the two men, likely in their mid-forties, sped over the puddle, skidded, slid, regained balance, and then went hilariously out of control, wiping out hard, tumbling head over wheels over pedals over each other, and finally into a dense patch of bearberry shrub. They were bruised and scraped and a little bloodied, but otherwise fine. They helped each other up, brushed each other off, made jokes about age and beauty, cackled, and limped their dented, twisted bicycles home, probably in nearby Washington Heights. Theo muffled his laugh so hard it gave him a headache. He knew Javier would piss his pants.

The next unwitting candid camera comedy star was a tall woman jogging with little mercy for herself up the same route. Theo had sprinkled the nails and screws along the path, pointing them upward, and covering them with dry leaves. The woman landed sole first on one of the nails, piercing her heavy foot, and precipitating a guttural, but painfully funny, howl. She buckled and dropped like a tonnage of bricks, and upon inspecting the source of her agony she discovered the nail, not too thick or long, but still a full inch embedded in her hefty right foot. She struggled back to her feet and with whimpers and a rosy complexion limped toward the exit, calling a friend on her cell to come retrieve her and drive her to First Med. Theo laughed out loud, throwing his head back, and allowing the tears to stream from his red eyes. The woman heard the theatrical guffaws from a distance, as she was now by the entrance of the park several hundred yards away from the sight of her misfortune but saw no one when she turned back to catch the unfeeling sadist who'd harmed her for amusement.

The next hoax was elaborate. Theo had filled four balloons with urine and hung them from an oak branch that covered the path. His long, patient wait was rewarded by a family, mother and father, youngish, likely in their thirties, and two children, a boy and girl, maybe nine or ten. Certainly, yuppies in clothes that looked too expensive. As the family crossed under the dangling sacks of piss, Theo shot his paintball gun with expert marksmanship, popping all four bags in under five seconds, the urine and the paint mixed in a sticky, colorful, stinging, stinking rainfall that doused the family. They shuddered in confusion and then cried out in anger. Theo covered his mouth and trembled as he giggled so hard that he gave himself hiccups. The parents urgently escorted their crying children from the park and back home to strip and incinerate their too-fancy, besmirched threads.

Theo reviewed the footage on his camera phone during the train ride home. He dashed past his parents who asked where he was and why he was late and why he was out when he should have been finishing homework. They had become so accustomed to Theo ignoring them and brushing off their questions that they didn't press for answers any further than their initial line of queries.

Theo uploaded his footage, logged into his accounts, and posted the videos. He tagged Javier in each of them and on all platforms. Even Tumblr. And then he waited. Javier responded quickly and according to his message, remotely.

Holy shit! You genius! I can't get over how quick you work! And how well! Poor suckers. These videos are funniest, Tristan! I mean it, Ace. You really know how to make idea come alive. Listen, I had another great concept. Since you have so many talents and can make videos as well as you can draw and make costumes, what about doing something really ballsy?! I won't tell you what. Surprise me!

Your brother from another mother, J.

Really ballsy, eh? Theo thought about the college students he had always seen hanging out in Washington Square Park, those pretentious punks from NYU's Tisch and the New School. They were artsy and weird and always had something to prove. And maybe if their faces were covered with his masks, they'd be down with doing what he asked of them. As long as no one got caught. He wrote an ad and posted it on the Dark Web. Surprise Javier, he would.

Furry-Like Performance Art Protest Video!
ACTORS WITH BALLS WANTED!!!!

Not literal balls, as women can apply, too! You think you're a badass with something to say? Star in my video and prove it! Dress up like our favorite cartoon characters from our childhoods and have wild, animal sex in public. Your faces will be hidden by my costumes, but your bodies will be seen and so will your sex organs and so will your intercourse. Ages 18-30. Any race. Men and women. Please have a nice body. No fatties. Sorry! Crazy pay!!! Plus, food will be provided and a copy of the video for your reel!

[59]

VIII

Darnell used his iPhone to record Risk and Dominick scale the fifteen-foot indoor rock wall in Harlem because Risk had told him to. The men had been climbing—bouldering, without a harness, without a belay—for over two hours, and their fingertips were chaffed and their toes sore. The team-building exercise was Risk's idea, but when he pitched it to his colleagues during their most recent Friday PD only Dominick, Darnell, and Marielle Granite, the athletic math teacher, elected to participate. Everyone else was too spooked by the tense intrigue shared between Risk and Dominick to spectate at their theater of morose machismo. Their competitive chemistry had become that readable and uncomfortable.

"Looking good, boys! ...and girl!"

Risk grimaced. *Boys.* Dominick had the energy and power of a boy. This escapade reminded him that he was a man. And one of a certain age, no less. Despite his many muscles and years of athletic victories.

"Just keep shooting, Darnell!"

Dominick's long, olive, hairless legs flexed and extended as he hoisted himself up to the next color-coded grip, an artificial ledge. He looked back—down—at Risk and smirked.

"This is harder than it looks, but do try to keep up, old man!"

"Little fucker!" Risk hissed under his breath and dug his fingers into the one-inch plastic cliffs jutting from the craggy walls and pulled with a desperate might, wincing and sweating through a perturbing ordeal. His index fingernails throbbed and for a moment Risk feared they might crack.

Positioned on the floor beneath them, Darnell captured awkward low angle shots, the soles of the men's feet, the contours of their buttocks, and the plumage of their packages most apparent. Had he been straight the point of view would have been lost on him. But he wasn't, and it hadn't been.

Marielle had been climbing parallel to the two men, paying attention only to the diagonal pattern before her. She was meant to maneuver laterally over the span of three feet, an arduous effort that required daring and agility. Luckily the ten years of Bikram yoga and childhood ballet classes had paid off. She reached the summit, slapped the ceiling, and began her slow, careful descent back to the padded floor.

Risk had hiked and scampered along many trailheads in New England and Tucson throughout his twenties and early thirties and thought he'd easily best Dominick at such a challenge. That he was falling behind on this, their ninth climb that Saturday afternoon, more than rankled—it incensed.

Dominick smiled and dug his toes into the miniature ersatz ledge as he ascended to his final victory. He grabbed the top lip of the fabricated cliff wall and with his free hand reached for the ceiling to palm it, but was stopped by Risk, whose hand was wrapped firmly around his ankle.

"What the hell are you doing?!"

Darnell and Marielle exchanged knowing, expectant glances, that familiar readable, uncomfortable tension making its inevitable return.

Risk gnashed his teeth and pulled Dominick's leg. Dominick lost his footing and both legs were suddenly dangling, as both hands had grabbed the lip of the wall. His feet kicked and scraped the phony rocks, angling for purchase. Risk made it two more feet and grabbed Dominick again, this time by his ample calf. Dominick screamed as his muscles had grown tender and the assault seared like a knife cutting through nerve.

Risk grunted and yanked Dominick down and backward, causing him to fumble his footing, and with palms that were raw and slick with sweat, the strapping science teacher lost his grip and fell. The drop turned his stomach and he thought he might vomit. The landing twisted his ankle and he screamed with a bitter fury. Darnell had caught it all on his phone. Marielle covered her mouth and rushed to her felled colleague's aid.

Darnell finally stopped recording Dominick's undignified weeping and writhing and looked up at Risk, still clinging to the wall and continuing his rise.

"Jesus Christ, man!"

"Just keep shooting me, Darnell!"

Darnell's compliance was no indication of his constitution. He suffered his friend's request only because he understood how to de-escalate an incendiary situation. Growing up queer and black in the ghetto necessitated such a skill.

Marielle watched in wonder as Darnell shot Risk's vertical crawl to the ceiling. She gawked with astonishment as her colleague and secret employer punched the ceiling loud enough for the other climbers occupying their space to look and snigger. *Had no one else seen what he'd done?* She scoffed at Risk's dainty descent. And shook her head at Darnell who never wavered in his cinematographic commitment.

Dominick too watched the embarrassing episode, though his pain was blinding and elicited tears that blurred his vision.

Marielle stood over Dominick and leered at Risk, who approached his coworkers and underlings with a compassionate urgency that smacked of inauthenticity.

"Are you insane?"

"What?! Is he okay?! Dominick, you're fine, right? The ground is padded. It's only ten feet."

"Fifteen," countered Darnell, who replayed the video he had just taken.

Dominick groaned and gripped his ankle. "I think it's sprained."

Marielle shook her head. "I guess we need to call an ambulance."

Risk recoiled. "An ambulance?! No. We'll order an Uber and take him to First Med. He'll be fine."

Marielle grabbed her phone and submitted the request for the ride as Darnell and Risk helped Dominick to his feet and toward the exit. Risk headed for the lockers to retrieve their belongings and turned back with a smile and big *boyish* eyes.

"It's a game, guys. I was just trying to win. Let's not be so precious about it."

As he stuffed his clothes into his duffel bag, Risk caught a glimpse of a bumper sticker affixed to a locker, red with white block letters that read, BE USELESS, OTHERWISE YOU WILL BECOME HARD. A typical piece of naïve pop art extolling the pseudo-wisdom of the charlatan and crook Osho.

"How dumb," muttered Risk as he adjusted his jock strap.

I X

"This one is called *Put That in Your Pipe and Smoke It*," said Theo to Charlie.

Charlie had been fingering the theme song to *Halloween* on Theo's keyboard with ferocious precision and mischievous speed but was now leering at the YouTube video footage of a twentysomething white yuppie in an expensive suit getting socked in the mouth while smoking a Cuban cigar in front of Trump Tower on 5th Avenue. The attacker was a homeless man, probably sixty or sixty-five-years old, and shorter than the victim. The assailant had to leap to connect with the gangly investment banker's lofty jaw, knocking the cigar across the street and the target on his ass.

Theo sniggered and replayed the video. "I happened to be there just as the altercation started," he said to Charlie who was practicing his ASL letters to himself. Theo wouldn't let on that he had provoked the incident by whispering to the homeless man minutes before a made-up insult he'd overhead the yuppie spew about him. "Dudes were arguing over money or Trump or something. And when I saw how heated it was getting, I just knew something amazing was going to happen, and sure as hell!"

"C-R-A-Z-Y S-H-I-T," spelled Charlie on his fingers with an easy grace. Theo winced and then chewed his bottom lip. "Try again, slower," he said. Neither boy was deaf, but they'd learned how to sign to help cheat on tests.

The second spelling was deliberate and slow enough that Theo was able to spell his friend's words. "I know, right! Check out this one!"

Theo played another video from his online catalogue. "I call this one, *Few and Far Between.*"

In the video a skater, a boy in his mid-teens, is achieving astonishing acrobatic feats in a crowded Chinatown park, balancing between metallic handrails when the board gets away from him and he falls hard on his crotch, squealing horrifically. Theo had slicked the railing with his mother's olive oil, of course. Charlie's chuckle was sudden and loud, but short lived. Theo feigned an amused, silent schadenfreude.

Charlie returned to the keyboard and played the theme to *JAWS*. "So, they're like all idioms, or whatever."

Theo was aware of his own specific handsomeness. His black mop of hair, high cheekbones, pale pallor, and full lips on a tall, thin body was a look reminiscent of the trendsetting English boys of New Wave. If only Charlie had the capacity to appreciate it, too. He mugged it up before his equally sangfroid friend, allowing his eyelids to fall heavy and his tongue to spill out of his mouth, the jaw too lazy to any longer contain it.

"Yeah, man, the whole point is to subvert clichés and, like, deconstruct formulaic language."

Charlie nodded, pretending to care, and continued poking at Theo's keyboard. It was theatrical, the boys' self-conscious expressions and measured exchanges.

Theo frowned and then laughed at his own demeanor. Javier's cleavage flashed before his eyes. Glimpses of eggplant-colored nipple and shaved abdomen. He wondered how many emails or social media messages lay in wait for him from the Spanish god. Writing to his "Ace."

"Yo, dude," said Theo, now in a spell. "Did I tell you about my dream from last night, Charlie? It felt, like, prophetic. Yeah … Like, so weird. I just think we … we're in for a hard time."

Theo caught himself and became morose, his heavy eyes cast downward, and his mouth wound up. Charlie stared and waited for the details of the nightmare.

◆ ◆ ◆

Down the hall of the two-floor 1920s-era Riverdale townhouse they rented from an old Ashkenazi Jew and his wife, Risk and Lorna were going through the paces of their own early-evening production. Risk thought on a regular schedule about his own Ancient Italian-Greek forebears and their campaigns into the Middle East and South Asia, spreading their genetic material like germs, littering the landscapes and their people with biological reminders. That vainglorious habit must still writhe within, he thought, in every unattractive narcissistic cell, through every unseemly, entitled molecule.

The question hung in the air for an excruciatingly extended minute, and Lorna stared with a look that bordered on admiring and accusatorial. Risk gawked, patiently dumbfounded.

"*Have you made me happy?*" she repeated. "Well, look, Risk, happiness is only an emotion, right? And emotions are ephemeral by nature, so I am often, sometimes happy, yes, sure. Of course, I am. Occasionally. Is this about what Worthingham said?"

Risk was an invasive species on an island close to paradise, upending the serenity of the indigenous wildlife. His wife and son would be the native fauna, and he the disruptive colonist.

"It has nothing to do with Worthingham and anyway we're done with her. I just want to make sure that you don't regret any part of it, okay?"

"Why are we doing this now? Did you have a run-in with that colleague of yours? Oh, wait. You had a PD today, didn't you? And I bet Darnell wasn't around to absorb your misery! Was it his PTO? Of course, this is why I'm being punished now. You do realize you don't have to actually even be doing any of this, right? It's all a vanity project. Playing at being a teacher."

"Yeah, he was out! And no, that has nothing to do with it. I just seem to be making a lot of mistakes, lately, and forgetting things, and ..."

"Yes, well, welcome to middle age! We do that here. Forget things. Make mistakes. We're never more human and limited than when we get smacked upside the head with this damn decade, the big 5-0 approaches, but it's fine, right? You're a mere mortal. Anyway, what's the point of it, to keep second-guessing yourself and us and your whole life?"

If he were a younger, newer man he'd quote her Socrates. That business about the unexamined life and how it's not worth living, but then he recalled all the new pop psychology so prevalent, even pervasive, on the Internet and big media about the folly of looking too closely within, the trouble with insight and self-awareness. It was tiresome, that whole age. He knew it would read as self-absorption, and he was already feeling dumb for bringing up this particular line of discourse.

"I just worry sometimes about not measuring up, as a father, as a husband, as a teacher."

"Obviously, you do, though. We have a good life. Our son is bright and doing well with the homeschooling. I'm often, occasionally happy. Why ruin the evening—*another* evening—by doing this to yourself? To us, really?"

"Are you happy in Riverdale? Is it okay that we're renting? I can put money down on a condo or co-op. See if the owners of this one will reconsider selling to us. You and Theo should own a home. Riverdale is okay, isn't it? I think I'd like to buy something in Inwood. Maybe a co-op. Something discreet."

Riverdale was fine. A perfectly fine southwestern Bronx neighborhood that was gentrifying like the other towns in the other boroughs before it, Staten Island notwithstanding. There were all variations of trees that provided sufficient tree cover. London planetrees, Norway maples, callery pears, honey locusts, pine oaks, willows, Magnolias, beeches, birches. It felt like an English village with a decidedly urban makeover. Replete with generous splotches of heath. The spirit was there. Multiculturalism. Close proximity to Manhattan. Inner city toughness. Respectable restaurants and cafes. Calf-challenging topography. Rolling hills and Hudson River views. It was the kind of place that inspired contentment if not felicitation. And their home (or rather, the home they rented) was canary-yellow with white half-timber trim. He could have afforded the house outright, but the landlord wouldn't sell. Risk could have afforded a dozen houses but was not ready to commit.

"Riverdale? Is this really about Riverdale? The house?" Lorna was pretty in a way that never threatened Risk, though he was proud to have won the devotion of such a woman. And when she took an incredulous tone with him her expression became warm and even goofy. It was endearing because it made him feel like she'd never leave him, as though the very idea that he had done—or could do—anything so egregious as to warrant abandonment was outside the realm of possibility.

Risk was pacing and balling his fists. Lorna's incredulous glare deepened and then softened but her voice retained a comforting firmness. "Risk, what is this? What's happening here?"

Associated memories flooded of male cousins and friends, his age but with a matured paternal instinct or maybe just common sense, lecturing him in front of Theo when his son was three or four or five about paying closer attention in supermarkets after Risk left the boy unattended for a moment to grab an item from another aisle or scolding Risk for calling himself "stupid" in front of Theo or paddling a canoe too far away from Theo when he was nine and swimming in a lake at dusk. Risk had been irresponsible, or perhaps preoccupied, during his son's formative years, and yes, there had been near misses due to his negligence, but none of it was done out of indifference or cruelty. He allowed himself that.

Risk sighed, the weight of a lifetime of missteps and blunders. "I just don't feel right, lately, with myself."

Midlife crisis, thought Lorna. Midlife *ennui*. All the fictions. Right on schedule.

"I just think about who I am and what I've done and what I haven't done and who I've *not* become, and I take a hard look at this man that I've amounted to and I just sort of, well, I don't know … can't help but to think that it's not enough."

Lorna's face was unreadable, and that spooked Risk. Had he struck some nerve too buried under compassion and strength to have been detectable? And then she looked away with what looked from his vantage point as a glimmer in her eyes. Could there be tears?

"Wait. What?" asked Risk, nearly stammering, walking toward his somehow wounded wife. "What did I do?"

When Lorna looked back at him her eyes were red and glassy. She had indeed been crying.

"Your life is a waste, in other words? You're grateful for nothing? You have nothing? *You're* nothing, Risk?"

For someone so cerebral and analytical, Lorna could be chaotically emotional. Unreasonably reactive. Risk assumed this was how she operated. A master of compartmentalization. Reasonable assessment was for work. Immediate, unthinking reaction for life.

"No, that's not what I meant, Lorna. Come on. There's no way you could have misconstrued it that way! I'm eternally thankful for you and Theo! Eternally! The only things in my life that feel like a victory!"

It was as though she were a tea kettle and all the steam that she amassed during her long days spent dissecting tricky literature, negotiating with administrative leaders, and molding eager young minds precipitated erratic whistles in the evenings.

"Then what is it, Risk? Why can't you just be okay with *this*." At *this*, Lorna slapped her chest with her left hand and pointed at the door with her right to indicate their son who was down the hall with his friend watching sadistic videos he had made of strangers suffering injuries and indignities.

"Clearly, we're not enough."

"It's the little things that I fail at, you see, like not being able to manage tasks incumbent upon men, or like, skills and experience that I'm lacking that the world expects of me, or kind of lacking a charismatic way with people and being able to endear strangers to me in an effortless way. You see, it's all so difficult. Everything is so damn difficult!"

Lorna's girlhood in Bronxville was idyllic. Equestrian games and trophies on weekends. Vermont in the winters. Cape Cod or Cape May during the summer. The moderate seasons were for weekend trips to Stamford, Connecticut, and the Hamptons. Her remote father Wilmer and dotting mother

Leona, both top-of-their-profession experts. He an architect. She an actuary. They had since retired and moved to San Diego. Lorna saw them once a year. They phoned monthly. Occasionally a text or Facebook message. In times of stress, regression into youth worked as a salve. The social justice warriors would not fail to uncover and dox Lorna on these fabricated background items in their social media campaign against her. She'd invented a past of some distinction.

Lorna shook her head and rose from the bed. She gathered herself and looked at her husband who was standing awkwardly in the middle of their faux-Edwardian bedroom. He had been talking dartingly and with his hands, which signified an agitation and self-pity that she had no interest in entertaining. His was the kind of narcissistic light that when shone on you left you euphoric, but when his sun set, you were alone, abandoned in the cold dark, the momentary elation revealed as a cruel joke. All shade. With shadow puppets. Despite his general bumbling incompetence.

Risk's pout hung hard and with a quiver. If he had the capacity to cry, he would have at the revelation: his unwillingness to give himself a break and accept his limitations and imperfections (there were so many), would continually rear up like a nocturnal predator in the brush and devour whatever bonds he would perpetually reestablish with Lorna.

"I work so hard every day to be a man you can be proud of."

Lorna scoffed; the new empathy had tasted bitter. Worse than her inexplicable infantile tantrums were her dissociative spiteful fugues. "I'm taking a shower and then heading to bed," she said, turning away, again, and entering their bathroom.

Risk was mystified by his own syndrome. His opponent was relentless and fastidious about striking nightly. It had its own witching hour. Every encounter with Lorna left him feeling wrong and reduced. And what was most frustrating was that their marriage in and of itself was perfectly healthy, and Lorna was above reproach. This was about how he felt about himself.

◆ ◆ ◆

Theo and Charlie giggled with mayhem from inside Theo's bedroom. Risk stood outside with his ear pressed against the door. He could hear the violence of the videos they watched, of people taking spills, incurring harm, and receiving bruising ridicule. What a time it was for the boys, to be so young and care so little. To be that free and reckless and have no concept of consequences. Their only principles pleasure and provocation. And everything in front of them.

Risk sat in his study a bit farther down the long hallway and flipped open his laptop. He groused to himself, all messy hisses in his own private echo chamber; the accusations leveled against him about being childish in his despair and sensitivity were irresponsible. The most you could say about him was that he was sad and recoiled readily from slights, however misperceived many of them might have been. But childish? That was unfair.

Risk perused Theo's YouTube channel, *The Future of The Species*. His boy's screen name was Ego-Physician (Risk had caught a glimpse once when Theo ducked into the bathroom in the middle of one of his editing sessions). As he assayed his son's cinematic achievements, inspiration crept in like an insatiable worm burrowing through a wealth of dirt. Though Risk had never forsaken employment with a dependable income, he had made sacrifices elsewhere in other ways to live his juvenile passions. The pursuit itself required a rejection of logic, for that's what Risk decided an artful life surely was. Anti-logic. Pure feeling. Excess and ego in the face of insignificance.

Through every groin shot, bone-shattering tumble down a flight of stairs, mortified public nudity, and emotional breakdown streamed in Theo's anthology, Risk cast Dominick in the role of humiliated and wounded subject. The germ of the idea was implanted. If Risk was to be ignored as a savior who dedicated many inequitable hours to the amalgamation of something noble in its intention and depth, then he would submit to the demands of this new age. Anyone could curry this level of attention. Theo's videos alone had tens of thousands of views and thousands of likes and they were each only a minute or two long and required little-to-no-skill to produce.

Why waste years on the formation of a noble figure when you could be the recipient of praise and engagement after a scant few minutes of amateur labor? Was this art?

Risk knew very little about art, but he had a fondness for the work of Matthew Barney and Damien Hirst. He had purchased original blown-up stills from Barney's *Cremaster Cycle*. One, a goat man with red hair in a white suit staring with a queasy curiosity at the camera; another of the same ginger satyr coated in semen; and a third of an athletic albino in a bushy red and white wig—an aristocratic Whig or Scottish tribal headpiece or stuffed poodle—gagged with a bloody rag. All the men were the artist himself, celebrating the animalistic instinct of maleness and artmaking. The pieces hung in the hallway and always sexually aroused Risk whenever he passed them, which was often. Blown up photos that Risk had taken himself of Hirst's sliced up and pickled cow lined the walls of his den. Theo avoided ever looking at them whenever he'd pop into his father's study, which was seldom.

Like the male creatures in Barney's work, the Ancient Roman emperors conquered demons by becoming demonic. Risk had recently taught his class about Caesar Augustus, who would wake in the middle of the night with a self-abasing start, berating his own worth and weeping over the accomplishments of his great uncle Julius Caesar. In time, Risk told his pupils, Augustus's envy would compel him to overcome the efforts of Uncle Julius, exceeding not just his own expectations but also those of the record keepers.

Before heading to bed, Risk uploaded the Harlem rock climb onto YouTube. Darnell was a loyal friend and honored Risk's interminable requests, no matter how self-defeating or insane. He watched it a dozen times before doing so and was relieved to see that it had received twenty views and nine likes within the first ten minutes. Violence sold. People ate it up. He waited with bated breath for comments, but none were to be posted that evening. Though he didn't tell Theo or Lorna, he imagined that his son would happen upon it soon enough, as it wasn't so dissimilar from his own collection of strangers facing failure and futility.

X

You. Are. A. Genius.

Javier had written Theo, or rather Tristan, on Facebook in response to his Furry-inspired cartoon costume sketches only two hours after Theo had scanned and sent them. Theo smiled and turned to the costumes hanging on a rack on the other side of his oblong bedroom; all four were about half-way complete. Rocky. Bullwinkle. Burt. Ernie. The masks were already constructed. Wire scaffolding under a gauze of stitched fabric. Multi-colored. The features were recognizable, but Theo had played with the color palettes and even some of the dimensions. They were somehow grotesque, no longer kid-friendly. Their hues putrid and their faces distressed, crusty with glue and paint at the frayed edges. They evoked a sense of death and decay. He had made them his own.

When Theo began drawing and designing five years ago, a prodigy at eleven, Lorna thought it advisable to foster her son's talents by investing in industrial-grade yarn, fabric, thread, needles, wiring, fasteners, ornamentation, paint, mannequins. Half of the boy's bedroom had been converted into a studio complete with a worktable. They hadn't seen his more lascivious renditions until recently; the choices were a new development. Lorna found his avocation unsurprisingly fey and she'd worked hard to put on an agreeable face.

Theo wrote him back on Facebook Messenger: Wait until you see the costumes! I'm more than halfway done with them!

[73]

Javier replied immediately: Wow. Like I always say, you work fast, Tristan!

Theo contemplated his next move, which shook his already nervous stomach. Knowing it probably premature to reveal his true identity, the boy succumbed to adolescent impulsivity and did it anyway. After all, he no longer had to hide behind a mask. He had proven himself to the matador and could be himself. Anyway, if the Spaniard had any problem with it, he could just blackmail him into accepting him by threatening to release the torrid emails exchanged between them.

Listen, Javier. My real name is Theo Bonaventura. This is what I look like. And I'm only sixteen. I still live at home with my parents. I'm no ACE.

He regretted writing the message and planned on deleting it, but for reasons that are still mystifying to even him, he hit "send". He attached a photo of himself posing queerly in the park, it had been taken as a gag by Charlie a few weeks earlier. It was Theo without manipulation, free of enhancement.

There was a long pause and Theo panicked. Suddenly the assuring three gray pulsating dots appeared in the PM window.

I'm even more impressed with you now ... Theo! And You're even more of an ACE to me now.

Theo exhaled; his body warmed and softened. Despite his sociopathic impulses, he could build a real relationship now.

Theo: Yeah, but I'm not a famous artist. I don't make a living doing this. I can't support myself. My parents buy me all my art supplies and fabrics and stuff.

Javier: That's cool. You still just kid. Give yourself time. Tell me about parents.

An entry. A passage. Theo rubbed his eyes and exhaled hard.

Theo: My father ... He thinks you're like a God or something. He's been studying you. He wants to come to Spain and become a bullfighter. But he's old and has no experience and can't speak Spanish, so I think it's really just a dream. Then again, he has enough money to make most of his dreams come true because all he needs to do is buy them. That type of rich!

Javier: Sounds like he might be ... what the word? Enterprising ... enough to do it then?

Theo: Maybe. Javier, how is your English so good? Are you using Google translate or something?

Javier: LOL! LULZ! No, no, no!!!! I grew up watching American and British tv shows and movies. And I always find American or British tourists, or rather, they find me! And I force myself to become good at English. Twenty years of practice, Tristan ... I mean, THEO!!!!LOL!!!

Theo smiled.

Javier: So, when do I get to see this masterpiece??? Did you find actors with balls big enough yet???

Theo: A bunch of art students are interested and not just because I am paying them so well. I hope to shoot it next weekend! I'll send it to you as soon as I edit it!

Javier: Can't wait! (smiling, winking emoji)

Theo was renewed and roused. He printed photos of Javier. The model. The nightlife lothario. The athlete. The killer of bulls. His printer was top of the line, of course, and the quality of the prints were professional. He assembled the images into an artful collage.

Javier knew him now and loved him anyway. He was excited by Theo's work and wanted to see more. He was, dare the boy dream it, a fan. Javier Forza was a fan of Theo Bonaventura's. A month ago, Theo didn't even know who this man was, but now he did, and now he had won his approval, his acceptance, and it was something his father would admire, covet, and envy. Something he couldn't have, wouldn't be able to win. Theo was besting his father, becoming his father's alpha. Dad emerged as a secret foe. Mother would have written an essay and given a sermon if she knew. She'd work it into her lectures, into another article. She'd validate him, too. Make him a man. His parents would be impressed. He'd continue to impress Javier. Theo's erection ached and he came swiftly.

X I

Three miles south of Riverdale, just over the Spuyten Duyvil Bridge, and into Northwestern Manhattan, the Bonaventuras' new community, Inwood, rivaled their old for greenest New York neighborhood boasting residents of rapid upward mobility. It was in this sleepy (by New York City standards) hamlet where the oddity in their son's desk hit them like a haymaker. Risk and Lorna weren't snooping—intentionally, that is—in Theo's desk. Lorna needed a pair of scissors to cut tags off a few blouses she'd just bought and knew that Theo had stashed them somewhere in his room. Though the discovery had been an accident, the images Lorna happened upon were macabre and lascivious enough to send a shiver down her spine. The otherwise composed and unflappable academic called her husband in from his office with a nervousness that caused him to stumble from his desk where he had been grading research papers on Nathaniel Hawthorne.

"Well, I guess I'm shocked that he can draw things other than costumes," said Risk, gazing sharply at his son's art. "Who knew?"

"I'll grant him that," said Lorna, flipping through the stack of illustrations done in ink and colored pencil with stippling, each entry more inflammatory than the last. The drawings featured nude male leaders of antiquity—Napoleon, Charlemagne, Nero, Caligula, George Washington, Genghis Khan—fornicating with muscularized all-male children's literature characters, including Tigger, Eyeor, Piglet, Mowgli, Shere Khan, Peter Pan, The Cat in The Hat, and others. "And creative, I suppose. Oh my, what is Nero doing to Mowgli?!"

Risk was especially stunned by the dimensions. The penises of the penetrating historical figures were gargantuan and threatened to tear through the beloved cartoons. "Do we confront him?"

Lorna touched her stomach, focusing only on the violence of the inter-actions. This looked like rape. Gay rape. "I mean, it could be awkward, but what else—"

"What are you doing?!" Theo snapped, standing in the threshold behind his flustered parents.

Risk and Lorna swung around, almost dropping the drawings. As soon as Theo saw what they had been doing, his face blushed a red so deep it bordered on burgundy. He rampaged with an unhinged confidence across his long room and snatched the art from Lorna's hands.

"Oh my god! How dare you?!" Theo's eyes were narrow, menacing. "This is a total invasion of privacy! What's wrong with the two of you?!"

Risk looked away from his son and found a dust bunny hiding under the dresser on which to comfortably set his sights. Lorna's eyes widened as she sighed and looked at her own feet, bare and manicured, but with dirt and dry. Theo busily gathered his homoerotic creations and stormed back across the room to where he stuffed them in a Manilla envelope and then a hunter green burlap messenger bag which had been hanging on his door handle. As he motioned for his parents to exit, Risk had already begun to speak. Really, hem and haw.

"Honestly, son, it's a little, kind of … what I mean is I think this is some-thing we maybe need to talk about, Theo, right?"

Emboldened by her husband's clumsy bravery, Lorna found the temerity to chime in with greater efficiency. "Why would you draw something like this, baby? Is it a cry for help, maybe?"

"Are you kidding me? I mean, like, are you both for real, or what? Consid-ering the shit you teach, Mom! I mean, the fucking bullshit in your books!"

"You're not in trouble, buddy," said Risk, now steady and uninterested in exacerbating the already volatile scene. "We were just surprised, and we weren't snooping. Mom was looking for the scissors to cut a few tags off some new blouses. We just found the drawings by accident."

"We can just forget it, Theo," said Lorna, combing thick strands of crimson hair away from her face with nervy fingers. "It's really not a big deal. We were just surprised. We didn't know you were interested in this kind of ... *art*. I mean, the fashion was one thing ..."

Theo continued to fume, his lanky frame imposing itself in the doorway as he stood with arms akimbo and legs wide, the satchel containing the unmentionable drawings slung around his back. He was a warrior ready for a battle to the bloody end. He shook his head at his parents who continued to stare softly with tentative eyes and awkward postures. And then left.

"I can't believe he just spoke to us like that," began Risk, hurrying from his son's bedroom as though the threat of persecution still loomed. "And I let him get away with it!"

Lorna sighed, mainly out of relief that the whole ordeal had ended, and she was temporarily off the hook. "Teenagers. Teenage *boys*, actually."

As he walked down the interminable corridor that was his early 20th century pre-war hallway, Risk continued to second guess himself. Had he been too permissive with Theo? Sons in other parts of the world would be more severely punished for lesser infractions. But they weren't in *other parts* of the world. They were in New York. A place where children were meant to run roughshod over their too-compliant parents. They were right on track, it would seem, in their unspoken, embarrassed efforts to always fit in, to shroud themselves in this new cosmopolitanism.

"A true man would never permit his child, especially his son, to talk to him like that," said Risk, now in the middle of his living room, his eyes cutting from the late Victorian wall molding to the crown molding running along his 10-foot ceilings. His home, though it wasn't a house, nor did he build it or even design it, would always offer him some measure of solace. He and Lorna did own at least a share of it, the apartment being a co-op. And it was old in that trendy New York City way where old things meant classy, and large, 2,500-square feet with three bedrooms and two baths. So, it was not nothing. They had bought and owned something. This alone provided satisfaction, however modest the success.

"Ah, there goes the alpha male I married, replete with all the attendant machismo I missed so much," hissed Lorna, fixing herself a vodka cranberry at the small floating oak bar in the rectangular living room's farthest corner, beside a window whose casement peeled and was over a century old. She stirred her drink and stared at the busy outside world seven stories below, where the Hudson met the park and the New Jersey Gold Coast settled beneath the emerald Palisades, where commuters raced home along the Henry Hudson Parkway, where Dominican boys chased Puerto Rican girls and gay white entertainers practiced show tunes or wrote poetry in the shadow of the Cloisters. The decanter shook in her hands.

"We've raised a bully," giggled Risk, plucking a bottle of Classico from a cedar wine trap and pouring a glass of the chianti beside his wife, who twirled away with her cocktail and sat down with a spastic forcefulness on a plush orange chair made of restored driftwood from India and fabrics from Burma.

Lorna had already downed two thirds of her drink and was allowing the spirit to take over. "I don't think we're so special, Risk. We're the dissenting voice of structure and consequence. We stopped raising him years ago. It's all TV and the Internet and school friends after they turn thirteen."

Risk took two long sips of his wine and then placed the glass with mindfulness on a tall cherrywood dining table, also restored wood from the subcontinent, on which rested his black leather messenger bag. He pulled from it a sheet of folded copy paper and walked it over to his wife, unfolding it along the way.

"So, get a load of this." Risk showed Lorna the sheet of paper. She read with expressions that veered from boredom to astonishment to confusion before finally settling on amusement. "What in the world!" And then she laughed with such an abrasive, sloppy enthusiasm that Risk took a step back and laughed, too, even though the joke had already been old to him, the discovery of the accidental note having occurred seven hours earlier while still

[80]

at work.

"Read it out loud!" chuckled Lorna, hurrying like a schoolgirl back to the bar to fix another vodka cranberry.

Risk cleared his throat and obliged his wife. He read in a bombastic, theatrical tone, his inflection grand and satiric.

"Risk appreciated Dominick's gift for accommodating people and situations, fully committing to whatever the environment demanded and giving to it as fully as he could. But he was finally also able to acknowledge himself for being stubbornly always only himself, and never trying to blend or glow or perform in any one setting. It wasn't a matter of better, right? Only different, right? Right?"

Lorna was back in her seat and halfway done with her second drink by the time her husband finished reading his embarrassing passage, an admission meant for only himself. Her eyes were wide with amazement, and she was attempting to bury another hearty guffaw. Risk giggled again as he reached back for his wine glass and continued drinking.

Lorna shook her head in awe, as though staring at an apparition. "Why do you refer to yourself in the third person?"

Risk studied a painting of a bellicose lionfish he had bought a few years back in Havana. Its beauty matched its archness. Forbidden in its approachability, it hung on the wall behind Lorna, dangling with threats over her head.

"I have no idea, Lorna. I guess it made it easier to write. Easier to admit."

"Has he seen it?"

"I must have accidentally sent it to the printer in the teacher's lounge instead of to the one in my classroom. Buffoon! Ha ha!"

"It's just so bizarre, that level of insecurity and competitiveness in a man of your age. I mean, you're not teenagers anymore. Don't you have other things to worry about?"

Risk shrugged as he pushed out his bottom lip. "Do you suppose I wanted him to find it?"

"People like you always want an audience."

From here Risk's imagination, usually reserved for his son's science fair projects and lesson planning and charter expansion and hedge funds, found itself exploring alien terrain: he thought about *people like him*, Risk Bonaventura, history teacher and millionaire and the most neurotic man he had ever known. Would someone like Risk find himself unequal to the demands of his job, the competition he fabricated between himself and Dominick, the sacrifices owed to his family, all the little pet peeves to which he found himself sensitive, and duly self-eject? Check out? Quit? Risk was sure that he must seem to a man like Dominick Truman like someone for so long passive and unconscious. He was the kind of man who could have a career for a lifetime and never fully grasp its central principles, its basic premise thoroughly forever lost on him. And little of the profession's processes and systems were retained. But maybe he was wrong. No one had full access to anyone else's phenomenology. Their secrets were not impregnable.

"Yeah," said Risk to himself, though Lorna looked up and stared at him with a queasy apprehension. "Right. How would I know."

Lorna squinted. "Huh?"

A photo of Theo at age nine hanging over the TV broke his hard assessment. He was smiling in front of a lion's den at Space Farms, a zoo in central New Jersey where regulation was a myth, ethics were nebulous, and safety was questionable, for the caged animals and human visitors alike. They had gone as a joke, to see how the local white trash who inhabited the outlying neighborhoods of their tony lake house community lived and played. Curio hunting.

Lorna, seven years younger, seven years lighter, had stood beside him and feigned fear with a comical expression. The lioness had just finished her lunch, which she had swiped from the trainer who placed the twenty-pound slab of dead deer at the edge of the cage, just beside a one-foot-high opening at the bottom of the bars. After no fewer than twenty-five heavy, sloppy licks of the bloody meat the lioness began to feast. It was brutal and elegant at the same time, savage pageantry, and Theo seemed perhaps too enthralled by it all. Lorna's faux horror was inspired more by her son's quiet bloodlust than by the beast's passionate feeding. The big cat began to chuff, and Lorna giggled.

That day Risk found himself succumbing to alarmingly uncharacteristic behavior. Reaching out for the baboon's coarse black hand as the primate extended his long phalanges through the bars after Theo tossed him animal crackers, poking the lemurs with a twig after they sneered at him, and spitting back in the Llama's face after one hacked up a ball of corn-enriched phlegm all over the history scholar's face, ordinarily so composed.

The zoo was private and therefore disregarded code, their animals showcased in enclosures that permitted shocking proximity to guests. The kind of place PETA would shutter should they ever catch wind of the conditions and policies. Risk and Lorna spoke about the "pedestrian" and "backwater" visitors loud enough for only Theo to hear it. They'd compared them to the beasts in the well-worn cages. Theo laughed mindlessly at the merry prejudice.

"What did you say?" asked Lorna, contemplating a third cocktail.

Risk cleared his throat. "Nothing. It wasn't important."

"What were you thinking?"

"Just about that trip we took to Space Farms with Theo when he was younger."

"You were so weird on that trip," said Lorna, choosing in favor of the third vodka cranberry, already at the bar and mixing her drink. "I couldn't understand. So … weird."

"It was rotten of us to do that. Go there for that reason." *To teach Theo to laugh at people.*

Lorna considered it. Carried on, untouched by the self-inflicted wound.

Risk weighed his own crude journal entry with his son's recent foray into gay erotica and the memory of that day at Space Farms. The considerations blended into a confluence of unfriendly revelations and unkind reflections. Risk was not the noble steady man his colleague took him for. He was fallible. As prone to fits of ego and failure and cruelty as anyone else. Risk Bonaventura—the world's saddest investment banker and imitation history teacher.

XII

Upstate New York. Dense, impersonal woods. Midday sun. Autumn chill. The obstacle course in the Bear Mountain region was not far from West Point and was more rigorous than the group had anticipated. Risk had already pinched a nerve in his neck and hyperextended a tendon in his left leg. Still, he persisted. Despite the sprain endured from his indoor rock-climbing mishap two weekends earlier, Dominick was outpacing Risk. A full five seconds ahead. It was a weekday, and the track was reserved for Risk, Dominick, Marielle, and Darnell, of course, recording all action on his iPhone once again. The only participants in these now weekly "team building" exercises.

The course organizers were a Serbian family with thick accents, grand gesticulations, brusque inflections, and little patience. They barked orders and defamed with an easy grace. Risk found himself more eager to please them than to triumph over Dominick. The obstacles were constructed from various types of wood, plastic, fabric, and steel, and were formed into a criss-crossing web of ladders, tubes, ropes, gangways, spires, nets, and walls. The Serbian family, the Boskovics of Belgrade, took credit for having designed and crafted the course themselves. Risk hardly believed them.

Marina Boskovic, the sixty-year-old matriarch, and Bashi, her sixty-five-year-old husband, ran the business with the expectation that their children, Djorje and Dragica, would inherit a lasting piece of their American dream. The "children" were stoic and hard. Risk assumed it was a show to please their parents, who were passive aggressive in their own stoic hardness. Marina and Bashi were initially congenial when they greeted Risk and co.; warmer still when they cashed the charter school's check for the team building program they had curated "especially for them," but then cooled once the exercises began. The Boscovics became controlling and militant in their guidance during the first few paces of the course, which required a jog up a muddy embankment and a scampering through a tunnel of twigs, leaves, and rocks.

Marina swung her heavy, outsized hands like lobster claws, screeching intermittently in Serbian at Risk, who lagged.

"Come on! Faster, you slow, middle-aged American man!"

Risk double-glanced at the homely, rotund woman with the kerchief around her head. It was daring on her part to berate her clients. Afterall, this wasn't Belgrade, and people took swift offense to such disparaging language.

Marielle, all nervy twitches and raw energy, clawed at the earth and endured deep scrapes and sure-to-be-long-lasting bruises as she slid past Dominick and finished the first course ahead of her colleagues.

This time it was Bashi's turn to demean. "You bitches just got beat by a woman!"

Dominick instinctively flipped off the short, stocky man who was built like a quadricep with sinewy appendages. All veiny, hard muscle and long, meaty fingers with an endless black hole of a mouth that filled his face above which a wisp of a black robber baron mustache rose and fell. He looked like some sort of creature from the brain of H.R. Geiger. Bashi giggled at Dominick's affronted posturing.

Darnell struggled with his iPhone as he recorded Marielle's victory dance. Risk turned back to him.

"You don't need to tape *everything*, Darnell."

Right, thought Darnell. *Only capture the moments where you revel in your own unembarrassed glory! People ought to have more shame.*

"How humiliating!" When Dragica yelled it was a masculine timbre. Her otherwise pretty face reddened and contorted and took on the aspect of a Halloween mask as conceived by Edvard Munch. "Pathetic!"

During the next stretch of Boscovic-built terrain, Djorje and Dragica impelled impetus through name calling and threats. What a strange approach to team building, thought Marielle. What dividends could such an orientation effectuate?

"Americans are so weak! Flaccid muscles! Flaccid brains!"

Risk's dad regularly accused his mom of being jealous of his entrepreneurial successes. There was always plenty of money, but the fights centered on who brought home more and who earned how much off whose own independent steam. Neither new nor old money, the Bonaventuras were middle money. To Dad, a.k.a. "Mr. Jonas Bonaventura," the only wealth that had value was that which was earned by one's own making, not under someone else's enterprise. Risk took note of his father's offense, his mother's defense. They played a cold game of math and philosophy.

Risk fought the fatigue and the pinched nerves and the shame. He trundled along the wobbly wooden bridge, leapt onto the hanging ladder affixed to the old oak, and swung chaotically from the fraying rope to the next landing, where he ceremoniously bypassed the gazelle-like Marielle and caught up to Dominick who had been in the lead for the past few minutes. Though it was cold, both men sweated profusely. Darnell was a natural athlete and his ability to keep pace while also managing the iPhone was admirable. Even graceful.

"New York City pussies!" Djorje grabbed his considerable package and flexed his underwhelming bicep. His pasty white skin against the raven black eyes, hair, and stubble made for a sharp contrast. He was handsome, but also unhealthy looking and the scars that ran over his left eye and lip and ear made one wonder what he had done to receive them. What would-be victim had beaten him away. What animal had had a go at him.

"Only the actual woman has any balls!"

With that final bit of goading, Risk, with the apace ferocity of a leopard, dove and crashed shoulder first into the small of Dominick's back. Both men grabbed at each other in a mid-air tackle, a savage tango, wrestling each other for safety and conquest and, ultimately, purchase. Their heavy bodies launched through brush, banged into steel structures, cracked planks of wood, and snapped several oak and fir branches as they fell from a platform through nature and man-made creations and finally landed face down in a mound of wet leaves, moss, and mud. Through their aerial dance and graceless descent all Risk could think of was how much worse the Serbians' lambasting would have been had they been privy to the machinations of his plot, had they known how much inner work he had to do to feel better about himself, to matter to himself, despite the financial successes, to feel like a man who could be counted among men, to stand beside builders and laborers, to be one with the gang, to win the love of an apathetic teenager, to succeed as a mentor, to pin an opponent and prove physical might, to be a regular guy who could win at regular guy stuff. Of course, Darnell had captured everything, save for Risk's elliptical internal monologue.

Marielle clutched her chest and stopped running. She wheezed and searched for the two men amid the squirming mass of broken objects, twisted limbs, and pulverized nature. The Boscovic Family gathered with wide eyes and abrasive laughter. They had insurance and every member from the charter school had signed a disclaimer that in the event of their untimely demise or dismemberment there would be no holding their business or family responsible, therefore obviating the risk of lawsuit.

Dominick, face black with wet dirt, moaned. Risk pushed himself off of and away from his younger, stronger rival who was by now cursing and balling his fists in menacing fashion. Risk felt certain that the generally well-comported man was presently planning on punching him.

Darnell continued to record. Marielle turned to him and shook her head. Her whisper was soft and hard at the same time. Maternal, but harsh.

"How could you be recording this? What's wrong with you?"

Darnell shrugged. Kept recording. "It's what he asked for."

Her disgusted scowl hit like a gut punch. "So?"

Darnell turned away from the sententious dancer-turned-math teacher and zoomed in on Dominick's face. Through the mud and rage he could see that the science teacher's lip was swollen and bleeding. He must have smacked it against a rock or log.

"Fucking crazy asshole!"

Risk nursed his right knee that had begun to throb. "Relax, Dominick! This is sport. It's a game."

Dominick now salivated. Literal salivation. "You said that the last time you almost killed me, motherfucker!"

"Such drama, these Americans," said Marina to Bashi, who nodded and chuckled. "All the theatrics. Especially when someone gets hurt. Such a big deal! Such little injuries!"

Dominick winced as he attempted to straighten his back, which ached as if it were broken.

"Darnell, you're taping this shit! I want that footage! I want to show it to leadership! I'll fucking email it to Mr. James! And to the network! And to the stakeholders! I don't care if this asshole owns the schools! The board will shit-can his sorry ass if they're not stupid!"

Risk's expression was now blank, unreadable, and that scared Marielle, who took a step away.

When Risk stood up, his right knee folded, threatening to completely give out. He grimaced, slanted, evened himself, and limped away. He said nothing else. Darnell recorded his exit. Risk didn't bother to turn back, but he did say, "You can stop now, Darnell."

And Darnell did.

Risk had received and uploaded onto YouTube the violent, shameful scene within the hour. The views exceeded nine hundred by midnight. Viewers included Dominick, who had shared the video with intolerant, exacting Velma Sanchez, his no-nonsense principal, by morning. And Theo had happened upon his father's channel and emailed the link to his mother by the following evening.

XIII

The wall closest to Lorna's desk was plastered with images of men. Prime men. Primal men. Merciless leaders. Libidinal warriors. Even Russell Crowe in *Gladiator* and the strapping Spartans with the airbrushed abs in *300*. The subjects weren't erotic in nature, however the emphasis was on physique and physicality. In fact, her entire office was full of paintings, drawings, and photographs of powerful bodies in glorious, gorgeous postures. She reviewed a stack of synthesized alpha biographies. Her connections between ancient rulers and contemporary athletes prompted many in academia to compare her to Camille Paglia, someone she had known for a short while when she taught for a year at the University of Pennsylvania as a visiting professor soon after earning her doctorate.

Lorna's notes on Sargon of the Akkadian Empire in Mesopotamia, Ghengis Khan, and Ramses II were as voluminous as her dossiers on Michael Jordan, Cristiano Ronaldo, and Roger Federer. Lorna was working toward building bridges between the men of their respective eras and the adoration and emulation they elicited in their followers. She considered modern male megastars to be on parity with the supreme commanders of history.

Her peers in the department had once supported her views, knowing that it would help her forge a distinction in the field; cultural studies was messy and turbulent and those few whose hypotheses could deliver the zeitgeist in palpable sound bites tended to reap a good deal of attention, appearing on *Real Time with Bill Maher*. Judith Butler and Jordan Peterson had been recent "co-stars".

It had been a week since the video had been leaked on YouTube. The faculty had since rescinded their initial encouragement, especially since FOX

News began airing Lorna's video with zeal, much to everyone's consternation.

"This bit goes too far, I think, dear," said Geraldine Herzer, a mainstay at Merriweather. She was closing in on seventy and had earned her PhD in the 1970s, a time when such grand accomplishments felt rarified and radical, especially for women. Her mentor was the eminent and still clandestine Julia Kristeva. Dr. Herzer's writings on "the abject" mystified her graduate students and sickened her critics who thought that she was too fixated on notions of good and bad breasts, authoritarian and inconsistent parenting and the instability it engenders in the needy, anxious-ambivalent, and highly emotionally disorganized children they raise.

Lorna stopped watering her succulents and turned to Geraldine. "Which?"

"Here." Geraldine poked the text with the tip of her red pen. "You state all-too-assuredly that even the most accomplished women ought to revere men as the chief builders and managers. That *all* women need to support their constructions and influence."

Lorna's eyes sharpened. "How's it *too far*, Geraldine?"

"Oh, Lorna, come on now, I know you value your provocations and polemics, but this is a bit much, no? Especially after that YouTube business. You know, our students complain to me. To us."

Lorna continued watering the succulents. One, robust and virile in purple, took the water aggressively. She thought she could hear it suck in the moisture. Everything thirsted.

"I mean, it's one thing to criticize men for their compulsion to fight and quibble over penis size, but it's quite another to suggest that women should worship at the altar of their narcissistic bravado."

"Okay, Geraldine. I get it. This has nothing to do with the article. Nothing about my work has changed. This is about the video."

Geraldine's eyes narrowed. "The video, yes, and the murmur across campus of students who feel unsafe here because of what you've said. You've no idea the number who want to file a class action lawsuit."

Though Geraldine's office had always been the warmest in the wing, Lorna managed to chill Geraldine with her gaze. The arctic atmosphere resumed its heat when the remainder of the cultural studies staff walked in ready for their monthly department meeting.

The men entered laughing. Thomas Chen was a short, sinewy Beijing exponent. Matthew Bowman, a ginger from Rhode Island, whose years of sprinting left him with disproportionately large legs and an easy strut.

Myriam Farshadi, a twentysomething Persian from Tehran, who had modeled her way through graduate school in Los Angeles and had only recently relocated to New York for Merriweather's appointment, sheepishly filed in after them. She was hoping to make tenure within the next three years.

"Weird tension here today," said Bowman, only twenty-eight and quicker with his tongue than with his brain. He'd done time at Harvard and then at Magdalene College in Cambridge, where debating was easy, fearless, and as natural as trained rowing on the Charles.

Geraldine bunched up her face in a mischievous smirk.

Lorna ignored the comment and instead reviewed her notes, the agenda for the meeting.

The staff assumed their jocularly fearsome circular seating formation. *Oh, these people.*

Dr. Chen said: "Your last paper, the one just published in *Junk & Noise*, was oddly confident in its assertions about homoerotic imperialism and role play, Dr. Hall-Bonaventura."

"Why was the confidence *odd*, Dr. Chen?"

Dr. Chen crossed his legs and spoke with a raised chin. "Well, there's not been a sufficient amount of data collected, yet. It's still just theoretical."

Lorna sighed. "But that's what we are. Theoreticians. Our work is rooted in observation and analysis. It's also largely guesswork. *Creative* guesswork."

Dr. Chen's dismissive smile, marked by bushy inverted eyebrows and dimples, caused Lorna to reflexively sneer. "Dr. Hall-Bonaventura ... Lorna

… Our students keep interrupting class to discuss the YouTube video … it's been over a week and it's *not* going away."

Dr. Farshadi sighed and, a little bored, thumbed through her students' research essays, which she had been grading before the meeting diverted her. These gatherings were always sullen and tense, not unlike a funerary repast, she thought. And it being the first since the social media bombshell, it was better to have work on-hand for the sake of healthy distraction.

Lorna took a breath before speaking. "It *is* the white elephant in the room today, isn't it? I get it, I do. But, really, what do any of you want me to do about it? I was just doing my job. I have no interest in being *that kind* of a teacher, who watches her Ps and Qs, censors herself, pleases the students and their parents and the community and the stakeholders. If I wanted to become *that kind* of teacher, I wouldn't have earned my fucking doctorate and I would have resigned myself to teaching high school or kindergarten! Do you have any idea how many emails and letters I've been receiving? People calling me a cunt and a bitch and a *self-loathing woman*, a *gender traitor*! A sexist and a misogynist? Do you?!"

Lorna was taken aback by how angry she'd become. It had crept up on her the more she talked, the more she thought about how useless and compromising the entire affair had been.

"And look!" she ventured on.

Lorna grabbed her laptop off her desk, smashed away nervously at the keys, and then spun the computer around for her staff to see the video playing on Vimeo:

Two suited women, both with close-cropped hair and chalky white skin, spoke chirpily about Lorna, the footage of the infamous video on mute in the background. It was MSNBC and the talking heads were self-satisfied in their tone and regal in their miens.

"She should be censured," said one woman. "Merriweather has a moral and ethical responsibility to patrol and discipline their own."

"I think she's dangerous," said the other. "And in the end, she'll just end up empowering the fringe lunatics that believe everything is a conspiracy. She's already all over the Alt Right sites and networks!"

Lorna stopped the clip, put her laptop on the desk, and combed her hair back behind her ears. Her wide, handsome face, often with little makeup and dark eyes with thin lips, wasn't completely feminine with her hair set back.

Geraldine fixed her stare on a Victorian weathervane and Colonial scale of justice, both patina laden, resting on a mantle close to Lorna's desk. Her office was stately that way, thought Geraldine. Quintessential in its Ivy League trappings.

"This is what we've been saying, Lorna," said Geraldine. "It's becoming a bigger story and it's not fair for us to have to bear the brunt as a department."

"It's not nice, the things I say, and I know that, but nice isn't something I aspire to be. *Right* is. I am only interested in being right, Geraldine."

Geraldine made a cartoonish, goofy face. A face that laughed at others, a face to be laughed at. "And do you really think you are, with all of this?"

Lorna's eyes widened in faux cheer. "Bowman, your ancestors were from England, right?"

Dr. Bowman's grin caused him to redden. His powder blue eyes even sparkled. "English, through and through."

Lorna nodded, played with her earring. "Chen, your family are Cantonese, though they moved to Beijing when you were in first grade, no?"

"Yes, that's right. Though we went to Hong Kong probably once a month to visit family. Kowloon."

Lorna's internal reverie quieted her, pulled her from the group. Remembering that time her father had caught her masturbating to a boxing match when she was fourteen. Mother had dismissed it as healthy. He was supposed to have been the more progressive of the two, but it was she who had better understood the ways of a young woman's impulses. What excited. What satisfied. She spared Lorna a discussion. Lorna would graduate to horror films and BDSM videos she'd find on gay websites by college. Popular, respectable teen girl and women's magazines would never explore these impulses. They were proclivities that no one wanted to touch, consider, or watch.

And then she was back, and her colleagues were staring.

Lorna stopped fidgeting with her earring and said to Bowman, as though they were faculty gathering friends: "They left Hong Kong, though, because they had trouble with England's imperial influence, right?"

Dr. Chen cleared his throat and mumbled when he spoke. "Even after the handover in '97, it still lingers. Like a stain."

Bowman's eyes narrowed as he chewed his cheek.

"*Like a stain,*" repeated Lorna. "What kind of a stain?"

Dr. Chen's compact body with aged muscle seemed to grow bigger as his childlike face took on a hardened countenance. He chuckled and pretended to annotate an article.

Dr. Chen, into his chest: "They arrived in 1841. It was a long time, their stay. They had occupied for a long time, Lorna."

Lorna tapped her pen softly against her bare left leg, slung over her right. "You're aware of the emasculation campaign that some British soldiers decided to spearhead clandestinely, aren't you?"

Dr. Bowman sat up. His jaw clenched.

Dr. Chen frowned. "I'm not familiar, no."

"Apparently, the young English soldiers of a small village outside of Hong Kong, I believe not far from Kowloon Bay, had decided that to make the Cantonese men easier to manage they'd have to break them first of their pride and pesky tendency toward self-defense."

Dr. Bowman slumped awkwardly as his stomach tightened. On his knees, Dr. Chen's fists balled.

"These young English soldiers would systematically pick out the strongest and most dominant men in the pack, the troublemakers, the agitators. Mostly fisherman or dock workers. Real brutes. And they would ritualistically rape them in front of the whole community. Shaming them. Feminizing them. Many committed suicide. Many others ran away. The British had their reign. As you said, Dr. Chen, it had lasted for one hundred and fifty-six years."

Dr. Chen spoke with a big, wet lump in his throat. "Fucking Limey bastards."

"Whoa there!" Dr. Bowman stood up on nervy impulse, dropping his folder to the floor.

Dr. Farshadi gasped and instinctively covered her breasts and closed her long tawny legs.

Red obscured Dr. Chen's vision and he shook. "Piggish white people. I could go on!"

Dr. Bowman snapped out the rancid epithet ("Chinks!"), and the word could not be unsaid. He knew he erred when he saw the faces of Dr. Farshadi and Geraldine, both of whom were wearing expressions of repulsion. But Dr. Bowman had only reacted and lost his sense of station, of place, of propriety.

Dr. Chen also snapped, but his explosion was not verbal. It was physical, and before he realized what he was doing he had already leapt to his feet and thrown one sharp knee into Dr. Bowman's ribs, causing his pillar-like legs to crumble, another into his face, and was soon on top of him striking with a crazed repetition the boyish redhead's swollen mouth, making it bleed.

Lorna's desk had been knocked over, two of her plants were left smashed, and at least one chair-leg was cracked. But she didn't care about any of that. In fact, she could barely contain her glow, the grin too bright to shade, and it shone on Dr. Chen, who was panting and revealed the faint outline of an erection when he stood. It shone too on Dr. Farshadi, who had a hand pressed against her right breast and another against her mons veneris.

Geraldine was breathless and flush, her hands out of view. Nothing like this had ever happened, though Lorna had always hoped and meant for it to. But it kept on happening, and delightedly Lorna wondered how she'd work it into her next book without condemning anyone at all. She thought of Plato's reverence for the Olympians.

Dr. Bowman groaned and coughed up a tooth and some of his lunch as Dr. Chen adjusted his tumescence and the female professors endeavored to steady their breathing. Lorna's inconvenient insights settled on the room's queasy inhabitants with an uneasy weight. Though it hadn't solved any problems, she was satisfied with the support of her thesis it had offered.

Then it was over, for now. It would prefigure future events, Lorna was certain.

XIV

Surrendering his true identity gave Theo the confidence to video chat with Javier over Skype.

"So, tell me more about your mom and dad!"

The cadence and enunciation of Javier's voice and words were smoother than Theo would have expected. His house was a safari. A museum of dead things. Javier's home was full of stiff animals. Theo couldn't stop staring into the Kudu's eyes, which seemed to gawk back at him.

"There's not too much to tell other than that I think I'm a big disappointment to them. My dad is this complete overachiever who's never that great at anything, except for maybe making money and even that, well, he's no Jeff Bezos ..."

"Well, that's a talent, though, right?"

"I guess, I mean, he's trying to be a teacher at his own school and he's not very good at it. And he has this weird competitive thing going on with a coworker, who's technically his employee, because dad owns the school, right? It's strange. And my mom calls him a beta."

"Always a bridesmaid ..."

"Yeah, like never the bride, never a winner. And she's really good at her job. Very successful, too. She teaches English and cultural studies at Merriweather and is always in the news because she makes these crazy-ass comments about, like, *gender norms*, or whatever, men and women and sex and shit. And she's in trouble for saying some fucked up shit about rape and machismo and it's all over the internet now."

"Interesting parents. *Very* New York City."

"It gets boring. *They* get boring. Always trying to prove something or be better than everyone else. It's like, grow up!"

"I bet." Javier fidgeted with something offscreen. "You should meet my father and brothers! Biggest weirdos ever!!!! Wild boys!!! So naughty!!!"

"What makes them 'wild' and 'naughty'?"

Javier ruminated with a sly smile, obfuscating something Theo bet was titillating, but then the Spanish bullfighter's eyes brightened, and he looked past Theo.

"Hey, Theo, what are those back there? Costumes?"

Theo had framed himself in the video so that the workstation and hanging Burt and Ernie, Rocky and Bullwinkle costumes read in the background. He wasn't subtle. Theo turned and headed over to them.

"Oh yeah, check them out." Theo lifted the masks off the hooks and carried them bread-basket style to his laptop.

Javier beamed. "Fuck, dude. Those look amazing. You really are a talent."

"Thanks, Javier." Theo rested the masks on his bed, beside the laptop.

"You know what, Theo, I knew you were lying to me all along."

"What? How?"

"For one thing, I can smell a liar from a mile away. I read animals for a living. Anticipate their motives and choices and strategies. Otherwise, I'll die. Literally, die. And for the other, I just knew you couldn't have been that older vain man with all the muscles and style and posing and crap. Your true personality shined through. You are too sensitive and creative and deep to look like someone like that. Behave like that. You know?"

Instead of exuding a quiet satisfaction with the compliments, Theo put on a plaintive pout. "Thanks."

"I mean it, though. You're not like everyone else, and that's what makes you worth my time. It's why I bit in the first place, even with all of those likes and comments and messages I get. Something jumped out about you that grabbed me. You said I seemed 'smarter and deeper than most people might think', that there was 'more to me than meets the eye.'"

Lorna knocked on Theo's bedroom door and tried to open it, but it was locked. Theo's eyes widened and he clumsily slammed shut his laptop, extinguishing Javier, who in his final seconds flashed a cocked eyebrow when he heard the knocking on the bedroom door and Lorna's voice calling Theo from the other side.

"What do you need?" said Theo as he swung open his door.

"I heard you talking to someone. Was that Charlie?"

"Yeah, he and I were just patching things up."

"Oh, good. Okay, well, dinner is in a few minutes. Your father cooked, if you can believe it. Steak!"

Theo laughed unconvincingly. Lorna's mask dropped and her face revealed itself once again as she turned away, caring more than she thought she would when she caught herself.

Theo shut and locked his door. Returned to his laptop, hoping to find Javier. He was gone. Theo called him again, panicking that he wouldn't answer. That it'd be the end once and for all. When Javier answered with a sinister smirk, Theo again felt like himself.

"Twerp!" said Javier. "I ought to bust your balls for that!"

"Sorry, man." Theo faked a sad face. "It was my mom."

"When do I get to meet her?"

Theo didn't detect Javier's perverted smile. He squirmed for other reasons.

"You don't. I think she actually hates me and doesn't know it."

"What? Why? No mother ever *hates* her own child. My mother adored me and my brothers when we were kids. Her death is still the worst thing that's ever happened to us."

"Wow. I'm sorry. I don't really know what I'd feel if my mom died. Possibly nothing."

Javier's smile was earnest, even loving. "That's rough, kid."

"Well, she's just like this actor who pretends to be a mother. It wouldn't have been her first choice, I bet. She has so many other things in her life that she cares about more than me and my father. Unless she's writing about us in one of her dull-ass articles. I guess her students must get a kick out of it, hearing her … make fun of us. The *cosmopolitan manliness, which is to say hardly a man at all.* She actually wrote that crap."

"For real?"

"In some interview, but she didn't call us out by names. It was just obvious. She's pretty fucked up. We're like lab rats or something. I don't know. She's just very into her job. And I think she thinks I'm a sissy or something. Like too feminine. An embarrassment, maybe."

Javier's face became soft, younger. "Pretty mean."

"Well, that's just it. She never does or says anything that seems mean." Theo looked down at his fingers, interlaced in front of the keyboard. "It's more like she just doesn't express normal behavior or, like, emotions that a mother should."

"She just sounds cold."

"Yes, that's it! She's cold! And when she does try to be lovey-dovey normal mom-type, it's just awkward and weird. I hate it even more. Because it feels *obligatory*, or whatever. Like because she thinks it's something she's supposed to do! Not because she really wants to."

"Got ya. Hold on a sec. Getting dry."

Javier got up from his computer and poured himself a drink at his bar in the distance. When Theo saw that he was only wearing a pair of briefs, he stopped breathing and nearly passed out.

XV

Lorna sat at her desk, finished sorting lecture notes for her class, which was about to start in ten minutes, did a cursory review of her inbox, saw and opened Theo's email, and read his message. Succinct, as usual.

Mom,

check out how dad plays with others.

−T.

(the YouTube link was pasted below)

Lorna clicked the URL and watched Darnell's footage of Risk assaulting Dominick on the indoor rock-climbing wall and tackling Dominick on the obstacle course. She bit her lip, frowned, squinted her eyes, readjusted herself, and watched the two clips again, a total of four minutes of footage. Darnell had edited the action into a montage that showcased Risk at his most athletic, most valiant, and most barbaric.

Ten minutes later, Lorna stood before her students, sustaining the pregnant pause that had become her signature, especially ever since the unfortunate YouTube video went viral. She thickened the silence between discourse to heighten the drama of her presentation, to engender discomfort, to retain power. Some students had complained in their evaluations that she sucked the air out of the room and created a cold learning environment (an "unsafe space") that triggered myriad anxieties. Most appreciated her theatrics, as she was the type of professor that college had held the promise of when they were still high school pupils looking forward to an elevated educational experience.

And when she spoke it was with an affected severity that made some students lean in and others slump with rolling eyes. Lorna was unmoved by all reactionary gestures. That is, if the students reacted, at all.

"So, Paglia's *Sexual Personae*. The first fifty pages. On nature. What did we think?"

A female student without makeup and in sweats raised her hand and spoke with a chirpiness that grated. Lorna thought she was pretty, but plain. "The way she puts down women, I don't know. She's internalized misogyny or something. I've read what she's said about college girls and date rape culture. Vile."

Lorna assumed the criticism was also meant for her, but she smiled brightly, even as her eyes blackened. "First, separate the creator from her own creation –"

"But that's ridiculous!" The student's scorn was evident in her expression, all bugged eyes and curled lips. "That's not possible!"

"—for the sake of this intellectual exercise! Second, is she really so off about *college girls*?"

"Of course, she is! No one deserves to be raped, Dr. Bonaventura!"

Lorna's correction was quick and clear. "*Hall*-Bonaventura."

The student blushed and nodded. Reticent, though respectful.

"College girls aren't the problem, at all. College boys, on the other hand. They are what they are. Dogs kill over seventeen thousand people a year. Snakes over sixty thousand. Mosquitos over eight hundred thousand. These creatures are behaving defensively, to endure, to survive, to protect themselves. It's instinct. It's not personal. College boys. Men. They're just doing the same."

The female student without makeup, in sweats, was now trembling with rage. Her lividness was borderline maniacal.

"Are you saying that … 'boys will be boys'?!"

The general air was one of: *have you not learned your lesson from the lec-*

ture that's now world infamous, professor?

"Don't be so simplistic." Lorna's cadence was a medley of stern and sing-song with an uneasy staccato. "I'm saying that men do what it is in their nature to do. That is, to take what they want when they want it. It's how our species propagates. The natural male tendency to fuck and fight. Their competitiveness. Their egos. Though vulgar, it's all necessary for the collective advancement of the breed."

"Breed" was carefully chosen, as the word intimated canines, once again. Lorna thought for a moment about the debunked alpha wolf study.

"Hold up!" A brunette with glasses and an athletic build rolled up the sleeves of her cardigan, agitated and ready to brawl. "What you're saying excludes from consideration that what separates humans from other species and enables our *dominance* is our cognition and verbal understanding and communication!"

Several more hands shot up. Incensed zeal parried with provocation.

Lorna nodded with a pout. She moved to her SmartBoard, turned it on, retrieved her email from Theo, and played the YouTube link of Risk.

The students watched, wondrous, bemused, captivated. Some laughed. Lorna replayed it.

"Watch again. Take notes. What do you see? What do you infer?"

A star swimmer, male, Latino, twenty, in a pink Polo, raised his hand and began speaking before he was called on. "I *see* an asshole behaving badly. I *infer* a white man with serious insecurities."

Lorna paused, reflected. "Yes. Your inference is correct. It's insecurities that compel such unnecessary and rough behavior. Inferiority complexes. Something to prove. Something to make up for. There is always a basis that they work from. Failure. Fear of failure. It acts as the engine for men. *All* men. And it drives them to rape, assault, war. But also, to Nobel prizes."

"Who is this guy?" asked the Latino pupil with the pink Polo, referring to the assailant on the SmartBoard repeatedly taking down the younger, better-looking man.

Lorna hesitated. Multiple strategies ran through her head. Would the admission serve as leverage, or a compromise? Would it add to the instruction, enhancing the lesson, making the moment teachable? Or would it be reductive to a persona she had carefully constructed?

Her words rolled off the tongue in a fashion so depersonalized that it even startled her. "A typical middle-aged American white man."

Half the auditorium laughed. The others gazed with a daydreaming sheen.

Constance De La Rosa, the chair of the cultural studies department, entered the classroom with thunderous authority. The students remained unmoved by her visit, even if her arrival was ceremonious and loud. The slamming of the heavy rosewood door against the bulletin board littered with flyers and announcements of service reverberated sharply. And the chair, closing in on sixty-five, was breathless and flush. As if she had run up the stairs from her office three floors below.

Lorna, obfuscating any hints of annoyance, looked at her. "Constance?"

"*Dr. De La Rosa*," corrected Constance in a smooth, unnecessarily breathy purr. The kind of feminine, neither sexy nor expedient, that always got on Lorna's nerves.

Lorna slouched, exhausted by the grandstanding. "What can I do for you?"

Constance turned to the scholars with a bashful smile. "I had misread your schedule. I thought you had already finished class. I can come back."

Unlikely story. Constance had her schedule and knew her office hours. This interruption was done for effect. Women with power, donning the masculine cloak, could be as theatrical in their grandstanding as men. Another case study, perhaps?

"You're sure?"

Constance glanced at Risk and Dominick's bellicose engagement on screen. "Yes," she said in a timid whisper, her eyes never leaving the action replaying on a continual loop of the wild, civilized men.

Class ended only twenty minutes after the discomfited exchange, with many of the students having pressed Lorna for questions about the peculiar man behaving badly in the video for the bulk of that time. Most of them would go back home or to their dorms to replay the clip and share it on social media, thereby creating a trend in their local circles by the weekend. Lorna would get a kick out of how quickly such things conflagrate, it being her vocation to track such fads.

Constance met Lorna by the door of the lecture hall as she exited with her valise slung around her shoulder and a bundle of research papers tucked under her arm.

"Really couldn't wait, eh?" Lorna slowed the pace toward her office.

Constance, her silver-black hair coming slowly undone from its bun, moved with majesty astride.

"*That video*, Lorna—let's get right to it, you know the one I mean—the one that's been all over social media since yesterday morning. It's going to cause some trouble. It *is* causing trouble!"

Lorna stopped and nodded, absorbing Constance's admonishment. "I didn't know I was being recorded, Constance."

"That's beside the point. The things you were saying shouldn't have been said in the first place! The department doesn't need that kind of attention. Not in this climate."

"The department doesn't? Or the *university* doesn't?"

"What difference does it make?" Constance's cheeks bunched when she winced. "The department *is* the university!"

Lorna's faux exasperation sent her moving again. "Oh, an honest and direct answer. I like that!"

Constance hurried after her. "We don't support your views, Lorna. Not on this one."

Lorna stopped again. "What's the problem, exactly, Constance? What's so threatening about—"

"You can't be serious asking me that? What you've said about women and rape and effeminate men, sometimes gay men … it's just downright bullying, Lorna. And frankly, bigotry."

Lorna's top lip curled into a livid smirk. "The hypocrisy is stomach turning."

"There's no hypocrisy, Lorna!"

"Constance …"

"And we won't even get into how you believe women secretly desire to be oppressed within patriarchal systems. From that ludicrous article you published last month! *The National Review* used to have standards when it —"

"I never said they *desire* to be oppressed. I said they long to be named, designated: 'Whore.' 'Mother.' 'Loose.' 'Frigid.' Women are like all other people. They require leadership."

"And that appalling thing you wrote about a woman's worth measured by how much they're willing to—"

"These kids spend upwards of seventy-five thousand dollars a year on a liberal education, to think freely, to expand their scope, and yet you're prepared to deny their educators the right to think liberally, to speak freely! It's the exact definition of hypocrisy, *Dr. De La Rosa!*"

Constance gathered herself, took in a deep, hearty breath worthy of a master vinyasa yogi, and spoke softly, slowly, with eyelids firmly half-mast. "And *Slate Review* just published an essay denouncing you. They criticized Merriweather for keeping you on staff. They say we're complicit. Aiding and abetting a criminal."

Lorna scoffed.

"And it's had nearly two hundred thousand hits already, Lorna. It was only released this afternoon."

Lorna sobered up. Retrieved her stoic mask. "*The Wanton Feminine* will be out in a few months. My words have been taken out of context and distorted. I'll be touring with the book, and I'll be able to clear up all the confusion."

Constance shook her head, her eyes heavier than before. "We're working on having the video taken down, but as far as the article … it doesn't help and now in light of what you said in class … We can't have it. Write a retraction."

"I won't do that."

"Then you're alone. The department and the president will send editorials of their own to *The Times* distancing ourselves from your views. And from *you*, Lorna."

Lorna pondered the threat with a demonstrative gusto. "I'm tenured," she said, shrugging. "And need to grade papers," she added, heading back to her office to grade papers.

XVI

Barefoot and in a tank top and sweat shorts, Risk again inventoried his myriad deficits. He couldn't play the piano. His penis never seemed quite big enough. He wasn't a forceful leader. He lacked an easy grace with children. The same limitations he ordinarily listed when suffering weekly professional development sessions, he now counted while facing Dominick, also barefoot, in a t-shirt that accented his torso, toned and vascular, and shorts that contoured his generous bulge. The mat beneath them was sticky, stank of dirty body sweat, and was splattered with multi-colored stains that formed a suspicious mosaic. It might have been "Manhattan-south" Brooklyn Heights, but the environment still smacked of all things outer borough.

Mr. Amudee, the Muay Thai instructor, was a tiny man with a black mustache, veins that seemed too large for his thin arms, and hard, heavy hands and feet. He stood between the two white men who lumbered over him, eyeballing them with a heightened melodrama that bordered on spoof.

Dominick stared at Risk with a mix of fear and derision. He'd challenged Risk to this dual under the auspices of a team-building exercise Risk felt the vibe. It hardened him.

Darnell, an ever-faithful videographer, captured the tension with his reliable iPhone. Marielle too was in attendance, if for no other reason than to witness Risk's latest competitive antics. They were both barefoot and wore sweat shorts and t-shirts, as well.

Principal Velma Sanchez and Executive Director Howard James stood beside Marielle, watching their history teacher carefully, taking their science teacher's admonishments seriously. They were fully clothed and in shoes, though the attire was, by their standards, casual: khakis with loafers and dress shirts sans ties.

"We're even being observed during team-building exercises now, guys?" Risk was beyond worrying about how obnoxious he might seem to leadership. Afterall, *he* was leadership. However silent. "Just take the fun out of absolutely everything, why don't ya?!"

"It's a formality, Mr. Bonaventura," said Mr. James. A didactic father in a teachable moment with a recalcitrant son.

Mr. Amudee cleared his throat impatiently. A bristly bark. Mr. James averted obsequious eyes and raised an apologetic hand.

"Strike!" Mr. Amudee's orders were guttural and acidic. This was no game.

Risk swung a fully charged fist that missed Dominick's mouth by inches. The science teacher stepped back athletically, which is to say effortlessly. He caught Risk by the right tricep and then by the wrist and flipped him in one smooth motion onto his back. Risk wheezed.

Darnell zoomed in from a full shot to a medium close up to fully express the impact.

Mr. Howard leaned into Darnell. "Is it entirely necessary, this recording business?"

"He likes me to do it." Darnell sounded shrunken, almost gimp-like.

Creepily dutiful, thought Mr. Howard.

Mr. Amudee slapped Dominick on the back. Congratulatory.

Risk's face was lousy with sweat and drool. He thought he caught Ms. Sanchez smirking in perverted delight. He knew she had never liked him and had a quiet crush on Mr. Truman. Was she turned on by this display? A travesty. Another shaming.

Risk charged Dominick before Mr. Amudee prompted another round of combat. Dominick received him in a wide stance, gripping him as he would a log barrel, and body slammed him again to the mat. Risk turned maroon and coughed up the undigested remainder of his breakfast. Egg and cheese on a toasted croissant.

Ms. Sanchez touched her chest. Darnell moved in on another close up. Risk spat up red phlegm. Grunted. Muttered obscenities. Rose to his feet.

"You didn't wait for my command." Mr. Amudee nodded disapprovingly. "It was instant karma. And your second fall."

Risk wiped his mouth, readjusted his jock, and balled his fists. He stepped back into fighting position. Mr. Amudee raised his hand and brought it down in a chopping motion while hollering in a shrill pitch.

Risk gnashed his teeth and rampaged gracelessly. Dominick swept his right leg in a swift roundhouse motion, catching Risk's thigh, causing the irate history teacher to shriek, clutch his leg and droop forward limply. Dominick smiled like a child, stepped back, and kicked again, this time forward and with a flat foot connecting with Risk's chest, sending him four feet back and onto his ass. Risk was still clutching his Charlie horse as he writhed on the floor cursing Dominick's mother.

"You might just be a natural," said Mr. Amudee to Dominick, who playfully flexed his bicep.

Risk stood up and winced. He wailed comedically and ran toward Dominick with a rage that sent a chill down Ms. Sanchez's steely back. Mr. Amudee caught Risk by the throat with fingers that were as thick as they were old and dense with calluses. Risk gurgled as the seventy-two-year-old instructor squeezed his trachea.

"Bad sportsmanship. Big ego. Fix your soul, white man."

Darnell's eyes bugged as he zoomed in once again on what amounted to Risk's fourth humiliation of the day. It had started as an outing that Darnell assumed would favor his interminably dishonored friend as Risk had previously studied Karate and Tae Kwon Do. Or so he bragged when he scheduled the team-building activity.

Ms. Sanchez exhaled, wiped her brow. Mr. Howard cleared his throat and turned to her with pursed lips. Marielle appeared between them and began hurriedly whispering. Their coffee clutch was an urgent and hushed affair. Risk watched them the way an abandoned child would his fleeing parents. Choice words popped. Their indiscretions came through in audio.

"Liability." "Unstable." "Aggressive." "Reputation." "Stakeholders." "Optics." "Asshole."

"You're talking about removing me?" Risk's face hung. He had become the abandoned child. And a tantrum would soon follow.

Dominick turned from leadership, they with whom he conspired and who made eye contact with affirmative head nods and conspicuous squirms.

It was all finally happening. Dominick cut his eyes back to Risk. The sullied, sweaty, sanguine face of a beaten man stared back at him, imploringly. And the science teacher couldn't help but to smirk.

Risk moved in, his glassy eyes and pouting bottom lip permitting disarmament. Dominick readied himself anyway. The science teacher knew well enough that all sociopaths invaded and infected with sheepish clothing that belied their wolfish intentions.

Risk stopped. "I ... you were ... I tried to ..." He swallowed hard.

Mr. Amudee watched Darnell record the suddenly bizarre and discomforting scene.

Though Risk's swing was maladroit, it was also exacting enough to set loose Dominick's left incisor and split open his top lip. It made a bloody mess all over the mat. The science teacher was on the floor holding his face, but soundless, by the time Mr. Amudee knocked Risk off his feet and planted a bony knee in his throat.

"See!" Marielle's hiss to Ms. Sanchez prompted a scowl from her boss that was equal parts appalled and frightened. Ms. Sanchez had known this kind of violence in her neighborhood growing up in the South Bronx among local gangs, but not between employees.

Darnell panned back and forth between Dominick, tending to his broken face and Risk breaking under an old Southeast Asian man's knee.

"When I let you up, you will leave my dojo." Mr. Amudee himself was on the verge of hysterics. Never had the insult been greater than what this history teacher had wrought in his home.

"Fuck that!" Dominick blew scarlet bubbles as he yelled. "I want to press charges!"

Mr. Amudee allowed Risk to get back on his feet. Ostensibly without a helping hand.

"There will be consequences, Mr. Bonaventura." Mr. Howard had never sounded so dire, thought Darnell, who moved into a chin buster of Risk to capture his wounded reaction.

"Mr. Truman," said Ms. Sanchez. "Are you okay?"

"Of course, I'm not! This psychopath has been coming for me for months! You'd better make good on that threat, Mr. Howard, or I will go to the shareholders and the media and raise holy hell about the kind of sick fuck you have running this school!"

Risk seethed. Marielle stepped behind Mr. Howard. "He's going to attack us, sir."

Everything white and pure in Mr. Amudee's formerly Zen-like space had been colored red. Risk growled. An actual primal gurgle. Diaphragmatic and full of bile. And indeed, charged toward Ms. Sanchez and Mr. Howard.

Mr. Amudee whipped his hand sideways, catching Risk in the ear and temple, sending him to his knees and wincing in agony. Mr. Amudee put a callused, tan foot to Risk's ribs. "Out! Now!"

Risk recalled the *New York Times* article he'd read about Apichatpong Amudee, Bangkok's premiere kickboxing teacher. He charged an exorbitant amount of money for these lessons and Risk was eager to show off for him. And impress Dominick, Mr. Howard, and Ms. Sanchez with his knowledge of foreign superstars and access to their insights. Things clearly had not gone as planned. As Risk stood, surveying the faces of the people he'd terrorized, and scrutinizing Darnell, who trembled, he remembered that in the article the journalist recounted an incident in which Mr. Amudee broke the collar bones, femurs, and pelvises of four burly men who had tried to rob him outside of a lounge. The incident had made him a legend in Thonglor, his newly-trendy, enduringly seedy neighborhood, and the men were left with permanent limps. They'd visit Mr. Amudee once a week at his dojo a few blocks from the lounge to offer their thanks for his instruction: humility was a lesson learned through immutable injuries.

"Fuck! Fuck! Fuck! Fuck!" Risk's blood red cheeks darkened in gradient, became maroon.

The unhinged history teacher pulled down his sweat shorts, swung his dick like a baton, and urinated on the mat. Darnell, a careful cinematographer of fine details, framed the penis in the center of the frame.

Mr. Amudee ran through a list of things he would do to Risk once the pissing stopped. He'd be damned if he'd let this nutty white man get urine all over him. He'd then have to kill him.

Marielle gawked. Ms. Sanchez hid her gasp with the back of her hand. Mr. Howard could only shake his head.

Risk, his underwear and shorts still around his ankles, stepped out of his clothing, over the glistening puddle of piss, and sprinted toward the full-wall mirror, which Mr. Amudee's students had used to watch themselves practice martial arts. Risk's punch was hard enough to shatter the mirror with one shot. The shards were yards long and the assailant's fist became a vermillion glove. The blood splattered against his bare legs and genitals.

Mr. Amudee had finally had enough. He took Risk from behind by his neck and between the legs by his testicles and walked him out of the dojo. Risk pleaded and grunted and walked with an uneven-tiptoe gait, bent over with his ass sticking up in the air to ease the tension on his scrotum, and through the doors and onto the street. Still naked. Still bloody. Still dripping sweat and piss and pride. Darnell was good enough to run his shorts and wallet out to him. Only a few passersby from the brick oven pizzeria and organic café caught glimpses of his immodesty.

The full spectacle in all its messy, maddened glory was uploaded onto YouTube that evening. Perhaps not the "full" spectacle. Before posting it, Risk carefully edited out the compromising moments—of Dominick besting him, of Amudee seizing him and tossing him through the door. But all else—the charged rampage, the threats, the unapologetic public urination—was there in cinematic celebration of his indomitable spirit. Theo watched it three times with Lorna and five more times on his own. By his eighth viewing, he realized he needed to step up his own social media game.

XVII

Lorna sat with the laptop screen facing Risk. It revealed his most recent You-Tube entry, the highly curated debacle at the dojo. Theo sat beside her, while his laptop played an older clip from Risk's channel, the obstacle course fiasco. The ambush was quiet. Pleasant, even. The living room was illuminated by their computers, bathing Risk in an electric blue that accented the dark circles under his eyes and his increasingly prominent cheekbones engendered by sunken cheeks.

He watched the videos, failing to initially realize the eventfulness of the moment. His wife and son had finally happened upon his new hobby and were presently showcasing the fruits of his efforts with an air of indemnity.

He sneered and took a step back. "So what?"

Lorna placed the laptop on the dining table behind her. It continued playing the violent shenanigans. "We're curious, honey. We don't understand it."

Risk watched himself being manhandled by Dominick and then by Mr. Amudee. "It's a performance art. An avocation, or something."

Lorna's face soured as she stood. "This compromises us." She clasped her hands together headmistress-style.

"You think so?" Risk's eyes were on Theo as he spoke softly and remotely. It was as though his thoughts were unmoored from his words. "I don't see how."

Lorna's tone leveled, and her face became cold. She got this way when situations that threatened her comfort arose. Her addresses during such moments occurred as patronizing and didactic, as though she were facing a freshman class.

"You're a banker at a respected firm, Risk. This charter is your investment. That you're acting like a teenager with something to prove is cause
for alarm. Yes, I'm worried about your mental stability, and so is Theo, but
I'm also uneasy about what your employers at Goldman will say, what the
board of directors at Perseverance Public Schools will do when they feel that
their pioneer and leader has an infantile inferiority complex that precipitates
violent confrontation."

Risk paced and shook his head, conversed unintelligibly with himself,
and then cleared his throat and looked at his patient, concerned family.

"We've managed to save a fair amount of money, Lorna. We don't need
theirs. Not anymore. We have enough. We can budget and learn to live comfortably for the rest of our lives with what we have."

"Only comfortably, though. On a budget? And what about Theo's future?
What will be left for him if we burn through it all maintaining our comfort?"

Risk looked at his son and thought that the boy must be judging him for
having stolen his idea of recording asinine episodes for YouTube uploads.
It was a teenager's game, wasn't it? What must Theo be thinking about him
and his desperation to feel relevant, vital? Typical, he'd think, no doubt. The
middle-aged white man syndrome. Tearing into old age like a cornered beast
fighting for its own survival.

"He will need to make his own way. Like I did. Like you did."

"Fuck that!" Theo spit when he hissed. "Selfish asshole."

Lorna turned back and touched her son's shoulder. "Don't, Theo. Not
like that. Not now."

Risk's heavy, wounded eyes found a crack on the floor, under the base
molding. His gaze nestled into a safe space on which to cover itself. He suddenly looked like a man possessed by a determined poltergeist.

"Be good to nature,' said Risk in a kind of fugue. "Obey the greater forces.
Fall in line. Stay small in the great plan."

"What is that?" asked Lorna, insulted and impatient. "Are *you* quoting
Emerson to—"

Risk gasped and almost cried, but managed in a sigh to say, "I need—"

"My God, *your* needs!" Lorna took a breath.

"My needs. Yes. I pay for them myself."

"We pay, too, dear." Lorna touched Theo's shoulder, again.

It was true. Risk paid well for his needs. Whatever it was he wanted had a price tag. A school. A teacher's position. A YouTube following. Even an improbable career as a matador. The itch could never be reached. He'd scratch around it, always just missing it.

Lorna readied herself. "In my class I sometimes teach the work of Emerson and Thoreau. The transcendental way. My students and I would discuss the grave admonishments they'd make to their readers. Not to stray too far from nature, God, the humble soul. Modest needs. They warned of disingenuousness, of flinging yourself too far from earth. The disconnected face unhappy ends. They fail at grace. Nature scolds them for their hubris, Risk. It's a note worth taking, you know."

Risk's red, sweaty face suddenly paled and dried. He looked unsteady but braced himself against the doorframe. Lorna moved toward him, and he laughed.

"Cold, Lorna."

"What? Dear, what?"

"Your dissertations are always so cold. Like you're at a lectern, playing to the back of the house. Like I'm always meant to listen to your elitist garbage, your intellectual ... what is it? *Pablum.* What do they say? *Drivel.* It's always so theoretical with people like you. Academics. So damned out of touch. Afraid of everything. Critical of everyone. Afraid to take big chances on anything!"

Lorna nodded and turned toward the dining table. She picked up her laptop and headed for the bedroom.

Theo watched his father with a ghoulish, hollowed-eyed glower, replaying the weird words he'd just said, possibly a quote, about obeying nature, and how strange, he thought, that such sentiments should come from Risk, the least natural person ever to live. Theo had previewed the haunting he'd master years later in Spain after the disappearance of his mother, when it was merely him and his father, alone in the big new house outside of Madrid. Incriminating silences would deafen.

XVIII

Theo stood before Perseverance High School with three buckets of flat finish—red, blue, and green— and a satchel full of spray paint canisters. It was 11 p.m. and the South Bronx neighborhood was uncharacteristically quiet save for the occasional cacophonous staples—hip hop blaring in the distance, car tires screeching on the tarmac around the corner, and mothers threatening their children to behave *or else!* Theo planned his project, assessed the amount of color he would need for the job, measured the dimensions, and got to work.

It had taken him no fewer than three hours to finish the first piece across the main entrance. Another two hours to complete the smaller work on the gym exit. And two hours to execute on his plans for the schoolyard ground. By the time he was done he'd been working for seven hours straight, all through the night. He was packed up and gone by 6 a.m., just in time for the arrival of the facilities staff and ambitious administrators. Some overeager teachers also showed up that early to get a head start on grading papers or finalizing lesson plans for the day.

Theo's masterpieces welcomed the charter school team in gory, still wet, and glistening delight. Across the main entrance a squat, musclebound Tom sodomized a lanky, lean Jerry. On the gym exit a well-endowed Fred penetrated a stout Barney. On the schoolyard ground a Bugs Bunny with a phallus the size of a baseball bat knocked a Playgirl-worthy Elmer Fudd upside the head with his purple glans.

The outrage was shared collectively with tears, obscenities, and swift demands that the surveillance video footage be immediately reviewed.

Ms. Sanchez, Mr. Howard, and Mr. Finn sat on scuffed, dented stools huddled around John Moran, head of security, in his cramped office on the ground floor. They watched the surveillance tapes of Theo defacing their school. Ms. Sanchez was the only one of the four to not register shock or disgust. She'd seen it all before.

"Holy shit!" Mr. Finn touched his heavy gut. "Isn't that—"

Ms. Sanchez frowned. "Yup. His son."

Mr. Howard wiped sweat from his brow. "Well, what the hell do we do about it?"

Mr. Finn chewed the inside of his cheek. "Puts us in a terribly awkward position."

Mr. Howard looked closer at the art on the screen. *We're always in a terribly awkward position*, he thought.

"Is that supposed to be Elmer Fudd?!"

Mr. Finn pressed his clammy hands to his knees. "Do you think this was about 'getting daddy' or 'getting us for getting daddy'?"

Ms. Sanchez turned with a sneer. "Stop saying 'daddy.'"

Mr. Finn cupped his gonads. "Sorry. But what're our next steps, folks?"

Mr. Howard turned to Ms. Sanchez. "The board is going to want to see this, and in light of what we've just disclosed to them about his behavior during the team-building outings, I can't imagine they wouldn't vote to remove him."

John Moran nodded in agreement. "Can't imagine they wouldn't. Right."

Leadership turned to John with unreadable expressions. Theo continued to toil assiduously on the small blue screen.

XIX

Theo watched Javier's kaleidoscopic array of expressions. Skype was their only mode of communication now. They'd graduated from posts and comments and messages. Theo had just sent his Spanish confidant a link to Risk's YouTube playlist, all the contests between him and Dominick. Rivals to the bitter end. As Javier studied them, Theo studied Javier.

"Your dad is twisted as you mom, dude."

Theo was adding the final details to his costumes. Hot gluing eyes onto Burt and Ernie. Double stitching ears onto Rocky and Bullwinkle. "Told ya."

"He's so bizarre, that he do this, especially consider his accomplishment. His wealth."

Theo surveyed his work. "Weirdo, yup."

"I mean, how insecure this guy?"

Theo wasn't looking up at Javier and the Spanish celebrity was becoming impatient. "You've seen the videos," Theo said.

"I mean, what does that to man, though? Chip so bad away at his confidence that he becomes loco … maniac man … who hurt people just to feel better about himself? Sound like my maniac father and brothers! Locos! Oh boy, they savages, all right!"

"He once misspoke at a dinner party that my mom hosted with her snooty ass friends from Merriweather. He was talking about *The Count of Monte Cristo* and accidentally said that the author was Cervantes. My mother didn't help matters by gasping and laughing."

"Cervantes, eh, *Don Quixote*. Alexander Dumas write *The Count of Monte Cristo*. You know, he half black."

Theo spoke volubly, a full monologue, exclusively to himself, into his workstation, addressing the threads and sewing supplies and ornaments and sketches, never once even glancing up in Javier's direction.

"Yeah, right, exactly. He made a mistake. A small mistake, but it doomed him for, like, a week. He barely said anything to us. He moped around the apartment. He would mutter to himself, like, really bent out of shape about the whole thing. I could never understand it. Such a small thing, ya know."

Javier took off his shirt, revealing the exquisite physique the photo spread in that European fashion magazine had promised all those weeks ago.

"I try to read you mom's articles. They hard. She's smart. Thanks for sending me."

Javier's alien motion caught by Theo's periphery caused the American boy to finally look up.

"Why are you getting naked?" asked Theo with a lump in his throat and a tent in his pants.

"Just about to shower," said Javier with the slightest suggestion of a smirk.

Theo's laugh was so nervous and joyous that it sounded like a squeal. Javier laughed, too. *Thank God.*

"No, but really, her words is so cold, too. I see what you mean. She must be hard … to live with."

Theo's expression was that of a cynical old man's, a hard-bitten drinker one might find at a local pub. "You see how I spend my spare time, don't you?"

Javier laughed again. Twice in one visit. Victory soothed.

"Well, I grateful. They make bad behavior but a good son!"

Theo smiled, but despite the Spaniard's naked splendor was again distracted by his outfits. The costumes had finished masks, but the bodies would remain undone, wide-open torsos from the throat to the crotch to showcase breasts, abs, and junk and snatch. The attention to detail was fetishistic.

"Okay, buddy, gonna shower!"

Theo looked back up and Javier was flashing the peace sign with a smile. A second later he was gone. "Shit." Theo hadn't been as present as he usually was, and he was sure that Javier had detected the preoccupation. It was rude and not like him. Sure, he was aloof around his parents and most other teenagers, but not with Javier. He deserved his full and undivided attention.

No matter. The next video would make it all worth it and Javier would forgive him.

Just as Theo was beginning to secure the ankle and wrist cuffs of the outfits, his phone started to jingle. He looked over and saw that Charlie was trying to FaceTime him. Theo swallowed hard and rubbed his nose. He answered.

"Charlie, man. What's up?"

Charlie looked to be on Christopher Street in the West Village. The sex shops in the background gave it away. "Theo, hey. How's it going, bro?"

"Uh, well, you know."

"Yeah, it's like, I know. Where have you been?"

"Where have *you* been? I thought you were pissed at me."

Charlie was nodding to someone off camera and then returned his focus to his friend. "Nah, man. I mean, I guess, I was, but I'm over it now."

"Hey, didn't that tournament at Stonewall happen last weekend?"

"Yeah, and well, I placed twentieth! Out of twenty!"

"Oh, shit, man, I'm sorry."

"No, no, it's okay. I was the youngest, by far. And the only straight one! Ha!"

"Ha." Theo's laugh failed to convince.

"It's hard being the only straight drag queen in the room, man. It's like, I'm doing this because it's cool and creative and fun to dress up. It's my art! Right? But all these gay guys take it so personally. It's like they think I'm doing it to be trendy or that I'm lying about my sexuality and … I'm just scared. It's like, hypocritical. They want to be all for acceptance and being yourself and this is who I am, you know, and they have to give me shit about it. Sucks."

"Right." Theo's disappointment was too heavy in his voice to not be detectable.

"Theo, look, I think that maybe you hoped that … *thought* … that I was maybe gay. And maybe I reacted like that because I could tell you thought I was. And I freaked out a little. And I'm sorry!"

Theo's eyes fell hard to something out of frame. The floor. His hands resting on the keyboard, itching to search for diversion. "It's okay, Charlie. No big deal. Not anymore."

Again, Charlie gestured to someone off camera before redirecting his attention to Theo. "Okay, cool. Wait, why not anymore?"

"Just, things changed. And I'm in a different place now. Like, emotionally."

"Oh, well, that's good, right?"

"Uh-huh. So, what'd you end up wearing?"

"I went to this thrift store in the East Village and bought all this tacky old crap. I looked like a hot mess. My makeup was a disaster, too. My face. Looked. Like. A. Mask. Yikes, man. Yikes. Not fishy, at all!"

Theo was genuinely okay with all of it and his tone suddenly intimated as much. "Ha! Well, you're new. You'll get it."

"Yeah. Yo, I saw your new videos. They were pretty dark, man. Did you set those people up? That family with the water balloons? Those guys on the bikes? That poor lady?"

Theo ran his hands across his costumes to get a sense of the texture. "I gotta go, Charlie. I'll talk to you soon."

"Okay, later, Theo!"

Theo hung up and returned to the costumes, now splayed out on his bed, facing up like limp bodies that had been eviscerated. He had already cast the film and the wardrobe was tailored to his actors' dimensions. If Charlie truly had an issue with what he'd already shot and aired, this new enterprise would make his blood run cold.

X X

"Okay, ready? Here it is! The world premiere of my *The Rocky does Bull-winkle While Burt does Ernie Homo-erotica-Spectacular!*"

Theo had shot the orgy in Washington Square Park at three am, having expertly snuck out of his parent's home and taken the red line into the Village. The four performers, three men and one tomboy, all in their late teens to early twenties, were students at NYU—the Tisch film school, precisely—and the School of the Visual Arts and took this project as an opportunity to shame their rich parents who had always given them what they wanted while also encouraging them to assert their individuality and artistic expression to a world that had cared too much about commerce and religion and propriety. Also, the obfuscation of their faces gave them license to entertain their moral depravities. Anonymity fed socially unacceptable behavior.

Javier leered, clapping his hands, and licking his lips. The video played, and Theo held his breath. He so badly wanted the matador to continue admiring his efforts. In the video, newly streaming on—but soon to be flagged and removed from—all of Tristan Goodman's social media channels, the girl in the group, butch with a lithe body, assumed the Bullwinkle costume as Burt, Ernie, and Rocky engaged each of her exposed entry points.

Rocky then did Bullwinkle. Ernie then did Burt. The park had been mostly empty except for the few homeless men who complained about the noise—the orgasms had been shrill, demonstrative—and the coterie of drunken frat boys who demanded to see more cock, yelling, "Throw more pickle, faggots!" The director ignored the criticisms. Theo had instead paid closer attention to the positioning of the masks, making sure that they read for the camera as well as his drawings had. The entire orgy lasted thirty minutes and was staged in the big dry fountain before the arch.

Javier leapt back at the collective climax in faux astonishment and applauded theatrically.

"Sublime! You're a damn Hitchcock or Kubrick or Almodóvar!"

"More like a dirty teen with too much time on his hands."

"Anyway. I'm impressed. See, you visualize a fantasy and you make it happen. You make it real. And now who knows how many others will be able to enjoy your work."

"I guess."

"When did you do all this?"

"The other night. I had to sneak out of the apartment. It's a good thing my parents drink themselves to sleep. Otherwise, they'd have woken up."

Javier chuckled. "Big drinkers, are they?"

"Kind of."

In Javier's generous moment of praise, Theo, the effeminate and awkward, weird and cerebral, *artistic type*, desperately wished he could be the corporate-minded, masculine capitalist his father and mother wanted him to be, the kind of man that his father was trying to be and the kind of man his mother wrote so flatteringly about. But he wasn't.

"You okay, kid?"

Though he had only posted the video twenty minutes ago, Theo checked his social media pages to count the views and comments. So far, a dozen on Facebook. Twenty on Instagram. Forty on Tumblr.

The comments were what he expected, they ran the gamut.

Disgusting! I'm reporting this garbage! This is dope! You're sickening!

"I'm okay."

"You seem sort of down."

"I guess. My dad is really cracking up, lately, and my mom, well, she seems more consumed with her writing than ever before, and I'm just really lonely, man."

Theo was an off-kilter American kid with a propensity for rash decisions, stuck with damaged, damaging parents, and a yen for maverick role models. Javier could provide him that much. And he loved his ugly hatred and ridiculous anger. It was refreshing.

"You don't need to feel lonely, Theo. I'm always here."

"Thanks, Javier. Hey, so, it's looking more and more likely that we might be coming to Spain sooner than we originally planned."

Javier's dark eyes lit up. "Oh, really?"

"Yeah, the people who run the schools my dad created, the board, or something, might want him out because he's acting like an ass."

"You mean, because of those videos on YouTube?"

"Yeah, giving the network a bad reputation, or whatever. It's a charter, so they're pretty uptight."

"Maybe then you'll be able to meet Dad and my bros. Those cavemen!" Javier scratched his genitals, though Theo couldn't see it. "Wow."

Javier's mind filled with possible scenarios in which he'd insinuate himself into the Bonaventura fold. How close he'd get with wealthy Risk, the frustrated, failed teacher, the wannabe matador, the half man, the unman, and Lorna, the castrator, the witch of letters, the baroness of academia, the adjudicator of what constitutes a true man. Javier thought he'd make a suitable consort.

X X I

Lorna was a bewildered, tender mess. It had been three days since Perseverance Public Schools pressed charges on Theo for his vandalism. Two days
since Risk had been called in to meet with leadership. And a day since he
was told by the superintendent and the board that they were removing him
from the network. Lorna's son was now a felon, her husband was suddenly
unemployed. The family was publicly disgraced. This last bit was in no small
part thanks to the fastidious coverage of unfolding events by *MSNBC, FOX
News, the New York Times*, and the *New York Daily News*. New York loved
a solid scandal and these developments, when strung together to tell a sala-
cious story, provided just that. And her own reputation was on the line. The
very undergirding of her place at Merriweather was tenuous. The YouTube
video was not going away.

More Internet-triggered seismic spasms. Risk policed the bar and drank
too much. Lorna was on the couch and replayed the events of the barbarism
in her office. She'd thought about it often since the melee.

"So, it seems that the board has a problem with my behavior," said Risk,
lumbering over a series of wine racks, gripping a bottle of beer.

Lorna was on her second highball. "No kidding?"

"They took issue with how I conducted myself during the team-building challenges and, you know, that I videotaped it, put it online. Fucking
shit. They think it reflects badly on me and as an extension on the network.
Whatever. Small, mediocre …"

How he *conducted* himself: those several awful months of team building nightmares, when Risk had pulled Dominick's ankle as he climbed the
tall, plastic rock wall, causing him to dislocate a knee. Or when he'd tackled

"Dom" into poison ivy near West Point after he was clearly going to reach the finish line first. Weeks later when Risk had broken his handsome colleague's nose during what had been a friendly Muay Thai sparring session. And then "Mr. Bonaventura" had elected to go ahead and upload all of these juvenile, violent shenanigans onto an internationally accessible website.

"And the Remington Associates, they're, uh, not happy either. So ..."

"So, they've both let you go, then? *Fired you?*"

"Yeah, but not without a healthy severance ... and then there's our savings, right? I mean, we're fine. Just fine. And this means that maybe now, you know ... we can seriously move forward with Spain."

Move forward with Spain. As though it were wedding plans or a military campaign. Lorna hadn't said too much more after his blasé pronouncements.

Lorna stared out the window and found a drab city below. She wondered if she ever thought their lives were anything but a contingency. Once Spain had seemed like a romantic fling held at bay while they found themselves. They'd never used the phrase *found themselves.* But that's what they were doing because both were now completely lost. The city was already forgetting them.

She retreated into her home office, smaller than the one at Merriweather by half, and checked her emails. The home office featured no plants, no posters of any Adonis or warrior. Just stacks of papers and shelves lined with books.

So many emails from former students and colleagues who wished to express their disfavor or support, scolding and sympathetic.

Though at fifty she wasn't all that old, Lorna was dazzled by how quickly the world had changed and how far behind it had left her. The new guard deemed her a relic of a primitive age. Not long ago her theories would be fodder for dinnertime discussion, stimulating classroom debate, and gentlemanly cross-examination in chambers of critical analysis. Now she was just labeled a cretin and a monster.

There had been multiple requests from legacy media, top brands wishing for interviews and profiles. Lorna would consider, but ultimately ignore the opportunities. She had no need to clear her name or clarify anything she'd said. The email from the publisher of *The Wanton Feminine* wouldn't arrive for another week. It would remind her of the morality clause in her contract and cancel the publication of her book, citing "too-tempestuous social headwinds". They'd allude to the Twitter storms, the Facebook fusillades, and the coverage on the 24-hour news networks, excerpting the comments and posts, likes and emojis.

But she was surprised by how grateful she felt for the momentary attention, negative though it mostly was. So what if the suicide requests and insults had started to chip away at her? She was relevant, again. Perhaps it was time to leave. Start over. Find a place in the world where they didn't martyr speakers of unpopular truths.

And then an official letter from Sherlyn Lopez, Merriweather's Director of Human Resources. Lorna urgently opened the email. She stared at the screen, rereading the words until her eyes strained, until they made sense. It took many minutes before they did.

Dr. Hall-Bonaventura,

We regret to inform you that your term of employment at City University of New York Merriweather has come to an immediate end. Due to your violation of our employee code of conduct Section 4.b) we have no choice but to end your employment with us.

You have until the end of the semester to clean out your office and vacate the premises. If you do not comply, your belongings will be packed up for you and you will be escorted off the premises by our security team.

Your courses for the remainder of the autumn semester have been canceled and all students have received full refunds.

We thank you for your service to City University of New York Merriweather and we wish it didn't have to conclude this way.

Risk watched Lorna cry in the bedroom. It had been the same week the police had mirandized, arrested, booked, fingerprinted, photographed, and held Theo for over two hours before Risk had bailed him out of Inwood's 34th precinct. Such drama was foreign to Lorna. She had never even been caught shoplifting, something she'd done during her college years because she savored the rush. She realized how much of a fraud it made her to cry about this situation, as a public thinker who'd made her bones extolling the virtues of masculine behavior, the naturalness of disobedience, the biological urge to buck propriety, to embrace the hot tug of hedonism. She had also written volubly about the need for public art, the social value of pornographic imagery, the healthful habit of tagging, the inevitable spread of graffiti. It was all hitting her now, days later. An accumulation of rescinded blessings.

Lorna stared at her termination letter. What were the odds that all of this would happen simultaneously? Theo's criminality and arrest? Risk's dismissal from the network? His removal from the hedge fund? And now her own termination. And dead book deal. It was more than even a woman of her emotional resilience could handle, and she wept for the sheer accretion of loss and failure.

Risk undressed, headed for the shower. "When it rains it pours, huh?"

Lorna grabbed his penis as he passed her. He gasped and gripped her wrist. She looked up at him with a defiant pout, brushed the notes she'd been annotating before opening her email off her lap and onto the floor. It felt like an assault, a challenge. She tugged too hard. It hurt. Risk began to sweat. For his callousness, she would hurt him.

Though Lorna initiated, Risk took control. He twisted her wrist as he hoisted her up and away from his stiffening cock. She winced and allowed the roughness. Welcomed it with a smile. Risk pulled off her teddy and underwear. He made love to her on the bed from behind.

As though conjured by a debased warlock, Dominick lay naked before him, spread eagle. His genitalia generous and purple, twitching and beckoning. His smirk made him boyish. Risk stopped fucking his wife, stepped away, and signaled for Dominick to take over. The younger, more virile man complied. Risk took his place on the bed, opened his legs, and masturbated with ardor. The fantasy felt realer than his real wife.

Science was alive, Risk thought. History collected dust, wanted to be forgotten. Dominick was living. Risk endured a coating of dead skin. The unctuous upstart laughed at him as he thrust into his wife. Consummated the cuckolding. Was complicit in the diminishment. Dominick flexed pectorals and biceps, tightened the abdominal wall, and pulled out far enough to showcase the quadriceps of a knighted Olympian, his best and only royal feature.

Dominick took Lorna with a braver agency. His sex lacked permission and apologies. Still, he was delicate and intuitive. Risk's thoughts turned biblical. Cain killed Abel because the envy was too great. Because God had granted him unfair favor. And Cain was spared death but remained Abel's keeper. Cain was only bad when measured against Abel's victimhood. But he was marked, anyway, and his lineage was spited.

Risk would be Cain. With Dominick. With his future fantasy, Javier Forza. He'd always be the one with the mark.

Lorna could read the hurt in her husband's eyes. She recalled Jerzy Kosinski's claims that an insult reduced more efficaciously than enslavement, burned worse than fire. All the wars. All the massacres. All the atrocities, mere peasants. An insult, the true and only king.

Risk came too soon. His climax banished Dominick. Atop Lorna, perched like a terrier, he shuddered, made an angry, choking sound, and slid off. He collapsed on the bed and squeezed out any remaining ejaculate. Milked an udder. Risk's imagination was vivid enough to allow the real physical sensation of another man.

Lorna wiped herself with her underwear and moved toward the shower. On her way, she only looked at Risk's feet. Only the lowest parts of him. It took work to find her husband attractive. She'd have to imagine lurid, sadistic scenarios or masturbate to pictures of him to condition pleasurable associations. Risk thought only about the weight and impact of Dominick's balls smacking into his wife's ass.

Neither one could sleep. Despite the harried, hapless sex. Risk tossed and turned as Lorna stared at the sole spot on the ceiling, illuminated by the cool yellow, pale blue streetlights. Her future, the next four years in Europe, shopping in Paris, weekends in Florence, day trips to the countryside or the beach, mixing with the Spanish intellectuals, finding equals in French and Italian professors, swapping notes, competing. She'd hold her own. Malaga. Alhambra. Cordoba. Andalusia. She'd host dinner parties. They'd learn Castilian and she'd improve her French. The days would be full, and she'd force her mark on the European media as thoroughly as she did the American. It'd be an easier game.

"How could we stay in New York?" Lorna's voice was raspy, as if she'd been yelling.

Risk would hunt down Javier Forza's agent. He'd pay for a face-to-face. Pick the superstar's brain. Spend efficiently on lessons and a place for himself in the sport. He'd live out this final fantasy, the uncharted frontier. Leave all of New York and his failings behind. Reinvent himself. Become the man he knew he'd eventually actualize. He'd pick up Spanish. It was the easiest of the Romantics, wasn't it? Add bullfighting to his repertoire, to the ever-burgeoning bailiwick.

"We could leave. Start over. We could do it." Risk's voice was light, as if he'd been whistling.

Lorna watched the streetlights compete for dominance across the ceiling. Blue parried with yellow. "Just run away. Like that."

Risk thought that only Darnell would be sad to see him go. No one ever counted him as one of their own. The students were awkward with him. He, with them. Being an English major and lover of old things, Darnell would allude to *Moby Dick*, say something about chasing a white whale. "Like that."

Lorna imagined only Dr. Chen missing her, and only because he would touch his crotch whenever he looked at her legs, revealed in a dress or skirt, or tight pants. Dr. De La Rosa and Dr. Farshadi would be glad to see her go. They never abided her brazen deliveries, her unorthodox lessons, her questionable teaching techniques. Her bad feminism. Most of all, her papers. That disastrously fast and loose scholarship. Lorna thought about their conversation. One would talk about the pretenses. The other about the hunger for men. A comment would be made about her efforts to appear younger than her actual age. Another about her stabs at fame. The only thing they'd miss is the grist she provided for their mill, and she seriously toyed with the idea of taking Joe Rogan, Laura Ingraham, and all the other conservative pundits up on their offers to appear on their shows.

The aspiration was feasible. They could abandon the unfeeling world. Start over in a better city, an older city. A new life in an old city. It was the great American tradition, wasn't it? Live off their trusts, savings, CDs, mutual funds, their stock market gains. Risk had built a sizable portfolio. It would get them far and keep them fortified.

Lorna remembered the faces of her students when she'd decided to throw them. How they were predictable in their awakenings. She could hear realtors picking up the phone and calling to ask if it was true, and how soon their place would be available for staging and showing.

"Okay," she said. "Let's do it."

PART II
THE GREAT
REDUCTIONS

I

The American fooled himself into believing he was something else. Something more. He had been an investment banker, a charter school pioneer, and a "teacher" in New York for a short while. All vanity projects and another life ago. He was now a matador. And it had been a good four years in this good new life. Though he had trained fast and hard and smart, he never quite got the knack for the sport. He had found his place among the Spaniards in Madrid, learned some Castilian, yet hadn't mastered the craft of fighting and killing bulls.

He hoped to move with speed and precision but was all thumbs with the cape and slow to steer clear of the picadors' lances. Had he been younger, born in Spain or Mexico, and begun training in his youth, like a typical matador, he would have been merciless, better at observing the bull's visual acuity and unusual head movements, smoother with catching the banderilleros' cape thrusts, and quicker with noting the bull's territory-marking. He had dreamed of putting on an elegant and brutal spectacle. Lacking any semblance of elegance, the fight was merely brutal, primarily due to the American's inaccurate foot work and faulty eye-hand coordination.

His redheaded wife—stark against the crowd of olive-skinned, raven-haired spectators—watched with clever eyes and a serpentine posture. Her cheers commanded, even scolded, rather than encouraged. And the imaginary envy the American occasioned from the other matadors excited him, made him feel proud. He had been especially tickled when the "Spanish fighter with the thick legs, lissome frame, and royal ancestry" fumed at what little attention he did receive. The American, *being American*, thought himself the best, so to provoke even made-up jealousy from such a celebrated—

native, no less—matador was satisfying. The American had a rich interior life, however threadbare its undergirding might have been.

And when Theo, ever present and recording all proceedings with his iPhone as he had in New York, described them in his YouTube video series now almost five years old, the primary players in his life—his parents and their lover— would be reduced to pronouns. Theo sat closer to the action than his mother and the family's new closest friend, those on whom he spied and worked into the ever-expanding and complicated plot of their lives, their new, old lives in Madrid.

Lorna, the redheaded wife, gasped when the bull charged, missing Risk, her able-bodied husband, by inches, its horns swiping upward and then down, so close to the gut and chest of the man she had tried for years to love. The crowd cheered when Risk sidestepped and snapped the red flag to his thigh in a mischievous mockery of formal Madrid manner. Javier, "the thick-legged Spanish fighter of imperial stock," balled his fists and bit his lip every time Risk goaded the bull, instigating an attack. They had entered the third stage of the fight, the "Tercio de Muerte," or "Part of Death," and the picadors had already stuck their lances into the bulky neck of the beast. Banderillas, bright flags fastened to barbed sticks, plumed from its shoulders like flaccid rainbow wings. It hadn't been a clean fight.

In between the life-and-death moments of man and beast locking horns and flag, or muscle and sword, Javier and Lorna would steal glances of one another. They had been seated close to the action, separated by a few fans seeking slapstick more than drama. Javier and Lorna could detect a nervy mix of terror and triumph in one another's eyes, their heaving and breathless bodies sending unambiguous signals to one another. Flush and dry-mouthed, Lorna couldn't resist picturing Javier fighting alongside her wide-shouldered husband, together besting the bulls of the country that stampeded toward them, perhaps rescuing her. Perhaps sharing her. Engorged and tense, Javier found it futile to shut out the fantasies of performing lascivious acts with the American woman before her magnificently built, though charmingly incompetent, husband and all the sneering, screaming, smoldering observers who had come to see a bloody good show. And he would show.

Risk had been "dressed to kill"—regal in his traje de luces, a diaphanous "suit of lights" coated in sequin and ornate embroidery. It had cost a small fortune and required the assistance of a squire to get into. He'd been too consumed by his appearance, boasting all the trappings of a genuine Spanish torero, and slid on a mound of dirt and pebbles as the bull trundled over his foot. The crowd screamed, but Lorna was cool. She knew the beast hadn't crushed anything. She knew by the smirk on her husband's face. She would always watch his face to determine how she should feel. Risk rallied and waved the red flag, prompting the bull to circle back around and without a beat rage through the flash of passion. Risk turned to the crowd and smiled, waved, and then redoubled his efforts to antagonize the increasingly maddened creature.

Javier and Lorna were beside each other. He had wormed his way past the impatient and hostile line of attendees to find his place next to her. She wheezed and tried to focus on the battle before her. The Spaniard brushed her hip with his swollen, misshapen knuckles. Her left leg nearly gave out.

Theo expertly, surreptitiously swung his iPhone back and forth, seizing the fight between the bull and his father and the fling between the Spaniard and his mother.

"He's cocky today," said Javier. "And he's not nearly good enough to be cocky."

"He's confident," Lorna corrected.

She had staked her reputation as an academic on the natural and necessary premise of male confidence. She'd become a reluctant ambassador since those embattled, eminent days in New York, and markedly less secure in her diplomatic abilities.

Javier leaned in, his hot breath blowing into her ear. "It's a treacherous sport. Confidence here *is* cocky."

In the four years he'd spent conversing daily with the Bonaventuras, Javier's English had vastly improved.

Lorna tried to smirk, but her cheek twitched spasmodically. She turned away.

"He'll be fine."

"He's a remarkable athlete. Clumsy and unfocused, but what a will! I'd love to fight him myself, some day."

"The bull?"

Javier felt a tingle at his admission. "Your husband."

"He'd hurt you," Lorna said, her voice quivering. She pictured Javier inside her. It had been too long.

"I'd count on it." Javier grabbed the matador's wife by the wrist. "And I'm certain that I'd hurt him."

Lorna yanked her arm away, watched her husband dance to a premature victory before the agitated horned behemoth that sought to kill him.

Risk turned to the crowd as the bull skidded to a stop just behind him, snorting and stomping. He would do this at the most perilous junctures, to find and make eye contact with Lorna long enough for a wink and a smile. And he did find her in her usual place, first row, center, but not alone this time. Not alone for the past few times. Javier, so easily provoked and enamored, challenged and charmed, stood next to her. Risk snapped to with enough time to dodge the return assault from the bull, whose horn grazed his shoulder, leaving a faint slash that stung. Risk winced and then laughed at himself for getting caught. Lorna touched her clavicle. Javier licked the sweat away from the black stubble of his top lip.

Theo zoomed in on Javier's mouth and caught the small gesture.

"This is the way it always goes, does it not?" Javier said, his accent making his voice heavier and angrier than intended. "With you Americans? Playing at being locals? Acting like you all own the place? Coming in and taking what's not yours?"

Lorna looked down. Blushed. She had left her tenured post at CUNY Merriweather for *this?* "We've distracted him. He can't afford any distractions."

The fight was at its mid-point, and the bull—its neck muscles duly weakened and suffering its first loss of blood—stopped and stared at Risk. Even with the picadores' lances jutting from its morrillo, a gnarled mound of muscles on the neck, the beast expressed a strange serenity. And Risk felt a stranger sensation. An ineffable, but unshakable, melding of guilt and compassion, soon overtaken by a menacing assurance—the bull could not hurt him. And he could no longer hurt the bull. There was personhood in the gaze of the nonhuman animal and Risk could not deny seeing him, for the beast was now surely a "him".

Miscalculating his abilities, underestimating the bull's bitterness, Risk lowered his red flag and waited. Lorna touched her breast and cocked her head. Javier crossed his arms and sniggered. The bull snorted, shook free the cobwebs, and charged. Risk looked at his wife, and then at the Spaniard beside her. He imagined multiple scenarios. Multiple schemes.

His arrogance engendered vulnerability. His jealousy permitted distraction.

What Theo recorded next would be a marketable sequence, so dynamic that it would yield the highest number of YouTube views in his short "career." Amid the pebbles and dirt and hoof shavings, there was a splash of crimson. Risk was gored through his groin. The horn went into the pelvis and punctured bone and intestine, tendon and muscle. Though it spared his genitals by inches, the pain the assault elicited caused him to cry out in unholy anguish and would leave disconnections between anatomy and desire. Lorna shrieked behind hands that shielded eyes that cried. She didn't need to see his face this time to know how to feel. Her husband's strong and tall body locked as it was impaled and went limp as it was tossed through the air.

Javier hid a smirk, though his eyes revealed admiration. Theo captured this, too. The American boy missed nothing.

11

Theo didn't listen, and he didn't fake it well, either. Risk sat beside him, reviewing stock margins on his laptop, navigating Bloomberg, discussing emerging markets and their currencies. Theo ate breakfast—tortilla Española—and scrolled through anime cartoons on his phone. Lorna cleaned the butcher block counter while composing in her head a new line of research that she'd whip into a series of articles, something she'd pitch to *The Atlantic* or *The New Yorker*. The remains of the ingredients—eggs, salt, brown onions, potatoes, olive oil, parsley—lingered.

They had only arrived in Madrid a few months ago, years before the bull would change Risk's gait, and readjustment was relative.

"They're called BRICS countries, Theo. Brazil—maybe not so much anymore—Russia, India, China, and South Africa. And their economies are something to watch out for. I've been studying the real, ruble, rupee, yen, and rand for a few years now."

"Uh huh. Wow." Theo zoomed in on the Japanese antihero whose squid-like arm vanquished a city corrupted by an insidious phantasm with a single blow.

Lorna scribbled notes for her article series. She considered the tastes of editors she'd known in New York. She had maintained cordial relationships with most of them, those who hadn't deleted her contact information after the ax fell on her academic career amid that YouTube business.

Risk sighed hard. He'd lost his breath. Indifference winded him.

Theo selected another image, a pink woman with antennae and gossamer wings who flitted above a demonic villain threatening calamity on a small village in the country. Risk pinched the top of Theo's phone and lowered it to the table.

"Does any of this appeal to you? Just because we're not in America anymore doesn't mean you get out of going to college, Theo. It's junior year and you need to get serious."

Lorna looked over with raised eyebrows as she chopped turnips for her salad and intermittently scribbled a few more ideas.

Theo pulled his phone close to his chest. "*If* I go to college, I won't be studying international finance, dad."

"What, then? Animation? Fine Arts? Comic books? Be practical, son."

"Like you? What, you get to act out *your* fantasies, right? You're a broker. No, you're a teacher. Now you're a bullfighter! You drag us through hell living out all your dreams—being whatever the fuck it is you want this week— but Mom and I have to sacrifice? How is that fair?"

"You're learning Spanish, Theo. You'll thank us for that skill!"

"*Peninsular* Spanish, Dad! Spoken by only how many?!"

Lorna stopped cleaning and watched. She waited to see what came next. She could have reprimanded Theo, stopped this tense exchange. She didn't. She elected to witness it, instead. Passivity had its power, too. Surrender was just as strong.

"Look, Theo. The money that's allowed me to live out *my* fantasies, as you say, was all earned by *me*! And you and your mother are free to do whatever the fuck you want! I'm not stopping either of you. But it's my job to look out for your best interests."

Lorna studied her ponderous, pondering husband and defensive son— lab rats in her cage. The discomfort would have thrown a lesser scientist, but her orientation was secured by years of finding rewards in troubling social experiments.

Theo nodded, shrugged, and stood up. "Sure. Always right!"

As he moved to exit, Lorna finally spoke up. "Theo, your plate."

Theo snatched his empty plate, brought it to the sink, tossed it in, and hurriedly left the kitchen. During his theatrical escape, Theo glanced at the acrylic portrait of Fiona, Lorna's long-gone West Highland Terrier, white with a blue bow, hung in the dining room just beyond the head of the table. She had died gruesomely seven years earlier of a rare skin disease that caused her to nearly cannibalize herself.

Risk made it a demonstrative point not to look at Theo, instead returning to his stocks. It was a mere diversionary tactic to keep his remembrance a secret. He regained his colleagues' quizzical expressions when he told them that he was retiring from finance and the teaching business to become a torero in Madrid. He had made his mark in New York as a banker in as little as ten years, right out of college, right out of the gate. Earned and invested more than enough money to retire well. Starting the charter school network and trying his hand at teaching was fun. *For* fun. His students wouldn't miss him; he was never present enough for true bonds to form. He only played at education, a noble role. At heart, he was a businessman. But even that inclination had begun to wane. Especially after that bad business with Dominick Truman. He confided in very few that the sterile suits and stoic suites were too luxurious, too removed from corporeal manhood, and he was beginning to feel unmanned by his white-collar comforts. And by Truman's innumerable abilities. The younger guys didn't get it as well as the older men, those who in their seventies and eighties were aged enough to have remembered what constituted true masculinity. Wars. Manual labor. Old fashioned life-risking sacrifices. Even if the feminizing too-tight pants of bullfighting required a changing pit and a staff and revealed outlines of testicles and buttocks.

Lorna thought about the day Risk told her of his plans. Though he had not expected her to put her robust, if not turbulent, career as an academic on hold for the sake of his indulgences, Lorna protested, anyway. New York. Madrid. In hindsight, it made little difference where they lived because she eventually learned that no matter where they landed, they'd maintain the lifestyle to which they'd become accustomed. Though the relocation was complicated by its association with Theo's run-in with the law, Risk's charter controversies, and her own YouTube fiasco.

Lorna didn't have to work anymore, though she was beginning to feel unfaithful to her advanced degree in English literature and mythology with a focus on critical theory. It was her other marriage, a lifelong engagement to scholarship. *The Journal of Literary Theory* had called her "a softer Camille Paglia, a sensuous Judith Butler." Her bright tenure at Merriweather had occasioned untold invites to tony parties for wealthy pupils. She'd met Risk at a summertime rooftop soiree on Park Avenue. It wasn't until after they had married that she'd secretly write erotic short stories about libidinous—and sadomasochistic—games played between mythological gods. Her creative urges were shot through with reactionary frustration.

The mythic tale Lorna most enjoyed discussing with her too-easily shocked and appalled students was the one about the Bull of Heaven. She'd stopped tormenting Risk with it when they moved to Spain, but it was always on her mind and frequently found its way into her writing.

◆ ◆ ◆

Javier and Theo approached the heavy mahogany doors, lousy with ornate Christian carvings. They were on the outskirts of Madrid. Toledo. Land of *Don Quixote*. The squat, sinuous Spaniard appeared even more utilitarian than before, more readily bellicose. A clean-shaven mega-muscle with a tan and a black-capped missile-head in the form of a shock of pomaded ebony hair, ready for the explosions and sinking that were to follow.

In the house, lingering in the grand foyer, stood three men, all similarly structured in height and proportion to Javier—Javier's father, Massimo, and bald brothers, Antonio and Rafael. They were made in the same cast as Risk's rival. Eerily similar; maybe quadruplets. Especially Massimo, who cut a young figure, ostensibly the same age as his regal sons. They held straps of wet leather and straight razors; foamy shaving cream coated their forearms and hands. The emancipation of each other's scalps had been that recent.

Theo thought only of his father and his carefully constructed reputation. In a moment it could all be dismantled. After all, it takes years to build a dream house and only hours to burn it down. And these men, these clones of Javier's shadow self, his father's future opponents, knew the timidity in Theo's eyes. They could see him shake beneath the sheath of muscle and shrink under the veneer of American exceptionalism. The infrastructure was weak. The United States was a house that could burn. Spain's flame had scorched for over five hundred years and left plenty of castles in shambles. A light for centuries unextinguished.

Theo was smart for his age. Perceptive. He had observed how Javier's light sent his father into dark corners. Javier had an easy grace with nearly everything. Risk had trouble negotiating even the most mundane of tasks. But heroes would entangle no matter what, smashing their iconic legacies against one another, exposing the narcissists cowering under the capes and cloaks. Their egos unmanageable, and their ruination imminent. Little boys with undeveloped testicles tucked between chicken legs. The menacing Mediterranean males were always men, but Risk was still a boy. It took a boy to see that.

Javier grabbed Massimo's meaty shoulder. "You know my father."

Rafael dried his head with a towel. Antonio continued to clean the razors. Massimo scrutinized Theo, evaluated his frame and expression, judged the emotional consistency and self-awareness with merciful cruelty. His examination was accusatorial. Theo found the scrutiny legitimate, and the silent recriminations substantiated.

Could Massimo and his sons see what Theo assumed Javier could see? The old man muttered something to Javier in Castilian, but Theo had already learned enough Spanish between living in New York City and then Madrid, even for just a few months, to know what he'd said: "He's the one whose mother you've been *counseling* all this time?"

The inflection on "counseling" confirmed things.

Theo squinted his eyes. Massimo raised dismissive eyebrows. "You are the American boy from New York that my son talks about?"

Theo's jowls flexed. "I suppose so, sir."

"Welcome to Spain."

Theo squirmed but smiled. "Thank you."

"Your father and my son have now become competitors before the bulls. Make your father be careful. After a while, the fighting turns men *into* the bulls."

It wasn't until Massimo began talking about bulls that Theo noticed through the glass patio doors a farm. Cows. Chickens. Pigs. And bulls. He strolled through the capacious house and headed toward the patio. He pointed at the caged animals. "Are those for fighting?"

Massimo turned away, sniggering to himself. His brusque reaction seemed to signal his sons. Antonio and Rafael sized each other up in a sluggish, creeping dance that culminated in a synchronized, smooth removal of shirts, shorts, and socks, leaving both brothers in their briefs. Legs as outsized as arms. They were Javier's kin, to be sure. Javier sighed and looked to the floor.

"Our mother loved me the most," said Rafael, in English for Theo, something else to show off. "Out of the three of us, it was *this one*, shit-fucks."

"She read me to sleep every night, dick-hole," said Antonio, also in English, another challenge to meet. "She read me nursery rhymes. In bed and alone."

Massimo remembered his wife's smooth legs in a nightgown. The touch of her soft, full lips on his ear, his neck. They fondled each other in bed and laughed about everything. Last month made twenty years since she had died. Liver cancer was their family's private demon. Massimo pursed his lips and prompted his sons to begin their performance in the theater of bravado and brawn. The men engaged, tearing into each other like poked rhinos.

The wrestling soon gave way to boxing and then to Krav Maga. The corporeal frames heaved and sweated and bled effortlessly and with a glistening beauty. Their assaults upon each other's bodies and faces and genitals spared no barbarism. Javier smirked and chuckled when he noticed his siblings' erections. The excitement of combat was arousing. Massimo dismissed the tumescence as natural physiological reactions to the friction and adrenaline surge.

Theo stared at Javier, expecting some manner of explanation. His secret mentor offered none. By the time the brothers finally concluded their demonstration of skill and fortitude through surrender with Rafael's heel on Antonio's throat, and his fist buried in his scrotum, a full ten minutes had elapsed and Theo had grown excited and worried that his excitement would be readable.

As Rafael and Antonio applied ice and bandaging to their swollen mouths and bruised flesh, Javier took Theo by the arm and led him out of the house and toward the livestock in the offing.

On his way out, Theo had heard a sound come from one of the bedrooms in the rear of the house, but Antonio and Rafael were still in the living room. Had there been more members of their gang hiding in the back with a gun or a knife? He turned to Javier. "Why are we here?"

Yellow meadows and brown mountains surrounded. Thin woods cut stark borders. They eyeballed the bulls that snorted and knocked each other around with affection or out of boredom. Or frustration. The argument with his father still preoccupied Theo, hours after the uneasy breakfast.

"My dad is such a selfish asshole," said Theo, picking apart a small, withered bale of hay.

"He's just looking out for you. That's what father's do." One of the first things Theo observed about Javier when meeting him soon after their arrival in Madrid was how well he spoke English, decidedly better than he wrote it.

"Nah." Theo's lip twitched spasmodically at the idea. "Not him."

Javier's wide, heavy hand rested on Theo's bony shoulder. "What do you want, Theo?"

Theo pointed at the bulls in the pen. "This."

The bulls turned to Javier, feeling his gaze.

"Come on," Javier said.

"If my father could—"

"You're *not* your father, kid. You can't pay for membership to the club. Your dad *bought* his way in. He's an unusual case."

"Who needs money, Javier? I'm younger than my father was when he started."

Javier pushed out his bottom lip, nodded sagaciously.

Theo patted Javier on the back, an impenetrable wall. "Plus, I have you."

Javier smiled wide enough for his crow's feet to become apparent, something he was proud of. He had earned them through a lifetime of laughing at reduced men, smiling at their beautiful women, stealing them from the men he'd reduced. He tousled Theo's hair, a thick mop of chestnut, and put the boy in a careful headlock. Theo giggled and became red-faced, wrapped his arms around Javier's sturdy, sinewy midsection. Javier shoved him to the floor, causing the boy to wheeze. Theo regained himself and stood, beating the dirt from his knees.

"Were you mad at me when you found out that I had been lying to you?" asked Theo. "Back when I was in New York, I mean."

"Nah. I'm a recovering young person," said Javier. "So, I got it."

Theo affected a goofy expression, thought up a clever retort. "I'm an ailing old person, so I didn't expect you to."

Javier gathered their gear and began walking back to the house. "Always with the quick comebacks."

Theo smiled and followed him, watching the super-heroic outline of his frame shift and flex. A Spanish Super-man. A Mediterranean god. Even the bulls abided.

"But if you ever lie to me again, little man, I'll cut your balls off."

Theo blushed but his heart thrummed to an awakened rhythm.

III

Risk is sixteen and in a wrestling singlet. His teenage genitalia under the elastic red fabric as apparent as an adult in matador pants. Always exhibiting manhood for proof of authenticity. Locking arms with the other boy, equally stout and sturdy with big eyes and oversized feet, veins pumping, sweat buds forming, and palms whitening against inner thighs and around stolid necks. Powdered fingers thrusting into groins and eyes, cheap shots for victorious postures. Entangled athletes grappling, pinning, chest thumping. Dominance and submission. And the nausea that would precede and follow the tournaments would follow him into adulthood, to Spain, into the ring. What was weird to him as a boy would become seductive as a man.

The weight and musk of Javier's sweat-dappled body snapped Risk back into the present. Despite his three-month old injury, Risk was proving a difficult opponent to pin. Javier tackled him into the couch, across the floor in flailing, squirming impatience, and through the screen door that led onto the backyard. Lorna grabbed her hair and grimaced.

"How old are you two?! Roughhousing like a pair of schoolboys!"

Risk threw back his head and laughed so hard the big veins in his neck popped. Javier laughed so hard that a string of spit slipped from his mouth and found itself on Risk's forehead.

"Vile savage! He spat on me!"

Risk pushed Javier off his torso with ardent, though jocular, force and wiped away his opponent's drool with the back of his hand.

The men couldn't have been more different in their pasts. Their experiences were shapers of persona and engineers of strength, as all rich and variegated backgrounds tended to be. The only thing they had in common was their unconventional and late entry into the community of bullfighters. A blood sport that had fallen out of social and political favor in Spain but persisted because there were enough affluent influencers who were determined to keep traditions alive.

Javier was comfortable with the label of bisexual from an early age, only twelve. He was fourteen when he had been put out of the house by his father for stashing French gray porn. Massimo was a Sicilian originally from a small farming town just outside Taormina who'd always abhorred the mincing cosmopolitans from the great coastal city. Massimo had moved to Madrid at sixteen to pursue work in labor and organized crime. He had found the orientation as despicable in his son as he had in the dancers and flight attendants who passed through his village on weekend holidays. Had he been fully gay, thought Javier, what penalty would he have suffered? Murder? And so, without a college degree and with a thirst for male bodies, he dove headfirst into the queer scenes of Madrid, Barcelona, Rome, and eventually Paris, raising hell in the snootiest of circles. He met and partied with the intelligentsia, deflecting their superior criticisms with an ease that made him seem impermeable, and he owned all the trendiest clubs in every city he conquered. Achieving a level of access and notoriety that few could imagine, as his facility with charisma and charm were things of gruesome grace.

He would play with scholars, actors, writers, doctors, and politicians with a quiet scorn. Each older gay man of some prominence would suffer the sins of Javier's father. Especially the closeted ones, who would be lured and baited, seduced and rejected.

Though Javier had flirted with homelessness and short careers as a stripper, go go dancer, prostitute, and opera usher, he knew that these episodes wouldn't last more than a few years, for by the time he turned twenty he had accumulated enough of a back story to put his loose and lascivious lifestyle to bed, retire his subterranean celebrity. Embrace a true man's character.

Before he returned home, Javier took a studio apartment in Madrid and apprenticed himself to the city's finest bullfighters, learning in a matter of a few months enough of their tricks to earn entry into a school of some distinction. Admission into the program provided sufficient confidence to face his father again, who welcomed his son back with a distrustful reservation. Being a matador was a working-class honor, a blue-collar privilege. It wouldn't make anyone rich, but it was sufficiently macho to win approval from the boys in the schoolyard, the men on the barstools, and the fans in the stadium. And it afforded an adequate living. Enough for Javier to buy a modest home and fill it with the big game he hunted in South Africa and North America, where he'd spent years enhancing the English he'd learned as a boy by watching American and British tv shows and movies. His English was tinged with a mild Midwestern accent.

Unlike Javier, Risk had lived a safer life, in every sense. He had attended a good boarding school, won plaudits in a respectable college, and introduced fresh theses in a noted graduate school, taking his MBA with honors from Wharton. His career in finance had begun while still in college when he started interning at an investment banking firm on Wall Street, a company that would offer him a position a week after graduation from business school. The acceleration had been unfathomable. He had outsold and out-earned even his superiors. And after fifteen short years found retirement at forty-two. His savings would last for half a century. His investments would provide for at least three generations, not that he banked on Theo ever actually having children.

Finance upheld an effete sort of masculinity. Risk realized it had not allowed him to get his hands dirty enough. It was as predatory as bull fighting, but far too antiseptic and not at all corporeal.

His partial paralysis, manifesting as a mere limp and impotence, was the first time he had been rendered less than unbreakable. The damage would be permanent. His gait would be no longer sturdy. And his posture would remain crooked. All his careers would find finality. His confidence would slowly wither.

"You two lunatics broke the screen door," said Lorna.

[154]

Javier helped Risk to his feet and smirked bashfully with high, inverted eyebrows. "I'll fix it, Lorna!"

Theo, his shopworn gunmetal gray sweater fraying at the sleeves and neck, appeared with tousled hair and a blush. Risk always assumed he was locked away in his bedroom masturbating, which would explain his near-constant rosy hue.

"You guys are weirdos." His tone was so flat and droll that the words spilled in an unintelligible mumble.

Lorna nodded and crossed her arms. "Your father and Javier, are, Theo, yes."

The knock at the door sent a chill down Risk's back. "The interview! I'd completely forgotten!"

"Fuck!" Lorna gasped. "That's today?"

Javier worked diligently and adeptly at refastening the screen door as Risk limped into the kitchen, grabbed a paper towel, and wiped away the remainder of the Spaniard's spit from his forehead and hand. Lorna gave herself a once-over in the mirror hanging over their fireplace and turned back to the men, who were in the process of ironing out their wrinkled shirts and mussed hair.

Lorna frowned crookedly. "I guess this is as ready as we'll be for her."

Risk shrugged, and Javier tucked in his shirt. Theo rolled his eyes and retreated to his bedroom, a sanctuary from adult apprehensions.

Lorna greeted the journalist at the door. A tall woman with expensive platinum hair and a singsong English accent. Her name was Lois Dealey, a freelance reporter for the *Times of London* who had flown to Spain for an interview with the famous and inscrutable American matador, his wife, and their close friend, the rival, the would-be favorite native son of bullfighting.

"You both have such unusual stories," said Lois.

"Mine is only unusual because I got a late start," began Javier, reaching past Lorna and smacking Risk on the shoulder, "but this guy, he started even later than me—by over two decades!—and came from another country. Another continent!"

Lois glanced at her notepad on her lap. "Yes, so, the average age for a matador to begin his career is around fourteen, is that right?"

Javier's eyes shone. "Fourteen, even thirteen!"

"And you began making your way at twenty?"

"Yes, ma'am."

"Still young, though it must have been awkward."

Javier's sideways smirk forced his left eye to squint, revealing the deep, cherished crow's feet. "To compete with children?"

"Well."

"I didn't compete with children. I *trained* with them. They had me in the ring years ahead of the boys whose balls had only barely dropped."

Lorna's eyes bugged. Her embarrassed silent scorn helped to mitigate Lois's unease at Javier's vulgarity. The platinum reporter smiled at the red-headed wife. Lorna touched Risk's thigh. The living room suddenly felt smaller, warmer.

Lois turned her smile to Risk. "Your ascension was certainly unorthodox, Mr. Bonaventura."

"That's what everyone keeps telling me." Risk grinned with faux humility. "No, in all seriousness, I appreciate that it was unorthodox. And that Madrid welcomed me anyway."

"Some say you bought your way into the sport." Lois spoke carefully, but with confidence. "Is there any merit to those claims?"

Risk assumed the expression of a mass murderer, and for a moment Lois thought she might become his latest victim. The American fighter spoke slowly and with an emphasis on every precious word.

"It was sheer will and natural talent that permitted such a meteoric rise in such an alien sport."

More like sheer will and *copious money*, thought Lorna as she smiled at Lois, who nodded and wrote.

Risk snickered. Lorna cleared her throat and looked down. Javier bit his lip and kneaded his thick thigh.

Lois closed her notebook and leaned in. "And they all embraced you."

Risk shrugged. His faux modesty was ham-fisted, and Lois chuckled at it.

"In our email exchange you mentioned that you also started a network of charter schools in New York and gave yourself a job as a history teacher."

"I was a highly effective educator. So affirming, touching those kids. Developing them." Risk's voice weakened when he gestured at his wife. "Lorna is a teacher, too."

Lois's eyes emitted a new, furious light. "That's right, Ms. Bonaventura. You left your career as an academic at Merriweather, even amid the scandal ... to live here with Risk while he pursued this fantasy."

Lorna smiled at the indelicate phrasing of Lois's statement. She was surprised and maybe even flattered that Lois had heard about it, the coverage being so paltry, after all, in comparison to the widespread attention other videos of its type had received. "I did, yeah."

"Have you had trouble finding work here because of it?"

"I haven't begun looking yet."

Javier and Lorna found each other. Their brief, muted connection almost announced a scheme.

"But your leaving ..." Lois looked at her notes, touched her chin. "It's curiously reactionary to the climate of today's sexual politics, no?"

"How do you mean?" Lorna picked at her earring. It weighed on her.

Lois's snark was delivered in her signature singsong tone. "I suppose nowadays there's a tacit expectation that the man will forgo his career or dreams to support those of his wife. But given your writings and lectures, I suppose it's *in-line* with your philosophy?"

Lorna turned to Risk whose smirk rippled with a bridled sneer.

"Speaking of history, I come from a long line of royals," began Javier, causing Lois to finally take the close heed he expected of her earlier in the discussion. "My great-great-grandmother was Mercedes de las Mercedes of

Orleans. Her husband, my great-great-grandfather was Alfonso the Twelfth. His mother, my great-great-great paternal grandmother, that is, was Isabella the Second. *The* Isabella the Second. Going farther back, all the way back, in fact, there was Carlos Antonio Pascual Francisco Javier Juan Nepomuceno Jose Januario Serafin Diego, that is, Charles the Fourth, and he was from Naples. So, yes, I have, like many Spaniards, a fair amount of Italian blood. I mean, my father is totally, completely Sicilian! There is also the very infamous Isabella the First of Castile and Ferdinand the Second of Aragon, of course. They are in the bloodline, as well. There'd be no United States, we all know, if not for their subsidized voyage. For better or for worse." Javier's wink was clumsy in its staged largeness.

Lois's grasp on history was firmer than Risk's, but not by much. It all sounded impressive and plausible. Lorna, though, being a student and scholar of things that happened long ago and their attendant mythologies, knew intuitively that the genetic connections were questionable.

Javier cleared his throat, stood up, and excused himself. Lorna watched him go with a quiet anxiety. Risk studied Lois's bare legs. Like Lorna's, but longer.

In the bathroom, Javier watched his reflection darken. He thought about his childhood summers in Malaga. His winters in Segovia. The tournaments with his father and brothers in Madrid. Their taunts when he failed at anything athletic, anything manly. He had grown up a delicate thinker and they despised him for it. When he finally pursued bull fighting at twenty (a full decade after most, as Lois had pointed out) and excelled at it, the men in his family provided him a place within their fold. Access to a fraternity earned through sweat and blood and muscle and achievement. Violent achievement. It was initially a sense of castration he felt when The American, a slapstick usurper, a sensationalist carpetbagger, appeared and took top rankings by sheer, dumb luck in a sport that was not his. An art that he would forge. Now the envy, the threat, was mixed with a quiet awe. Lois popped back into his head. *Bitch, who are you?!*

Then the incident three months ago. His friend's flaccid figure tumbled through space. The bull kicked back and forth, making its angry victory sound. And by the time it was ready to return for another engagement, the picadors were on top of it, sticking lances into its throat and chest, bringing it down before it met again with The American, whose punctured body twitched in the dirt four yards away. *Incompetent fighter, but what passion!*

Javier suffered from a glut of passion. He was made of passion. Passion for Risk, passion for Lorna, passion for Theo, passion for bulls, passion for fighting, passion for killing. Sometimes the passion was too great, and he was outmuscled by it. In such moments he would have to regulate his desires by introducing pain. Like a kettle letting off steam or a borderline letting out blood.

The Spaniard punched himself twice in the stomach and once in the balls. He buckled and wheezed, but at least managed to calm down. It was a reliable method he'd used since he was thirteen. And it left no visible marks, thereby proving itself a sustainable tranquilizer. Outside the door Theo listened to the strange sounds of knuckle beating hard and soft meat and cringed, though on the inside he relished the dysfunction with a smile.

By the time Javier returned to the living room, Lois was saying goodbye to Risk and Lorna.

Javier touched his stomach, feeling a bruise forming already. "Leaving so soon?"

"Yes, Mr. Forza," said Lois, guarding her breasts with the notepad. "Early deadline. I need to type up my notes and spend the night editing. You know how it goes."

Javier nodded with a smirk that questioned. "Not really."

"The life of a freelance journalist. We never sleep."

"Requires stamina." Javier pursed his lips as if to blow a kiss.

Lois turned quickly toward Lorna and shook her hand as she was led to the front door. She had already shaken Risk's. Javier's would be left untouched.

[159]

"Uptight bitch," muttered Javier.

Risk turned to him with a frown that suggested he'd inhaled a foul stench. "She's a professional, Javier."

"*Professional* bitch."

Lorna shook her head as she moved into the kitchen to begin prepping dinner. The meat was defrosting on the counter, but a bucket of peppers and onions required chopping. Risk hobbled across the living room to a chair closest to Javier, who stood with his back to him, staring out the oblong-shaped window beside the front door.

"You're just sore because she changed the focus to me when you got obscene."

Javier picked at the thin strips of wood splintering off the doorframe. "I said nothing obscene."

"You talked about boys' balls dropping."

"To make a point!"

"It was unseemly, Javier. She's a journalist. Not your buddy at the pub."

"Whatever. She's a phony, like all women are phonies."

"Careful, Lorna is within earshot."

Javier turned to Risk. Thought about tackling him again. Or perhaps lifting him off his chair, hoisting him over his head. Though Risk, at six-foot-one, exceeded Javier's height by eight full inches, the Spaniard had the sturdier, stronger body, and an advantageous center of gravity. Javier shrugged.

"They're all the same, my friend. None can be trusted."

Risk's scowl was devoid of anger. More an expression of confusion. "What's on your mind, man?"

"Why not ask your wife?"

Risk gritted his teeth. "About what?"

A chaotic crash and sloppy series of thuds bellowed from the kitchen. There followed a string of expletives. The bucket of onions and peppers had fallen off the counter and Lorna cursed them. Javier and Risk hurried to the threshold in time to see Lorna urgently refilling the basket. She was winded and red-faced. Javier knew she had heard their conversation.

I V

Lorna saw Javier out. She kissed him on either cheek, as was the custom in his country. He waved again to Risk, who staggered in the background, tipsy on too many glasses of red wine.

The American slurred his Spanish. "Adios, amigo!"

Javier nodded. By the time his eyes cut back to Lorna, she was staring down at the ornate, patina doorknob, waiting for her guest to finally leave.

"Buenos noches, Senora Bonaventura." His Spanish was sharp and slick, even drunk as he was. "Frente su marido."

Lorna did indeed face her husband, but not until her friend had left.

The Grenache had already begun to give Lorna a headache and she knew she wouldn't sleep soundly. "Looks like we might have overdone it tonight."

Risk belched, staggered some more, and limped to the couch, where he fell limply into the oversized European pillows that Lorna had picked out when they first moved to Spain all those years ago. Stitched by an elderly woman who lived down the road from their first, interim apartment in Madrid, the pillows meant something to Lorna, who had insisted on paying four times the asking price for them.

Lorna took off Risk's shoes and began to rub his feet. He smiled and stretched into a long and obnoxious yawn. She thought about Javier, what she had heard. And her mouth became hot and dry. Risk had been good enough not to bring it up during dinner. Javier had been smart enough to introduce multiple new subjects throughout the evening to keep the focus elsewhere. Theo had been good enough to sulk demonstratively enough to provide adequate diversion. The white elephant in the room changed shape and color. It had become a red bull. The shape of a single-focus animal. The

[162]

color of blood and wrath.

"What did that fool mean?" Risk's eyes were shut.

"What?" Lorna's tongue grew thick. "I don't get it."

"Before dinner, when we were out here."

"I have no idea. I was in the kitchen. How could I have heard what you were talking about?"

Risk's sigh sounded more like an irritated grumble. "After he called that reporter a bitch. He said all women were untrustworthy. And then he said I should ask you about that."

Lorna held Risk's feet close to her gut, almost hugging them.

"Javier is a chauvinist. You know. He says things."

"Uh-huh. Right. He does. Usually when he's drunk. But we hadn't been drinking, yet."

Lorna squeezed Risk's toes. He winced in frustration, never pain. She could feel her husband scrutinize her blank expression, searching it for a clue, an admission.

"Well, those dishes aren't going to wash themselves," she said, and proceeded to lift Risk's legs to free herself of his heft. Though he could only fully exercise the might of one limb, Risk kept Lorna pinned to the couch, to the over-paid-for European pillows. She turned to him. The blank expression was gone. In its place was a stare that meant this business wasn't amusing and warranted anger.

"What are you doing?"

Risk bugged his eyes and cocked his head. "What are *you* doing?"

"I'm trying to clean up the mess we all made this evening."

Risk snort-laughed and then abruptly stopped. "So am I."

Lorna exhaled and pushed the big, weighty feet away from her. The lame leg drooped limply and the good one relented, reluctantly permitting the prisoner freedom.

Risk spilled off the sofa and crawled toward his wife, who was in the kitchen and at the sink scrubbing dishes by the time he made it to the threshold. He used the frame to rise. Once he was on his feet he leaned and gazed with a pasty, sweaty mask-like glower.

"Are you sleeping with that conquistador because my dick is broken?"

Lorna gasped. An actual gasp. Risk found it a comedic affectation. Like something she'd rehearsed. And he laughed at her. She still hadn't turned around to face him when she brought the china that she was rinsing down to the lip of the sink hard enough to chip it.

"What is wrong with you tonight?"

"Tonight? Or for the past three months since that fucking bull turned me into a limp-dicked gimp?"

Lorna turned with a face that had become a mass of wrinkles, teeth, and bloodshot eyes.

"I don't like this!"

"What did that fucking envious cocksucker mean? *Ask your wife?*"

"You *let* that bull gore you! You just stood there and let it happen."

"I had that fucking beast in my sights! It wasn't going to ever get me!" Risk wiped his mouth and nodded. "But then you and that fucking conquistador distracted me! You and he should have been at the receiving end of the bull's horn!"

Lorna tried not to cry, and the more she tried the more she cried. She flung the dishtowel at her husband and beat his chest. He barely registered the blows. And with one hand he took her wrist and twirled her across the kitchen into the cedarwood island.

"We could dance all night, darling."

Her hands ironed bunched fabric and wiped away tears and snot. Lorna gathered herself. "I told him that I was staying with you out of pity, Risk."

"Dear God." Risk's color vanished. He was a ghost. "That's even worse than if you'd fucked him!"

"Theo will hear us!" Lorna's whisper was heavy and freighted with fear. A hiss wet with venom.

"He already knows how fucked up his parents are!"

Lorna swallowed the rest of her tears. "I don't understand why you did what you did, but what's happened to you is awful and I would never leave you because of it."

"So, let me see if I got this right, you *choose* to suffer? To stay with a man with a broken cock and a funny gait, so that you can play the martyr? Saint Lorna! And that's supposed to make me feel, what? Better? I should be grateful? And you tell that rotten, hateful Iberian—"

"Who else could I talk to about it? You're so goddamned arrogant and entitled! *So arrogant.* Like some fucking— ! Damn it ... It's just ... I have to always spare you, your fragile ego."

And then Lorna gasped. Shocked by her own words. Troubled by them.

Risk flinched, shook his head. Like a remediated child confused by a simple arithmetic problem. He thought for a moment about Javier, and about his own chaotic mix of competing needs. Hearing Lorna confess her compassion and misgivings unbuckled a safety belt that had kept him fastened to a seat of a car careening toward a concrete wall. And then an indecorous truth occurred to him. A deranged fantasy that he would never say out loud. To hear it would be too humiliating. His problem was that he desired a man. Not just a man to hold and love and exchange pleasures with. That would be too simple. And it wasn't even a problem that he pined for a man to dominate him, to act as the alpha to his omega, to make him feel inferior, and to turn him into an un-manned slave. The problem was that he also resisted such a wish. Resisted the tug toward submission and worship, deference and supplication to a superior. Risk's impossible dilemma found itself squarely between the drive to be broken and the demand to stay fully formed. After all, his being contained a glory and a defeat, an invincibility and a failure. He built a fortune in record time, assumed the role of an ordinary man, a schoolteacher, erected a community of schools, and conquered a foreign game, but he was also now lame and impotent. A superman castrated.

Risk winced as though gut punched. "Do you know about his family? Who they are? What they can do? Or his fans? Their derangement. How much they hate me! How dangerous this all is for me!"

Risk's stomach dropped when Lorna touched his shoulder. The vomit was maroon, scolding, and ejaculated in a hard, messy stream. Most of it hit the floor, but a fair amount also splattered on Lorna's mustard dress from Florence. She screamed and stumbled backward into the cedarwood island, once again. Risk gripped his gut and dropped to one knee, the good one. As Lorna watched in disbelief and disgust, her face a crisscross of sharp eyebrows, deep frown lines, and twitching, snarling lips, Risk endeavored to stand again and walk, but on his first step his heel hit the puddle of vomit, and he slid, caught himself, and then slid again, careering headlong into the cupboard above the sink. He lay on the floor with a bloodied nose and fluttering eyes. Lorna was at his side and tugging on his collar before he settled into his new slump.

"Jesus Christ, Risk!"

Theo had been at the threshold witnessing his parent's baroque theater for the past few minutes, long enough to have ascertained the gist of their performances.

"Fucking gross, guys."

Lorna gasped and turned to her son. His expression confused, a quietly perverse thrill. She was oddly relieved to know that Theo was cynical and "unconventional" enough to withstand such displays of hysterics with minimal damage. Or minimal *additional* damage. Theo shook his head and returned to his room. Pornography, colored pencils, and footage of mocked strangers awaited.

Risk's expression bordered on daffy. "What just happened?"

"You got drunk, had a fit, puked all over the floor, slipped on the damn vomit, and smashed your face. That's what *just happened!*"

Risk shook away the cobwebs and touched his nose. He examined the blood on his fingertips, let his head fall back, resting it against the counter, and gazed sadly at his wife.

"Do you have any idea what you've done?" he asked Lorna.

Lorna slouched, her shoulders folding over her breasts. "I haven't done anything, Risk."

Risk nodded at her as though she were his child and had just told a lie. "You have, though. You've violated something sacred. A trust. You've compromised me. In front of *him!*"

"I haven't done anything wrong, Risk! Javier is a friend. To us both."

"He is a rival." Risk bared red teeth. "And what you've done. You may as well have slept with him because *this* is worse."

"Please, be reasonable. It was words. Only words. Of concern, and about you. And *us.*"

Risk's eyes became as flat as his voice. "Words do the most harm, Lorna. Please get out."

"Get out?" Lorna hugged herself and stood up. "Of our home?"

Lorna worked toward symmetry. Structure and clarity contended with formlessness and ambiguity. She was a creature of logic but also of intuition, at constant odds with rational mindfulness, undergirded by calculations and strategies, and an ardently artistic soul, shot through with acidic recriminations and scorned betrayals.

"*My* home. You're not here anymore. Go stay with him for all I care. Or fuck off back to America. Back to Merriweather. I'll take care of our son."

Lorna turned and waited. Taking stock was in order. What she had put up with. For him. What she had accepted. On his behalf. What she had given up. In honor of *him*. The study of the worship of men. Everything felt dreamlike, and she spun. She walked slowly out of the kitchen. Risk could hear her crying as she packed a suitcase in the bedroom across the living room. She blew her nose and filled a smaller bag full of toiletries. He could hear this, too. She closed the front door behind her but did not lock it. Risk would have to do that himself, as well as soak up his own vomit. In fact, he would be doing everything for himself from here on out.

[167]

V

Lorna hadn't left that night. She had packed her things and walked out of the house, making sure to slam the door as she did. This had all been for effect, though. She'd returned after twenty minutes. Standing outside in the front yard, staring up at the moon and contemplating her next move, proved a tedious production. Risk had been busy cleaning his vomit off the floor and rinsing the dishes.

That next morning, Risk had attempted to pretend the whole incident hadn't occurred or if it had it couldn't possibly have been his fault. It was the alcohol. It was the pain in his hip. It was the painkillers. It was Javier's provocations. It was his sleeplessness. Lorna wasn't one for prolonged confrontations, so she had been civil, even contrite, in her way. But there was a palpable distance that grew throughout the day, if not outright stonewalling.

Theo milled about, editing his videos, drawing his pictures, doing homework. He was always busy doing something productive. Prancing, rifling, sighing, theatrically demonstrating the rigors of coming up with ostentatious new enterprises.

Lorna started to miss New York. All the typical New York nights out with lovely people. Gay jokes and beautiful women. Musical theater folk from places like Asheville, Memphis, and Kansas City with deep narratives about finding their place in the world and using myriad self-help—or, self-*improvement*—manuals as guides.

She had kept her luggage, still packed and ready to go, in the closet, and wrote at her "desk," the teakwood dining room table. What had originally begun as an essay morphed into a short story, a satiric think piece that she'd send to *Playboy* or maybe *Harpers*. They'd like the sort of thing she was outlining, a parable about a frustrated middle-aged man whose social media profile—so different from his real-life persona, so much happier and more successful and more interesting—comes alive and escapes the confines of tweets and posts and status updates and announces itself to the tangible world. The social media creation tortures the actual man, the dull fibber, by living its best life out in front of him, dangling what could have been, had he been bolder and braver to seize such a life for himself. Though Theo was the one more in tune with the avatars of cyberspace, it was Risk who provided the inspiration for this one.

"I thought maybe we could go out for dinner tonight," said Risk as he rubbed Lorna's shoulders from behind, not stopping even after she pulled away and cringed. The offensive obliviousness rankled.

"I'm working."

"Okay, good. I'm glad you are, again."

Lorna would make her protagonist an investment banker who by all accounts seemed victorious in his life but who had merely achieved someone else's forced version of conventional victory. Her sad, ridiculous husband had been that type of hero, someone who seemed to find a roadmap outlined by another traveler, some imaginary cartographer of material gains and shallow renown. He followed the criteria set by derivative teachers; mentors and role models who themselves had no idea about signposts and detours, who could only encourage in their misguided tutelage to go one way, setting sights on only one direction, simply desiring one destination.

It wasn't just people like Risk who misled. She often thought about who she was versus how she was perceived. The image that one held of her in their mind and how precise it had been. The impossible task of changing perceptions, of permitting portal into one's subconscious to show ineffable but honest portrayals. All the students and colleagues and administrators and journalists who had judged her for something she'd said. Those people and their limitations would come to regret their reactions.

Risk was watching an old movie, something from the early 80s. Lorna half-paid attention to it. Some comedy with Bill Murray. She had trouble focusing on the plot and dialogue but instead found herself fixated on the actors' teeth and then their skin. Yellow, pockmarked. The advancements in HD technology and photoshopping were only partly to credit for their beautification of celebrities. Cosmetics, health care. Lorna thought, we've never been more beauty- and appearance- and age- obsessed than we are now. And never as old and ugly.

Theo was whining about corporate sellouts as he paraded a new series of embarrassing drawings around the house. Ever since she and Risk had happened upon his stash of cartoon erotica, the boy had become emboldened to show them every sordid sketch, no matter the quality.

Theo held up a drawing of giant penises intermingling with modernist architecture, as though the penises were buildings, too. "Look, mom, a new one. It's all about how big companies make profit—"

"Give me a break, Theo. Just let me work."

Theo's eyes conveyed hidden wounds. This hadn't been the first time his mother had dismissed him, and it wouldn't be the last. He knew enough about her philosophical positions on conventional gender roles through her books and lectures and the scandal, but she was also an intelligent, educated woman and his mother. He retreated with his phalluses and skylines. Lorna watched his effeminate gait as he shuffled his lithe carriage back to his bedroom. She couldn't help but to sneer, though secretly she admired the artwork. The masculine drive to plant a seed and watch it grow was the very basis of architecture itself.

Risk turned to her from the couch. "He needs encouragement, honey."

"After what he did? The last thing we ought to do is encourage that sort of work."

"That's surprising."

"What is?"

"You not approving of renegade behavior. Having a problem with that *sort of work*. I mean, it's art. I thought you supported all forms of—"

Despite the growing seed, despite the masculine drive, despite the phallic glory of steel erections, the art was queer, and Theo had already made a mess of his life and identity and of theirs with queered art.

"It's *not* art."

"That's harsh."

Theo had been on her nipple for too long, until he was almost three, and cried too much, until he was four, denying her and Risk adequate sleep. He tormented them with delayed toilet training, leaked stool, and bedwetting. A too-sensitive child. The burden.

Lorna had tried to take care with the words. "He's just a little … still forming … and he needs direction from us."

"Right." Risk resumed watching his old movie with actors with bad teeth and skin.

Lorna looked up from her laptop and stared at the back of her husband's head. The dining room table was positioned behind the sofa. Risk had never really wanted a wife and child. He only took them as accessories to bolster his brand. She wondered what it must feel like for him, how hellish his days must be, limping around, ruined, watching mediocre movies, knowing on some hidden level that his wife and son did not love him. That they were using him for security. Poor, stupid Risk. He must have so desperately wanted to believe that he was loved, that his wife was devoted, and that he was safe. He would fight and kill and be humiliated for her, and maybe for his boy. But neither she nor their son would ever reciprocate the sentiments.

She watched Theo from the threshold into his bedroom, a place of comic books, drawing pads, homoerotic cartoon characters doing unspeakable things to each other, nests of wires and gadgets and old cell phones and laptops, walls of rapidly outdated video game systems, classic comic book, superhero, and horror Funko Pop figurines, caringly framed posters of the drag queens, Adore Delano, Sharon Needles, and Lady Bunny, vintage board games, and all the stuff he'd held onto from childhood. He was the child of a nationally vilified cultural studies professor and stunted investment banker living out boyhood fantasies, after all. Lorna should appreciate that much, Theo always thought to himself that he might be a sissy, but at least he was interesting.

His back to her, he intermittently drew naked male cartoon characters mingling with chaos and edited together camera-phone footage of strangers enduring disaster on his computer. Lorna attributed his creative multitasking to a nervous mania. Or a megalomaniacal neurosis. Sissies worked harder than anyone else. A kind of angry, scared sublimation.

She cleared her throat. "Didn't you want to show me something?"

Theo turned with a perturbed gasp. He didn't like being surprised, or as he saw it, *snuck up on.*

"Forget it, mom."

Lorna glanced at Theo's work, a messy mound of drawing paper strewn across his desk and floor. Figures twisted in repose and penance, unapologetic in their sin, sodomizing and surrendering, swallowing and singing. It was Dante and Goethe. Virgil and Homer. She at least felt a twinge of relief that her son had a sense of myth and history, that his acumen could extend that far back. Unlike all the other children of his generation who knew nothing beyond today and couldn't care less about events that hadn't occurred on their watch, along their timeline. Her new story would reclaim the 21st century. It would hold a mirror up to the faces of all who commodified and mass marketed *it*, that undefinable thing that seemed to possess all who succumbed so fully, breeding apathy through diversion and self-satisfaction. The Internet did this, rendered art, history, knowledge, and fame inconsequential, and thereby unimpressive. It ghettoized the rarified. This moment only ... or the abyss.

She nodded and left Theo's room, but not before covertly snatching from Theo's dresser an old plastic figurine of Yoda, a gift Risk had given him when he was seven, something from her husband's own *Star Wars*-fetishized youth. Lorna thought about Fiona, her West Highland Terrier, her plush teddy-bear white fur and blue bow, fondling her and loving her as she never could Theo.

In the kitchen, where she spied on Risk as he ate an egg salad sandwich, Lorna pocketed off the refrigerator a ceramic magnet from Casablanca, an item she'd bought as a gag when she and Risk had vacationed there a summer ago. The outline of a Dromedary camel set against a sand dune and sunset.

Her husband ate quickly, burped occasionally. She studied his gorilla-like mannerisms, his heavy nose-breathing, open-mouth chewing, hunched shoulders. It sickened her, and she thought of the hero of her new story. It would be as though the disingenuous, posing character bore the brunt of the transgressions of so many, those who lived life carelessly, selfishly, egotistically, hedonistically. Falsely. As though their days were meant to be spent dreaming, walking in a fantasy of their own making, relishing the construction of their own singular reality, without regard for others or for consequences. The social media branded persona would be the penalty, worked through by God or the universe. Doling out a cosmic consequence. Designed to teach lessons.

"Should we try talking about last night?"

Risk gasped and shuddered. He too was easily spooked. "I thought we already decided that it wasn't worth talking about. It was like … a weird combination of the painkillers and wine."

"Okay, but it was worse than anything you've—"

"Lorna. Don't keep pushing it. You push and push and push, and then I become like an animal, and then I'm the bad guy. It's like entrapment!"

Lorna pursed her bottom lip and nodded, agreeing to nothing. "Uh huh. Uh huh, right." And then she drifted ghostlike into the living room where she collected a small canvas oil painting of herself and Risk in Alexandria rendered five years ago. It was no larger than a greeting card, no thicker than a paperback novel, and was propped against a clay lamp on an end table.

Would he even miss it?

She'd felt as though her marriage had been a furloughed career. She put in the work but never felt compensated. She wished she could send in a proxy to do the heavy lifting, clock the hours.

Her reduction was criminal, and this life was the culprit. She couldn't fully blame Risk as she'd been complicit in his felony, abducting a once-promising academic from a career that was conflagrating. It had been one thing to support him in his athletic, masculinist endeavors, basking in a spotlight, and wiping away blood, but the new arrangement of playing nursemaid, imprisoned by pity, bound by obligation, stretched the parameters of reason. The nonsensical despair of duty. It was unfair to expect so much.

Lorna reviewed the reproductions of Artemisia Gentileschi's strident women taking no nonsense from bullying men. The ones she would share with her students at Merriweather. She had always seen herself in the paintings. She was Judith, cutting the throat of the Assyrian warlord, Holofernes. She was Susannah, shoving away the elders. She was Salome, grinning at the head of Saint John the Baptist. She was Jael, about to drive the spike through Sisera's skull. She was Boudica, rallying the Britons against Rome. And she imagined cutting throats of a condemnatory media bent on sensation. Shoving away needy students. Grinning at decapitated heads of colleagues. Driving spikes through the skulls of her son and husband. Lorna, like Gentileschi and her women, was strong but suffering, ready to exact gory, virile vengeance.

In the bedroom Lorna stole a pair of Risk's socks from his dresser drawer. Black with white dots. Well stitched. He only ever bought the best of everything. Exorbitant price-tags promised quality. Lorna's patience was furious, her educational excoriations methodical.

Lorna stuffed Theo's Yoda, the magnet from Casablanca, Risk's socks, and the portrait from Alexandria into her luggage, still in the closet, tucked away, and under a plumage of furs. She calculated her departure and timed it to Risk's doctor's appointment, a mere morning away.

During peer review of her journal articles, Lorna's colleagues at Merriweather would often criticize her tendency to write subjects as stereotypes. She'd argue that she'd been alive for too long and knew people too well; she was well-equipped to generalize and comfortable with cliché.

Amid that tumultuous period when the Social Justice Warriors wanted her head, Lorna would, against her better judgment, periodically check in on the Twitter storm and Facebook fusillade that broke out over that unfortunate YouTube video. She was good about not commenting, but she had screenshot some of the harsher criticisms. And sometimes when she was feeling low, she would revisit them. Lorna, in bed on her iPhone, found the three posts that had stuck longest, one from a college student in Chicago, a male, who had written about her sermon: "Do you really hate yourself that much?" Another, a female high school student in Tucson, called her out in a post: "I would kill myself if I had a mother like you!!!" Another, a law student from Philadelphia, provided advice: "Get help. You're sick. Fix yourself."

The culture was as much a misguided sham as her marriage and family. Leaving meant living, and what surprised her most was how little it troubled her to do so.

VI

Risk knocked on Javier's door hard and long enough to bruise at least two knuckles. By the time the Spaniard answered— after several, long, unhurried minutes—the American's right hand throbbed as ceaselessly as his pulverized pelvis and limp leg. Javier wore a bathrobe that hung open at the chest, showing off a bare, tawny torso. Risk braced himself. The early morning sun was heavy, and it weighed on him. He used a cane as his hip and leg were having a particularly bad day.

"Where is she?"

Javier scratched his crotch. "Who?"

"My wife, of course."

Javier scratched his head, rubbed sleep from his left eye. "Shouldn't she be at home?"

Risk looked at the tips of his Bruno Maglia lace-up loafers. "I threw ... I told her to leave. Two nights ago. That night we had you over for dinner. The day of the interview."

"And so, she just left?"

"I was at the doctor for a checkup yesterday and she just ... she just left. She'd cleaned out her closet. I haven't been able to reach her ..." Risk second-guessed himself about sharing so much about his family with Javier, but once he started talking, he couldn't stop. "She's not answering her cell. I barely slept last night. You know, Theo doesn't seem at all bothered by it. I think ... he's not really ... Look, she's done this sort of thing before. To punish us."

"Well, she didn't come here, and I—"

"Oh, no?" Risk's face was red, almost purple.

Javier hid a nervous smirk and studied Risk's crinkled brow as though it were an untamable thing. "No … And I haven't seen or heard from her since I left your house. Two nights ago. After dinner."

Risk gathered himself. He leaned against his cane, his head hung, and he silently lingered before Javier's threshold.

"Look, come in. Have a drink."

Though it wasn't even noon yet, Risk accepted Javier's invitation and entered the ranch-style house with an uneasy waddle. It was modest, perhaps small. Especially by Madrid standards. Contrary to popular thought and by dint of the sport's fading luster, bullfighters had become working class, and Javier's home signified such status. Despite all the followers and fans on his myriad social media accounts, Javier lived comfortably, but not with any degree of wealth. Inside, dead animals hung on walls or were spread out on the floor. Heads and pelts. The aftermath of mass murder. Risk had been to Javier's house several times before, but something about this visit made him take stock of the North American and South African deer heads mounted as trophies throughout.

Javier had told him during his last drop-in that the South African deer—the Duiker, the Kudu, the Oryx—boasted sleeker, thinner coats and more elaborate and elegant horns than their North American cousins. And the Wildebeest skull resting on the floor beside the grizzly fur and head appeared even in its skeletal form to be stronger and less clumsy than its counterpart to the west. There were also an assortment of stuffed cranes, egrets, and herons. Javier had explained the differences—in size, beaks, and feet—to Risk on numerous occasions, but the American never committed them to memory. Javier had done all the hunting and taxidermy work himself. Such skills made him proud. His father had been subsidizing all his hunting expeditions since he was twenty-nine, as the old man regarded it as an investment in his son's manhood.

Javier poured cognac. Risk looked into the black eyes of the oryx, a gemsbok.

Risk drank his cocktail, and Javier sat on a loveseat across from him, being sure to keep his legs open. It was clear that he wasn't wearing any underwear beneath his bathrobe and Risk quickly averted his eyes. He had already seen too much. Enough to make him feel instantly inappropriate. And insecure.

Javier's eyes followed Risk's discomfited shifts. "Where else do you think she might have gone?"

Risk thought about the countless times Lorna had compared him to Javier. Always unfavorably. Always with Risk coming up short. Ever the inferior. The gays and the gals celebrated Javier's singing voice, his dance moves, and his impossible stomach. The true men accepted him as a true man, someone who could discuss fishing, hunting, football, and carpentry.

"There's that bar downtown, near the stadium. Where all the matadors go. And their fans."

"I've seen her talking to Diego and Pedro. She's friendly with them and their wives. Maybe they might know something? I can ask my brother and father to start—"

Risk looked at his host. "Your family?"

Javier grinned unsurely and sipped his cognac. "Yeah. My family. They know a lot of people in the city. They can ask around."

What did the Spaniard's charisma matter to Risk? Others relished it, but he couldn't care less. Risk had accomplished a great deal in a short time. People admired him. Idolized him. And he never felt the pressure to perform for others, to curry their approval, their fandom. Though he received it, anyway, and it rankled Javier. During moments when he was gentle and generous with himself, Risk admitted that perhaps that was why Javier needed to show off so badly and win everyone's attention and praise at parties and in barrooms. These were embarrassing and petty concerns worthy of junior high school boys, not grown men. Adults were meant to outgrow such issues as low self-esteem and public perception. All the promised, unfulfilled glories.

Risk poured himself another glass of liquor and when he looked up from the bar, he saw in the hallway three stuffed giant birds, almost standing as sentries into the kitchen. He stared in a disgusted wonder at them.

Javier watched him with sinister amusement trying to puzzle them out. "The biggest and most surly one is an ostrich, from Africa. The emu, next to it, is its smaller, more refined cousin from Australia. And that little one is a Rhea. It's from South America, as grungy as its big African relative."

Risk's boyhood in Brooklyn Heights had been preppy and pedigreed. His father Jonas had run a profitable tutoring agency, his mother Sara was a medical director at a prestigious hospital in on the Upper East Side. They fought often and had loud, celebratory sex. Risk and his brother Roland, with whom he hadn't spoken in three years and who also worked in finance and lived in Tokyo with his wife and daughters, would cover their ears and make irreverent faces through the ordeal. The memory found its own reason to push its way through.

"She took a small painting of us." Risk whispered it to the kudu, but Javier heard.

Javier raised an eyebrow, cocked his head. "That's strange."

Risk swallowed the remainder of his drink and began walking toward the door. "Please let me know if you hear from her."

Javier smirked and shrugged. Risk caught the motion from the corner of his eye.

"What? What was that?"

Javier cleared his throat. "It's like I said the other night. There are things we don't always know about women. What motivates them. What they're thinking."

Risk grabbed the handle of the door and endeavored to double time his escape. The talk of women and their mysteries began to nauseate him. Especially when the talk was nonsense being espoused by a known lothario.

"Listen, Risk."

Risk stopped in the threshold, steadied himself on his cane.

Javier crossed his arms. "Does Lorna have her own credit or bank cards,

[179]

or are they all under your name?"

"No, they're all in our name. She withdraws from a shared account. Why?"

Javier put a warm palm to Risk's shoulder. "So, she's still using your credit card, then?"

"Yes."

Javier bowed his head, raised his eyebrows, and put on a soft pout. It was the face a father would make to his young son when counseling on a personal failing. Risk realized that he had left his own young son suddenly motherless.

"Maybe that's where you want to start. Perhaps she's about to begin leaving a breadcrumb trail for you."

Risk nodded and left, traveling down Javier's majestic path like a man old before his time, though navigating with his cane like a furtive warrior. Javier returned to his bar and poured himself another drink.

VII

The concierge at the Hotel Conquistador on the Gran Via said he remembered a tall redheaded American woman checking in, but not out. He said she had tipped both himself and the bellboy well and asked to hold all calls and not be disturbed. Maybe it was because he was focused on the mission of finding his wife, but Risk didn't need the cane that day and his gait was become incrementally steadier, sturdier. Risk nodded at the concierge and asked to see Lorna's room. The concierge, a young man with a showy mustache and a soft, lilting voice, waited for Risk to match his wife's generosity before doing so.

Lorna's room, 327, was empty. It appeared that she had left but didn't formally check out. Risk searched under the bed, in the drawers and closets, throughout the bathroom, and even behind the desk, TV stand, and armoire. The cleaning ladies who were currently in the next room had just finished straightening out Lorna's, and when Risk asked them if they had seen her at any time, they said that they had spoken with her only briefly soon after she had checked in when she asked for extra shampoo. They hadn't seen her since.

"I suppose she left without returning the key," said the concierge in measured English. "Which means that maybe she will come back."

"But all of her belongings are gone." Risk searched the room again, as though this repeated effort would suddenly turn up a clue or turn out differently. "Why would she take everything with her if she planned on coming back?"

"I don't know, Sir. You Americans have funny habits."

Risk's eyes cut to the young man who smiled sweetly, obviating Risk's impending sneer. He'd have to pay a small fee for the missing key.

In a fog and fatigued, Risk shuffled through the throngs of shoppers, commuters, tourists, and workers intermingling along the Gran Via. He wondered where Lorna had gone, if not why. The "why" was clear. He had been unreasonable and arrogant. Too proud, too righteous. He would have left, too.

As though she were beamed down from Heaven, a redheaded angel loitered in the distance. Her back was to him as she window-shopped artisanal Christmas ornaments. Risk hurried to her, elbowing and nudging his way through the crowd. Even with his limp, he was able to move faster than usual. The woman managed to make it two steps away from the display of holiday decorations before Risk grabbed her arm and spun her around. The woman yanked her arm away and hissed a string of pejoratives in Castilian at him before slapping him in the mouth. The incident had elicited the attention of onlookers, and two young men began moving in Risk's direction.

"I'm so sorry! Lo siento!" Risk turned and ran off, his aching hip occasioning an absurd stride, though it was the first time he'd been able to move that quickly since the incident with the bull.

"Te rompere las pelotas!" yelled one of the men. He and his cohort then tended to the woman who was left breathless.

It was the first time a stranger had threatened to smash his balls, thought Risk as he caught his breath several blocks away from the scene he had created. He felt foolish. Too old to be causing such problems in public.

He called the bank and asked for a freeze on the shared account. Lorna would have to return home if her ability to spend was cut off. It was a harsh tactic, but Risk had no better ideas. He feared that she had a separate, secret account, or perhaps stashed cash in the house. Still, how much could she have saved? How long would it last her? He would also have to pay regular and unannounced visits to Javier's house to make sure she hadn't come to him for sanctuary.

Risk was still frustrated that he hadn't thought to check the bank or credit card statements first. That it took Javier mentioning it bugged him. He cut himself some slack and reasoned that his head had been fuzzy these past few days and thinking clearly was the last thing he'd be able to manage.

It was wrong of him to have scorned Lorna for such a minor offense. An emotional misdemeanor, at most. What had she really done? Confided in a platonic friend concerns she was having about her marriage? All women did that. Though, the confiding was usually between girlfriends, not a man known for his sexual prowess and promiscuity. Still, he was brusque and sententious. His ego had done this. Distorted sympathy into pity. Twisted sacrifice into deceit. Corrupted friendship into betrayal. Risk believed that he had gotten what he deserved. And still he hesitated to call the police.

VIII

Risk stared at Javier, swallowed hard, and shook his head. The Spaniard had kept him lingering in his doorway and refused to explain his cryptic text, sent and received an hour earlier.

"Well … are you going to invite me in, at least? It's hot as Hell out here!"

"Yes." Javier looked back, over his shoulder and into his house. He had been awaiting a signal to proceed. "Come in, Risk."

Risk thought that Javier had sounded uncharacteristically congenial, even soft, possibly concerned. Javier opened his door and stepped aside to permit his guest entry. Amid the stuffed beasts that Javier and his father had slain abroad, sat Lorna in a pair of distressed jeans, a white blouse, her hair in a twist, little makeup, and barefoot. She had been drinking. Her martini glass was nearly empty, and her face was pink.

"Jesus Christ, Lorna. Where the fuck have you been?"

"Last night at The Conquistador, but you already knew that."

"Yeah, only because I had to track you down by following your credit card charges. What're you doing here? Why didn't you come home? Was this some sort of a lesson? Well, you've more than made your point, so, just, you know, come on home, now. Theo has been worried."

"I doubt that. And I'm not coming home."

Risk flinched as if slapped and took a clumsy step back. It would have been funny if it weren't so sad, thought Javier, knowing the gut punch that would come next.

Risk wiped his brow and turned to Javier with a menacing frown. "Why the fuck not?"

"I think I'm happier here … with Javier."

"Is that what this is, then? An affair? So, you *are* fucking him! You *did* lie to me! You *are* a tramp!"

Lorna rolled her eyes. "Don't be so self-righteous! *You* threw *me* out! And for nothing! And so now, yes, now I *am* fucking him! You expected the worst of me, so now I'm behaving the worst!"

Risk balled his fists without conscious intent. It was Javier who now took a step back and readied a defensive campaign with his powerful arms folded in front of him.

"I can't believe you took any of that seriously. *Seriously?!* I was drunk and I was in pain … I was exhausted, and my hip was acting up, so I was in pain!"

"You said that already."

Risk was red-faced. "Well, underline it!"

"I've made my entire career worshipping at the altar of machismo, finding something virtuous to write about and discuss—all bullshit, I suppose—about toxic masculinity, trying to find romance in men's boorish, brutish behavior!"

Risk had already walked over to Javier's bar and fixed himself a drink, a whiskey neat, downed it, and was in the process of pouring a second highball glass for himself.

An unexpected flash of tender mercy surprised Risk as much as anyone else as the words left his lips: "Don't do that. Don't knock yourself. You did good work there. It made you famous and brought in a lot of money for us. Just don't degrade yourself—"

"You don't understand." Lorna had to stop him before it got any sadder. "How do I articulate this? Despite all your embarrassing efforts, making a fortune at the firm, opening the schools, casting yourself as a history teacher in the ghetto, and then those *horrifying* videos of the team-building exercises that you put online—that business with Dominick Truman in New York. None of that made you the type of man I extolled in my writings or lectures. You were desperate and you failed, Risk. And you made a mess of our lives doing so."

[185]

Throughout her long, awful diatribe, Risk had filled and emptied his highball glass no fewer than three more times. Javier thought it would have been more efficient to just down the whole bottle and jettison the highball glass. His face too was now rosy and his stance uneven. He shuffled across the room and to the sofa, where Javier attempted to assist a soft landing, but Risk swatted him away with grunts and growls and drool.

"Get the fuck away from me, you wife-fucker!"

Javier raised his hands. *Mea culpa.* And stepped back, permitting his drunken houseguest to fumble for purchase and land inelegantly in a teak chair.

Lorna looked down and put a fist to her mouth as if to stop herself from laughing or crying. Maybe both. Probably both.

"And I've been a hypocrite, you see. But now, here in Madrid, and after all these years of doting on you and starting articles and essays that I'll never finish and never submit to magazines that don't want to hear from me anymore, I think I'm ready for a change. You helped me see that the other night. And Javier is who he says he is."

"Fuck you. Fuck you, bitch. Fuck you both. Fuck both you bitches."

Lorna could not verbalize what it was about Risk that left her wanting so much more.

"He doesn't hide, Risk," she said. "He isn't pretending…"

In his house of dead beasts, Javier began explaining to Risk that red male cardinals follow brown females to protect them.

"Fascinating." Risk's tone was performative in its drollness.

"And also, this." Javier paced with his hands clasped behind his back. Pomposity suited him surprisingly well, thought Lorna. "Whenever zoos put animals together, they avoid mixing the sexes to obviate the males competing for the female's affections. They also avoid fights over territory when introducing a new animal into an established environment by gradually joining them in a new, isolated, neutral space."

Risk wondered if that's what Javier was currently doing. If his lecture had been in the service of a relevant life lesson. It hadn't mattered, though. Not at this point.

Javier was expounding on his zoological acumen, when Risk was on his feet again and busily clawing at his belt and his button and his zipper and in seconds his dick was out and he swung it wildly at Lorna, who looked away and sighed, and at Javier, who looked right at it and sniggered, and Risk turned to the nearest beast, the stuffed kudu, and he peed on it. His stream was thick and yellow and long and hot, and it saturated the furry African antelope. Lorna gasped and jumped to her feet, turning to Javier with reticence. Javier laughed heartily and shook his head with sweet eyes at Lorna, indicating that it was fine, a mild offense if anything. Such possessions could be shampooed.

Risk smiled, pleased with his work. Zipped up, careful not to catch a testicle or foreskin, and turned back to his targets, beaming with pride. They stared back, intrigued.

Risk gripped his gut, stood, walked toward the bathroom. "I'm going to be sick."

Javier turned away from the awful, wet sound of Risk retching into the toilet bowl. Lorna folded into Javier. He held her. Risk emerged from the bathroom, wiping his mouth with a wet washcloth. His pallor raised Javier's eyebrows.

Risk looked at Javier with a goofy tenderness that would have been comical if it weren't touching.

"I suppose that takes care of that, then?"

A pang of guilt-addled relief washed over Risk. To be rid of her. To be free. Free to leave. But go where? Do what? Be with whom next? Risk's lip twitched, and he pressed his chin to his clasped hands, as if he were praying. *Poor Lorna. Poor, poor Lorna.*

Risk turned toward the front door and took a step to leave, but then stopped as if paralyzed. Javier approached him and stopped inches away, paused, and then threw his long, lissome arms around him, pulling him close, holding him tight. Risk and Lorna gasped. Risk surrendered to the victor and went limp. Risk wept. Javier held him. Lorna bit her lip and turned away.

"It's okay, man. You'll get through this. Everything will be okay. You'll see."

In this moment feelings rotted. No longer concerned about his wife, Risk now noticed how large and strong Javier's hands were, how massive and vascular his forearms suddenly appeared. This revelation gave way to an unstoppable inventory of all the ways Javier would be superior to Risk.

And Risk devised his plan. The unmanning would be documented and put online for public consumption. The selfishness of this anxiety sickened Risk and he fought to reorder his priorities. It would be a repeat of Dominick Truman.

Javier kissed Risk on the back of his neck. A small, friendly peck that signified support. Risk wheezed, grabbed his friend's forearm—his massive, vascular forearm—and took a deep breath.

"I saw that fucking bull and all I felt was shame. I really hoped it'd kill me. I deserved death. It deserved my death!"

Javier rubbed Risk's biceps, steadied him on his feet. The Spaniard stepped back and patted him twice on the shoulder.

"You did what felt necessary in the moment. That's all we *can* do."

After Risk left, Javier and Lorna discussed how strong Risk looked and how well he'd walked. It was as if the injury had never befell him, or if it had, perhaps the resulting limitations it occasioned had only been in his head the whole time.

Risk barely slept that night. He tossed and turned, writhed within sheets soaked with sweat and self-loathing for hours, until he finally succumbed to exhaustion. Periodic waking throughout the night struck like shrill gongs. Like clockwork, he'd shoot his eyes open in a hypervigilant mode, fear and nausea commanding forces that would prompt him to rise, look out the window, and pace restively.

In the living room he'd find Lorna, bound and gagged, on her belly in the middle of their arabesque Persian rug. Javier was hogtied beside her. Both were naked. And the shadowy figure that lurked behind them before the French Tudors that led into the backyard was illuminated in a cobalt moonlight. His silhouette suggested a plaid suit and a bowler cap, and a barely detectable face made hideous by crisscrossed scars and a hair lip. A crookedly groomed handsome beard covered much of his large, ungainly jaw. The man held a pistol trained on the back of Lorna's head. Then the crashing and snorting stirred in the kitchen. The beat of heavy hoofs on the wood floor barreling toward them. A black bull shining in the cobalt tore through the house and came for Risk, but only after stamping on Lorna and gutting Javier.

Risk wet himself and gasped. The sheets were now also soaked in urine. The nightmare aged him. He sat up panting and took off his t-shirt, shorts, and underwear. He stripped the bed. Did a wash. Showered. And made himself coffee. Theo had been watching and recording from his iPhone the entire morning, but Risk either had no idea or hadn't cared. The only new thought on the bold American man's mind was how little his hip hurt and how able his wounded leg had become.

IX

Aside from homeschooling Theo through his junior year—a task that had cost her many hours a day back in New York but one which her pride had insisted upon—and ruminating on unrealized writing endeavors, Lorna had felt bored and purposeless during the first few months in Madrid. One Tuesday morning during her daily walks around the still-new adopted neighborhood, she had happened by chance upon The Eva Peron School for Girls, an all-girls international school only four blocks from their home. A little red brick schoolhouse looking more British than Spanish. The website claimed that the English headmaster's grandmother had founded the school in 1971 after her husband had died and bequeathed her a small fortune. She had left her family in Manchester and began anew in Madrid. Eva Peron only accommodated fifty-seven pupils, all English, Irish, or Scottish, with a handful of Americans and Australians, no Canadians, and had on payroll six teachers. That put the student-teacher ratio at 1:9. Much more manageable than Merriweather's unwieldy lecture halls with their myriad sections, too often neglected by absentee teacher assistants.

Lorna had walked in and inquired about any positions that might be available. And it so happened that the role of English teacher had been recently vacated by a young woman, just married and emigrated with her husband from Glasgow, who had become pregnant and would soon go off on an indefinite maternity leave.

The interview with Samuel Quilty, the headmaster, the grandson who had inherited the school, had been marked by an ineffable strangeness. Dr. Quilty held his PhD in English Literature from Cambridge's Trinity College and maintained a tenured post as a writing instructor at the university's

Corpus Christi College. Lorna had fidgeted too often during the interview, but he had offered her the post, nonetheless. There was something strung-out and creepy about the man. He looked much older than his reported forty-eight years, closer to sixty, thought Lorna, and his shocked white hair, still lustrous and dense, was only further accented by his gauntness, a face of too-large cheekbones and too-thin lips, a too-pale complexion with too-sunken cheeks. A nose like a hook and eyes that were red, rheumy, and tired, possibly jaundiced.

"Grandmother Margaret gave her whole life to this enterprise, and it's been my pleasure, my privilege to run it since her passing," said Samuel, with the slightest suggestion of a tic, his left shoulder twitching forward in unison with his head, which bobbled momentarily. "People find their place here in Madrid. It lacks the tourism and glamour of Barcelona or other major European cities and still carries the weight of London, the bleakness, I think. The parents of the students come to us from England and Ireland, Scotland and North America, rarely Canada, sometimes Australia. They are businesspeople or statesmen or those who just want to faff about with money, you know, looking to run and hide, reinvent themselves, perhaps. We all deserve a space to remake ourselves and take refuge from those mistakes that hound us, no?"

Lorna would have taught English at the junior and senior year levels. She would have liked it. The appointment would have been good for her, but she turned it down, and not just because there was something undefinably spooky about Dr. Quilty. She had decided that she ought to dedicate her time and industry to her own writing. Throughout the past three-plus years since that first meeting at Eva Peron, Lorna had started and stopped two short story collections, three essay collections, and a big non-fiction book, a memoir that married her fall from grace in New York while at Merriweather with the power of social media in distorting reality and ruining lives. She just could no longer commit to the completion of any writing task. Nothing felt worthy enough to finish and send out. Besides, the prospective publisher was put off by her incendiary material about victim blaming and romanticized masculine brutality.

Now that she had at last left Risk, maybe it would be a good idea to either revisit the post at Eva Peron or at least conclude any one of her abandoned projects.

Javier had been brushing his teeth in the en suite while Lorna lazed in bed, scrolling through the titles of her incomplete tomes on her laptop. She watched his semi-naked body stand contrapposto before the sink, the wrist of his free hand folded and pressed against his raised buttock, not unlike Carol Burnett. Only his briefs between them. She considered pulling them off, pulling him into her. Risk rarely elicited such desires, except for that night when they finally decided to leave New York and run away to Madrid. And even that encounter had been fueled by anger and perhaps a little hatred.

Instead, she visited Eva Peron's website. Three white girls in matching uniforms stood shoulder-to-shoulder, all smiles as they bearhugged their textbooks. The school was further now that she no longer lived at home. It was still "home," wasn't it? She would now have to take a car or ride a bus, should she pursue employment there.

Someone was pounding on the door and Javier spat out his toothpaste, grabbed his robe, and threw it on as he bounded across the house toward the entrance. Lorna followed him with an empty mug, bypassing her lover on the way to the kitchen to refill her coffee, until she saw who it was who stood in the threshold.

"Risk?" she said. "What now?"

Her husband had arrived unannounced and had been staring at Javier with eyes that could not be read. Was he here to murder them? Could he be that cliché? Javier's hands made fists and his legs were wide and springy at the knees, ready for a tussle if it should come to that. Risk studied his body, boasting an always-prepared elasticity and easy grace of whatever required movement, to fight, create, or kill.

"May I come in? I've been doing some thinking. May I please come in!"

Javier glanced back at Lorna, and she shrugged with a pout that Javier read as frightened.

"I won't do well alone," said Risk, five minutes later. They had been in the living room, Javier holding Lorna on the sofa, with Risk sitting in a chair across from them. The same blocking—as if this were recurring theater—as the day before during the awful ordeal of hearing his wife say she was leaving him for his best and only friend. Risk looked at the urine stain on the kudu. *His* urine stain. He shook his head. He could be an asshole, but he could also be contrite. "And neither will Theo, Lorna."

"I don't understand what you want, and I thought I made myself clear yesterday. That's it. We're done. I'm here now. With Javier, now. Theo is a grown man. And so are you. Don't try to pull a guilt trip on me, Risk. We're too smart for that sort of thing, aren't we?"

Risk had it in his mind since he woke up in a puddle of regret and panic that morning. He'd come to Javier's house to propose it. And now that the time had come to articulate it, speak it out loud, the very notion sounded lunatic, and completely laughable. He expected them both to laugh.

"Maybe we can come to a new arrangement? Maybe there's an *arrangement* … that can make us all happy? Or at least content."

Javier seemed more interested than Lorna. She just appeared increasingly exhausted by all of it. "What? What is it?"

"You and Javier move into our house. And we live … together. Like, *together*. And you can maybe come here on weekends to have time to yourselves. I can live with it. I can live with it. You're free to have her, Javier. You're the better man, clearly. The always winner. And I wouldn't want to lose you as a friend. Despite all of this. I suppose much of the mess has been my fault. And I'm ready to own that. Ready to *pay* for that."

Javier's expression was downright cartoonish in its goofiness. Lorna sucked in air as if she had been kicked in the gut. She opened her mouth to say something, but Risk whimpered, and she gasped, again.

"Losing you both would be too much at once. Maybe my greatest failure.

Lorna, please."

Risk may as well have been a crippled puppy or a crash-landed alien as the stares he elicited from Javier and Lorna were informed alternately by adoration and perplexity. Javier, touched and appalled by Risk's proposal, looked at Lorna with a beseeching smirk, as if to implore she take the chance of this adventure. Lorna, fascinated and disgusted by both Risk's audacity and Javier's willingness, stared back in wonder at her new lover, the replacement, and played through what this bold new life would look like, how she would feel within it, what it might do to her or to Risk or Javier. What it would do to Theo.

Risk was now on his knees, again, and had slithered across the living room, and was suddenly groveling at Javier's bare feet, again. Begging. *Begging!* Lorna pulled away, tucked her own feet under her legs and stared down at the man who for so many years had made it a habit to seek out other men to secretly challenge, clandestinely best, overcome, even if they hadn't known he was their undercover competitor. His stealth duels were his art, though he was artless in their executions. And now here he was, for the second day in a row, kneeling prostrate before another man, grabbing his feet and *begging!* Was this who he had been, after all? Always a needful beta, a broken omega? Had she been right all along?

"Risk, stop it," she said, though he didn't stop it. He instead grabbed Javier by his heavy, hairy ankle and continue to rub his face against the vascular, muscular top of the Spaniard's size-twelve foot, and she thought she would vomit when she heard Javier giggling and huffing and puffing, as if he were getting off on this obscene display of queer subservience, of sadomasochistic submission. Her husband and her lover embroiled in something torrid.

Is this what the prospective threesome promised? Had it not been obvious what Risk was doing?

X

Theo, never one to allow an unusual situation to pass him by without adequate documentation, watched quietly but with his iPhone camera always on and always pointed at his parents and their new addition, the man who had been discreetly mentoring him for the better part of four years. The first few weeks played out like a situational comedy, sitcom-style: "Mom, Dad, and their Spanish Lover."

They knew that Theo had been shooting them and allowed it, but in moments of discord or affection they instructed their son to turn off the camera or to go away. He often complied, but not always, and sometimes caught interactions that were arresting in their tenderness or malice. They were one unit, the three of them, and Theo couldn't find the tenderness, only the malice. He was most comfortable outside their lurid fold.

The first time Theo and Javier trained together was just a week after the Bonaventuras had moved into their majestic new home. The European house version of their New York apartments. Maybe even nicer, thought Theo. American money went far here. One day when Lorna had gone for a walk and Risk and Javier were alone watching a soccer game in the living room, Theo, nibbling on baby carrots while considering dad's glorious turmoil, clacked away at his laptop on the kitchen table. He passively listened to the Spanish commentator announcing stats and plays and scores and fouls while reviewing damning footage he'd amassed over their years in Madrid that would wound dad.

Earlier that day Risk had done something to upset his son, scolded him for not cleaning up after himself or chewing with his mouth open. Whatever the infraction, the reprimand had been done in front of Javier, and embarrassed the young man.

During a commercial break, Risk, tipsy on his fourth glass of bourbon and coke, casually picked up the remote from Javier's thigh and changed the channel to a CNN *Business Insider* program. Javier, still sober after his fifth glass of Chianti, looked at him as though he'd just been groped. He snatched back the remote and put his soccer game back on, which had just returned from the commercial break.

"Rude American."

Risk turned in Javier's direction and moved closer. "I don't feel like watching this anymore."

"Too bad." Javier stared at the television. Not even the courtesy of looking at him. "Go garden or something, then. This is what we're watching."

It had been nearly a week since Lorna had moved back home with Javier, and the new arrangement had clearly proved problematic. Risk slept on the sofa and Javier and Lorna slept in the master bed. Though Risk could hear Lorna and Javier going at it nightly, and sometimes also in the early morning hours, she and Risk hadn't had sex at all. In fact, Lorna was not even affectionate with her husband. She'd been civil. Pleasant, even. Dinners, with maybe too much alcohol, were friendly and felt communal, like they were all recent college graduates on a backpacking tour and living together in a hostel somewhere in Southeast Asia. There were the uncomfortable pregnant pauses and long silent spells, but they were inevitably broken and filled by Javier discussing soccer or bullfighting or Risk bringing up financial news or Lorna testing the waters on a new literary endeavor.

At first, Lorna refrained from touching Javier too often in Theo's company, but she soon couldn't help herself. She had asked Javier to do his best for Theo's sake not to make the situation any weirder than it already was and to try to get along and just keep the peace. Lorna had also pulled Theo aside on the evening of her return and spoke with him about what they were trying to do. He wasn't a child anymore and she expected him to understand and accept the somewhat awkward new reality. He said he was fine with it and went to his room to draw and edit videos, though Theo knew it would be difficult having Javier share a roof with him and a bed with his parents. Lorna was satisfied with her son's reaction. He hardly ever really reacted to anything, anyway. She was less concerned about Risk and his reactions. He was the one who had pitched this deal, of course. However, without having anticipated it, her husband had become a guest in his own home. She drank more chardonnay than ever before. Javier drank more Sangria than he had in years. Risk, his primary source of caloric intake sourced from hard liquor, wondered if he had implored them to move in with him as a means of self-abasement, even if that was a fatuous musing. The American Man knew what he was doing—undoing an upstart and winning back his property.

Whatever the case, everyone had begun to drink more.

Risk reached again for the remote control. "We've been watching your fucking soccer games all day and I want to watch *Business Insider!*"

Javier swatted Risk's wrist hard enough to leave a pink welt. "And I said fuck off!"

"Fucking dick!" Risk again went for the remote and accidentally scratched Javier's bare thigh, as he'd been wearing only boxers and Risk hadn't cut his fingernails in a week.

Javier instinctively slapped Risk across the head, stunning him and then settling him, and spilling his drink.

"Enough, little bitch!" Javier had forgotten—or didn't care—about Lorna's request to maintain harmony.

Risk took a deep breath and pouted with crossed arms and mussed hair. A little jobber who'd been once again sorted out by a bully. He soon began regarding himself as a battered spouse. If this arrangement was at all a type of marriage, then the description would fit. The weekend was fast approaching, and Javier and Lorna would be gone, and he'd be able to watch whatever he wanted on television without fear of reprisal from a slap-happy dominator. Risk looked at the spilled bourbon and coke on his knee, sofa, and floor, and thought about letting it air dry and leave stains, but then came the snapped tether.

He was on Javier with fists and spit. The matador reacted quickly and dodged Risk's sloppy blows, grabbing his striking hand and elbow and twisting his arm close to breaking. Bones cracked and a joint may have fallen out of socket. The American pursuer begged for a reprieve, and Javier granted it, but not without admonishments.

"Do it again, and I'll break both arms."

He would get this prime specimen one day. He would bring him down a peg or two. He would keep him locked into a permanent kneel with unrepairable damage.

Theo, having overheard the tiff between his "fathers," rushed to the threshold to see it go down with his never-failing phone camera. He felt a tickle in the pit of his stomach when Risk had submitted to Javier's command. He knew who wore the pants now, and he'd once again caught it on camera. He'd upload the footage later, but for now, he sauntered into the living room with his laptop and sat between the two men. The tension made him breathe heavily and caused armpit sweat. Spiteful and pleased with his unadulterated spite, Theo waited for Javier to leave for the kitchen and then played for his father on his laptop footage of Theo and Javier at a bullpen, discussing the matador way, and then footage of coached pig wrestling, and finally weightlifting exercises. It was then that Risk figured out what had been going on. Another betrayal. Theo had been under his rival's and now "partner's" tutelage of all lessons in manliness for the duration of their time in Spain. And it hurt. Theo, ever the impresario of the candid camera, had recorded all his mentorship sessions with Javier, and he played it for Dad. He spared Risk other recordings.

Theo fought to hide a callous smile. "He succeeded where you couldn't, Dad."

Javier watched the interplay from the kitchen's threshold, an apple in one hand, and his mouth in a violent frown. "That's even colder than I could ever be, kid."

As Theo passed him, scoffing, Javier reached down and grabbed his genitals. Theo winced and jumped back. "What the fuck, man?!"

Javier had him pressed against the wall and squeezed his manhood just enough for it to hurt a little, to remind him of his fragile position in the world. Javier moved his mouth close to Theo's ear, spat chewed apple when he spoke.

"You know where my dad is from. Crazy Sicilian fucks castrated boys to make them sing soprano. Forced them to carry their shriveled balls around in a satchel stitched to their waistbands. Couldn't be buried without 'em. You're twenty now. No longer a boy."

Javier let him go. Theo scowled, cupped himself, and limped away with a reddened pout. As he uploaded onto YouTube his day's accumulated data—compromised scenes played out between his parents and the new father—Theo couldn't help but to recall that awkward first meeting four years ago between Javier and his dad. It was in the lavish lobby of a Marriot in Madrid. Javier's agent—a tall, thin man, young, maybe twenty-five, with a heavy but stylized handsome beard, in a pinstripe suit, and bald, a Spanish hipster—sat beside Javier and nodded and pouted with fatigued eyelids; his snootiness had made Theo laugh under his breath. Risk had kept asking asinine questions. Theo had been embarrassed by how banal he'd come across. Lorna, keeping her virtual affair with Javier a secret, wrote notes into her smartphone about some article or another, ignoring the whole ordeal. Javier had caught her glancing up at him on several occasions and registered the gratitude in her eyes for his guidance. He and Theo had exchanged knowing smirks more times than was probably advisable, too. Risk had been too enamored of Javier and intent on learning as much as possible about becoming a matador as soon as possible to have noticed either his son or his wife making eyes at his new mentor.

Back in the living room of checked dominance, Risk watched Javier discipline Theo, however unorthodox and inappropriate the lesson, and accepted that his own love was tepid. He hadn't loved with the same abandon as

Dominick or Javier. He liked things, was amused by things. He had interests but no passions. This was why he'd always come up short. Shorter than other men. Men who loved with a blind, reckless fullness. Risk would cry if he felt anything at all, but he was out of tears for himself.

Besides, there were plots that still required planning and men who warranted undoing.

XI

Javier regaled Theo with stories about his family as they pruned the bushes and weeded the intersecting cobblestone walkways in the backyard. "Did my weird brothers freak you out, little man?"

"What? When? Oh, that wrestling stuff? Nah, I thought it was kind of funny and cool."

"They haven't been totally right since our mother died when we were kids." Javier wiped his brow and licked his lips. "And they always go on like that, competing over who she loved more, and naturally it was me, though, right? But then they become like funny and gay when they challenge each other to fights, like the real, actual fist fight you saw that time. And they always strip down to their underwear, like that, and it doesn't matter where they are. They don't care if it's awkward or unsafe."

Theo imagined Javier's brothers, as powerful and beautiful as he, depending on the day, maybe more so, maybe less, tackling him in their youth, atop their bed, fumbling with each other's pricks and asses. To be on each other's bodies, almost naked, and sweating and drooling and groping and tussling. Theo began to get hard and had to shift his erection down and obfuscate it by crouching over the walkway to yank up the unruly weeds. He didn't think Javier noticed anything off in his behavior.

Javier smirked like he was keeping a secret and eyeballed the young American man, no longer a boy, but still every bit as unusual and effeminate and eager as he was four years ago when they first saw each other via Skype. "You'll meet them some day."

"That would be great." Theo almost whimpered with delight. He was grateful that he was able to subdue the sound.

"Hey, look, I'm sorry if I hurt you the other day when I grabbed you, but what you did to your dad was unnecessary and totally fucked up."

"You did hurt me." Theo gathered his gonads and made a face that Javier could not read: a bashful smile but with eyes that promised retribution. "I got what you were trying to do."

Javier looked dumb. He stared with an open mouth, catching flies. "And what was I trying to do?"

"I'll bet you twenty Euros that you don't figure it out by the end of the day."

Javier opened his mouth with a ruby-lipped snarl but before he could get the words out, Lorna's scream from inside the house brought the scene to a premature close. Theo and Javier hurried to the backdoor and filed into the house, tracking mud and dirt and pulverized bush and grass. Lorna and Risk were as drunk as they had ever been, and the theater was in full swing.

"Oh, it's another show," sighed Theo. "George and Martha are at it again."

"You fools," giggled Javier. "We thought someone got hurt."

Red-faced, slack-jawed Risk hiccupped and looked at Javier with crossed eyes. "I *am* hurt! Oblivious cretin!"

Lorna set her sights on her boy, the soft target. "Everything is just a joke with your aimless, bored, trite generation, isn't it?!"

"Don't start in on the boy, you cow!"

Javier was already in the kitchen, fetching his fourth beer for the day. Theo had already set his camera phone on his parents and began recording but in a way that looked like he was instead reading something or perhaps texting. He was very good at surreptitious surveillance.

Lorna spilled her cocktail and began to pour herself another. "You killed my career as a film actress! Selfish bastard!" She staggered and then braced herself against the floating bar. "I could have been iconic."

Javier smiled. Theo looked at him. His trousers tugged once again.

Risk stumbled onto the ottoman and made it look intentional by laughing and then posing like a centerfold across it.

"And you killed our goddamned child! Harridan! Vicious, seething harridan!"

He put his drink down too hard and half of it splashed out onto the Persian area rug.

"Theo would have had an older sister. You hate women! Or have you forgotten?!"

Javier gasped loud enough for Lorna to hear and look at him. She made a sorrowful face—a perfected expression, he thought. He believed her.

"I haven't forgotten, mongrel! And it was an abortion. An abortion! I don't kill anyone."

Risk leveled his gaze, sat up with a scowl that wrinkled his face and made him dark and ten years older. A menacing middle-aged man twisted and distressed by time and insult.

"She was nine years old, murderess!"

Theo rolled his eyes at the tired, old, recycled script.

"It was an abortion." Lorna whimpered and then gathered herself. She turned to the bar and refilled her glass. Downed it.

"You were both trying to take my career away from me. The only thing I had left!"

"You slept with my father, Lorna." Risk's voice was monotone, and it gave Theo a chill. "Ruined my parents' marriage."

"It was only payback, scum." Lorna sighed and sat on a nearby chair. "You drugged and molested my sister. Payback, you see?"

Risk scoffed and then chortled. "You don't have a sister! Daffy shrew."

Javier gave the couple an inscrutable stare. "Is that all true?"

Theo didn't look at him. His eyes were on his mother and her bent posture in the chair, an old woman distorted and diminished.

"Just the abortion part. It was four years before she had me. She was working on her doctorate and teaching and didn't have time for a kid, yet."

Javier now looked at Lorna, too, and saw the old lady that Theo had been studying. He had never been more attracted to her.

"Have they ever acted this way?"

"They do this occasionally." Theo began to turn away. He hadn't finished weeding the path. "They've always been George and Martha."

Outside, Javier continued to watch Risk and Lorna through the Tudor doors that led into the yard. Lorna was slung over the chair and crying, and he thought about rushing in to scoop her up and carry her to the bedroom and make love to her, but then Risk was beside her and touching her and rubbing her shoulders. He had rested his head on her legs and was massaging her bare feet. She had her fingers coiled around his hair and was touching his back. Javier considered for a moment killing them both. Or at least giving Risk a sound thrashing, crushing his pelvis and penis. But instead, he just continued to watch as he sliced larger and larger swaths of twigs and leaves and then whole branches from the bushes that formed a lush perimeter around the yard.

Theo hadn't been watching him, too engrossed in yanking the vines from between the cobblestone and remembering how his mother looked in that chair to pay any attention to the Spanish bullfighter who infiltrated his dreams and demanded his full attention while awake.

"Hey Theo." Javier's voice was a soft purr. "I think I can win your bet."

"Go ahead." Theo didn't sound excited, but listless. Maybe even bored.

"You think I was trying to … *emasculate* you … that day. That day when I grabbed you."

Only Theo's eyes smiled. "Nope." His mouth remained fixed in a knot. "You lose."

"So, what then?"

Theo didn't answer. He worked faster to finish his chore for the day and Javier only stared at him for a few seconds before shaking his head and turning back to the bushes. The Bonaventura clan had cost him enough that day, and he hadn't even considered the twenty euros he owed Theo.

XII

Risk was ghoulish. His episode with Lorna the other evening had taken its toll—an irreplaceable piece of him. He was also still battling a near-lethal alcohol toxicity. The weary American sat across from his son in a cramped, jovial tavern. More Teutonic than Catalan, though flamenco dancers clapped their castanets while throwing crimson legs and stamping scuffed heels.

Theo assessed Risk's haggard cheeks and blemished mouth as his father stared soullessly into a glass of red sangria.

"I don't care or anything, but I still don't get why you're doing this."

"It's a tough thing to put into words. I'm just trying to keep my family in one piece, I suppose. You know, we're in this foreign country and we're all alone here and I just thought—"

Theo's eyes rolled and his mouth went crooked. "What the fuck are you doing, Risk?"

So, it would be 'Risk' now? "I'm not a fan of this discussion, so then, as I was saying before we ordered, the big firms are JP Morgan Chase, Goldman Sachs, Bank of America, Merrill Lynch, Morgan Stanley, Citi Group—"

"This is riveting."

"Credit Suisse, Barclays, Deutsche Bank. There are others, but these are the big boys."

Theo's expression screamed at the top of its lungs that his father was wasting his time but was too self-obsessed to know it.

"I don't care. In fact, I *couldn't* care less. This is the least I've *ever* cared about any subject. *Ever.*"

Risk was small. His meekness screamed, too. In fact, it begged.

"I need to do this with you, Theo."

"Why? Because you fucked up again? Every time you fuck up, we have one of these *mentoring sessions*! But now you've brought some dude into your marriage! Into our family! And you're embarrassing yourself and us with more stupid videos of you making an ass of yourself!"

Risk didn't mean to grab the bread knife and point it at his son with a murderous sneer, but that's what he did. Motives were unimportant. Intention, masturbation. Action mattered. To Theo, all that would be remembered in his old age was that Dad had once pulled a knife on him when he was still just a young man in public during dinner. And to that, the vindicated teenager smiled with unforgiving eyes and a pink wide-open mouth.

The exasperation. The amazement. The disbelief. Theo declared the proclamation in stereo.

"Holy shit! You're gonna stab me, you psycho?"

Risk lowered the knife, pulled his hands back into his lap, and sat forward. His eyes were on the breadbasket and his timbre was low but curt. He measured every word to a cosmic metronome that permitted a slow, deep beat.

"I'm. Your. Father. And. You'll. Watch. Your. Fucking. Mouth. With. Me."

Theo feigned interest for the rest of the dinner. Risk bloviated for an hour about the differentiation across American, French, German, and English investment banking firms, their histories, their growth, their busts. He talked about mergers, acquisitions, and bankruptcies. It was an impressive history lesson of world finance. Theo wolfed down his patatas bravas and faked care with dead eyes.

Risk barely looked at the boy, though when he did glance up from his squid sandwich and cocida madrileno he could tell that Theo was phoning it in. Perhaps it was fear or shock—of himself, of what he had begun doing, again—that compelled him to go through the motions of civility and respect. Risk's shame made him talk fast and avert his eyes whenever contact was clumsily, accidentally made.

Theo wiped his mouth, looking at his father's hands and the knife beside his plate.

"Okay, sure, Sir. I'll look into … that guy …"

Risk used the knife to cut into his dinner. "The Niall Ferguson book."

"Yeah."

Risk watched the flamenco dancers on stage beyond Theo. "*The Ascent of Money*. It's worth your time."

They were seated three feet from each other, but it might as well have been a thousand yards.

◆ ◆ ◆

Javier cheered Theo on as the American kid threw his legs around the swine. The pig was heavy and strong, but Theo, exerting every fiber of tendon and muscle and ligament, put up a good fight. Human and porcine slid into each other, grunted, snorted, yelled, kicked, squeezed, rolled, and splashed. They were coated in a film of brown. The mud in Massimo's employer's Toledo farm outside was rich and dried quickly. Hours after his father had threatened him with the knife, Theo had taken off with Javier to ostensibly train; really, it was to sublimate his fear and loathing. The regrettable pig, the target.

"Get that fat bitch, Theo!"

Theo put his back into it. He exhausted muscles he didn't know he had. He got on top. Pinned the hog, pushed her face in the mud. Flashed sharp canines. Spat at her. Howled. The pig squealed in anger and surrender.

Javier took a step back, aroused and disgusted by the boy's savagery. The Spaniard was impressed with himself to have broken something hard through an otherwise soft shell.

"Okay, kid. Okay, good! Now, get the fuck off my pig." Javier yanked Theo by the collar of his saturated t-shirt onto his ass.

Theo coughed and shoveled a mask of embedded dirt from his eyes and nose. Javier patted his head like a puppy and rubbed his neck. The gesture was thick with a paternal jocularity that Theo hadn't felt before. He turned to Javier and smiled, a face of white teeth peering through a mask of brown glob. The pig looked at her attacker with genuine anguish and a sense of real betrayal.

"You made me proud here today. This was just a hog. You'll never wrestle a bull, not like this, but it's important to, number one, start conditioning your body, and number two, make regular contact with wild animals. They have to start to feel like an extension of your own hull, your own body, cock and ass, arms and legs, face and head. Your back. All of it."

Theo nodded, cleared his throat. Javier helped him to his feet.

Theo wiped mud off his mouth. "Why don't your brothers ever train with us?"

"That's up to them, Theo. They're shy around strangers, especially smart-alec American kids like yourself."

"I thought I wasn't a *kid* anymore. Plus, they certainly don't seem shy!"

Javier readjusted his bulge. Theo eyeballed the gesture. "I wouldn't bother them until they say it's cool, little man."

"My father actually pulled a knife on me last night. A bread knife! During dinner."

Javier stretched and spat. He seemed unfazed. Maybe he'd known worse in his life?

"Your mother thinks he's cracking up. He's my friend, so I won't drop him like that. What he's doing doesn't make sense to us, but I'll play along because I'm a good sport and a true comrade. Everybody wants to always cut and run. Cut and run! Nobody sticks it out anymore with anyone else. Well, I'm going to stick it out with your pop until this bad period passes. I'm man enough to handle his bullshit."

Theo nodded and stared at the bulls in the offing. Javier studied him.

"Do you know how they castrate bulls now?" asked Javier.

"They don't just cut them off?" said Theo.

"It's bloodless, more humane. They zip tie the balls, cutting off the blood supply, and they eventually just fall off."

"Jesus." Theo winced, covered himself. "Isn't that more painful?"

"Yes, of course it is."

Javier led Theo back toward the house, where his brothers would be grappling in their underwear or less, his father would be boiling a stew, a hot shower would be awaiting the little guest, and Theo would hear strange sounds emanating from a back bedroom that he'd dare not investigate.

XIII

Though Risk had made a sweaty, twitchy, profanity-filled, and in his way, valiant, effort, he could not line up the prefabricated peg with the pre-drilled hole of the bookcase Lorna had had delivered earlier that day. Javier had offered to help on three occasions as Risk's efforts quickly went from endearing to sad to plain irritating. Lorna had asked him why he just didn't pay the deliverymen to do it and he had grunted something to the effect of "because I can do these fucking simple things myself!" Her query made him remember a similar line of questioning from his colleague/ employee Darnell all those years ago back at Perseverance High: "Why do you insist on teaching history classes here when you own the whole damn network?"

Neither his wife nor his friend had understood. Why do needless work? Why toil on unnecessary tasks? Why get one's privileged hands dirty?

When she asked why he didn't allow Javier to lend a helping hand, Risk pushed the disagreeable, misshapen, "incorrectly manufactured" wood panel into place with such force that the peg cracked clean off. Lorna hadn't seen that temper-triggered misstep. Had she, Risk would have had no choice but to allow the hyper-competent Spaniard to save the day.

Risk tried again and once more failed. The boards slipped out from under one another, and Risk pricked his finger on a screw. It punctured his thumb just barely and left only a pinhead-sized red hole. But it hurt, and he was having more trouble with this mundane business than he'd expected.

"Son-of-a-bitch!" Risk punched the panel and gnashed his teeth. "Motherfucker-cocksucker!"

Javier sighed, rose from the sofa, turned off the soccer game he had been watching, and knelt beside Risk. He snatched the tools and wood panels away from him and in a matter of minutes smoothly, with precision, without sweat, without pejoratives, without miscalculations, set all prefabricated pegs into all pre-drilled holes, fastened them with the Allen key, hammered the outer casings into place, and stood the seven-foot overpriced Crate & Barrel bookcase on its tenuous legs, while mumbling in Spanish something about "cheap American crap" that celebrated its "lack of romance" with "cookie cutter designs" and "pedestrian surfaces".

Risk didn't speak. He gathered the cardboard box the shelf had arrived in and clumsily, hatefully folded it, punched it, stomped on it, and tore it until it was reduced to a stack of considerably smaller dented squares piled atop one another. The action had less to do with recycling than it did Risk's requirement for instant sublimation. Lorna and Javier ignored the tantrum and fastened the bookshelf against the wall between her desk and an antique apothecary chest.

Theo was perched on the edge of the sofa with his poised iPhone like a gargoyle on a ledge with carrion. He shot his father's fit with an expressionless, dutiful stoicism. The budding videographer felt the relationships in the odd house turning once again, and immediately began to plan a new collection for social media.

In his YouTube series, Theo narrated that it had been a week of minor failures and major meltdowns. He supposed that it being almost a month into the new arrangement, the situation had begun to wear on his father. Lorna seemed to float through unscathed, focusing more on her many writing projects that rarely came to fruition. Theo had noticed that she cared more about conceiving and developing and outlining than she did executing and completing and submitting. Javier drank too much and worked out in the gym Risk had installed when they first moved in, as extensive as any Equinox back home with weight racks and treadmills and murphy racks and a host of machines designed to make the workouts less arduous, and a whole ab section. Sometimes, the Spanish bullfighter still fought bulls, but his bouts were few and far between.

Risk had been trying to figure out how to retrieve a finance news program he'd recorded on DVR for ten minutes to no avail. He fumbled with the two remote controls, hitting more buttons than were necessary, getting lost in the labyrinth of multiple guides and settings and features he never even knew existed. Theo could have helped him, but instead secretly recorded him from the foyer, where he made it look like he was reading an article from his phone, too deeply absorbed to tear himself away.

Javier, post workout, still in his wet sweat shorts, sans underwear based on the movement in the crotch when he strutted in, and already on his third glass of Sangria, snatched the remotes from Risk's hands and in a second landed on the DVR page which showcased all programmed recordings.

"This what you were looking for, old man?"

Risk played the show and watched it with anger. Javier chuckled and sat beside him, spreading his legs wide enough to encroach on Risk's space, forcing him to shift further down the sofa. Theo's cinematography was more obvious now as he zoomed in to capture expressions and body language. Javier's unexpected mix of satisfaction and annoyance. Risk's unsurprising medley of rage and inferiority. Such a small inability and gaffe, such an exaggerated effect. Javier began to find Risk's buffoonery tedious and his misperceived insults tragic, or what's more, insulting in and of themselves. Javier knew Theo had been shooting them but didn't care. He enjoyed his rival's son's admiration. Risk was too wrapped up in his own frustrations to notice.

"Risk, these are unimportant things." Javier slurred his speech. "Don't get so worked up over them, buddy. Don't make them mean failure. They're not failure. They're nothing."

"Right." Risk's chin tucked into his chest, his arms crossed across his belly, his knees brought up to his gut, and his feet pressed against the wrought iron coffee table had become his go-to posture, his prepubescent defensive lockdown pose. He'd soon go into the kitchen and get quickly drunk on far too many vodka cranberries. And he'd go to bed without dinner and wake up with a sour stomach the next day.

◆ ◆ ◆

Failure struck yet again the following evening when Risk attempted to light the outdoor grill for dinner. He had attempted to barbeque steaks for everyone but could not get the disagreeable apparatus to ignite. He had pushed the button to release the gas and turned the knob to raise the flame, but still nothing caught fire. And Risk was becoming dizzy on the fumes.

Lorna, tipsy after several gin and tonics, editing at the teakwood patio table, filling her printed pages with red ink, ignored her husband's interminable sighs, hisses, and profanities, and knew that Javier would appear soon enough to complete the task Risk had inexpertly begun. As was becoming the custom around the house. And like clockwork, Javier, in a pair of speedos to show off his every square inch of aesthetic fastidiousness and ample packaging, exited the house in a pair of flip flops and a tall helping of freshly made sangria. Theo trailed with his iPhone and laptop. Everyone had decided to work outside that late afternoon in honor of Risk's rare effort to cook.

The steaks had started to attract flies, and Risk had begun to sweat. Lorna looked up from her pages and made a face at Javier, as if it were time to step in and get this show on the road. He sighed, took a swig of his drink, and headed over to Risk. He gently nudged his friend out of the way, uncovered the issue—a simple matter of a regulator reset after a tank disconnect and reconnect—and began grilling the sirloins. He nodded at Risk and made a faux-empathetic face with comically inverted eyebrows and a big pouting bottom lip.

Theo, in full cameraman mode, figured it had been the combination of the humid early evening air, the gas inhalation, and yet another stunning defeat at the mundane, daily functions of living that put his father over the edge. Risk lifted two of the four pieces of cooking dead meat from the grill and launched them across the yard as though they were frisbees. A stream of blood and marinade splattered across Javier's bare chest and some even got on Lorna's manuscript pages. Javier made a fist and cursed in Castilian as Lorna gasped and sneered at her daffy husband.

Risk growled, "Enjoy dinner, motherfucker!"

Theo steadied his frame. Risk moved to lift the two remaining steaks from the fire as Javier slammed shut the cast-iron lid, catching Risk's fingers. Bruised, swollen, the American screamed and danced spastically around the patio in agony as he fanned his hands out in front of him as if he were on fire. Javier laughed hard at this. Lorna did, too, but didn't mean to, didn't want to. Theo held in his laugh with such ardor he gave himself heartburn.

"Motherfucker! Motherfucker!"

Risk fled the scene, into the guest bedroom, which is where he had been living, and flexed his fingers for an hour to make sure they hadn't been broken.

"Well," began Lorna, dabbing her pages with a moist paper towel. "At least you salvaged our dinner. Theo, I'll share mine with you."

Theo shrugged. He didn't care about dinner, not really. The footage was too good and had been worth the wasted food.

Javier minded the meat. "He is completely crazy."

"Our therapist in New York said he was having a midlife crisis, but that was four years ago! How long are these things supposed to last?"

"I think I had mine in my twenties."

Lorna continued working with a cocked eyebrow. "That's a quarter-life crisis, and I thought only Americans had those."

Theo reviewed the scene on his iPhone and began to upload it onto his laptop. Tonight would be an especially long editing session.

Javier retrieved his drink and downed it. "I thought you were the expert on all things masculine, Dr. Hall-Bonaventura."

"All my training and experience couldn't properly prepare me for my husband, darling. The man is a complete enigma to me."

The next few days had been uncomfortable for nobody except for Risk, as usual, as Javier and Lorna consumed themselves with myriad interests and rituals—exercising, drinking, writing, cleaning, drinking, shopping, watching movies or soccer games, drinking, reading, drinking, drinking, drinking—and Theo was wholly engaged with his social media collections, the videos of which had grown a fan base well into the tens of thousands, 14,000, then soon 22, 000, and currently, 33,000, with so many comments that he lost the dedication to read and respond to them all. Most of his fans were in America and Western Europe, but increasingly South American and East Asian viewers began to follow along. His work was on the brink of going viral.

Risk's only occupation, in addition to occasionally reading financial news and checking his stocks, was drinking. He had introduced several blends of beer into his diet, in addition to his staple cocktails, gin and vodka and bourbon being the go-to beverages. He drank alcohol like an athlete would water. And his belly began to show signs of bloat, his skin started to suggest jaundice, and a promise of cirrhosis.

It was a lazy, breezy Thursday afternoon when Risk, just coming from their gym after an arduous series of leg presses, challenged Javier to an arm-wrestling match. His confidence was likely owing to the adrenaline and testosterone surges that the violent workout had engendered. Shocked legs had always made for a steely will. That and the fact that the nerves in his damaged hip always acted up on "leg day" and the pain made him prone to irritability.

"You can't be serious with this chickenshit bullshit?" Javier hadn't been drunk enough for such nonsense. And it rankled that Risk would even put forth such a challenge.

"Scared?' Risk stretched his arms and still-sore fingers.

Theo excitedly fumbled with his iPhone and began recording. Lorna, overhearing the farcical situation from her desk, shook her head and continued chipping away at the article she'd never finish. She had long since abandoned the short story based on Risk's social media avatar come alive but had suddenly found herself reconsidering its merits.

The gentleman arm-wrestlers moved from the living room, which is where the battle had been pitched, and into the dining room, to the corner of the table closest to the living room. They took their seats, placed elbows on the table, joined hands, braced themselves with their respective free hands and began. And Theo was on top of them, demonstratively capturing every grunt, swollen neck vein, blush, bead of sweat, whitened palm, tremble, spittle, and foot slide.

For a moment, Theo thought his father might win as he brought the top of Javier's grasped hand just a few inches from the tabletop, but then the Spaniard rallied and with a shocking show of strength, wrenched Risk's entire arm quickly and easily back to the point his knuckles smashed into the tabletop.

Though she remained at her desk, pretending to work, Lorna could overhear who had won, and she wasn't surprised, but she was regretful as she also knew that she'd now have to contend with her increasingly unhinged and reactionary husband. She wished Javier had let him win. They'd all be paying for his umpteenth failure now.

Risk's eyes, bloodshot and glassy, narrowed, and he yanked himself away from Javier.

"Fucking snake!"

Lorna arrived in the dining room in time to see her husband wipe away what could have been sweat or tears, and retreat once again into the guest room, mumbling something unintelligible under his breath. She covered Theo's iPhone and nodded, negating his intrusion.

"Fucking joke!" Risk's words had become clearer. "What a fucking joke!"

The time to strike and crush was forthcoming, and Risk's plan of attack would have to be accelerated. This humiliator would lose one day. That day couldn't come soon enough.

Lorna turned back and saw her husband turn down one of the house's many cavernous hallways and heard a moment later in the distance the door slam.

"Give him a break, Theo."

Theo rolled his eyes and stuck out his tongue. He too skulked away mumbling unintelligible complaints.

Javier proffered a humble surrender but with a boyish smirk. Lorna looked at his giant hands, red and raw.

"I want to get out of town this weekend."

"I'll bring you to my father's place in Toledo." Javier stood up and kissed Lorna on the mouth, grabbed her by the waist. "You can meet the family, at long last."

XIV

Lorna sat quietly in the backseat of a 1987 burgundy Peugeot. The drive was long and much of it was over rough terrain. It hadn't "floated along as though on a cloud" like her Mercedes 500 S class with its exceptional shock absorbers back in New York. Javier sat beside her. Massimo drove. Theo was home with his father for the weekend, as always. The weekends promised much needed breaks from one another. By Friday, everyone—mostly Risk—was ready to degrade into unmitigated brutality.

Antonio and Rafael would greet them when they arrived at the palatial estate in Toledo. The countryside provided a jarring departure—burnt umber rural vistas with the occasional mountain or hill and maybe a lone stark hazelnut tree.

Lorna found Massimo's accent when speaking English more Italian than Spanish. "What else, Lorna? You been so quiet."

She said the first thing that came to her. "We're all getting along well."

Massimo had been hoping for compromising biographical details about her husband. Javier smiled.

"It's an interesting arrangement your husband has worked out with you." Massimo eyeballed her through the rearview. "And my son."

Lorna sighed, discomfited by the prolonged labor of righting a spouse, and by the fact that her lover had shared such information with his father.

"Yes, well, we've never cottoned to convention, I suppose."

Massimo looked like he might slap her and spoke to Javier in Spanish. "What's more conventional than an American family relocating to a European city to find themselves?"

Javier confused and then alarmed Lorna. "One must humble oneself to the point of humiliation and moral surrender to survive, dad."

"What makes you an exception?" Lorna's voice softened. Timidity was a new tone.

"Will. And a lack of tolerance for oppression. My father is Sicilian. So, I have Roman soldier and mafia in my blood. We tortured and crucified Christ. And wiped out whole families. I'm okay with horror."

Massimo mumbled something in Italian. Javier laughed so hard he snorted and coughed. The matador was different with his family, and Lorna's future suddenly seemed less certain than before. Even though the car had been cool, she had begun to sweat.

"You know," began Massimo, "Spain is the only country in the world where anarchism became a true mass movement."

"I am aware," said Lorna, taking care to display due respect.

"It became part of the very DNA of industrial labor and rural poverty."

"I read about the trade unions during the Spanish Civil War." Lorna studied the landscape outside, rustic, alien to her despite her time in Spain.

"The CNT, they had two million workers, and that was almost a hundred years ago. The idea of anarchism only came to Spain in the 19th century, after most others, but it surely took root."

"I read Giuseppe Fanelli brought Mikhail Bakunin to Barcelona after meeting in Ischia."

"You know your history, Dr. Hall-Bonaventura."

"It's my livelihood."

"It was 1866, yes? And Fanelli, our Italian brother, was responsible for introducing Spain to Bakunin, whose revolutionary ideas would help this country stage the greatest demonstration in all of Europe of workers and peasants."

Lorna nodded and gathered herself. "Why are we talking about anarchy, Massimo?"

"Life is anarchy. The poor are life. The rich are death. They will lose in the end."

◆ ◆ ◆

Inside the compound, the once-orderly, considerably curated arrangement of expensive furniture and rarified bric-a-brac collected from around the world was in disarray. Lavish gowns and dresses, designer suits and couture casual wear were draped over chairs and sofas and tables. The place suddenly looked impoverished with an affluent flair. Shabby chic. Pasolini peasantry. She felt like the unsuspecting visitor—and thereby target—in one of the Italian provocateur's numerous cinematic takedowns of mid-century bourgeois decadence. *Teorema*, mostly. But now also maybe *Salo*, which really terrified her with the possibility.

Antonio and Rafael, in tattered t-shirts and stained underwear, fidgeted with cameras, tested lenses, replayed footage. Massimo began scolding them in Spanish. Lorna understood that they were being reprimanded for having made a mess and for playing with prohibitive possessions that were not theirs. They'd not be able to pay for repairs if damaged. The sons were contrite and returned the cameras and lenses to the master's den.

"Where are they, your employers?" asked Lorna, sitting on the corner of the long leather sofa that wrapped around the area of the sunken living room.

Javier poured himself a bourbon neat at the bar across from them.

"In Paris and then Munich and then New York. Hopping around. They're opening new warehouses. They obsess over everything. Scrutinize every little detail. They're infamous for their micromanagement, but they turn these tours into holidays, so they'll be gone for a few more weeks."

"They have the luxury," mumbled Massimo.

"We are the dauphins now!" exclaimed Antonio, drunkenly.

"The *marquises!*" corrected Rafael, drooling and hiccupping.

"No, *Javier* is," said Antonio. "He's the favorite. The little prince."

Lorna studied Javier for a reaction, but he demonstrated none. He stared at his brothers, turned to his father, who shook his head at his sons, and then retreated to the kitchen to forage for a late lunch.

Three bottles of wine and several pounds of chorizo later, Javier and Massimo stage-managed Antonio and Rafael in a re-enactment of Jakob wrestling the angel, and then Solomon proposing to tear the child in half, and then Cain killing Abel, and then Rachel envying Leah. Lorna sat in the middle of the all-engulfing sofa and tried not to emote. These were volatile people and any indication that they were getting a rise out of her could send them into violating territory. She donned her professor's cap and observed, filing away mental notes for an eventual essay. A survivor's story that would raise her profile.

Javier belched in Lorna's face. "My father is Jakob wrestling the angel!"

Lorna nodded, feigning interest.

"He is King Solomon splitting the child in two to teach the greedy women lessons in honesty and sacrifice. He is Cain killing Abel. He is King Herod murdering all of Israel's children."

Lorna mouthed "okay." That's what men do, she thought—they internalized and projected their fathers, but only after deifying them.

Rafael used a marble statue of Remus and Romulus suckling The Wolf to mime stoning Antonio. Cain slew Abel. Massimo laughed at their drama. Lorna couldn't tell whether it was intentionally ham-fisted or if the brothers just lacked talent. Javier seemed bored, fidgeted with his cell.

By the time the brothers were imitating Mary cradling Jesus *Pieta*-style, Lorna's fascination had become earnest and her reservation fearful. Antonio, playing the role of Mary with a dish towel draped over his head, lifted his shirt to allow Jesus, Rafael in a bed sheet wrapped around his torso like a loin cloth, to feed from a nipple. Javier giggled and resumed fussing with his phone. Massimo became impatient and smacked both of his sons across the neck, commanding them in Spanish to cut it out and get dinner ready. The sons obliged with petulant pouts. The bizarre biblical theater had ended.

Lorna watched as Antonio and Rafael butchered Massimo's masters' chickens and a pig. They were preparing a banquet. She was the guest of honor. On the drive over, they promised her they'd host a dinner fit for a queen. Sustenance up until then had mainly consisted of lettuce, tomatoes, eggs, breads, and beans. It had been a long, lean week at home wherein nobody bothered to shop or cook, and Lorna now craved more significant fare, though she regretted the barbaric killings and felt like a hypocrite.

Javier approached her from behind. "Does it bother you, to see your food killed hours before you will eat it?"

"No, not especially. My uncle had a farm in Upstate New York, and we'd spend time with him during the summer. He even hunted and that didn't bother me, either."

"You like your men manly."

Lorna moved on without giving him the satisfaction of a reaction, gesturing toward the caged bulls in the offing. "And those, they're bulls, no? For the running? Fights?"

Javier nodded. "Awaiting slaughter like the rest."

Lorna watched Javier's brothers decapitate and defeather the birds. The pig was a messier ordeal. Gutting swine was unpleasant. The smell and the sound. The imagery. It was a horror and Lorna grew bored of horror. She turned to reenter the house as she had been loitering at the threshold.

Javier stood in her way. She grew bored of his machismo, too.

"Javier, I have to use the bathroom."

"Shall I open my mouth?"

This man she had fallen for all those years ago when first arriving in Madrid *was* different around his family: creepier, cruder. Crueler. Lorna scoffed and pushed him out of her way as she walked through the capacious home that was neither hers, nor Javier's. Nor his father's.

She paused before turning the bend into the hallway that wound toward one of the house's four bathrooms. "Won't they mind that we're all here while they're away, eating their food, killing their livestock?"

"They treat my father like a son. He's been with the family since he first came here from Taormina at seventeen. He and their children are as close as siblings."

Lorna's voice lilted in a condescending whine. "But he takes advantage, anyway."

"The only person taken advantage of is *him*. They stand on his back."

"Right." Lorna's smile occurred to Javier as a smirk, a gesture smacking of sarcasm and therefore disrespect. He could feel both his penis and his fists stiffen.

"We all take advantage, Lorna. Don't we?"

Lorna knew he was right. She turned away meekly and retreated into the bathroom where she'd take several minutes to catch her breath. Javier managed to regain a steadier mien. He offered his brothers a hand. They told him to pick vegetables. A daintier affair than felling farm animals.

They ate a late dinner that evening at nine. The mahogany dining table was covered with bowls of Paella Valenciana, Gazpacho, Fideua, Jamon, Torillas, and an array of sofritos. There were even desserts. Flan, Catalan cream, and churros filled the floating bar beside Massimo, along with bottles of Frangelico, port wine, and Anisette. The sweets had come from the walk-in freezer below, just beside the wine cellar. Antonio quipped that Massimo's masters wouldn't be happy to find them gone. The patriarch shrugged and implored everyone to leave no traces. No leftovers.

"If there's no evidence, they won't be able to holler at me for nothing," said Massimo in a singsong tone with a mouth full of meat.

Lorna couldn't help herself. She'd never shrink from confronting hypocrisy. She'd spent too much time building a reputation calling it out.

"So, then, you *are* stealing from your employers?"

Massimo stopped chewing. "What?"

Javier cleared his throat, drank more wine.

"Javier said you were like family to these people and that you'd be welcome to whatever they have here, but now you're sounding like someone who is trying to get away with something, someone who is stealing something."

"Little American woman with big mouth," began Massimo in Italian, chewing now with wide chomps to show the mangled mess sitting on his tongue, "like all little American women with big mouths."

Lorna looked down, knowing she'd upset him. Antonio and Rafael smiled at each other, though their eyes intimated apprehension.

Javier suddenly remembered all the times Massimo had taken him and his brothers to whorehouses to watch the matadors fuck prostitutes. The one time he took them to see a performance-endurance artist get fucked by a horse. The fist fights between the brothers that he had refereed. The way he'd encourage dirty tactics and humiliating defeats. Bad sportsmanship was his game. Javier was naturally sexual, but the violence was conditioned. Ensuring masculinity made the boys grow up weird.

Lorna often figured that Javier played up his ancestry. His bloodline couldn't be as royal as he claimed. This family was shabby-genteel, if anything. Minor nobility.

"You know, the word 'slave' derives from 'Slav.' As in *Yugoslav*! The Eastern Europeans were the Moors' slaves. So were the Sicilians. Almost every civilization has practiced slavery or had slavery practiced upon it. Though it's true that most African nations enslaved their own and did so as a product of tribal warfare, the colonial transatlantic business was a mere blip in the long history of slavery, and the whites didn't even invent it."

Massimo's delivery was almost too articulate and precise to be off the cuff. The English too clean and elevated. Lorna suspected that he must have scripted and rehearsed it for occasions like this, where he had a captive audience. *Captured an audience.*

"That's what all white people say," said Lorna, without irony or a flippant tone.

Massimo continued eating. "Americans are so arrogant."

"I'm not arrogant." Lorna's tone was friendly, almost lilting. She hadn't been offended.

Javier looked at her with wide, angry eyes. "You're oblivious and indifferent."

"That's *not* arrogance."

Massimo swallowed his food. "Isn't it?"

Lorna wanted to tell Javier that he likely revered his father for an imaginary, cowardly roguishness, but even she knew when to draw the line and not cross it. Javier's family pretended rich well, even as they spanked it. Their delusion infuriated. But Lorna and Risk's and maybe even Theo's wellbeing were on the chopping block, and she'd have to refrain from doling out every criticism that came to mind.

"When I went to school, until I was thirteen, I had to walk three miles back and forth in shoes with holes in them, getting my feet scratched and cut up by pebbles and concrete."

Lorna glanced at Massimo as he recounted the rigors of his impoverished youth. She nervously averted her eyes, fixing on the banquet; she couldn't weather the old man and his sententious self-pity. Her deference granted him permission to rant.

"My parents and I lived in a cousin's car for a time, a 1963 Buick Riviera, and then in a park for a while. With bums and junkies. And other poor families. We stayed as long-term guests with various friends and family members. They would make us feel like shit. Broke my father's pride and his spirit. Crushed my mother. That neediness. That dependence. We would steal groceries. Commit robberies. Mostly old ladies. The easy ones. We would break into farmer's estates and take their crops and sometimes their livestock. My mother prostituted herself for a time. So did my brother. So did I. But I only ever jerked off the men. We would knock over rich shoppers after they left department stores to take their clothes. My aunt could sew. She would make the clothing fit us. We would rummage through dumpsters for food that was thrown out by restaurants. We lived for a long time on bread and beans. Sometimes rotting vegetables and fruits. My father lowered himself as a rubbish worker. Cleaning up people's rubbish. My mother became a politician's maid. We dirtied ourselves. To keep eating. To spare our feet the pebbles and concrete. To sleep somewhere dry and warm and safe. But … you have no idea what I'm talking about. How could you ever?

Javier and his brothers waited for Lorna to reply, not realizing that their father's question was rhetorical.

Lorna, on her third piece of flan, couldn't help herself.

"But what about your royal bloodline? Javier has told me so much about his ancestry. It all sounds very impressive."

Javier thought he might vomit up his dinner. He turned to his father, whose rheumy eyes were already on him.

Massimo's voice sounded suddenly older, gravely and with a rasp. "They cut us off before my time. Before my *father's*. My grandparents began the low living, well, thanks to the war, and we continued it."

Lorna glutted herself. More flan. More chicken. Too much pig. It bordered on performance art and sent signals that Massimo had trouble digesting.

Alone in one of the seven masters' guestrooms, Lorna surveyed the keepsakes she'd taken from home. They had been kept at Javier's house, but he'd brought them here. He mentioned it on the drive up but didn't say why. He told her where they were kept and that he could take them back to his place in Madrid if she wanted, but they were better suited to remain with his father and brothers. Again, he would provide no explanation. Theo's Yoda. The magnet from Casablanca. The painting from Alexandria. And Risk's socks. She allowed herself a moment of sentimentality, a weakness she abhorred. But the vulnerability felt right, if just for a moment. What she'd built and earned, what she'd given up, and how much it would hurt if it should all be lost.

She had first heard from Javier a few weeks before she moved to Spain. It had been through email, rife with endearingly flawed English.

Lorna,

My name is Javier Forza. I am 'Madrid's premiere matador'. I think I speak well English because I was raised on American and British movies and television shows. But still I make sometimes mistake. Your husband found me on Facebook and begin friendship. He intend to come here someday and pursue new career as bullfighting. It ambitious agenda when you think about his age and nationhood, but his wealth will help him a good deal. Your son is Theo. He has also found me, on Instagram. He present a different person at first, a heroic kind of figure. A big, great, beautiful man. "Cat-fishing" is how you Americans call it. We only call it "deception" in Spain. But it okay now. This was all many months ago and he has "come clean", show me his true and full face. He is a lovely boy with a potential and you should be proud. He told me about you, and so has Risk. I research you lectures and articles and books, and you are obvious quite brilliant woman. Theo and your husband have turned YouTube videography into art. Maybe even as form of psychotherapy, as I humble see it. This how I come to find the YouTube video of you ... "less-than-stellar" as media call it, moment in class. As a favor to Theo, I alert you, though you should know how bad your words and work bruise him. I also see that your situation has not improved. Have you thought at all about considering how effective your husband and son's creativity have been? The creation of reality. The stealing of support and love and sympathy. I sure you have receive hate mail. Why not reclaim tools of your near demise? Why not make art of your own?

This is with full love and deep understanding of how business work. It all entertainment now. So be entertainment!

I look forward to your arrival here in Madrid.

Best,
Javier

In hindsight, Lorna should have been offended by what Javier had written, but she remembers having been instead intrigued. She'd found the provocation erotic. And then she wondered if Javier had only presented himself as a different person all those years ago or if had he truly changed? Had they changed him? Still, she had been grateful for his suggestion. It would course-correct.

Massimo was at the threshold, watching her inventory her personal effects. She moved toward him and attempted to push him out, giving it a go at slamming the door in his face. He chuckled and forced it back open. Lorna continued through the house but felt Massimo's rancid stare hounding her. His entitled manhood was a cage, and he relished imprisonment.

His mere presence did things to her. He'd been inside her now, under her skin. Lorna removed herself throughout the ordeal of the dinner and watched with circumspection the bitter poetry recited with a sense of sour irony. The lies she'd told. Her sensationalist theories. All in the toilet now.

She hosted morbid fantasies.

Older fabrications hovered. Ancient histories loomed. Weeks back, she had entertained a sordid story. She had devised a plan with Javier, Massimo, Antonio, and Rafael. The beautiful, boorish Spaniard Italians. The Tournaments would not be her idea, but she would more than intellectualize them—she would abet them, help shape them. Crimes of degradation and domination, to teach her insecure, egotistical, selfish husband a goddamned lesson!

Massimo and Javier would descend while she was out shoe shopping. They'd follow her that afternoon. Watch and wait. She would go into and out of four stores and try on a dozen stilettos before they'd approach her. They'd give her that space, that respect. They'd bring her to lunch, somewhere cheap and obscure, somewhere away from tourists and people that mattered, somewhere in the dusty country. She'd listen to their plot. They'd relay it with too many details and a clear purpose. They'd provide a schedule. And assurance that she and Theo would be safe. Lorna would listen and do the calculations. She'd contemplate the benefits versus the risks over three glasses of white sangria and a fish entrée—fresh tilapia, for once. The obstacles themselves, as outrageous and vile as possible, would be her brainchild—eating live cockroaches and livestock, fist fighting naked in a popular sports bar, digging up and making love to long-dead matadors, and fighting four bulls blindfolded at once. And all would require video documentation for upload onto YouTube for the world to consume. She composed the messages. Javier, always his father's mere foot-soldier, would have reached her in a moment of pettiness, when spite would win out over compassion and reason. The lure of vindictiveness would give her a rush, regardless of its damages. Though she would buy no shoes that day, the decision to go forward would be an impulse purchase. And it would cost more than she could afford.

Lorna returned to her senses, stared down at the trinkets from home. She sickened herself with the daydreams. All the creative ways to punish herself and torment her husband. Her criminal imagination. *Gender traitor.*

She was not this person. She was not this person. She was not this person.

XV

The pond was murky because the gardener hadn't treated it in weeks. The algae conjured a putrid cloud that obscured the dozen foot-long koi thrashing about beneath the surface, periodically popping up for food with their sucking mouths that sent ripples around them like wet halos. Risk stared into the brownish-green water. Theo sat beside him on the cobblestone perimeter, picking at a coat of moss.

Theo began fingering a beetle that scurried onto the patch of green, rolling it over onto its back.

"So, have you heard from them yet?"

Risk stuck his index finger in the water, traced a figure eight, hoping for a fish to nibble on it.

"They never answer on weekends. It's their time alone."

In the back of his mind, Risk began hoping Lorna and Javier would run off and never return.

Theo rolled the beetle back onto its legs. "Don't forget, Dad. This was all your idea."

A koi, named Big Boy by Risk, began to suck on Risk's finger. "I know."

"I'm sorry that I've been uninterested in finance, Dad. It's just very … *uninteresting*. I know you've been trying to get me into it, but I'm just not. And I'm not gonna be."

"I was only looking for something to teach you. Something for us to talk about. You're always on your phone or drawing or making *those videos*. Or disappearing to God-knows-where."

Theo lifted the beetle and poked it while it ran in circles on his palm. "I know. And I'm sorry I stopped talking to you."

"You just seem … so contemptuous, Theo. Of me. And then there's this, where you make an actual attempt to be kind. Like you're doing me a favor."

"I'm a teenager, Dad." Theo flipped the beetle onto its back, touched its kicking legs. "I'm entitled to my weird mood swings."

"A *teenager?*" The koi submerged itself. Returned to its depths. Risk sniggered, stroked the surface of the murky pond. "You're twenty. No longer a teenager."

"Close enough." Theo flipped the beetle back onto its legs. Set it loose on the mossy patch. "I'm meeting a friend. I'll be back by tonight. I promise. I'll be here when they come."

Risk touched Theo's leg. "Where do you go, Theo? Who is this *friend?* Why haven't I met him? Her?"

"*Him.* It's just someone I met at the comic book store in the city a few weeks ago. It's important that I have some sort of social life, right? Being cooped up with you and mom and Javier doesn't leave me much of a chance to do that. Make friends."

"I know. Okay, go. Have fun."

Theo moved to leave, but then paused, and turned back to his father with a precocious smirk.

"Skittish markets behave unpredictably before major elections. And always react dramatically to the results."

Risk's eyes lit up. He nodded. "You remembered something."

"Of course." Theo was already at the patio door, entering the house when his voice trailed off, but Risk heard it, anyway. "You're a good teacher."

The beetle lost its footing and fell into the pond, whereupon it became fodder for Big Boy.

◆ ◆ ◆

Lorna had gone shopping that afternoon, a Sunday. No one knew Theo had come to Javier's place in Madrid. Javier had invited him over via text that

[232]

Saturday evening, on his way back from Toledo.

Javier taught Theo how to do barbell curls. Then preacher curls. Then squats. The gym in his house was as state of the art as Risk's. And clean. It had a starched antiseptic smell, as if Javier treated the equipment and floors daily. Despite the filthy nature of his work, Javier was fastidious about hygiene and managing odors. Theo, obsessive compulsive about cleanliness, appreciated this neurotic tendency. With every lift and tissue tear, Theo thought about folding his father.

"Your form is good but stick out your butt even further and arch your back," said Javier, as Theo struggled with a hundred-and-ten-pound plates, wobbling into an uneven squat. Javier took him by the hips and adjusted his stance as his protégé autocorrected and completed a set with ideal structure.

"Good. You need a strong core to do the work we do. *Become the bull,* remember."

A few minutes later they were doing deadlifts. Javier could pick up a significant amount of weight—five hundred pounds—at which Theo marveled. "Damn, you're strong, Javier!"

Javier's pump was obscene; his arms, shoulders, buttocks, and back popped. The simple act of lifting heavy things made the already dark beauty that much more exquisite. Theo lost his breath.

"It took a while. I was a scrawny kid, Theo. You have to slowly condition your body. Your tendons, ligaments, joints, bones, and muscles only get stronger … by increments … slowly. You must have patience. You're starting at a good age, though."

Javier guided him through four sets of ten repetitions. Theo found deadlifts more arduous than squats and winced through the last few lifts, fearing he might have torn something in his shoulder. Javier rubbed and iced it.

In the kitchen, Javier made them both protein smoothies: bananas, blueberries, whole milk, peanut butter, kale, ice cubes, and whey protein powder. Theo drank it too fast and gave himself brain-freeze, at which Javier laughed, rubbing the boy's temples to soothe him.

After cleaning the counter and washing out their glasses, Javier and Theo watched video clips of Javier's greatest moments in the bullpen. A montage produced by the local sports news network. Theo spied on Javier through the corner of his eye, getting a kick out of his mentor's boyish reactions to the glory that was his career. *Is* his career.

"Gosh, you're kind of a king out there. A real gladiator. So graceful and swift. It's, like, totally majestic."

Javier shrugged. "Hard work. Some talent. Luck! We'll get you there, Theo. If you stick with it. You have to really want it."

Theo didn't think, just acted. *Reacted.* His skinny fingers were wrapped around Javier's bulge. In his excitement and nervousness, the American boy squeezed his hero too hard and made him grunt. The Spaniard shot forward, grabbed Theo's thin forearm. The American boy was hard when he realized that Javier hadn't been wearing underwear. The large, sloppy genitalia firmly in his grip made Theo pant.

Javier, wide-eyed and bewildered, stared at Theo in disbelief. Hot, wanting pupils, dilated and intoxicated with lust. The need bordered on impoverishment.

"What are you doing?" Javier sounded more confused than angry.

Theo shook. Squeezed harder. "Please."

It hurt. Javier was in pain. The come-on was assaultive. He let go of Theo's wrist and sat back. Theo gasped as he yanked down Javier's sweat shorts and gasped again when he saw how suddenly huge and erect Javier was. He drooled. Slickened the lance. Javier turned away. His rival's eager son fought for satisfaction. Javier watched the "glorious" montage of himself besting the bulls, earning the adulation of the stadium. Theo jerked him off with a vigor that made the man quake and whimper. And then a quiver.

The ejaculation happened too quickly and in a nervous spasm. Javier's semen shot impossibly far, traversed the room, and found itself splattered Jackson Pollock-style across the mounted plasma flat screen. Coating his televised countenance like Risk's Matthew Barney photo of the albino, suited

[234]

satyr.

Theo dashed with urgency into the bathroom to wash his hands as Javier tucked himself back into his shorts and remained mesmerized by his own image enhanced and blurred under his sparkling ejaculate.

XVI

Javier stared at the Matthew Barney photograph that had always hung over the sofa but that he had just then noticed. Maybe it had been on account of the queasy association he'd made over the weekend when Theo had come to visit and done what he had done. Whenever the young man appeared with his iPhone and laptop, Javier became small and palpable in his discomfort. Risk, too wrapped up in his own plots and paranoia, was oblivious. Lorna hadn't noticed, either, too mired in the memories of the unpleasant exchanges with Massimo and Javier's brothers and the awful fantasies that followed. She had also been preoccupied with the trinkets she'd stolen from home and why Javier felt the need to bring them to Toledo, to a stranger's house.

She stood beside him, pretending to regard the Barney. She whispered in his ear, "Why did you bring my things to your father's place?"

"I didn't want that shit in my house."

Lorna glanced at Theo, who had appeared with his various and sundry electronic media, all the troublemaking accoutrements. Javier looked away and cocked his head. Lorna still hadn't noticed the weirdness, still too fixated on her own business.

"Why not?"

"It just didn't sit right with me, Lorna. Either bring it back or throw it all out."

Lorna returned to her desk with a sigh and continued to mark up her essay collection, every piece of which would prove problematic in the current political climate. She thought that perhaps she should write a non-fiction book defending her positions, or at least clarifying them. She had *not* been a proponent of rape. She was *not* a self-loathing misogynist. She did *not* believe that men were superior to women. She did *not* seek to romanticize masculine aggression. She was *not* a war hawk.

All she had been attempting to say was, "Hey, Defenders of Freedom, let's not forget that we're still animals and like animals we are driven by prehistoric impulses to fuck and fight, and no measure of civility or pretty rhetoric or social enlightenment is going to change that beautiful-ugly—and very fundamental—fact".

And almost on cue, Risk appeared in his underwear. Javier and Theo looked at him, waiting for the next asinine pronouncement, the next exhibition of manliness. They all knew there would be more to come, that the arm-wrestling defeat would engender a litany of desperate displays of butch behavior.

"Laundry day?" Javier had been unimpressed, unintimidated.

Lorna, for only a moment, thought that her husband's body looked good. Many imperfections, to be sure—patches of hair on the back, too-thin ankles and wrists, a slight paunch, but there was also ample musculature, long and lean, fresh skin, still young looking, and a not woeful manhood. For fifty-two, he was still attractive, sexy if no longer handsome, powerful if not necessarily young looking. We all bargain and compromise as the years wear on.

Risk had read a study recently about the associations between hunting and spousal abuse. Clinicians reported that during the fall season North American hunters reach peak "buck fever," and incidences of domestic violence and wife-beating were highest the day before each season of hunting opened. A vegan publication, no doubt. The findings inconclusive, but intriguing: sexual deviance was afoot within those who got off on killing for sport. Shocker!

"I want to wrestle you right now. Outside. Strip down."

Javier, Lorna, and Theo all shared the same thought, as if suddenly interpsychically symbiotic—had Risk somehow known about Antonio and Rafael and their nearly-nude wrestling shenanigans? Was he making a mockery of the whole thing?

Javier snickered and then yanked off his t-shirt and dropped his shorts. "This is stupid, but if you want it."

The two men were outside and circled each other. Risk thought back to his high school days when he reigned over the other boys and had won myriad trophies. He had no trouble beating friends, but strangers were another story. He'd always become sick with nervousness before tournaments, as performance anxiety would make him vomit. With friends, it was just playtime, and he had been in control, and undefeatable.

Theo had beat Lorna to the yard and was, quite naturally, already filming the showdown. She rose slowly from her desk and took her time walking across the long house to witness the farce.

"Oh god," she whispered to herself, not believing the life she was living, not believing she had agreed to it. Not even a book out of it. Not yet, anyway.

"This is really dumb," she said, but no one listened.

The gentlemen wrestlers locked arms and exerted pressure against one another, their bare heels digging into earth and cobblestone and grass, multiple scrapes and cuts instantly forming, and they tore at each other like a pair of heated apes, intent on covering and crushing, and it wasn't long before Javier had the upper hand and Risk was on his back and pinned.

"Best of three," Risk muttered.

And again, they locked, and again they angled for domination, and again the scrapes and cuts, and again the slipping and pinning, and again Risk lost.

Lorna could only imagine the blowback from this current defeat. He'd likely set the house on fire and burn them all down with it. He'd not be recovering from this one, he'd not be able to live with himself now. Not a loser at his own sport.

Risk's penis had become hard, small, and closer to his body. And Javier wiped his brow and laughed. That self-satisfied laugh that meant to belittle his conquered, his reduction. Risk would always be his conquered, his reduction. And again, after Dominick Truman, the lesser man.

Risk made no sound, but was off his knees, and on his feet, his toes burrowing into soil, and he leapt like a wild cat through the air and into Javier, taking the better man down with such force that Lorna screamed and covered her throat and Theo exuded such an explosion of joy he thought he might cry as he framed the frenetic action as best he could, despite his tremors.

Javier was too strong, too beautiful. There needed to be violence. And the fight was now real and gruesome, and it went quickly, but for the two men having at it, it felt like ages. They writhed through bushes and flowers and fingers were in faces and around necks and knees found themselves planted in ribs and groins. The men made animalistic grunts and wheezes and Lorna covered her mouth to muffle her own primal sounds of arousal and of disgust.

Javier landed the first blow. A fist to the jaw that sent Risk stumbling. The swelling was instant. The yard spun. Javier engorged. It was a thrill to dominate publicly, nakedly. The novelty and the attention sent adrenaline and blood through flaccid tissue. Theo stared at Javier's elephant-trunk-like appendage swing obscenely, and grinned. A hungry hyena. He was sure to capture it.

Risk returned the assault with a set of long, boney toes to Javier's fat, low-dangling testicles as the Spaniard crumbled to his knees, fighting back tears and breakfast. Theo grimaced and touched his own groin sympathetically. Javier's tawny face reddened, and he began to sweat. The smack bellowed, sounded like a bat hitting dead meat. And Javier's semi-erect penis went limp as Risk enlarged, grew mighty.

Lorna touched her breasts. Moistened. She hated this reaction and didn't understand why it was happening. Even in the midst of his ass-kicking, Risk thought that she might write an essay about the spectacle. He'd read and heard her critical analysis on women who unconsciously crave alphas, seek the winning specimen, pine for the victor's seed. Entered estrous when spectating male bellicosity.

Risk yanked his nauseated, hobbled opponent to his feet by his ears. Javier answered the effrontery to his sex with a flurry of quick and precise gut punches, some of which made contact north and south of the sinewy target. Risk's sternum and genitals ached, quickly bruised. He doubled over Javier who caught him in a bear hug, lifted him inches from the floor, and body slammed him hard on the earth. They had both been drinking earlier in the day and the alcohol had gone only so far in mitigating the pain.

Javier seized a handful of Risk's still-thick, lustrous hair and pulled his head back. Risk screamed in a womanly way and thought about the time he took Lorna and Theo, then only nine, to Adventure Aquarium in Camden, New Jersey. Gritting his teeth and pausing the memory, Risk sent his right thumb into Javier's left eye socket. As Javier tumbled backward palming his poked eyeball, Risk remembered how happy Theo had been when visiting the hippopotamus. He had pranced down the ramp alongside the giant mammal who had been separated from the boy by a full-wall glass partition. At the top of the ramp was an artificial rocky shore, the descent leading into a giant pool lousy with algae and little fish. The ecology was realistic and hewed to the demands of nature. And Javier punched Risk in the face with his full might, destroying what beauty remained.

The blood was heavy, but Risk still thought about the Camden aquarium. The shark tank, this time. Theo had pressed his hands and face against the glass and marveled at the carnivorous fish that swam before him. Even Lorna had found amusement in their son's joy. Thresher, Mako, and tiger sharks circled the smaller fish—remora, tuna, and mackerel.

Though Risk was whimpering, and the damage was extensive, Javier did not let up. He would put an end to these absurd games. The primed matador was upon the American imposter, grabbing his balls. Risk shrieked and leapt to his tiptoes as the Spaniard squeezed. Risk hissed, emitting a new guttural sound that was one-part whine and one-part gurgle. Javier unhanded Risk's genitals. Theo zoomed in on the suffering. Lorna was still dizzy from the intensity of the skirmish, and she trembled like her son.

Theo had asked for a saltwater aquarium, which Risk would end up buying him. The first few fish would be the ones he took the greatest number of photos of while at the aquarium, including flame hawks and mandarin gobis. Lorna had warned of the maintenance and time and tedium required of such a hobby. Risk promised he'd help their son as much as possible. Theo had been responsible with other pets, tarantulas, Nile monitors, and ferrets in the past, and he'd be prepared for this new exotic endeavor.

Risk nursed his testicles with one hand and his mouth with the other, taking a seat on a teakwood bench to gather himself.

"Dumb ... fuck..." Javier caught his breath. "Are we done ... dumb fuck?"

Theo's videography had taken on a cinema verité queasiness, which served the gruesome scene respectfully. Everyone was quiet now, and patient. The reverence was palpable. It was akin to the bated breath with which they had grown accustomed to witnessing the final moments of a bull fight, those last few seconds in which the outcome was unclear. Peril was rich in the air. The nervy mortality of the moment silenced everyone.

The Camden staff had not been happy with them. Theo had been scolded by an employee at the aquarium who had caught him lifting a starfish from the petting tank. Risk had paid the young docent a considerable sum to walk away and ignore the engagement. Theo continued to grab and lift other creatures in the tank. Sea urchins were a favorite. Lorna took pictures. They were exceptions. Money afforded them such rarified experiences.

Panting, wheezing, huffing. Theo fought to catch his breath as this most current assault of his father left his knees weak and his heart racing. Not even the seven vodka cranberries could mute the deafening stinging of dad's disgrace.

Sea life had agreed with the boy. Theo drew representations of the stingrays with exceptional accuracy. Lorna had commented on how much creative license he had taken, how abstract and unique his rendering. Risk had encouraged Theo to replicate other sea life in his pad. His illustrations of the sea anemone were especially striking, as the liberties he took with form, proportion, and color were uncommonly artistic. Upon returning to New York, Lorna had discussed with Risk enrolling Theo in specialized art classes. Theo's love of nature would wane but his passion for bold, liberal aesthetics would only wax.

Lorna covered her face and shook her head. The immediacy of the brawl in her backyard intruded on restorative memories. She thought for a moment that it might have been she who had facilitated the altercation, but then put the thought out of her head. Her husband had been this way long before they ever even met. It had only been a matter of time before he'd shed his assured exterior.

Theo's camera filed away every second of his father's hobbled, hurried crawl toward Javier. The beaten, bloodied man took the victor by the ankles and bit into his left foot. Lorna's blood was curdled by Javier's unapologetic screech. Lorna felt nauseous, once again. What monster had she married? How deep had her husband's pathology and self-loathing gone? How much further could it go?

Defeat—this most current and significant of losses, a culmination perhaps of all his surrenders—changed Risk. It reshaped his brain. As though cut down by a stroke or malignant diagnosis. He now only sought to own Javier, lord everything over him. Now he just wanted the prized matador under him, under his foot, beneath his body, and bent to his will. He wanted the greater man to love him, admire and knight him. Risk had earned that much. Absolute devotion and adulation. Reverence to a self-immolating extreme. And Risk could take that much. Become the master. *His* master. The savagery comforted, mollified like a salve. Javier would accept his velvet cage, cozy up to his pair of plush handcuffs.

Blood filled Risk's mouth as Javier stomped hard with his other foot on the crown of Risk's head, sending his chin into the pavement, loosening his toothy grip. And again, this time on the temple and jaw, knocking him unconscious. A purple, oozing outline of Risk's teeth covered the top of Javier's foot, far from the toes, closer to the ankle.

Theo turned off his camera and his breath was no longer bated. Maybe it was time to return to other, long-abandoned pursuits.

XVII

The week following Javier's unforgiving thrashing of Risk, both men found themselves inexplicably, irrevocably, irrationally beguiled and affectionate. As Risk's jaw and Javier's foot healed, though poorly, with permanent dislocations and scars—Risk's jaw would forever bear the malformation at the point in which it had met Javier's heel and Javier's foot would hold for the rest of its existence the marking of Risk's maddened chomp—the combatants had, beyond all reason, become gentlemen, speaking regularly and at length.

But before the love, there came temporary turmoil. In the immediate minutes following Risk's knockout, Javier had packed his bags and tore through the house, hissing and muttering obscenities in his mother tongue, banishing Lorna and Theo from his sight. A wild animal tired of its cage, clawing for freedom. And in bare feet, freshly marked by the captor's teeth. Risk regained consciousness at the terrible sounds of Javier cursing in Spanish, slamming drawers and doors. Slamming colonial culture, his own included.

The American found his footing and then his bearings. Finally, he found Javier at the front door. And in that emergence from the fog of the battering, Risk formulated a new plan, a better agenda. The titan would still fall. Risk would be the David to Javier's Goliath. He rushed wobbly, drunkenly into his house and stopped Javier at the threshold by dropping to his knees, grabbing the Spaniard's ankles, and kissing, once again, his bare feet, kissing the wound he'd pinned on him.

"Please don't leave. Javier, please! Just ... please! For the love of God. I'm done with this shit. I'm done hounding! Jesus Christ! You've won. I submit, for the love of Mary! I submit to you. You're the God. You're *my* God! God,

Jesus Christ and Mary! Fucking stay here, you bastard! God damnit!"

Javier, his own colossal ego in chronic need of inflation, fell victim to the flattery, the self-abasing idolatry, the undignified pleading. And he stayed. And the relationship over the course of the days that followed softened by the hour, warmed by the day until Javier barely detected that he'd succumbed completely to the adulation, the devotion, the subservience. Risk proffered much, professed even more. And the true bullfighter ate it up.

The suddenly civilized men alternated television programs—sports and finance—and discussed them like fanboys at a comic book convention. They spotted each other during workouts and complimented each other with hyperbole. They gardened together. Ate together. Cleaned together. Took walks together. And to Lorna and Theo's chagrin, cuddled with each other on the sofa and in bed.

Javier took it as straight guy business—the winner of the schoolyard scrap earns the loyalty and respect of the loser and they become best buds after a thorough beatdown. Risk saw it as a new direction, a smarter ploy. And the always-victor would eventually drop to his knees. In time, Risk would be his upstart underdog to Javier's dethroned top dog.

"I'm sorry I'm having such a hard time with this." Lorna sat with crossed legs and a hunched back with tangled arms and a wrinkled brow at her vanity across from the California King, on which Risk massaged Javier's feet with fragrant lotion, lavender. "I know that I agreed to this ... whatever you want to call it. I just didn't think ..."

Risk sneered. "Would you rather me angry and petty, again? A narcissistic monster?!"

Javier sat up, grimacing. "Do you like us better when we're fighting? After what you saw last week? What we did to each other, Lorna?"

"What does it matter, what I think?"

"Don't make it about you," said Risk. "What should we do? This feels right. I mean, Lorna, are you jealous?"

"How ludicrous!" Lorna jeered. Javier swayed in her direction. "*Jealous!*

ally laughable!"

ie of the many perks of Risk and Javier's new union was that Theo had become bored and stopped recording them—though they had not known he'd been uploading all the footage he shot of them onto YouTube. The boy thrived on carnage and bitterness. It made for compelling cinema. The tenderness was off-putting and not at all dynamic enough. It was unworthy of production. He had instead taken to posting his defiled renderings of cartoon characters—the very illustrations that had mortified his parents four years back in New York—around the house. Lorna ignored them, Risk was disgusted by them, and Javier celebrated them, commending the boy on his bravery and creative expression.

"Your drawings have real guts, little man!"

Lorna stared at a recent depiction of Woody from *Toy Story* taking it biblically from Buzz Lightyear's buzzing light-stick clipped to the Moorish armoire on the far side of the bedroom. He'd snuck in before the threesome found their way in for their congress. She'd sometimes found room in her heart and in her bed for Risk.

"Lorna!" Risk broke his wife—she was still his wife—from her spell.

"Yes?" Something else had suddenly found itself on her mind. A new project. If she were to explore her own biases and theories through memories and experiences, then surely this new dynamic would provide sufficient material, even *evocative* material. A gender studies professor so thoroughly excoriated for her ideas of women complicit in their own violation and men's entitlement as the engine of their own ascension finds herself in the middle of an erotic affair between her husband and her lover.

Straight men could fall in love with each other, could be gentle with each other, share femininity, exchange sweet sentiments. The agreement was bending, and they were all entering uncharted territory. The book would sell itself. Something she'd perhaps finish this time.

Javier scrutinized her noncommitted eyes. They seemed everywhere and nowhere at once.

"Lorna, my darling, where are you?"

Her roaming found a mark and she smiled at it, her posture suddenly straight and her limbs no longer entangled. "Everything is fine."

"You're sure?" Risk worked Javier's toes with uncanny finesse, glanced at Theo's drawing.

Lorna had reached the threshold of the bedroom before she turned around with a new ebullience that both soothed and disquieted the amorous men.

"Yes, I just need to get back to work."

While Theo began taking on a haunted aspect, and Lorna donned once again her pedantic cap, slipping right back into full-on professorial mode, observing and taking notes, conducting secret experiments and recording her findings, producing conclusive evidence and testing hypotheses, Risk and Javier spun a cocoon, encapsulated themselves in a sweetness so rich they soon became exhausted.

Washing cars, Javier would turn the hose on Risk, and Risk would douse him with suds from the bucket of soapy water. They would manhandle each other gracefully and slip their hands into each other's pants, pushing one another against the Renault and the Aston Martin.

"I'll scrub you good," hissed Javier, soaking Risk with a sponge against the hood of the Aston Martin before sticking his tongue in his ear. "Filthy homeless man!"

Risk imagined all the ways in which he'd unman Javier.

Spectating at bull fights or soccer games or operas or movies, they would sneakily slide their hands between each other's legs, knead one another gently, accidentally poking testicles and massaging phalluses, touching feet in sandals, rubbing bare ankles in capri pants and loafers. They were surface friends, undercover lovers, quiet partners. They enjoyed the game they played with society, on holiday from Theo and Lorna. Risk was suddenly happy he'd proposed the threesome. It had worked to his advantage, after all. So much more than he had ever expected.

In the opera house, Javier whispered sweet plans. "I'm going to fuck you in the janitor's closet."

Risk ran through scenarios in which he'd ruin Javier's reputation.

Clothes shopping, the men would comment on the styles and cuts that best suited each other's frames and compromised on fashions that would satisfy both of their aesthetic particularities. They tended toward the same shoe size and all purchases were made by committee. A committee of two. Most heterosexual clerks and tailors assumed they were adopted brothers or friends, but the queer sales representatives knew better. They could smell the heat they exuded for one another.

"Maybe we can ask him to join us sometime," requested Risk in reference to a salesman whose beauty matched his interest. "I'd love to watch you drill away at him."

Risk pondered procedures that would leave Javier paralyzed.

Risk considered that the root of his lifelong discontent could have been repressed need and misplaced passion. Maybe he'd been in love with Dominick Truman. And the male cousins and male colleagues and male friends by whom he'd felt neutered. Maybe this would be the ticket out. The way to shed the old persona. The heavy, moldy personality that had never served him. Except for the sublimated drive toward wealth. He'd been an expert at that.

During a walk through the city, just exiting an ice cream parlor: "This feels like a dream, Javier."

While finishing an ice cream cone: "Don't spoil it by saying shit like that."

Risk sketched out techniques that would disfigure Javier.

The undergirding of this new wisdom and tenable faith would be threatened whenever Javier withdrew from his gentle touches and loving kisses, all studied affectations, anyway. The romance and kindness sometimes revolted the bullfighter, whose machismo was as restrained and natural as it was imposing and unquestionable. The mercurial shifts in mood, the out-of-nowhere protests and urgent nudging away. The sex had been effortless, and Javier received pleasure well, making little mewling sounds whenever Risk would lightly stroke his arm or thigh or neck or kiss his cock. But in matters of true connection, Javier held Risk at bay.

And it had begun to challenge his mission.

Getting a manicure-pedicure: "Do you still love me, Javier?"

In response to the ladies who'd been working on their toes but were not studying their exchange: "Let's not talk about this here."

Risk knew he'd loved Javier in a way Javier never accepted. And in a way he could never reciprocate. The bullfighter was in it for the sex and for the praise and for the dutiful massages. Risk, for the first time in his life, was on the receiving end of half-hearted attachment. Maybe no attachment at all. No. The sentiments were incorrect. Love was not the right word for what Risk had been feeling. Envy was more like it. Possibly covetousness. He sought to imprison Javier, or at least jail him—a temporary ownership if nothing else—and then maybe love could follow.

On a picnic in the Royal Botanical Garden, a crowded park in the middle of the city brimming with arid shrubbery commissioned by Charles III in the late 18th century, they found a secluded corner, shaded by Japanese raisin and pomegranate trees and off a path that rose above boulders and wound behind dense blackberry shrubs and peony bushes. Javier rested his head in Risk's lap as his American fed him grapes. They'd both gotten drunk on cabernet and full on brie and crackers. Risk brushed Javier's heavy, ebony hair with his fingers off his forehead and studied his brow, not as prominent as it used to be.

Javier made a face. "What are you smiling at?"

Risk now fingered his ear. "This. It's just ... really... oh, I don't know. Right, or something."

Javier sat up. "Maricone," he chuckled, with a softness in his tone. Good

[249]

humor had been successfully intimated.

"No. I mean it." Risk moved closer as Javier crept toward the basket of fruits and cheeses.

"These past few weeks have been maybe the best of my life."

"Yeah, it's nice." The lack of commitment in his voice panicked Risk. Had he not been fooled?

Risk massaged Javier's back, as the bull fighter went into a child pose and stretched away from his American pursuer. "What is it, babe? Lorna? Theo?"

Javier scratched his forehead hard enough to leave a mark. Risk wasn't sure if he was getting a heat rash or if he were agitated and was breaking out in hives.

"I mean, they're not making it easy, of course. I love Theo's drawings—you know how I feel about bold brains letting it all hang out—but the way he mopes around, and Lorna, well, you know, we don't have sex anymore, and she's writing about us. It's weird, man."

"We go to your place on weekends, and she used to do that with you, I get it." Risk was suddenly too confident, and it turned Javier's stomach. The sense of security grated. "Well, I used to be married to her. And even—"

"You still are."

Risk spoke slowly and with enunciation, as if he were steering a wayward child. "… Had a son with her."

Javier finally turned to Risk. "It's not really … *only* them, Risk. I just don't know if this is something I want to—"

"Don't. Let's take it one day at a time and see where it goes. If it means moving into your place permanently, or getting a new place, Hell—I can afford ten houses for us!"

Risk secretly marveled at his own talents. He pretended masterfully.

"If my father or brothers ever found out about us, Risk, they would—"

"Your father? Your brothers?" Risk looked around to make sure no one had been listening. "Javier, you're a grown fucking man."

Confusion had found its way in, if only for a moment. Had Risk been acting his role so well that he'd forgotten what he'd been doing, and why? Could envy and covetousness spill over into love if the emotion were performed, even without genuine ardor?

"This is not America." Javier poured himself another glass of red wine. "It's not *New York City.*"

Risk became quiet and stopped protesting. He drank with Javier and together they got drunk and picked blackberries and peonies and jerked each other off behind the dense shrubbery to the sounds of teenage boys playing soccer and mothers and fathers bickering over dinner and weekend agendas.

When the improbable couple returned home that evening, Risk began his search for a hitman on the Dark Web. It was time he'd implemented his new scheme, a crueler deal. Risk would cut down the towering offender. He would be the Spartan to Javier's Xerxes. The American had managed the ruse more convincingly than he'd thought himself capable.

XVIII

Theo continued to plaster the house with drawings of cartoons in libidinal trysts: Snoopy with a swimmer's build sodomizing Charlie Brown with a bodybuilder's physique, Daffy Duck with humungous genitalia impaling long, lean, vascular Speedy Gonzalez with sexy runner's legs, and a vampy Dumbo with a porn star's torso skull fucking a brawny Prince Charming with a purple dildo. Risk was nauseated by the art, but he left it all up as he found it a sort of atonement he ought to endure. And to please Javier, of course.

"These are monstrous, Theo." Risk had muttered the words under his breath, but it hadn't mattered, as Theo wouldn't have acknowledged the remark anyway.

"She took my Yoda toy you gave me," said Theo, only glancing at his father.

Risk would take whatever he could get from his son in the way of communication and replied with an eager exclamation of his own. "And our magnet on the fridge from Casablanca! Don't think I hadn't noticed. Why don't you ask her where they are?"

Theo's haunting was comprehensive. He also streamed clips of strangers falling, flopping, failing. Bystanders. Spectators. A theater of mortification. The very YouTube videos that had inspired Risk all those years ago in New York to document and present his exploits with Dominick during the team-building fiascos. There was the aged businessman who tumbled (was tripped?) down the subway staircase, the professionally dressed woman who had a screaming match with a homeless man in the park (instigated?), and the young hipster trying to move boxes of books into a presumably new apartment who crumbled under the weight of the heft (a compromised box?). Among a dozen others.

Though Risk had spoken to Theo, the boy wouldn't respond verbally. He'd answer his father's questions or comments with grunts, sighs, shrugs, smiles, eye rolls, giggles, chortles, claps, snaps, and hisses. Theo had become a ghoul, a specter, arrived and trapped within the cavernous hold of a man who'd never believed in ghosts. However, blame and shame were real monsters that could stare and scare. Risk had stared back, but he hadn't been scared.

"How much longer, Theo? How long do you intend to ignore me, Theo? Theo!"

It was a quiet, humid night when Risk read the response to his inquiry on The Sicilian Hitman, accessible only through TOR, a software browser he'd spent weeks researching. Risk had been shocked and amused to learn that such a site really existed. It had been true—everything you could possibly imagine existed on the Dark Web.

And it was now time to take the crown from the king.

"It can be done. What you've requested. I have a background in anatomy and physiology. I know how to leave a person with permanent disabilities. And the disfigurement is the easiest part. It'll require two men. We only accept payment through BITCOIN."

Javier entered the kitchen, uncharacteristically sullen. The Spaniard looked haggard, somewhat sallow, and sad. *Remorseful.* Risk slammed shut his laptop and hid his gasp but swallowed hard.

"I just need some company, friend." Javier's voice was meek. It was an alarming reduction.

Risk made tea. Javier requested it be spiked with rum. Risk complied. The men drank too much and were drunk within the hour. They spoke little.

"I'm not much for conversation tonight," said Javier. "I hope it's okay for us to just sit here and drink for a while."

"Of course, Javier. It's okay."

Theo would peek in on them, hoping for a sudden burst of violence or dominance testing. But, without fail, nothing interesting ever again happened during that dry period. He'd retreated to his bedroom for the evening to masturbate and make more art.

"He's having trouble with all this," Risk said, gesturing to Theo's drawings and video installations.

Javier studied the artwork, raised his eyebrows. "None of it is unlike the twisted shit you have hanging out there."

Javier was referring to the blown-up Barney and Hirst photos that filled the walls in the living room of the suited satyr slimed with sperm and the excessively divided cow. Javier scrutinized them with performance, making clear that he was having an appreciative reaction to the horror of the artists' statements.

Some Comfort Gained from the Acceptance of the Inherent Lies of Everything. It was quite a title, and Javier found himself in agreement with it.

Risk smiled, sipped his tea. Appreciated the rum. Javier stood and limped to the stove to refill his teacup and add another few shots.

Risk bowed his head, awaiting his return. Javier placed his teacup on the table and touched Risk's wound he'd given him days earlier, still tender and hot on his neck. Risk recoiled, turned to him with a defensive glower.

Javier nodded and continued to stroke Risk's scar lovingly, softly. Risk turned back to the table and exhaled. The touch felt good. Soothing. Javier slid his hands to Risk's shoulders and deeply, caringly massaged the bunched muscles and twitching nerves. Risk closed his eyes. Javier was conscious of the wounds and worked the tissue around them. He moved his hands around to Risk's heavy, hard pectorals and kneaded them. Risk's nipples hardened. His penis did, too. He didn't care. This all felt too good. Javier leaned in and kissed Risk's ear, then his cheek, and then faint old burn marks on his neck, ones he'd never noticed before. Risk wheezed.

Javier reached down farther and patted Risk's tight stomach, pulled up his t-shirt, and stroked his aged, tough abdominals with the tips of his fingers. Risk pushed his head back into Javier's cradling shoulder, turned his head, and kissed his mouth. Javier smiled and slowly pulled away. Risk watched with wide, wanting eyes.

Javier choked up, wiped his nose. He crouched and cleared his throat. His eyes reddened, and he cleared his throat again, but this time whimpered when doing so.

Risk took his hand. "Javier?"

Javier pulled Risk's hand to his face and kissed it. Took a finger in his mouth and sucked it. Risk gasped in ecstasy. Javier's eyes were always on his American opponent as he again kissed his knuckles. "I'm sorry, Risk."

It wasn't until the bullfighter had made his way to his feet and lumbered back into the bedroom that Risk spotted Theo standing in the threshold watching the entirety of the affectionate interplay. The fondness was terrifying.

And in a flash Theo was back in his room dreaming up a new tableau, this one of his father and the Spanish fighter in a coital entanglement. Their bodies super-heroic, their lovemaking mythological and warlike. It was sex and it was murder. Risk wouldn't see the piece, but it would no doubt fail to mystify him as deeply as the man he'd come to love—not love, not yet, but envy, covet—and plot against. Even art couldn't eclipse the mysteries of people.

Risk opened his laptop and responded to the reply on The Sicilian Hitman.

"Done. The money will be in your account by tomorrow morning."

XIX

Risk had made breakfast for Javier, Theo, and Lorna. Spinach and onion omelet with asparagus and English muffins with jam. Blueberries, oranges, and bananas. Everyone ate heartily and the tension that had for so long covered the house had lifted, at least slightly. Theo had still been strange, however, doodling at the counter in the kitchen. Risk had overheard Javier compliment his latest sketch, this one of a Dumbo with sprinter's legs being infiltrated by a lithe Simba with an impossibly gargantuan appendage. Lorna had yet to be impressed with the cry for attention.

Lorna had spoken first that morning and with an uncharacteristic chirpiness. "So, we're going out for lunch, Theo and I, this afternoon."

Risk nodded and looked at Theo, whose back was to his father as he continued drawing from inside the kitchen.

"Good, I'm glad you two are spending some quality time together."

Lorna shrugged, sipped her black coffee, and resumed editing the books she'd been writing about Javier and her husband's relationship.

Javier began tickling Risk's foot with his own. Both were bare and freshly washed. Risk smirked up at him from his plate, romance on his mind. Sexual chaos on Javier's.

That afternoon, with Lorna and Theo out for the day, Risk had begun to make love to Javier in the living room. It was carefully done, with adoring whispers and sensual caresses. Risk had to maintain his affection and adulation, keep his body and his mind on the platter. Though the sex had been smooth and lively, something upended the passion. Javier had initially been game, through foreplay and into the undressing and the entanglement, but as Risk began to slide himself in, Javier suddenly cringed and pushed the

American away. He exhaled with a brusqueness that killed the mood.

Risk crossed his arms and sat forward on the couch, not quite looking at Javier directly, though eyeballing him obliquely. "Is this ending?"

It was in these moments, when Risk could feign emotional injury and find nuance in his performance, in his improved character, that he really came alive.

"I don't know."

"Was it a phase or something? Were you just fucking with me? Trying to get Lorna? Embarrass my son?"

Risk wanted more than anything to reveal his charade, if for no other reason than to gloat about how authentic his acting had been, how pure a performer he was, how expertly he'd duped Javier, and Lorna, and even cynical, perspicacious Theo. He'd made fools of them all and he wasn't even trained or had any aspirations to be a thespian. It had all come naturally. Like jazz. Exact, yet on impulse. He could do anything well if he set his mind to it, even invent a personality and sustain a show like this.

Javier looked at him, at the strange confluence of expressions playing out on his face, from scared to angry to excited to maybe happy and then back to scared.

"It's nothing like that."

Risk shrugged, allowed his movements to inform his language, his gesticulations to lead his expressions. "Well, then what is the matter with—"

Javier drove his body into Risk's with such agency that Risk gasped and panicked, assuming the greater man was about to throttle him yet again, to punish him for his backtalk. But no, that wasn't it, at all. Javier had been aroused and wanted to fuck. It was the lovemaking that had made him squeamish. Risk submitted quickly to Javier's advances and remained docile through the loud, merciless, sodomizing affair.

Javier hadn't gone easy on him, and throughout the ordeal, the bullfighter grunted such adorations as "Take it, you sad, fucking faggot!" and "You want it, don't you, you little pussy!" and also "Take it up the ass, up your little flower!" and finally, "Feel what a real man is like! How a true man fucks!"

Risk's anus was chapped and bled. He had been penetrated without lubrication. Without comfort or care. Without fondness. And he had been shaken by the interaction. The debasing role play, though he hadn't meant to play this rough. Javier took his submission, his limp body, his willful surrender as permission, as a performance, as play itself. This was an engagement to which he could become accustomed. Not the silly lovemaking. Not the tender touches. None of that limp-wristed mixed messages crap.

Javier Forza was *not* gay. He was a man. And he was okay with occasionally fucking a close buddy. That was the benefit of the bi, or pan, as he'd sometimes prefer to call it, identification.

Risk had resigned himself. Slipped back into the original mode of subservience and smallness. Quietly folding in under Javier's arm, creeping at his ankle, between his toes. Much less than he, the premiere warrior of Madrid and the favorite son of Spain. The absolute athlete, the unbeatable fighter.

Over the course of the next few weeks, the tonal adjustment had not gone unnoticed by Theo and Lorna. Dr. Hall-Bonaventura was herself, again. Her writing had become sharper as her interests in the subject of Risk and Javier's unequal, uneven, unhealthy relationship elicited a deeper curiosity, produced a richer text. She also, during her darker minutes, when she'd been lonely and desperate and seeking an exit, visited the website for The Eva Peron School for Girls and thought about reaching out to Samuel Quilty, despite the years that had already passed and his inherent crepiness, his cryptic intimations.

And Theo had quit drawing, stopped posting the obscene illustrations throughout the house, and once again, continued to record the peculiar goings-on around home, between dad and dad's dominator. Nothing too queer. Except for their periodic bouts of sobriety. The most disarming hours.

Risk, the character he'd molded, pined for closeness. His false Self fought for it. Slaved himself for the affection. But even the real Risk kept Javier's scent inside. And the sensation of his skin close. The tactile memory of his lover's body would adhere for the rest of his life, even if the bullfighter had no further use for his affections and romance and even if the American hadn't truly loved him. Envy, covetousness. The finery and thickness of his fingers and toes, the cleanliness and fastidiousness of his fingernails and toenails. The taste of his mouth, the texture of his stomach, the cold rubbery fullness of his ears. His warm crotch, his hot, minty breath. And then the gravely hum of his voice, like a trash compactor's zoom or a garbage truck's rumble.

Javier only romanticized Risk's worship, his doe-like obsequiousness and dutiful deference. The American—performing love and service, knowing only grudge and greed—wished he could devour the Spaniard's skin, fingernails, toes, ears, mouths, calves, veins. His romantic imagination tended toward the macabre, but it felt true. The sexual for Risk was ego-edifying for Javier. Risk's worship fueled something quiet and sick inside him. Possessing a full man, subjugating him, twisting him under his thumb. It exceeded even the rush of downing a bull.

"And you don't mind any of this, Risk?" Lorna scribbled notes. Too copious for such a minor question, thought Risk, though he couldn't care less about what his wife wrote about him and Javier.

Javier sat between them on the bed in the master bedroom. Theo had been recording from the threshold. He smiled and felt like his old self. At this point, no one was anymore uncomfortable about anything in the Bonaventura Household. It was one of those rare instances where everyone had been sober, and the stale air hadn't been too abundant.

"I'm not sure how to explain it, Lorna. I know it's odd, but it feels okay. If this is all Javier can give … in this way. It'll have to be okay, and I'll have to adapt."

Javier eyeballed Lorna with suspicion and impatience. Too engrossed in the material to acknowledge his taciturn tics, she nodded, staring at her notes, and wrote. She was no longer an active participant in this threesome, but now a clinician assessing a pair of patients that required understanding and possible therapeutic services and strategies for healthful outcomes. Before, her short stories, novel proposals, academic texts had been remote, impersonal, and disingenuous masturbations. Now, she was writing something real, personal, and immediate, something of measurable consequence, something that felt anthropological, like the discovery of a new tribe or virus or species of wild animal. Even the finding of a new continent. She was the Vasco Da Gama of forbidden human behavior. This was real sex.

Lorna wrote furiously, spoke at a disorienting speed. "Do you think it's because you actually love Javier and therefore will sacrifice yourself for his happiness or is it rather a matter of your self-loathing, a *punishment*, if you will, or better yet, a *confirmation* of your low feelings about yourself? Or, maybe this, just maybe, do you believe you require being brought down a peg because you're arrogant and have a superiority complex? So many possibilities, really!"

"I haven't given it much thought, Lorna." Risk sounded dim, or at least mousy, shrunken, and he reached for Javier, naked under a towel, fresh from a shower. "Like I said—I only like how it feels, being there for him, being there ... and ... *less than* him."

Javier slapped Risk's hand away and flicked his nose, causing his American subaltern to recoil and wince. Lorna made notes. Perhaps her husband had been too deeply in a state of submissiveness to resist her questions or Javier's punishments. Maybe he sought compliance to any dominant figure in that moment, and indeed, during this prolonged period. Maybe, Lorna imagined with irritation and pride, he'd finally accepted her as a mother figure. Risk sniveled and wiped his nostrils. He played poorly at jocularity, and so badly wanted to be a brother to the man who ruled the household and his spirit. The sway he held over his realm, controlling body, thought, and impulse, bordered on the magical. And without ever actually issuing a single command. The reduction would come soon, and it would sate his insatiable palate.

"Javier …" Lorna became tentative and scribbled slower now. "What is this doing for you? Treating Risk this way?"

Javier removed his towel, exposing himself to the married couple. Theo became weak and though he knew he'd have to edit it out of his video for the sake of YouTube sanitization he took a closeup of the dusky, hefty, and hardy mess of genitals dangling between the bull fighter's great legs. The matador's pose, spread-eagled and reclined, demure and even dainty, was as much an invitation as it was a denial, even an intimidation. The naked bully, quietly coercive.

Risk's eyes fell softly on his victor's manhood and his mouth became dry. For a moment he believed in God. God as an artist. And when Javier flexed, Risk heard angels. But then the diminished New Yorker envisioned his faux lord's gonads on fine china. Risk's drive to destroy Javier's genitals was equaled only by his hunger to devour them.

Lorna fumbled with the pen and pad as she regained the interview.

"This is your husband's doing, all of it." Javier touched his sex, engorging it. He looked at Risk, who whimpered and moved an inch toward it, like bait, a lure with an outsized worm. "Look at how starving he is. Look at what I've woken up. He's a dog. And like all dogs, he seeks to be broken. And that's okay, Lorna, because he's a grown man. And he knows what he's doing. *How should I feel?* I feel good. Proud."

Theo imagined that this is what prison must be like for straight men. Men who would be denied women and freedom to choose. In prison, you made do with what you were given, with what, or whom, you were stuck. Walt Whitman called it cohesion. A love between men. A brotherly kind of love that grows into something more, something physical and daringly affectionate. He'd observed many cases during the Civil War. Now they just call it "gay for the stay."

"And I'm done with this." The bullfighter cringed as though afflicted with an instructive urge.

Javier stood, leaving the damp towel draped over the bed, and put on cotton shorts and a t-shirt. Lorna and Risk held their breath as they waited for him to leave the bedroom. Theo recorded him push past as he exited and brooded and seethed and swore down the long hallway.

"You're okay, Risk?" Lorna closed her notebook. "With me writing about you?"

"I'm not ashamed of it. And I've nothing to hide."

Sad, silly Lorna. One day you'll perhaps know what a fibber I could be.

Lorna nodded. It hadn't been lost on her that she and her husband and son were reliving a lurid version of their New York lives. A fantastical theater of their former selves. A penance. Repetition. There was dignity in the danger, a sacred peace in the peril and the debauchery. She felt at home within it, as she knew Risk had, as she knew Theo had.

They were not a conventional family but that didn't matter. Convention had failed to please.

◆ ◆ ◆

That evening in the kitchen, Javier made sangria, Lorna fried Merluza, a fish easily found throughout the country, and Risk read financial news on his phone. Theo stood at the threshold, hugging his laptop, and contemplated the scene, the family, the subverted tableau that had become normal, expected, and even relished.

He knew that he was about to complicate matters and possibly upend the harmonic, dysfunctional filial moment, gossamer as it had always been.

"I guess I'm ready now. Ready to show you all what I've been working on this past year." Theo walked to the breakfast nook, flipped open his laptop, accessed YouTube, and played his videos. When one ended the next began. A long loop, interminable and ghastly.

"My big, not-so-secret project."

Javier saw it first. "What the fuck did you do, you little shit stain?"

This prompted Risk to look up from his phone and rise with an angelic expression, as if he'd just been visited by the maker. "Oh, Theo. Oh … son …"

"Thoughtless, careless boy!" Lorna, moving urgently from the stove and across the rectangular kitchen, panted, wheezed. "Jesus Christ. Now you've done it."

Theo sighed. Waited. Rode out the storm. A comprehensive review of their most private and undermining minutes. Risk's failed attempts to best Javier at constructing the bookshelf, managing the remote control, barbequing, arm wrestling, and fist fighting. And all the subsequent, attendant fits and degenerations. Coital moments between mom and Javier, dad and Javier. The George and Martha scenes. And then their eyes collectively dropped to the number of views, the number of likes, the comments. *Oh, the comments.*

BOREDBOT1977: "Not too bad for a middle-aged guy. Even with his skinny ankles and back hair!!!! LOL!!!!"

BROWNBUTTHOLE2002: "That's Javier Forza!!! Hot Insta stud! Sickooooo!!!!!"

FRATFROG: "I'd do that old cunt! A MILF I'd actually fuckkkkkk."

MARCUSMAYHEM: "A DILF for a gang bang!"

ILIKEBIGTITS1996: "Risk Bonaventura, that's you, man! Doing that perverted bullshit! Get it, old man!!!!!!"

NELSONNONSENSE1989: "HOOOTTTTT Mexican dude!"

TABITHASMALLS: "FUCKED UP family!"

EUSTACIA1998: "Euro TRASH!"

ORWELLJUSTICE77: "I know that feminist bitch from New York who said women want to be raped! Maybe her husband and that spic take turns plowing here hardddd!!!!!"

LUKE&BACCA: "Ugly American assholes!!!!"

They only read the ones in English, and Javier couldn't bring himself to translate the Spanish, though Lorna, Risk, and Theo had learned enough to grasp the main ideas of each crude sentiment.

BESAME-EL-TRASERO99: "Quiero fijar tu madre!"

Lorna couldn't speak. She'd avoided social media and especially YouTube since the trauma of her own short-lived infamy. No wonder she'd never happened across Theo's collection. She had been too busy running from the Internet to see what was being sent out into the world from under her own roof. And Risk, he'd been too spellbound, too turned around within his fugue, to have ever noticed something like his son's web-based magnum opus. And after his own YouTube troubles, the last thing he'd want to get sucked into was another social media shit storm.

Theo surveyed the faces and sniggered. "I mean, what did you think I was doing with the camera and all that footage I shot?" Theo chuckled, pointed at them. "You guys! Your faces are—"

"You think this is a joke, you little cocksucker?" Javier stepped forward and grabbed the laptop, hoisted it above his head, and snarled at the trembling boy before him.

"For fuck's sake!" Lorna hissed as she snatched the laptop from Javier, yanking it away with such ferocity she banged her elbow on the counter. "What is wrong with you? Barbarian!"

Javier made fists and his temples bore giant beating veins. "Your son is the barbarian! Your husband is the barbarian! *You're* the barbarian! What the fuck did you raise?"

Lorna hurried past Javier with the laptop, grabbed Theo's iPhone from his hand, and fled the terrible scene.

"You're done with all this now," she said as she sped past her son, who nodded in horror and was for the moment cowed. "Take it all down, Theo!"

As Lorna bounded down the hallway and into the master bedroom, Theo thought, but how would he "take it all down," now that she'd removed any means of deleting the footage. He'd kept the smart-ass remark to himself for fear of further reprisals.

Risk sat back down and continued to review his financial news articles, but his mind was elsewhere. He'd deposited the first payment to the hitman weeks ago already and had yet to pull the trigger on the service.

Javier slapped the phone out of his hand. It hit the table hard enough to bounce across it.

"Aren't you going to say anything? Aren't you ever going to be a whole man, again?"

With a mannequin's affect, Risk reached across the table to retrieve his phone and resumed reading.

Javier laughed. Moved toward Theo, who covered his genitals and face, turning away as though the bullfighter were about to assault both fragile destinations. Javier laughed again and was gone.

Theo and his father had not said anything, though they sat together at the kitchen table for another hour.

Risk returned to The Sicilian Hitman site and pulled the trigger.

X X

Javier and Risk had dinner in Barrio de Las Letras—huevos rotos, oreja a la Plancha, and pincho de tortilla. A lot of pig and eggs.

"I like this part of town," said Javier, picking his teeth with a toothpick. "Great literary history."

"And a lot of tourists." Risk wiped his mouth, sat back. "Like all of Spain. Tourists everywhere."

"Everywhere is a tourist destination these days, buddy. The world is shrinking."

The men walked along the Calle de Santa Catalina, turned down Ateneo de Madrid, and window-shopped the countless cathedrals, boutiques, and galleries that filled the tiny, trendy, literary neighborhood.

Risk cringed. "It all feels too curated, somehow too self-conscious."

"*All* European cities are. You've been here long enough to know better."

The men maneuvered past the timid tourists mingling with the shameless cosmopolitans, contemplated al fresco restaurants, and browsed the old homes—now museums—of Cervantes and Quevado, before deciding on the oldest, smallest, quietest tavern in town. Really, on the outskirts of town.

Risk had spotted the unassuming storefront, all weathered wood framing with blue slate and overgrown ivy, as they turned a corner, dimly lit and with uneven pavement.

"It's been two hours since we've had anything to drink."

"Let's fix that."

A soccer game played on television, an antiquated heavy box tube set which sat on one end of the bar as a bullfight flickered on another, a busted LED flat-screen that slouched on a shelf by the bathroom door.

"Lorna thinks we've gone crazy." Risk drank his beer too fast. He was intent on sustaining the buzz that he'd started that afternoon. "That we're getting along so well, suddenly. And being ..." Risk surveyed the bar. ".... The way we are with each other now."

"I thought it was strange, too, my friend. At first ... it's been many years since I've been with a man ... like this, right? And even then, hey, it was just fucking around, right? Nothing too serious. But then ..."

"But then ..." Risk was being cute, putting on a too-endearing face, and it annoyed Javier. The opposite effect Risk had hoped for.

"But then, I figured, fuck it—sex is sex, and a hole is a hole, and the more the merrier, right?"

Risk frowned. Refilled his beer at the bar and, of course, drank it too fast. Javier snickered. He knew how to get the American, especially when his guard was down and he sought validation.

A woman—maybe seventy, with sloppily administered makeup, deep blue eyeshadow and purple rouge, and heavy, red eyes—scrutinized the couple.

"¿No es eso Javier Forza y Riesgo Bonaventura?"

The corpulent man—possibly eighty, in a suit presumably stitched in the 1940s—who sat beside her continued to puff on his cigar and shrugged.

"¿Quién sabe? ¿A quién le importan esos homosexuales, de todos modos?"

Theo's social media broadcasts of them had apparently leaked into the mainstream outlets if old people had known of their trysts.

When they finished their last round of beer, Risk and Javier muttered to each other drunkenly that they ought to duck out before anyone else recognized them, hounding for autographs and photos, though both men would have been flattered with any positive attention at all at this point. It had been a while since either had been in the news.

"No one here is going to want our autographs, Risk."

"Great job, my son did."

The dejected matadors headed back to their Aston Martin parked in the lot behind the tavern. Risk began making a crude joke about gay sex and Spanish culture and old people, but before he could deliver the punchline (an awkward meeting of Paella, nursing homes, and Fellatio) he heard a rustle from a nearby dumpster. A shadow danced across the hood of the car and then came the sensations.

The impact of the assault swept Risk off his feet and sent him hurtling into a botanical island of trimmed hedges ornamented with white lights, leaving him scratched, poked, and entangled.

As he pulled twigs from his eyes and ears, Risk heard violence—a chaotic medley of bones bashed against metal and shuffling feet across concrete and huffing and grunting and clothes tearing and then the distinct sounds of Javier, growling, howling.

Risk regained his footing and rose from the bushes and beheld the source of the ambush—a great beastly figure. All fat and muscle and big bone and in a ski mask and gloves and boots. He brandished a crowbar. Risk gasped and then recoiled as the behemoth swung the weapon repeatedly and with a surgeon's exactness into the small of Javier's back.

As the Spaniard writhed on the ground, groaning and salivating, the figure again raised the bar to threaten Risk.

"Esto es entre nosotros españoles. Este maricón tiene que pagar por sus traiciones."

Even as he was being pummeled, Javier was most struck by the accent of the man assaulting him. It was unmistakably Italian. Sicilian, specifically. The assailant sounded like his father, but it was not Dad. This voice had been too soft.

Risk raised his hands in surrender and then another figure emerged from the darkness. Shorter, square-shaped, and with a ducky waddle, also gloved and masked. He was calm and deliberate in his movements but muttered unintelligibly in peninsular Spanish. The smaller figure pulled a glass vial from his coat pocket. He popped the lid, rubber and tightly sealed, and doused Javier's face with the liquid inside.

Dense, acrid steam rose from the Spaniard as he screamed—his face had become a kettle spout. All sizzling, roasting sounds. And Risk knew what it was that the stranger poured on him. From the smell. Acid. *Nitric* acid. The most common type of corrosive substance used in acid attacks. Also the type Risk had ordered.

The two figures then left with a steady urgency, but they didn't run. They simply walked away, got in a red van with peeling paint waiting for them on the corner, and were gone.

By the time Risk reached Javier, the matador's face was oozing puss. Flesh bubbled. His skin and muscle were cooking. The Spaniard made no more sounds. His mouth opened and he was toothless. His expression, an Edvard Munch painting—an eternal, silent, twisted shriek.

Javier's face hung from his skull, his eyes changed by fright and shock. He gazed at his American, untouched, unblemished.

XXI

Risk had become Javier's nursemaid. It was a role he played well. He had been dutiful and compassionate and attentive to details and medication schedules and infection risks. His diligence had turned the home into a clinic, or, at the very least, one wing of their mansion had taken on a semblance of a clinic. Drugs. IV drips. Crutches. Canes. Ointments. Spools of gauze. Heart monitors. High-tech thermometers.

"Come on, old buddy, take your oxycontin. Believe me, you don't want your hip acting up on you before bedtime!"

He treated Javier's grisly scars and burns with the ointment prescribed by the physician who examined and operated on Javier when Risk brought him to the hospital only two miles from the site of the attack. The location had been strategically chosen.

"We need to try walking, as per the doctor's instructions! We don't want your other leg to lose its strength, now do we?"

The attacker left Javier's lumbar nerves, specifically L2, L3, and L4, crushed, and therefore his right leg paralyzed. The matador would now require a cane or crutch to walk.

"Rest, I'll bring you your dinner. Just don't move. Here—watch your soccer game. Is Madrid playing tonight?"

It had been a week since his discharge from the hospital, almost three weeks since the attack itself, and Lorna had not gotten used to the sight of her erstwhile lover struggle. Or her husband infantilizing him.

"Let's rub these sores down. We don't want them to attract any bacteria!"

Risk, the actor, had demonstrated astounding versatility and range, segueing from the obsequious lothario to the dispassionate caretaker. He fibbed with such depth that he even believed his own performances.

"Time for your bath, old chum. Here, let me help you into the tub."

Theo, quite naturally as per his instincts, recorded the new life, his new mentor in his new role, his new father in his new lie, and his new mother in her new revolt. Indeed, against her better judgment and in a moment of extraordinary weakness, Lorna had given Theo back his laptop and iPhone. What further damage could the boy do?

On Javier's first night home, the bullfighter's morbid transformation had become the favorite subject of the Bonaventura family. As Javier soaked in the bathtub, Risk made him tea spiked with Whiskey. Theo sat at the table fumbling with his iPhone, waiting for something worthwhile to happen for him to record. Lorna washed the dishes, turned to her husband.

"I still can't believe this happened."

Risk boiled water and grabbed a mug. "Yeah, a real tragedy."

Theo looked up from his phone. "Do you really think it was my fault? Because of my videos?"

Risk snatched a teabag—oolong—and honey and lemon and a cinnamon stick, and then turned to his son and made an expression as if to convey suspicion, as if to say, *Theo, stop pretending that you care. Stop faking your concern. Stop suggesting that you're not getting off on the power of your shitty video collection on that awful website.*

Theo leaned back, cringed. "What?"

"Of course it wasn't your fault, Theo. No one is ever influenced by the media. Not even *social* media."

Lorna moved closer to Risk and spoke softly, too low for Theo to hear. "His face, Risk. It's … I'm not at all…"

"I know." Risk dipped the teabag several times, pulled it out, and tossed it in the trash. "It's a lot. He looks horrible. But he's our friend. And he needs us now. He needs *me*."

"And he's… You said the doctors said … That his …"

"He's impotent now." Risk lifted the mug. The aroma comforted. "That,

[271]

too. Yes. He's lost so much, Lorna. In the matter of one evening, he lost practically everything that mattered to him."

Lorna touched the ring of condensation on the counter left behind by the hot mug. "The poor man."

"Yes, so, you know, he can't lose us, too."

He'd used this tone on her before, whenever he suspected her of concealing true feelings.

Risk had left the kitchen, but Theo lingered, staring at his mother with covert eyes signaling self-satisfied recriminations. She wiped down the counter and retreated to her bedroom.

Javier sat in the yard and scrolled through the news on his phone. Local headlines stopped reporting on his attack, and none of them were able to get a hold of photos of his new face and altered posture. He was grateful for that much. But the journalists had reported the extent of his injuries correctly. Doctors in Madrid surrendered confidential information for the right price. He hated the pity but relished the attention.

Lorna joined him with two glasses of sangria. She sat beside him, and he muttered "thank you" as he received the glass from her.

"Do you want to get out, Javier? I can take you to a movie or maybe we can walk around the park."

"I'm not going back into *that city*." Javier's mouth was tight, as if masked by duct tape, and his words were slurred. Lorna thought it looked painful to talk. "Where people who could do this to me live. They can all go fuck themselves forever now."

"It's not that bad, you know. Your face." But Lorna's voice quivered when she said the word *face* and Javier knew that it was *that bad*.

"Right." Javier downed the sangria expertly and took Lorna's hand. He pulled it toward him and put it on his crotch. Lorna gasped and pulled away as if she had trodden too close to a cobra.

Javier pushed up from the arm of his seat and strained to kiss her, but she cried out and shuddered as she nearly fell off her chair to escape.

Javier frightened her now. His bottom lip had become misshapen and was too big. It drooped into his chin as if his face were a candle with running wax that had become permanently stuck mid-drip. His nose and left eyelids merged. One nostril remained of original size, the other, on his left, was two sizes too big, a giant, gaping hole. The top row of teeth, big and still white, that ran along the right side of his mouth were permanently exposed as the upper lip had been burned off. His left ear was mostly gone, as was a sizable swath of hair above his forehead, doubling his hairline. The flesh itself was now purple and scabbed like roasted eggplant. He was a hideous aberration and Lorna could not fake it.

She wept and Javier laughed. She attempted to explain herself and he laughed harder. She apologized and he cursed at her. She moved to touch him, and he spat at her.

Theo had been on the far end of the yard, crouched down within gooseberry bushes, recording the interaction in a shaky, but clear, zoomed-in medium close up, framing his mother and Javier as imperiled lovers destined for bloody calamity.

When she went back inside without her half-empty glass of sangria, Javier fought his way to his feet, gripped his cane, and hobbled to the garden, where he found beetles and worms and butterflies to seize and squash and azaleas and daises and bougainvillea to pluck and shred.

Theo had caught all that, too.

XXII

Theo recorded his father as Risk blotted Javier's tender skin with antibacterial lotion, a nightly ritual. Some of the scabs had darkened and hardened like turtle shells. One already peeled off and left behind a violet blush across his chin. Despite Javier's long list of medications and Risk's newfound set of responsibilities, both patient and nursemaid drank whiskey and coke.

"Motherfucking shit!" Javier grimaced and snapped his head back. "It fucking stings! And stinks!"

"Well, it needs to be done, my dear." Risk dabbed more gently, with less ointment. "We don't want your whole damn face rotting and falling off, do we?"

Lorna reread passages she'd written the day before and found countless failings in her work. They were small and probably inconsequential, but she convinced herself that the research and the composition were both categorically flawed and beyond fixing. She considered giving up on the project, tossing the whole endeavor. The self-criticism went some way in mollifying her horror. Javier's grisly aspect hadn't grown on her, and she was still rattled from their clumsy, boorish encounter days earlier.

Lorna filed her chapters into a folder and brought it to her desk. She'd been sitting in the dining room with the nurse and his patient.

Lorna picked at the edge of the folder. "I, uhm, think I may go for a walk, get some fresh air."

"Oh, really?" Javier turned to her and smiled. It made him scarier. "Maybe I'll go along with you."

Lorna wheezed and bumped into the desk as she instinctively backed up. Risk raised his eyebrows, disarmed by her terror. Javier sniggered and looked at his hands, always trembling now.

Javier's eyes dimmed. Everything about him now seemed dimmer. "I was fucking with you."

"Oh, well …" And then Lorna laughed, too nervously, thought Risk.

Theo pushed in on his father's incredulousness—another raised eyebrow and a kind of half scowl.

Risk looked back at Javier, whose dimness was now too dark to ignore, and then back to his wife, who was visibly shaken. "Is there a problem, Lorna?"

"No, no problem, Risk." Lorna gathered herself. There was no threat here. Nothing by which to be so flustered. Her behavior had been overblown. Even she could see that. "I just wanted to be alone."

Javier's mouth tightened, gargling his words. "You're creeped out by me now, aren't you, dear, beautiful Lorna with the functional leg and the regular face?"

Javier had been quickly drunk and Risk was getting there. Theo zoomed in on Javier's unfortunate face and focused on pockets of puss, on his melted chin, now a little nub. How could his mother not be disgusted by this man now?

Risk shook his head. "Shallow, shallow, shallow Lorna. High priestess of intellectualism and moralism and profound things beneath the surface. *Deep bullshit things!*"

Lorna was now tucked into the corner of the living room, seemingly hiding behind her desk, and burrowing into the corner.

"That's not fair," she whimpered, a little girl, unsure of her own mettle.

"It's *not fair?*" Risk had been drunker than she thought. His face was red, and he spat when he talked at increasing speed and inflection. "It's *not fair* that this has happened to our dear, beloved Javier! It's *not fair* that some bigoted monsters attacked him and fucked up his face and left him a fucking cripple!" Risk balled his fist and banged the coffee table. "That's *not fair*, either! And it's *not fair* that now you're acting weird with him!"

Lorna reached for her keys and her cell. She began putting on her shoes when Risk whistled at her. Reluctant, she looked up at her husband. He was crouched before Javier, touching the Spaniard's neck—still strong and sinuous, but with deep pock marks now, places where the splattering of acid had hit—and leaned forward, opened his mouth, pushed out his tongue, and kissed him on his mouth, the mangled orifice that had once been his mouth, and the deformed matador received him, and their kiss made sounds and was wet and Theo said "Ewww," which broke the 4th wall for the first time of his video series as it was caught on camera, and Lorna gasped.

Risk pulled away and Javier sneered at Lorna, but his sneering was menacing now that his face looked like a Halloween mask. Like the devil. Or the star from some 1950s creature feature.

"Surface." Javier's voice changed. As if emergent from the pit of his gut. "Fucking surface bitch."

"I haven't even been a part of whatever it was that you two were doing for—"

"Ah, but you *wanted* to!" Risk was giddy with righteousness. He bounced on the balls of his feet. "You still checked him out. You still dreamt of his cock and face and strong, strong legs wrapped around you."

"You don't know." Lorna finished getting her shoes back on and paced in the foyer. "You have no idea what I—"

"Just save it, Lorna." Risk put his arm around Javier. "We both deserve better than this. We've both been through enough. How about a little compassion and kindness?"

They'd been through enough? Compassion and kindness? The proclamations were outrageous. Lorna just nodded, but the men couldn't tell if she was surrendering or agreeing. She left and went for her walk, got her air, and on her stroll decided that the arrangement no longer suited her.

Theo hadn't recorded his mother's departure. He instead kept the camera trained on Risk and Javier, on their cuddles, their inside jokes, their affections, their very brave closeness.

[276]

XXIII

Lorna packed just the essentials. Three large pieces of luggage. One for professional attire. The other for casual wear. The third was for toiletries. A duffel bag for the shoes. Another for her most prized books and the possessions she'd absconded with during her first escape. A final bag, a valise, held her writings and laptop. She was ready to go.

A day earlier, on the morning during which she'd awoken from a nightmare about Risk and Javier turning her into their maid and mother, which itself followed the day Risk and Javier berated her for losing any attraction to Javier, she wrote Samuel Quilty from The Eva Peron School for Girls an email, asking him if he had remembered her and requesting an interview. He wrote back almost immediately and said that he did and would love to. She set a date.

After that exchange, she began checking listings for an apartment and scheduled a visit to see a furnished studio on the top floor of a three-story walkup. Lorna was ready to move on.

Without even attempting surreptitious strides, she'd managed to see the apartment, take it, pay first and last month's rent, move her six pieces of luggage into the space, and even shop for flowers, plants, and paintings. It was a mere three miles from "Javier and Risk's house," and still close enough to the school to walk, should she get the job that had been offered to her well over three years ago. The apartment had no WiFi capabilities, which suited her just fine. In fact, Lorna appreciated the lack of connectivity with the world. She'd needed a break from the internet, anyway.

Throughout her many comings and goings, neither Javier, nor Risk, nor Theo paid her any attention. They never questioned her. Never stopped her.

Never suspected a thing. Risk and Javier had become morose and sad, like middle-aged American couples found in the Deep South or the Midwest, thought Lorna. They'd both begun to take on paunches and stopped grooming as closely as they once had. Javier's lack of interest in life and presentiment were understandable, but not Risk's.

Theo, so deeply involved in his YouTube series and "heinous" portfolio, stopped speaking entirely. Lorna considered that Javier's degradation might have left her husband and son shell-shocked and maybe Javier had regretted ever getting involved with them, or maybe the brutal violation in the parking lot behind the tavern had cut him that deeply, after all. Or maybe he'd just grown bored and indifferent. Maybe there was truly nothing left to pervert.

The interview at Eva Peron went as well as the first one had all those years ago. Samuel Quilty was still creepy and still as charmed by her as he'd been during their initial meeting.

"Dr. Hall-Bonaventura," he began after reviewing her submission. "Why didn't you take the job when I offered it to you back then?"

"I'd just moved to Madrid and was busy with my own writing, Dr. Quilty. I guess I wasn't ready yet to make time for a day job."

Quilty raised a mordant eyebrow. "And your situation has changed?"

She smiled politely. "I'm ready to make time now."

"You know, Dr. Hall-Bonaventura, when you—"

"Please, Dr. Quilty. It's just Dr. Hall, now."

"Oh." Quilty's quizzical expression made Lorna smile. It was the look of innocence. Of an innocent man who had trespassed and suddenly felt very sorry.

"Well, I apologize, madam. I had no idea that you—"

"No, no. It's quite alright. Situations change, right?"

"That they do." Quilty's eyes were warm and understanding and they suggested that he knew what Lorna was getting at. That he was not merely being sympathetic, but rather empathetic, that he'd somehow been to where she was going.

[278]

"And that's just what I was about to get to, you see. I didn't mention this back then, during our first encounter, because I felt it gauche, but I knew of your *scandal* … or dilemma, rather … in New York. I had seen the YouTube videos and, well, you see, you received a lot of press, and the conference in which you discussed your *history*, it was all rather, relatable, to me."

"It was?" Lorna sat up. At first, she'd been nervous and then bothered, but now she was composed, if not still curious.

"Yes, you understand, I too have had my … history. I am only now sharing this with you because I have also seen your husband's videos from New York and the ones your son has made. His channel is quite popular among the students in our school. The girls here just love that sort of *mayhem*, and they all talk, you see, and so the faculty and I know what's trending and we investigate it all for ourselves, right? And …"

Lorna had begun to stand up, assuming this would not end well, and she'd be damned if this neurotic English weasel was going to decline her offer to work at his sad, small, sanctimonious school for wayward brats whose parents were too busy or rich to give a damn about their—

"Why are you standing, Dr. Hall-Bonaven— Dr. Hall?"

Lorna looked down at Quilty, his receding white hairline, his rosy cheeks with broken varicose veins, his liver lips, his—

"I was just arriving at my point, madam." Quilty's voice took on an authoritative timbre.

Lorna sat back down and listened.

"I, too, have had unfortunate, uhm, embarrassing…" Quilty cleared his throat, removed his glasses. "I'm afraid maybe I really don't know how to put this."

Lorna studied his sweaty forehead. "I'm not so easily shocked, Dr. Quilty, so just say what's on your mind."

"In London. I was a philosophy professor at Cambridge. The Corpus Christi College. And, well, you see, I happen to be homosexual, and—"

"Maybe this isn't necessary. I'd just like to know if I have the job or not, sir."

"Well, that's just it. You have the job, Dr. Hall. There was never a question. Our current English teacher's contract will be ending shortly and she's off to China with her fiancé soon, so it's yours, naturally. But before you commit to working here, you should know this about me, as I already know so much about you and your husband and your son, and I think this will help bond us."

Lorna exhaled. "Thank you, when do I start?"

"I'll introduce you to the girls shortly, but first let me complete my thought, please, madam."

Lorna had humored him but grew impatient with his ethically dubious rambling.

"I am a homosexual, right? And that didn't matter, I didn't think. But my writing wasn't getting the attention I thought it deserved and I had been passed up for tenure, repeatedly, after three close calls, and I did something to get everyone's attention, and it worked, and I had a good, long ride, secured tenure, and my books and papers prospered. *I prospered.*"

Lorna pursed her lips and narrowed her eyes. "You ... *did something?*"

"I fabricated a story." He'd said, at last, plainly. "And everyone paid attention. Paid attention to *me.* Oh, dear Dr. Hall, it did wonders for my career. My ... victimhood, for lack of a better term."

Lorna's mind went to her own collapse in New York and the bad days at Merriweather. Could Quilty have been feeling some compassion for her?

"After all you've been through, the blows to your name and career and reputation..." Quilty trailed off and for a moment Lorna thought it looked like he might cry, but he rallied, and composed himself. "I just want you to realize that you have a friend here, Dr. Hall."

And now it was Lorna who almost cried, but she steeled herself. Keeping company with the English stiffened her upper lip.

The girls in the class that Lorna would inherit looked like miniature versions of herself, she thought. Maybe it was a tad solipsistic, she allowed. They were old fashioned in that *Prime of Miss Jean Brodie* way, proper and polished, with ironed plaid uniforms and carefully coiffed hair, bangs and ponytails and plaited, and knowingly blended, soft makeup. Something out of a 1950s advertisement. Anachronistic. But charming in its faux naivete. *Little Lolitas.*

Lorna categorized the students by appearance and demographic. Her silent fixation on background, region, and race was fetishistic and likely problematic should it ever be announced. "Mixed race and London-reared Mila," "white-bread Kristen from Boston", "Chinese American Aileen from Upper Saddle River, New Jersey," "Colombian American Ramona from Manhattan," "London-bred white girl Gloria," "Southern California biracial Mandy," "Manchester-raised English Irish Rebecca." They ranged in age from 17-18. Newly adults, laying to rest their girlhoods.

The young teacher at the head of the classroom was short and petite, smartly dressed in gunmetal gray and light brown, with a chic Peter Pan haircut and very little makeup. Her name was Samantha and she'd soon be off to China with her fiancé.

"Sam," said Quilty. "We're sorry to intrude, but I'd like for you and the girls to meet your new teacher—Dr. Hall."

Samantha, with a glower masked by a put-on smile and unconvinced eyes, led the charge. The seven girls smirked and whispered amongst themselves. They had known of "Dr. Hall" from her social media stardom and all the insidious press that followed. Quilty hadn't exaggerated their knowledge base.

It had been years since Lorna assumed the studied maternal posturing of a schoolmarm.

"It's a pleasure to meet all of you and I look forward to becoming your teacher."

Mila and Kristen smiled at each other. Aileen spoke furtively to Ramona. Gloria and Mandy sniggered together, reacting to a joke that all the girls had apparently been in on. Rebecca remained solo in her unknown, knowing response to the announcement.

For a moment, Lorna thought that she had made a terrible mistake. These little demons would eat her alive. It would be a reenactment of her unbearable final days at Merriweather. Hounded by too-clever scholars who tolerated too little and criticized too much.

Quilty and Samantha exchanged faces that were suggestive of the sentiment—*Well, we'll see how this goes!*

◆ ◆ ◆

Lorna stood in the foyer with her purse and one overnight bag full of bathroom necessities and final garments.

"So, I've made up my mind, I'm leaving."

Risk had been massaging Javier's "good foot" on the sofa while Theo reviewed footage he'd recently uploaded on his laptop. After all these months and despite the traumas and tragedies between them, the tableau hadn't changed one bit.

Risk looked at her stupidly. "Where are you going?"

"I took a job as an English teacher at a school and rented an apartment." Lorna looked at Theo, not even giving her the courtesy of glancing up at her. "I won't be far. Still in the neighborhood. But I can't live here with you like this anymore. I thought I could. But I can't. And I'm sorry, but I have to go."

Javier sat up and frowned. It was a dismissive frown. A reductive frown. A frown that meant to say, *Lorna, you're being ridiculous.* And that this is a *completely overblown reaction.* He then shrugged and reclined once again and allowed himself to enjoy Risk's footwork.

"Underwear drawer." Javier's tightened mouth mumbled the words, but Lorna understood. "Under my briefs."

Lorna hesitated and then went into their bedroom and opened the dresser drawer that contained Javier's many pairs of underwear—boxers, briefs, boxer briefs, silk, cotton, mesh, solids, striped, animal prints, cartoons, humorous, erotic, Christmas themed—and felt around for whatever cryptic items he'd suggested she'd find there. And then she felt it, seized it, examined it—the satchel. She held her breath, opened it, and exhaled when she pulled from the bag her stolen belongings: the magnet from Casablanca, the painting from Alexandria, Theo's Yoda, Risk's socks.

She returned to the foyer, and decided she'd not thank Javier for giving her back what was rightfully hers. Lorna nodded at nobody, to herself, perhaps, and left. For a moment, Theo thought about asking her not to go, making a scene, throwing himself at her feet and telling her how much she was needed, how much she had been underappreciated, and that they had been wrong, and that she had been right, always right.

But he did no such thing.

Javier and Risk shared a blending of freedom and regret. They'd loved each other—yes, it was love that Risk now felt for Javier, no longer envy, no longer covetousness—more than they'd ever loved Lorna, but they had also felt an ineffable responsibility for her, for having dragged her into this mess of their lives. Risk, especially. By now, she'd have been well on her way to resuming her prominent position at Merriweather with all the sympathetic support systems firmly in place. He'd taken that from her. The chance to rise from the political grave, a Phoenix from the academic ghetto, to play at victimhood and sovereignty.

None of it mattered now. Too many years had gone by, and they were all too devoted to the recreation of their discarded lives.

XXIV

Lorna held her breath at the stench of the travesty. She loitered in the threshold, unwilling to see more. The ransacked foyer was enough. Broken vases, holes in the wall. Uprooted plants. Mounds of soil. Piles of shit. The flies. And then the odor. This was not what she had expected. It had gone further than planned. Then again, the variables associated with such endeavors could never be planned for adequately enough.

Murmurs emanated from the kitchen, bathrooms, bedrooms, living room. Her house was full of strangers. By the time she reached the dining room she had come across no fewer than ten squatters, though she could hear the others laughing, arguing, fucking elsewhere in the ample chambers. Her romantic mind found connections with literature. The squatters, the invaders, Javier's dangerously abiding fans, were not dissimilar to The Suitors who took control of Odysseus's house in *The Odyssey*. This was an inversion, though, as Odysseus was away on his journey back when the locals stormed and seized his oceanside hold. Perhaps she was Odysseus in this iteration. Risk was Penelope, the bride that endured the oppressors and their seizure. Theo, Telemachus? Possibly not. Risk was cast in the roles of wife and son, emasculated and feminized. What would Homer think?

Her examinations remained literary as she surveyed the damages. She replayed the afternoon a few years back when she shared with Risk her work on Pearl-as-signifier-of-uncannily-perceptive-youth-piercing-the-deceptive-veil-of-the-adult-world in *The Scarlet Letter*. She stepped over broken wine glasses, near which maroon blotches made ornamental patterns across her area rug and parquet inlaid floorboards. Wine? Blood? Two squatters played Gin Rummy while eating avocados at her dining room table. Upon revisiting

Hawthorne's knowing material, Lorna saw Javier as the morally weakened minister, Dimmesdale, and Risk as the dominant "doctor" Chillingworth feigning "treatment." Like those condemned Puritans, Risk and Javier were coupled in domestic defeat purposefully. There was a design. A fashion.

The defensive allusions spinning in Lorna's catalog of letters stopped at Shakespeare. *The Tempest*, in which the colonized Caliban is diminished and learns to love his oppressors, internalizing them, felt relevant to the situation. Had Javier begun to love Risk? His fans and family? The squatters who had put him on a leash, housebroken him? Unmanned him? Had he internalized their indignities, their feet on his face, their heels in his back, their words, their neutering?

Rafael and Antonio were taking turns boxing the biggest, strongest male fans in their underwear in the backyard, while their father recorded it on his iPhone. The fight club was queer as all the men sprouted in their briefs brawny, insistent erections. The Forza brothers talked about making love to their mother, competing, arguing, bragging—with whom did she have the most passionate sex. Massimo giggled drunkenly at the entanglements as the pugilism gave way to grappling, close, gyrating wrestling matches in which appendages and sacks intermingled with mouths and fingers and toes. Mr. Forza remembered his wife's orgasms and singing, her drawing and cooking, her cleaning and crying. Lorna would have written a masterpiece about the scene. She imagined how a Renaissance master would have captured it, in this early daylight with the mildew and sweat glistening off the brown and beige skins.

Javier, his paralysis and disfigurement worsened, was on the other side of the yard regaling a small group of young men with his sexual exploits, sharing his catalogue of conquests, naming the women and their dimensions, their ages, their hair colors, their races, their ethnicities, their accomplishments, their gifts, their perversions, the quality of their vaginas and orgasms, their labias and desires, their reactions to his abandonment, their spite. *The Gilded Cunts*. He saw Lorna watching and listening, but he dismissed her recriminations. He smiled and went into greater detail. The young men cheered and punched the air. Javier savored his role.

Lorna's parents were an uneventful couple. Neither had ever cheated. Their fights were clean, they respected each other. Had patience for one another. Remained married after forty-seven years.

"Hi, Mom," she said into her mother's voicemail as she moved through the house. It felt like possession, making the call at the least opportune time. "Just wanted to check on you and Dad. Miss you. Love you."

Who was Lorna in this parable? She thought again about The Bull of Heaven myth. Was Javier Gulgalanna? The Great Bull of Heaven, himself? Was she both Inanna, the one who was rejected by Gilgamesh and on behalf of whom Gulgalanna was sent on his murderous mission, and a gender-inverted Enkidu—Gilgamesh's male companion? Was Risk Gilgamesh? Surely, these modern characters were echoing something ancient and eternal. Some recycled and classic narrative of the asinine humans and their petty gods. We're all only archetypes in the end, thought Lorna. Come alive to clash and smash each other apart. The victory would be pyrrhic. The damages and losses after the win, significant.

Theo grabbed Lorna from behind and held her. She held his hands. He cooed into her buttocks like some damaged hatchling. She rubbed his forearms. He prostrated himself. Cooed harder.

Lorna's humanity, when faked, came across as weird and studied.

"You were such a difficult baby, Theo. But I loved you, anyway."

Lorna petted Theo and made plans. She planned to return to New York, with or without Risk. She planned on taking Theo with her. She planned on resuming her work at Merriweatther. She planned on making a study of victimhood. She planned on orchestrating a similar scenario. She planned on defacing her office with the words "CUNT" and "WHORE" and "RAPE BAIT" scrawled on the walls in red paint to edify the narrative seeds she'd planted before leaving. She would do this to bolster her brand as a new feminist writer. Lorna had only ever written about men—and on rare occasion, women—who acted and made the culture. Whose *actions* made culture. She would now take action that made culture. The rape was now real, and she'd deserve remuneration. It would boost sales of her eventual book of scholarship and journals in which her articles appeared. The accusations that she wouldn't deny would include celebrating male bravado, violence, and competition. Toxicity had utility. She would claim she'd also been receiving harassing phone calls and texts, which she would send herself from a burner she'd destroy. She'd be martyred, a sacrificial lamb of free speech and intellectual honesty, a sacred patron of bold thinkers. Saint Lorna.

Theo sat on the floor and with wounded eyes, watching his mother drift away. He thought about his mother's fondness for Artemisia Gentileschi's women. Surely, she saw herself as one of her brutalizing bitches. His father and Javier, the men who would be impaled, beheaded, pushed under foot, and castrated. She could hear her son's thoughts in an amplified murmur as if through an old stereo.

Her surreal tour of Home concluded in the upstairs bathroom, where she found Risk draped over the toilet. He was pale and red-eyed with chapped lips. He wore boxers and a tight white t-shirt. Had he been crying, or vomiting? Maybe both. Others gathered in the hallway. They filled the threshold, building a wall of rosy cheeks and purple lips and hard nipples. The bizarre, deranged orgy was continual, and bodies accustomed to smashing into each other were now bodies dripping wet with seminal birth and fiery afterglows. Lorna smelled the vulgarity. She'd have to burn all her sheets. Toss the furniture. Have all surfaces steam washed. The house wept for a deep cleaning.

"Honey," she said, touching his shoulder.

Risk shuddered and winced, recoiling violently enough to crash into the bathtub. "What do you want?!" And then he saw who it was that touched him, and he rambled freely. "Remember that fucking dog you loved so much and how it started eating itself? You gave more to that damn mongrel than you did to us."

Lorna smiled and knelt beside him. The invaders squeezed closer for an improved view.

"It's over, Risk." It dawned on Risk that she looked too good. Too good for a woman who had been held against her will. Too good for a woman whose husband and son had been in harm's way. Too good for a pawn in a madman's game. Too good as a victim of abuse.

"I'm glad. This has been … difficult. A nightmare." Risk sniffled, choked back snot.

Lorna touched Risk's hand. "Hush, babe. It's done now."

"Why did this happen? What did we do?"

Lorna's eyes danced. They surveyed Risk's face. Swung horizontally with incriminations. The edges of her mouth curled mischievously. Risk watched the odd expressions like a child staring at a firework show. The array of tacit assessments panicked him, though he didn't know why. He sat up, shifted his position, crawled closer to his wife, eager for anchoring.

Lorna sweetened, though her thoughts belied her affectation. *We didn't do anything. You did everything.* No need to say anything reductive.

Risk's squinting eyes rounded, saddened. "I don't know. I don't understand."

Her words would have killed, and so Lorna only ran them through internally.

Risk scoffed and rose, leaning against the wall. "This was nonsense."

Lorna sighed and stood beside him. *We fabricated the entire scenario. It's laughable. And mean.*

"It's over. They've released me."

Risk took three steps toward the mass of faces and nipples. The wall of watchers. "Get out of my way, you fucking violators!"

None moved. Risk shoved and slapped at them. Hands thrust forward, shoving him back into the wide, marble-laden, pinewood-finished lavatory, back into the arms of his wife with her confession, her silk scarves, and her victory. The squatters formed an organic mess of limbs and teeth, an ethereal, phantasmagorical, Gothic chimera as dreamed up by Dante. Life was an

Italian farce. Scaramouche was everyone.

"Did you steal my favorite pair of socks? The black ones with white dots?"

Lorna held him. "Yes. They're back now." *You were spoiled. It was a lesson. Just a lesson.*

Risk pulled away, sat on the sink, a pouting child in the throes of a regressive revolt. "When will they get out?"

She tried again. Grabbed his wrist. "They'll leave now."

Risk was still a boy, and his tantrum was implosive. He reeled. Banged into the medicine cabinet.

"It's a joke. A fucking joke. What a fucking joke. Lorna, they were fucking joking."

Lorna wanted to laugh. Nervously. A relief in its way. She shook her head and tried again. Grabbed him again. He stepped back. Touched his wound. The mark left by the bull's horns.

"I didn't deserve any better."

Lorna pulled up his shirt, inspected the scar, kissed it. She pushed out her tongue to feel the hard, knotted permanence, and kissed it again.

Risk wheezed. His eyelids fluttered. He slid off the sink and fell limply into her arms. She supported him until she couldn't, and they were both on the floor, sloppily, absurdly. The watching squatters, the pulsating wall of judges, gawked. Rafael and Antonio and their father and brother emerged. Javier's alarming face, growing more gruesome by the minute. Massimo assumed his title. God or King, depending on the day. Javier's confused look occurred comically—no longer scary. Theo took shape. He held his camera phone. He recorded his parents' theater of dutiful indictment.

"I did it," Risk mumbled into his wife's breasts, smearing them with mucus. "I did it."

"You did," she said, cradling him. Her babe. Her baby. "I hate you, Risk. I hate you."

Risk pulled back, looked at her. A man stuck in boyhood. "Then why'd you marry me?"

"Because I hate myself more."

Lorna woke from the nightmare gasping and gripping the sheets. She'd fallen asleep on the sofa of her new apartment. She wiped her brow and knew that things would have to change yet again.

XXV

Theo reverted to a gloomier iteration. The frustrated filmmaker began once again drawing lascivious toons. But no one was anymore in the mood to deal with them, and Javier, once so supportive and even encouraging of the kid's expressive hobby, tore the illustrations from the doors and walls and cabinets and balled them up and tossed them in the trash.

"Dumb fucking kid." His mouth was a tight pulsating hole. "Bitch ass garbage! Fucking cunt bitch boy! Stupid bullshit scribbles!"

Javier and Risk spoke more to each other than they had in months, mainly about Theo's "dementia," Lorna's "abandonment," and their "odd" situation. And those videos that showcased the domestic passion play for the whole world to see. Javier existed in two modes: the grumbler and the ineffectual fornicator. When he wasn't complaining about America and Americans, he had frequent, spastic sex—mainly fumbling and slurping and awkward gyrations, never hard, never coming—with Risk behind closed doors and out of earshot of Theo, to spare him the horror. The boy had enough troubles.

The monotony broke when a coterie of unannounced, unexpected visitors came knocking. And they had been pounding on the front door with an impolite and harried urgency—a flurry of heavy, clumsy fists beating expensive wood. Risk hadn't fully recovered from what was the worst hangover of his life, clinging like a tenacious leech, but he answered the caller with the vigor of a man half his age, if not the belligerence of a retiree advanced in his years.

The three men who stood at the entrance were strangers to Risk, though well known by Javier, and even acquainted with Theo. And with Lorna, despite her absence. Risk immediately saw vague similarities between them and Javier in the eyes, the bridges of the noses, the fullness of the top lips, the wideness of the jaws, and the squat body structures. Of course, it would never have occurred to him that these visitors had been Javier's family.

"Javier is home?" asked the oldest of the three men, his gravelly voice making his question sound more like an order.

"Uh, who should I say is … I'm sorry, who are you?

"His fucking father," said Massimo, and then chortled, smacking Rafael in the chest with the back of his hand. Antonio turned his head and spat whatever he'd been chewing into Lorna's azaleas.

Risk, no longer a man in control of himself, considered punching the boorish visitor in the throat.

Instead, the American took a step back into his house and readied himself to yell for the first time in two days.

"Javier! Oh, my son! My sad, fucked up son!"

The bullfighter appeared—his face masked behind yellowing, crusting gauze, and the lame leg, dragging like a hefty tail, his bulk leaning on the crutch—and in moments there was an explosion of cheers and chuckles and Italian words and Spanish sentences and the three strangers were suddenly in the house and helping themselves to the television and bathroom and refrigerator and whatever was in the cupboards or on the counter, making messes with fruit and beer and wine.

Theo, already apprised of the Forza men, nodded and faked a smile as they slapped the American's son on the shoulder and back respectfully, if not with a too-familiar entitlement.

After a few hours, everyone was drunk, including for once Theo, who had once been so adept at refraining during the bouts of abuse and absolution. He'd only ever been a spectator and capturer of the spectacle of the drink, but now, motherless and tired of merely, quietly, obediently spectating and capturing, had decided to give in and partake.

"My son and I had a good laugh about you, Senor Bonaventura!" gurgled Massimo, face purple and belly distended, on the sofa with open pants, sans shoes. "A grown American man thinking he could come here to Spain—to Madrid—and pay for his way into bullfighting! Something our boys have been made for since childhood! They began doing it with serious balls as teenagers! With *serious* balls!"

"Right. Sure." Risk swallowed hard and imagined hurling a gob of phlegm in the bloated, bloviating man's sanguine face. He gathered the spit and swallowed it back down, even drooled a bit, the alcohol doing its job with admirable efficiency.

Massimo had waited for a rebuttal, but after none was to be had, he sniggered and lurched to his feet and trundled across the living room and helped himself to the remainder of Risk's Jack Daniel's. Antonio and Rafael began to strip down to their briefs. Theo had wondered how long it would take before they bore their assets. Risk was first mesmerized by the mass and shape and vascularity of their thighs and then found repugnant how close a semblance they bore to their brother—the man with whom he'd fallen in love, if not cupidity—especially along the patches of white, hairless skin of the inner thighs, closest to the crotch.

For a moment, he thought he might proposition all four Forza men to skewer him. The lust and the longing, the punch and the kick.

Risk turned to his mighty warrior, the American's wrinkled brow intimating uncertainties and quick condemnations.

"Javier?"

The Spaniard smiled and closed his eyes, put out his bottom lip, and raised a hand, as if to assuage the concerns, or perhaps to suggest that he'd handle it or maybe to just sit back and enjoy the show—*it can't last forever.*

◆ ◆ ◆

Hours passed and the situation only got worse. Downright grave. Risk waited for the uninvited, unwelcome intruders to leave, but as the day wore on and the moon supplanted the sun, the three drunk men became drunker, lost additional items of clothing, spilled alcohol, broke plates, knocked over plants, damaged priceless art, alleged that they'd come to the house only after watching Theo's YouTube collection of what "degenerate horseshit was going down with their son and brother" and how "the perverted Americans had been corrupting him" and "how it was the American man's fault that their heir and golden child had been left an ugly cripple," and finally passed out on the sofa and living room floor. Theo stood silently and watched with a petrified and uneasy glower from the corner, a captive in his own house. Risk had pleaded with Javier to ask them to leave.

"They're my family, Risk, I can't do that." Whenever Javier got nervous now his mouth would become taut, more than what had become the usual, and his words would slur and collide into each other. He was sometimes only barely understandable. "Where are they going to go? Their employer came back home and now their caretaking jobs are over. I can't put them out on the street."

Risk watched the three bullish, naked men snore and drool and fart and fend off nightmares. He wondered what they had been dreaming about as they grunted and swung fists and cowered in their sleep. Javier was unfazed by their night terrors. He knew his kin. He knew what plagued them. Risk suspected that their demons were shared and unconquerable.

XXVI

Theo was five years old the first time Risk and Lorna had taken him to Walt Disney World. His eyes widened when the actors who played Goofy, Minnie, Mickey, and Donald Duck circled him, waving and dancing. He posed gaily for photos. Touched their faces in wonder. Pleaded for merchandise with their likeness. Toys. Mugs. Posters. Coloring books. He even began drawing them during that initial trip. Though rudimentary, the style and representation were evident. Lorna remarked that his talent was natural, though he wouldn't return to it until that trip to the aquarium in Camden years later.

Lorna and Risk chased Theo around the Tree of Life on Discovery Island, the center of Animal Kingdom. The trails seemed labyrinthine and interminable. The boy jumped and laughed and squawked at the macaws and poked the glass of the Komodo dragon enclosure in Asia, the culture-themed section of the park not far from the manmade baobab tree. Risk and Lorna were spent by the end of the day. Any time Theo encountered wild animals he'd occasion a manic episode and interface aggressively with the fauna.

Risk thought he'd take to the bulls of Spain before flying his family out to Madrid. It was a miscalculation engendered by self-interest.

It was at Disney World where Theo got sick on too much cotton candy and vomited while on the *It's a Small World After All* ride. Lorna had held him and rubbed his head free of its sweat as Risk mopped up the puke with tissues and a handkerchief he'd kept in his pants pocket during those days. They had left the Magic Kingdom earlier than planned and watched *Snow White and The Seven Dwarfs* in the hotel room. They'd visited Epcot Center the next day. It would more than make up for the prematurely ended outing.

And as the grunting, inconsiderate bulls—Mediterranean men and their musk—tore through his house, Risk's memory of happier times had ended, and it dawned on him that he was indeed through with this trial.

If only he'd had the guts to stand up.

The Bonaventura story had taken uncountable implausible turns, but this recent event was the most improbable. He had permitted the invasion of guests—participants, not mere spectators. Though Risk's house was expansive, the quarters felt instantly cramped once the squatters colonized.

Theo faded into the background, a nosy, meddling specter, a spying apparition with his condemnatory ever-roaming eye, the camera that would never be turned off, like Pearl, Hester Prynne's daughter in *The Scarlet Letter*. Risk thought about Lorna's paper on the character. A postmodern feminist reimagining of the girl born of adultery in the milieu of Puritanical New England, Lorna remade her as a quiet youth who evaluated and devalued the adult world. The child in her paper knew adult society was flawed, a betrayal of her own generation, one the grownups resented and subconsciously planned to doom. In Hawthorne's darkly romantic mid-19th century novel, Pearl existed as guilt embodied, shame made flesh, a demonic interrogator of liars, a hobgoblin of hiders. Her mother, unable to escape the girl's barrage of questions and suspicions. Theo, with his private estimations, was Risk's Pearl.

The invaders adjudicated, too. They lambasted Theo's queer illustrations, tearing them off the walls, crumbling them into damp balls. They didn't mind the lampooning of the boy's father, but their heroic Javier would be spared the ignominy.

Risk made fatuous demands. "Lay off the Hirst and Barney!"

The invaders scoffed at the admonishments, stuck thumbs and forks into the priceless art collection.

"Stay out of my bedroom," Risk hissed. The invaders jumped on his bed, peed on his bathroom area rug.

"Don't touch my journals," Risk insisted, as the invaders rifled through his chronicles and tore out pages while mocking him in Castilian. Their chaos was circus-like, a carnival of defacement.

"Don't ruin the interiors, these are imported fabrics," Risk pleaded, as the intruders masturbated onto his sofa and chairs, leaving their marks. Abstract expressionism, organically.

"Don't disturb the garden," Risk ordered, as the squatters trampled the roses, yanked down the bougainvillea vines, and dug up the lilacs. They tossed worms and rocks at one another with glee.

Risk anticipated them doing unsayable things to him and his hold. He wasn't sure if Theo would be spared, but could he care about his son's welfare any more than his own? Risk had endured abuses. The only recourse he had left was defensive apathy. The trance was deep and mammoth. He resigned himself to a quiet reticence in which he meditated on his chronic need for self-reinvention and all the trouble it had gotten him into.

Javier, Antonio, Rafael, and Massimo had stripped down to their stained designer briefs as soon as they moved into Risk's mansion. They remained that way for the duration. Risk imagined it was to show off their vascular, sinewy mass, their outsized bulges, which often gave way to performative tumescence, with the occasional appendage gratuitously popping out from beneath the fraying waistband. The Forza men were well constructed, with considerable endowments. They made it a point to remind as many people as often as possible of their corporeal advantages, their godly gifts.

An olive-green denim duffle bag rested on the ottoman. Risk eyeballed it and imagined draconian weaponry hidden inside.

"Mother massaged my feet and sang me lovely songs every day," said Rafael. "She even rubbed my shoulders and back."

"Mother cradled me to sleep and kissed me for hours afterward," said Antonio. "She made me feel warm and safe."

"You're both liars and remember everything wrong," said Javier.

Massimo recalled his wife's pumpkin pies and apple crumbles. She fed him like a baby and wiped his mouth. She would shave his testicles and anus.

She would give him pedicures. She was dutiful that way. Welcoming the filth of his feet on her clothes. She was irreplaceable.

Rafael turned to Javier, poked him with the toes of his bare foot. "Let's see your fucked-up face, brother!"

Javier looked away and scoffed, but still unwrapped the bandages, winced and whimpered at the wounds that stuck to the cloth as he pulled it away, and revealed his new face. His brothers gawked and laughed, but both in the reverential service of horror.

"Santa Maria!" Antonio made an expression of played up terror. "Jesus Christ, man! You look fucking brutal!"

Javier laughed it off. Nodded.

Massimo shook his head. "What did they do to my son?" Massimo spoke Italian. "What did this American fucker do to you? You were once a full man, Javier. You were once a beautiful and strong *full* man. And now what? I bet your dick doesn't even work anymore, does it? And the people of Spain worshipped you! And now they do this to you! Does your dick work?!"

Though Risk didn't know the language, he understood that Massimo was berating and blaming him for what had happened to Javier. The anguish in the bullfighter's eyes translated the message with arch clarity. He wondered what had taken the Sicilian tough so long to ridicule Javier's misfortune and Risk's complicity.

Theo, with his customary fixed flat expression, recorded his father ambling through the new rigors. Rafael and Antonio were also ever present with their camera phones. All the data ready for dumping. YouTube beckoned. Risk was certain that penance would cost him whatever he had left.

Javier kept apologizing to him from afar, whispering reticence in the din of the intruders' carnage.

"What is the defining mark of a true man?" said Massimo, reading with an affected inflection from his cell phone.

Massimo, Antonio, and Rafael—the squatters—stood up and formed a circle in the sprawling living room, surrounding Risk, who in cotton sweat shorts and a t-shirt, trembled. It was the dawn of the second day and the "activities" were officially beginning. The lambast required veracity, which Javier had decided was verifiable through journals, testimonies, and micro-expressions. The omniscient brood waited.

"Responsibility." Risk answered. A meek schoolboy.

"More," said Javier, granting Risk his foot to rub.

Risk's elaboration was a medley of deeply buried truths and quick, convenient fibs.

"Bravery. Making plans and executing on them. Having integrity. Doing what you say. Providing for family. *Protecting* family."

Massimo smiled paternally. "Have you done these things? Have you become a man? Do you think about the Bull of Heaven, anymore?"

An altar boy ready for communion, Risk inverted his eyebrows beseechingly. Lorna had told *him* about the Bull of Heaven. Javier's disgusting father?

Antonio and Rafael reached into the olive-green denim duffle bag and pulled out rubber masks of Tigger and Eeyore. They put them on but continued to film the stately, ceremonial proceedings. Their father reached into the bag and pulled out a rubber mask of Winnie the Pooh. He donned it and approached Javier.

Risk stared softly at the men in their masks. His stomach dropped. Theo fought off a smirk. He relished the spectacle, the gruesome charade.

"I don't understand." Risk's voice broke as he leered. "What is this? Why?"

Massimo's words were muffled from beneath the mask. "Your son's imagination, so vivid, so criminally neglected. As neglected as my son now in his motherland. By his own fans. His own people. Now that you've turned him into a freak!"

Javier reeled, scowled as if struck, flashing a black gap, a placeholder for a missing tooth, something lost in a bar fight years earlier. His lack of lips made the sight more terrifying.

Javier, Antonio, Rafael, and their father took down their briefs and exposed long, heavy, threatening erections to Risk. The men began to chant a masculine battle cry, something between a soccer stadium rally and a cult-ish cooing. Theo wiped his sweaty palms on his jeans and licked his lips. He didn't understand his own excitement. He worried about his father but wanted to see what happened next. His vivid glory made his heart race and his knees weak. At the end of the day, Javier was still a Forza and a very angry, bitter man, to boot.

The strain of interrogation brought Risk to heel. Massimo had run this nightmare like one of Risk's charter school professional development work-shops, replete with role playing and team building exercises. The American had divulged more than he should have to the Spaniard about the nuts and bolts of the PD session after too many drunken afternoons. Had he told his father?

A montage of Risk's YouTube uploads replayed on a continual loop in his head—the ones wherein he had harassed and bullied Dominick Truman in the mountains of New York State, the Brooklyn dojo, the Harlem rock climbing wall, all the tense days at the school in the South Bronx. It was pur-gatory, Risk accepted. It was all too thoughtfully curated. The orchestration had a knowing mind at its center. His own center would barely hold.

This ridiculous, petty theater of derangement!

"That's it!" Red Risk trembled with a revelatory wrath. "I've had enough! Get the fuck out of my house!"

The men closed in on him. Risk, alert now, and even wily, with old blood and skin still caked under his unclipped fingernails, remembered who he was and what he could do when pushed into a corner, when insulted, when reminded that he was a man who lusted after the man he wanted to be. Risk snarled, a feral, mangy cat, and clawed at his pursuers, inadvertently slapping Antonio's dick hard enough for the Spaniard to squeal and drop his iPhone, disrupting the recording.

Massimo, affronted and titillated, drove a knee into Risk's gut hard enough for the American to buckle and collapse.

Javier struggled to his feet to get between his family and Risk but was shoved back down by Antonio. There was still room in Javier's heart for un-expected changes.

The Forza men adapted Theo's cartoons with a creativity that made their imaginary crowd roar with locker-room delight. Even the fantasized women among the invaders screamed like cheerleaders. The "audience" knew merciless heckling, celebrated Western degradations. Their reductions were espoused with such gaiety and abandon that Risk felt more chilled by the joy of their pitiless pronouncements than by the molestation and penetration he was presently experiencing.

"Carpet bagger!"

"Fraud!"

"Charlatan!"

"Coward!"

"Pussy!"

"Take his nuts!"

"Impale him!"

"Strike him down!"

"American intruder!"

"Imperial!"

"Colonialism is dead!"

"Yuppie fuck!"

"One Percenter!"

"Faggot!"

"Great fool of history!"

"Loser!"

"Shame on you!"

"Half man!"

"You've abandoned your family!"

"Weakling!"

"Failure!"

"Kill yourself!"

As Risk was manhandled, his shirt, shorts, and boxers ripped from his writhing, bruised, scarred body, his gaze falling on Theo who watched with a stone face, a gamer's glower, and on Javier who again ambled to his feet and cried and tore at his brothers and begged Massimo to make this all stop.

Theo remained a silent, dutiful spectator. The boy witnessed his dad's ignominious defeat as though it were an action film or one of his video games.

Risk was passed around as the Forza men dropped spit, feces, and urine on him. They owned an endless supply of excretions that insisted upon blessings, a degrader's baptism. Occasionally, Risk could fetishize his beta status. He could make his mediocrities and deficits erotic. Magical masochism.

Javier disembodied, witnessed his own participation in the act. Pampered and poor. Wanted and wanting. The brothel and its whores. The stable and its horses. Massimo and his sons. Javier and his brothers. Markers of men. All the lessons rushed back in a hot flood of sensations and smells, signs and sighs. The memories of boyhood had been dimming but this event brought them back in a blast of bright need.

The swirl of faces that surrounded were spiteful. They exuded contentment and shared wonder. Risk hadn't understood that this was dissociation. He was feeling the blows and the insertions and the fingers and the chaffing, but he also registered no emotion. Prison made suitable demands on the imprisoned. He could be compliant, offer up his orifices and bulk—his surrender to the bull was no different.

Risk felt himself slip on something wet as he bolted away from the latest blow. In moving suddenly, Risk knocked his head against a teakwood armoire and dozed. While the Forza warriors continued to plunder his unconscious body, Risk dreamed up a disorienting tableau: there was the day Theo was born, Lorna loopy on epidural, her blush deep, a sanguine pulse. Their olive son with small ebony eyes and bushy, ink black hair. Lorna joked about having mated with the Native American registrar at Merriweather. Risk cried onto Theo's head, another blessing, another baptism. The strong newborn squeezing his father's clumsy index finger. And then the intrusion of big bull balls dangled into frame. It was now a Polanski terror, a Pasolini picaresque. The animal's testicles filled the foreground of the frame in a yellow meadow; the background pictured a bride and her groom, Lorna and Risk, younger and unfettered, childless, and fresh. The marriage day in the New York country, a honeymoon to Vietnam soon to begin. Alone with the photographer for the album. *Conventional*, joked Lorna, about their following of standards, the reception with family and friends, the cocktail hour awaiting them, the Viennese hour promising sugar rush and bloat at evening's end. An affirming event. And then another coterie of Velazquez figures, a family portrait as rendered by Bacon, the ugly mass of kin in a handsome lounge, Edwardian furniture, wine traps, colanders, roots, canned fruit, curios boasting wooden figurines from a Medieval year, a Puritan's hold, wainscoting and moldings on base and crown, and the faces like wet paint running, like fractured and cubist bastardization, a non-representational work, a coterie of humans fell afoul with nature. The father, a minotaur. The mother, a stroke-suffering disfigurement of monstrous aesthetics. Both nude. The child, a boy, also naked. Theo, clearly. Younger. Scared. And obedient. Risk denuded atop a wild bull seeking to toss him free, trundling past a tawny man—Javier in year two with his brother's Tigger mask—championing him on with a raised, balled fist. And then the yellow meadow in Upstate New York with the bride and her groom, young Lorna and abiding Risk, and the big bull balls draped at the top of a European master's frame. Then the sickle. And the chopping. And the castrated bull bucking with an oceanic burgundy splash drowning the landscape. Lorna and Risk in the distance covering their eyes at the awful future ready to come. Barreling toward them like a colossus intent on pulverizing. And Risk regained himself. Woke with a gasp as Massimo gasped. They had come together.

Risk panted. Massimo pulled away and wiped himself with Risk's t-shirt. The Forza men left for the showers, ordering Theo to continue recording the payback.

Though the Forza-family-shit-and-piss party felt like a climax to something, a cinematic conclusion, it was merely the prologue to a host of indignities to follow.

Javier had fallen from the sofa, his crutch tumbling from under his frenzied attempt to reach his felled friend, who lay on the floor, naked and bruised and bloodied, and trembling. He covered him with a throw and spooned him until he stopped shivering, all the while fearing his brothers and father would see and penetrate him next. He had already lost his place at their table and on the filial crest.

"Why?" asked Risk, searching Javier's eyes for reason. "Why, Javier?"

"I don't know," Javier answered as he damned his submission to his father and considered burning the house down with his family inside as they slept.

XXVII

Javier had not burned down the house, but he did contemplate *The Rape of The Sabine Women.*

The ancient mythology of Roman men abducting and possibly violating—depending on the scholarship—young women of other outlying cities, had been a favorite subject of his, and Risk's recent victimhood at the hands of the Forza Men made him revisit the story. Maybe he'd learned how to find parallels by listening for too many years to Lorna prattle on didactically about everything, even that which she knew too little about. The associations and allusions went some way in mollifying personal horrors. It was a reliable defense mechanism.

As Massimo, Antonio, and Rafael made fun of Javier's weakening and sullying—his leg, his face, the only valiant parts of him now marred irreparably—Risk watched his lover/victim fake badly his imperviousness to their mockery. They then set in on Risk, replaying the beatdown and the infiltration of fingers and cocks. They'd shrunk him as thoroughly as he'd shrunk Javier.

Risk found momentary shelter in the memory of mom. All boys crept back to their mothers in times of defeat and decimation. His parents had divorced when he was in college. His mother had been reassigned to a sister hospital in San Francisco, and Risk talked with her a few times a year, even saw her roughly every three months—quarterly like clockwork. His father had recently died. He had been seventy-four and "expired after a brief, but catastrophic illness." He'd left his estate to Risk. Roland had been estranged for too long to have earned a share.

"I'm moving to Madrid because I've exhausted New York," he had said to his mother the night before flying to Spain. "It's just time to go. Try something new."

Sara had said that she understood—though she knew the truth, having read all about his and Lorna's awful relationship on the loveless monolith that is the internet—and asked him to stay in touch. He had tried. In his way.

Risk had spent no less than a thousand U.S. dollars a day on breakfast, lunch, dinner, and snacks for the intruders. Massimo had taken the American's credit card and had deliveries arrive at eight a.m., one p.m., and seven p.m. The entire Forza stay had cost Risk over seven thousand U.S. dollars in catering by the end of the seventh day. To add slur to grievance, the squatters ate in front of him but denied him his share. They permitted scraps, but only from the floor, and only after their bare feet had stamped it. He had been moved to suck the leftovers off their toes. He'd been a dutiful host.

"Material"—footage—from Theo and Antonio and Rafael's phones were uploaded onto YouTube as the world watched the sordid scenario unfold soap opera-style. Authorities were intrigued, but no official action had been taken. Investigations were theoretical. Prosecution was fable. The too-indecent imagery was deleted by the host, but the bulk of the scenes remained intact. It was an edited horror movie, a pornographic film with the best parts lopped out. Little did it matter—the views increased reliably. In intimate, deviant circles, Risk had become an international folk hero. Viral and iconic. Ironic, too.

Risk and Javier tended to each other as the Forza men watched like prison guards—drinking and eating and farting and scratching their balls and sniggering. Javier had been replaying his own imagined threat, considering it fatuous. Hid his tears from his father and brothers. They'd kill him for sure if they caught him crying.

Risk attempted a conversation with Theo, occupied by his camera and "material."

"I've been thinking a lot about when you were young. The trips to the aquarium in Camden. That place, Space Farms, by the lake house. The people we laughed at. The shitty things we used to do."

Theo smiled at his father. But his mind was elsewhere.

Risk could see in his eyes that he had not been paying attention and he retreated into the kitchen, his limp worse than it had been in months. The beating and the rape had left him with deficits.

Theo sat at the dining room table editing on his laptop. He'd periodically look up and survey the room to determine if his cinematography had been required.

Massimo and his sons sat beside one another in their underwear as had become the house's dress code. They whispered with large gesticulations and smiles and knee slaps and neck grabs and kisses and soft fists to the chin. Risk watched but could not hear anything they said. Antonio and Rafael stared at him as though he were freshly grilled meat, ready for the devouring.

"Mother bathed me with her own hands until I was sixteen," said Rafael, now in Spanish. "She even washed my genitals."

"Mother hired a harem of women to bathe me until I was twenty, and she watched and instructed them on how to do it correctly," returned Antonio, in Italian. "She inspected their every scrub and rinse."

A minute later, Massimo rose, found his clothes, and got dressed. He barked orders in Italian at his sons, and they too dressed. Javier rose wearily, grunting all the way, and slowly disappeared into the bedroom as they did so, and Risk could barely contain his excitement and fear. He trembled, and his breathing was shallow. He began to sweat, and it stank instantly.

When Javier reappeared after what felt like ages, the four men hugged and kissed in a way that made them seem momentarily human and not so threatening. Risk was sickened by the affectionate goodbyes. Javier handed his father a ring of keys.

Massimo muttered something in Spanish to Risk, and he only understood half of it. Something to the effect of, "Thank you for accommodating us. You Americans are more hospitable than people say." And then the three intruders left.

Risk stood weak legged in the living room, his face that of a young boy who'd just been devirginized.

"They've gone to my house," Javier began, his mouth tight, the ruined flesh constricting, signaling tension. "They'll live there now, as *this* is now *my* house. They said they were *satisfied* with what they saw. They said that— satisfied. That their … faggot son … and brother … was … no longer … a man. No longer in control. Ready to be under … any other man. And that the Americans were … destroyers. They're satisfied now."

And then Javier fell into Lorna's writing chair and wept hard and painfully.

"They think I'm done."

XVIII

Risk mastered multitasking. It had been three months since Lorna moved out and inherited a class of superior, entitled teenage girls from China-bound Samantha. She'd sent emails every few days to Risk and Theo, updating them on the new developments in her new life. It had been two weeks since Massimo and his sons had left their lives upended, infecting them both with the incurable twin maladies—insecurity and self-loathing.

Risk never asked Javier again why he had done what he had done with his brothers and father and Javier never broached the subject. It was a wound the two men would ignore, allowing it to fester. Maybe on some level Risk felt it was a cosmic punishment for his own crime. Maybe Javier had on some unconscious level knew Risk was responsible for his attack and so had meted out retribution. Both of their cruelties had been embedded in the bedrock of their union.

Risk had been clipping the toenails of Javier's lame foot on the back porch, while also frying eggplants, tomatoes, onions, and peppers in olive oil for Samfaina, managing laundry, and intermittently dusting. He'd become Javier's servant as the patient became master and he'd been an especially ornery and demanding one at that.

They could have afforded a staff to do the cooking and cleaning, but the bullfighter insisted upon Risk doing it all. It was their game. Their relationship. Theo documented thoroughly. He was a dutiful and tireless recorder of their lives. Javier and Risk not only allowed him to record them and upload their untenable—though forever-in-misery-soldered—union onto his YouTube channel, but even encouraged it. They'd review the likes and comments ritualistically every night as a family.

Risk collected the toenail clippings with a paper towel and headed for the kitchen to sample the Samfaina

"Where are you going?"

"To check on the—"

"You haven't even filed and moisturized." Javier sat up with an impatient sneer, his tight mouth spasming. "What kind of a pedicure is this?"

"I'm tired, Javier. Do it yourself."

Javier's voice became uneven, unequal to the challenge. "You know I can't."

The video footage of Javier—so changed, so "monstrous"—returning from the hospital, Lorna's "abrupt and unreasonable" departure, the arrival of Massimo and Sons, their rape and beating and insults had all yielded a predictable spike in views and comments.

Risk and Javier, and Lorna from afar, avoided checking in, though they'd wanted to, their curiosities eating away at them, how they'd been received, how these new developments played, how they were read, what their "fans" had been writing about them. Theo reviewed the likes and comments hourly. He'd never tell his father or Javier or Lorna what people had been saying. He still had enough humanity left to spare them that.

No one spoke during dinner. Javier's injuries only looked worse, and they'd still been "off-putting". There was new swelling and discoloration. His face was a basket of produce: eggplant, tomato, and cauliflower. Deformed and ill hued. Risk felt sick, but also right. He'd saved the relationship and maybe even his own soul. If he'd really had one to begin with. No, his thoughts were for once clean. A surge of assurance. Blasts of competence. Though even those had been short-lived.

Javier watched Risk eat. The men had suddenly become un-men. And Javier knew the commander—his father, well equipped with the mindless bulldogs that were his sons—had meant business. He'd made their house his home. No—he'd made *their* home his butchering veterinary clinic, and he'd left them, Javier and Risk, his dogs, neutered. Pissed on them. Hamstrung them like strays. Put them in their places. Their *low* places.

Javier was able to get a few words out, though they were garbled by his swollen mouth. "The Bull of Heaven myth—"

"We're done with that bullshit." Risk slammed his fork against his plate, left a crack. "Fucking bullshit!"

Javier nodded and found comfort in the deference. Like a rest. A reprieve. A luxury to be small, a gift to be conquered. Subjugation had its advantages. Being led was a blessing.

Theo had been recording, but Risk plucked the iPhone from his paw. "And also, *this.*"

Risk tucked Theo's iPhone under his left thigh and continued to eat. He'd put on the pants and the other men of the house would have to abide by the trousers. This was all a performance, too, as Risk no longer believed himself worthy of the title: Man.

The days that followed "Massimo's rectification," as Risk was fond of regarding it, but only to himself, were solemn though smooth. Risk had given Theo's iPhone back to him, and the young man was permitted to shoot whatever he liked, however, there was suddenly nothing worth shooting. Javier and Risk had become warm again, and demonstrative in that warmth, which bored Theo. The tenderness was a letdown. The kindness, a bummer.

The men cuddled and massaged one another's shoulders, cut each other's hair, showered together, watched movies (romantic comedies and superhero adventures) and read in bed. Javier helped him cook, clean, and returned the favors of clipping his toenails and rubbing and moisturizing his feet. He also offered up his orifices, something he'd denied him in the past. They discussed regularity of bowel movements and waxed each other's backs. They shopped together for clothes and groceries and washed the cars as a couple; well, Javier had assisted from a garden chair. They gardened together and went for walks through town. They attended bullfights and movies. Theater. And Javier took to opera.

Their routine had been broken by an irregularity. Weeks now since the Forza barbarousness. Months since the hitmen had done their work on Javier. The matador brandished his wounds like badges from some civil war in which brothers from a divided motherland had taken too much from each other. His jaw was swollen, his eyes blackened. Javier's temple was unsightly and covered by a gauze that had turned an unknown color—yellow blended with burgundy. His nose looked even more deformed, nostrils now closing, but he could still breathe through it. The body had been riddled with other scars and contusions and abrasions—infections from the droplets of the acid that had cooked other parts of him—but those had been hidden by his attire.

◆ ◆ ◆

The reluctant, much-to-prove warriors were at the sidelines of a ring, staring at four bulls circling impatiently and kicking up dirt amid snorts and nasty looks. For now, Risk and Javier were safe behind tall, thick, oak partitions. This would be the most dangerous of all tournaments. They wore complete torero regalia: monteras, customary black hats, corbatins, narrow black neck ties, chaquetillas, short, rigid jackets with exaggerated shoulders, taleguillas, tights, secured with decorated gaiters, medias, two pairs of socks, cotton, then silk, zapatillas, the flat ballet-shoe-like slippers, and capote de paseos, the 19th century promenade capes, short and made of silk with luxurious embroidery.

Theo, acting the part of a picador, bore calzone de gamuzas, chamois boots with steel armor on the right leg, castorenos, beaver-fur hats, and chaquetillas, while manning his iPhone camera as the action would be demanding and require multiple angles, simultaneous setups.

Javier, less sturdy on his crutch, his useless leg dangling heavily beneath him, already tasted dirt and blood. Risk's body was small and tight. The bulls welcomed the guests into their home.

Javier thought it high time to say goodbye to Risk and Lorna, his ego, and these outrageous farces. He turned to Risk, who smiled back. Javier's smile bore a missing tooth and swollen, split lip, his face a grisly horror-show that summarized the journey of the past four years.

The bulls had only gotten angrier. They smashed and kicked and bucked and charged at nothing. The ether itself goaded. The firmament cracked in half. Javier watched, but his mind was stuck on Risk's warm, wet mouth, his dry, hot hands, the kiss, the suck, the fondling. It had happened, and it was all that Javier could think about. It magically covered the assaults, the blows, the incendiary, murderous gestures. Risk could be a source of pleasure. He could be a light. A savior.

Javier sighed. "These animals might just kill us today."

The thought unsettled as it entered his mind. He could tell Risk to walk away with him. Forget Lorna. Let her go. Give her to the girls' school in all his unkind, sadistic perversion. Theo was progressive enough, and likely gay enough himself, to accept it. Two fathers. Save themselves. Build a new life. He could plead with Theo to dismiss his castrating father and the fraternal unmanning.

When would this all end, anyhow? What more was there to prove?

Risk and Javier took their red flags and entered the ring. The bulls wasted no time and met them with ardor. The wrath felt personal. As though the animals had been waiting for them. Eight horns swept and slashed the spaces between Risk and Javier as the two men deftly sidestepped and leapt out of the path of carnage, Javier dropping his crutch and springing off on one mighty leg. The matadors had been surprised by their abilities. Despite their convalescence—mental and physical—they were still capable of fighting and surviving. They mutually attributed the athleticism to adrenaline. Fear was the great motivator, a remedy to sluggishness and injury.

Theo double-timed it across the rows of stadium seating, doing his best to shoot the melee. The young man sniggered maniacally as though his urge to see either his mentor or father fall increased and the threat—the promise—of doom seemed more and more inevitable. The boy had become increasingly earnest and stoic. It was as if he served as his father's ballast, leveling a quiet, steady seriousness, an appreciation for the gravity of the troubling situation.

Javier's body throbbed as he picked up his crutch. He stunk of antiseptic ointment. His limbs moved with a heaviness that sought to betray their intentions to keep the body to which they belonged animated. The men moved well. Their motions were nearly balletic. Even Javier's—a semi-paralytic butterfly. They knew they'd pay for this exertion, should they survive. Frustrations mounted. The bucking bulls took on a frenzy that spooked their would-be slaughterers.

The horned beasts conspired on a new strategy. They surrounded their pursuers. The creatures' consciousness seemed elevated, thought Javier as he wiped sweat from his eyes, touched his temple. It singed. He shook his head in disbelief. They would willingly butt heads to neutralize their opponents. They would sacrifice themselves for their bloodlust.

"I'm sorry, Javier," Risk whispered under hot breath that tasted of copper. Javier glanced at his American. "Huh?"

Javier saw Risk turn to the exit and sprint with a lame gait. Javier gasped. The bulls charged. They launched themselves at the American, who reached the gate with seconds to spare. He slammed the ring door shut with an emotional anarchy that disquieted the bulls. They rammed the gate. It rattled. Risk stumbled back into one of the bleachers. Theo was above him almost instantly, recording the cowardice as Risk panted and began weeping. Theo also continued to record the bulls in the ring. Javier gazed in disbelief at Risk, who stood in unfair safety.

The bulls turned their attention to the only remaining target. They got in each other's way, barreled into one another, butted heads, and snorted snot. Twisted stout legs entangled.

The musk of disrespect filled the arena. The footage would be online an hour later. YouTube would nearly crash with all the views. The fans would replay it numerous times until it sank in that the husband willingly surrendered his pride and forewent the fate of his wife.

Javier could have escaped at this point, but he did not. After that final blip on an otherwise straight line, everything would have gone back to normal. Risk and Javier would never have discussed Javier's inscrutable request to fight the bulls as a couple, nor Risk's plea into the wind for Javier's forgiveness. Those things would have been filed away. They would have settled into being a couple. A family for whom dinnertime would have been sacred. Even if Theo had become intolerable in his attitude, in his revolt against the man who insisted upon being called "Dad." Javier would have told him to respect his father. Or leave. Get a job and a place of his own and be a man and go out and make a living. Risk would have gotten hard every time he did this. Sucked him off before bed as a reward, as a thank you.

Javier imagined that Risk would have fucked him hard, and Theo would have sometimes heard them when Javier groaned and yelled. He would have been a good groaner, a better yeller. Javier imagined that Risk would have enjoyed making him groan and yell. These sordid theatrics would have forced Theo from the house. Perhaps it would have led him to begin taking long walks as often as possible, searching for a new subject worthy of his YouTube channel, but everything and everyone everywhere would have taken on a conservative reticence.

But instead, Javier surrendered to the bulls, and they impaled him, and his death was noble and glorious and appropriate and predictable. It was quick, if not clean. No, not quick either. They gored him. Tore him wide. Tossed his ravaged corpse around the pen. It was a graphic horror movie. Buckets of blood and entrails and howls and cries. And the end of a fabled bullfighter.

Javier sat on the toilet in the master bathroom and completed his death-by-bull fantasy. It had been elaborate and with many details and nuance and presumption about Risk's perceptions and Theo's motives.

As it turned out, Javier could spin an original story, too. It would have been a suitable demise, but he lay dying in a more conventional, maybe sensible, way. Downing a month's worth of oxycontin with half a bottle of whiskey. And he waited, sure of his decision. Why live ugly and crippled? Better to be dead. Risk would find him soon and the whole terrible ordeal of his farcical life—and the disastrous involvement with the Americans—would be over.

XXIX

Lorna greeted her son at the entrance of her tenement. It was early, seven in the morning, before classes would begin for the day. Inside, Theo walked in a circle, looking over all his mother's borrowed things. He thought the apartment looked small and poor and couldn't for the life of him understand why she would want to lower herself by living in such a dump. It wasn't really a dump, but rather a charming apartment complex, and the neighbors included painters, writers, teachers, and musicians. An artists' colony, really, with bougainvillea vines draped from the window planters and hydrangeas forming a perimeter in the patch of grass serving as the front lawn.

Theo again scrutinized the tiny studio, sparsely furnished, but with sparkling flourish. Little instances of his mother's touch. Trinkets taken from home.

"This is it?"

Lorna lifted her valise, brimming with papers, and a novel, *Walden*. "Yeah, isn't it enough?"

And then he saw his Yoda figurine but pretended that he hadn't.

"I guess. Are you happier here?"

"It's only been a few months, but I think so."

"At least you don't have to share it with anyone."

Lorna looked down and smiled to herself. The boy was wiser than she thought. But he wasn't a boy. Not anymore. It had only been a few months, but she felt like she hadn't seen him in years. And it was fine, that absence. Something earned. She'd probably been too permissive as a parent, or at least she'd always imagined as much. Too hands off. Too involved with her own interests and research. The child had been an ornament and then a burden.

And now a man, somewhat self-sustaining.

"How is your father?"

"He doesn't understand why you didn't come to Javier's funeral."

"Oh." Lorna stared at Theo, thinking about his answer, but put all the questions about his response out of her mind. She'd had enough of that sort of thing.

"Or why you didn't come back home after he died."

"I send him emails and texts, Theo. I write him a few times a week. But this is my life now. I'm done with all that."

"*All that?* All that is done now. Javier is dead."

Lorna was no longer mother. "I'm not sure what you want me to say."

"He's different now." Theo widened his eyes for effect. "Like, sick and old. Like, really fast."

She recalled the incident at Merriweather. The attention and social media outrage her lecture had elicited occasioned big sales of her books. Of course, it was awful to be the recipient of that much ill will—and troubling to learn that people could regard her as a bigot, one emboldened to exercise loathsomeness in a city as liberal as New York—but still, Lorna pondered, it had worked wonders on her career, previously on life support. She wanted to scream at her son that at least she'd not followed through on her original scheme. Abandonment wasn't such a crime in comparison.

Theo sat and Lorna looked out the window onto the street, where an old woman with a handkerchief wrapped around her head was pushing a carriage full of breads, fruits, and cheeses. She thought about her own mother, a seamstress, and her father, a postman, and their ramshackle row house in Queens, and the close calls with the attendant eviction notices and suspension of utilities due to delinquent payments. She revisited the rough blue collar neighborhood and its equally tough upbringing and the cottoning to the man-focused leadership of household and community by fathers and husbands who were the ultimate providers and the rolling up of sleeves and the sliding under cars and the "doing-it-yourself" attitude and the plain black and white law of vengeance and the defending of one's own turf and the hot dogs and hamburgers and the clearly defined gender expectations, and she valued the cleverness of her own mind in its revision of history, remaking of the past, and reconciling of biography for employment pedigree and media entry.

"Your principal is okay with me coming to the school today?" asked Theo.

"The *headmaster* is excited to meet you, actually." Lorna grabbed her keys and headed for the front door. "He's happy you're visiting."

Theo nodded, following. As he approached the foyer, he glanced back at the Yoda figure and nearly snatched it but decided against doing so. His mother should keep a part of him close.

The girls stared inquisitively at Theo, who stood awkwardly in the front of the classroom as Lorna introduced him. Quilty entered as she began. He loitered in the threshold.

"And he's a budding filmmaker and artist," Lorna concluded about her son after stating his name, age, and where he was from, before noticing her prowling boss.

"Dr. Quilty?"

"It's a pleasure to make your acquaintance, Theo!" Quilty rushed over with a stiff hand and a hot, firm handshake. "Your mother has told me so much about you."

Theo smiled cordially but pumped the headmaster's hand nervously. The son's palms had been sweaty. Lorna appreciated that Theo hadn't understood the extent to which Quilty knew about him, and was a fan of his "filmmaking" and "art," and the young man squirmed as the headmaster evaluated him before the girls, all of whom chuckled and whispered about his blush and discomfited tics.

Quilty found a seat at the back of the classroom. "I'll be sitting in again for a bit today, Dr. Hall."

Lorna smiled at him, at ease and in control. It had been the third time that week he'd observed her lesson; it was standard operating procedure to heavily monitor new hires during their first few weeks. He'd make no exception for the superstar from New York.

Theo sat beside him, behind the seven girls who'd periodically turn back and smile and give him a hard time with phony winks and soft air kisses. Quilty would intercept the mimicry with sharp points and curled lips and narrowed eyes—all the trappings of a true school leader. He had approximated derision well.

Lorna projected her slides onto the Smart Board. A painting of Henry David Thoreau sitting on what could be presumed to be Walden Pond. The girls took out their books and opened their notes. They wrote their names and the dates in the heading. Lorna appreciated their ritual. Obedient, with little prompting.

"We began discussing Henry David Thoreau yesterday afternoon and his great meditation of nature and solitude and morality called *Walden*."

Lorna hit the keypad on her iPad and a new slide appeared, a quote: "Our whole life is startlingly moral. There is never an instant's truce between virtue and vice. Goodness is the only investment that never fails."

Lorna eyeballed the girls. "Who'd like to dissect this quote?"

She allowed appropriate 'wait time' to build intrigue.

"What is Thoreau saying here about morality?"

Mila raised her hand but began speaking before Lorna could call on her. "Well, I think it's obvious, isn't it? Be a good person. Full stop."

Lorna shrugged and called on Kristen, who quipped, "But who's to say what *good* means? Isn't it a matter of opinion?"

Lorna folded her arms and stood wide-legged. "Well, that's what I was hoping you'd all be getting at."

Aileen crossed her legs and leaned forward. "That's ultimately the difference between morals and ethics, though, right? Morality is mostly personal,

[320]

subjective?"

Lorna lit up. "Yes, Aileen, good, that's right."

Ramona played with her many silver rings, taking them off and putting them back on with a nervy cosmopolitan verve. "But who cares if you're immoral? Why put so much importance on something like that? Being good? Why do we always care so much about that?"

"Beyond the law and religion and social condemnation, Ramona, you're right." Lorna sat on the corner of her desk. "Why do we care?"

Gloria cleared her throat and with a hunchbacked mousiness struggled to get the words out. "I don't care about what religion or the law or society says is right or good. I think we should trust our own compass. Even if everyone else thinks it's wrong."

Mandy tucked her heavy, blonde hair behind her ears and sat up straight, perhaps in reaction to Gloria's slouching. "I'm not a fan of people judging me. No one is perfect."

Rebecca pulled her copy of *Walden* to her chest. "But I worry about people not liking me. I worry about going to Hell. I worry about bringing shame to my family."

"That's understandable, Rebecca. I'd venture to say that most people would agree with you. Maybe what you're talking about is taking responsibility for our actions, right?"

Theo had been doodling fornicating, anatomically exaggerated cartoons, though Quilty hadn't noticed. He'd been too entranced by Lorna's command of her pupils and their eagerness to share thoughtful musings on Thoreau's postulations. Lorna's eyes briefly met his for the first time; she'd mastered the art of ignoring observers ever since Constance De La Rosa had made it a habit back at Merriweather to spy on her, waiting and wishing for her to trip herself up.

"But what responsibility for your actions, Dr. Hall?" said Aileen with obvious difficulty.

Lorna stood again. "What's that, dear?"

"Sure, you had the right to do and say everything you did and said in New York," began Mandy, "But why did you?"

Lorna glanced at Quilty. He looked both curious and unnerved.

"How's that?" said Lorna, her palms and armpits sweating.

"I mean, you were pushing buttons and getting attention, sure," began Mila, "But what about the people you hurt? Like, I bet there were students in your class who had been raped and assaulted and they probably didn't need to hear you blaming them for it."

Lorna now looked at Theo, who had stopped doodling and begun indiscreetly shooting the discussion. "Oh, I see."

Her humility was demonstrative, maybe too studied and performed. Specious eyebrows raised. If they could only know how much she regretted.

"Those videos …," said Kristen. "I'm not sure how to say it …"

"We don't want to …," said Ramona.

"You were defending bad behavior," said Gloria. "The worst behavior."

Lorna couldn't hide her frown, not even when she saw Quilty rise and hurriedly excuse himself from the classroom and her son recording the trial in plain sight.

X X X

Risk had aged badly. Javier's death, the lack of Javier, the deprival of Javier with the lessened face and body, made him old too soon. He'd finally attained a man to handle, to stand above, to put under, and to own, and now he was gone. A dog, a bull, a man. Love, ownership, and harm shared a dance and a bed.

The American shuffled around the house in briefs and slippers and in an always-open robe. His beard had grown out heavy and gray. He drank and smoked and ate poorly. He watched too much television and stopped exercising. He'd stopped cleaning and refused to hire a cleaning person. He'd bathed infrequently and smelled like weeks old cabbage. He'd let his chest hair grow out. Let his back hair grow out. He never cooked but ordered three times a day. He quit tracking stocks and bonds and reading financial news. Stopped following bullfighting and college wrestling. What's worse than the things he no longer did or cared about was the return of his pained hip and lame leg. The effects of the old injury resurfaced, and he was once again anguished and limited. With that emergent reminder, it was the end of all pursuits. Hell, the end of all interests.

The only thing Risk did with any regularity was mumble and mutter and sigh and recite encounters and escapades and endeavors and blame everyone by name for his downfall—Dominick Truman, Massimo Forza, Antonio Forza, Rafael Forza. Lorna Hall-Bonaventura. Javier Forza. Theodore Bonaventura.

"Fucking vultures! Fucking leeches! Motherfucking cocksucking motherless vermin! Pieces of shit losers! They should fucking rot in hell inside their mother's—"

[323]

Theo, left to his own devices, closed his door whenever his father's "psychotic rantings" got too loud. He prepared mom's lecture for upload onto his YouTube channel, but before he could bring himself to post it, something had disconnected. Nothing electronic. Nothing technological. Rather, something intellectual, maybe emotional. A fuse had been blown. A bulb had gone out. He'd lost interest in the routine, the charade.

Like that, there was suddenly a violent opposition to sharing the video with the world. It might have cast Lorna in a good light. It might have reignited the animus the world had for her. It might have won her favor at Merriweather. It might have been the final nail in her coffin. Whatever the outcome, Theo didn't care. He just knew that he'd not be posting this video. In fact, he knew that he'd be removing all his videos from the social media site and deleting his channel and maybe even his account. Maybe he would.

And then Theo found a clip he'd never uploaded—one of the countless "George and Martha" presentations, an episode of false allegations, made-up memories, and pretended histories. He'd not manned the camera himself, but rather propped it against a bookshelf.

In the video's frame, Theo drew pictures of his parents in the throes of yet another drunken breakdown, which he'd occasionally hold up to the camera to chart his progression. His mother's hair frizzy and heavy before her eyes, in her face, her blouse too loose and low and without a bra. His father's hair equally mussed and his shirt and shorts wrinkled and stained and with skin extra sallow in the middle of a bright day. They belched and slurred and threw coasters and magazines and knocked over pedestals and cried intermittently and laughed on occasion and leveled operatic allegations. They fell into each other's arms and rehashed old stories.

"They think I need to tone down my rhetoric," said Lorna, barely coherent.

Risk nodded in agreement. "You tend to say the wrong things."

"They're much too sensitive," said Lorna. "I only speak freely about what I observe."

"You say antiquated things, though, my dear," said Risk, losing his face in her bosom.

"They want my head, but the things you've done, you're no better."

Risk had been the orchestrator of similar transgressions and so he nodded in agreement.

"There's been something wrong with us," said Lorna, plainly.

"So wrong," said Javier.

Lorna stood, trying to walk, and immediately tripped over her sandals, spilling her drink. It shattered against the floor and Javier cringed. He'd been battling a headache. Lorna was red faced and began to cry again.

"Yes, a sad, confused *mother!*" Lorna wept.

Risk dropped a pair of dirty socks that had been left out—his or Javier's—on top of the spilled drink and shards of glass because he was considerate that way.

Lorna punched the wall, knocking a framed antique drawing of 1920s-era canopied stagecoaches parked on the Champs-Elysees to the floor.

Risk fixed himself another drink and drank it. He sighed and sat down on the sofa, beside Javier, who pushed him away with a scowl when the American put his hand on his thigh and tried to kiss his neck.

Lorna found a new glass and began filling it with vodka. "Even *he* doesn't want you anymore."

Risk reclined, spilling what was left of his liquor onto his stomach.

Theo continued to draw his "George and Martha." Their sad reinterpretation of Albee's horrific, tragic, clownish duo.

At first, Lorna stared steely eyed at him, but then her expression dropped and hung, and her eyes went dim, and she had not cried, not only because she'd run out of tears, but because the weight of the melodrama and the truth of the lie had crushed her. Or at least winded her. She gasped and held her belly and sighed. She had run out of material. The show demanded too much creativity, too much depth or imagination, and she was plumb out.

"George and Martha" vomited and sobbed and drifted off and woke up and showered and wept some more and then properly rested as Javier studied their mess and Theo inked his drawings. He even colored them in, and the quality was on parity with a *New Yorker* satire. Tall figurines composed of fine lines and soft watercolors and inflated, outlandish features, and all done with a minimalist flourish.

Risk rose, and in a fugue mumbled, "I'm too big for this nonsense."

In her unsteady inebriation, Lorna rambled too, prattling on about Thoreau and Emerson. Perhaps a response to Risk's assertion. *Be good to nature. Obey the greater forces. Fall in line. Stay small in the great plan.* She'd regained their admonishments. *Mother's* admonishments.

All the warnings. All the writings. All the foolhardy bold strokes.

END

Special thanks to Luba Ostashevsky and Michael Carroll, careful readers who offered constructive feedback of early iterations, Dr. Alexis Cohen who advised on the clinical aspects centering on sociopathy, sadism, insecurity, and narcissism, Chris Campanioni, editor of PANK, for publishing a short version of the novel in his journal. A final and very grateful nod to Laura Schleifer, who provided a rigorous and generous edit of the material and was instrumental in helping me shape the final draft.

Additional gratitude to my husband Tommy, my mother, Anne, my late father, Anthony, and Sven Davisson, my publisher.

Brian Alessandro has written for *Interview Magazine*, *Newsday*, *PANK*, *Huffington Post*, and has recently adapted Edmund White's *A Boy's Own Story* into a graphic novel for Top Shelf Production. Additionally, he co-edited *Fever Spores: The Queer Reclamation of William S. Burroughs*, an anthology of essays and interviews about Burroughs for Rebel Satori Press. He is also the co-founder and editor in chief of the literary journal, *The New Engagement*. His first novel, *The Unmentionable Mann*, was published in 2015 by Cairn Press and his first feature film, *Afghan Hound* was produced by Maryea Media in 2011.

CPSIA information can be obtained
at www.ICGtesting.com
Printed in the USA
JSHW031103130223
37452JS00016B/10